THE ONES THAT ARE WANTED

THE ONES THAT

UNIVERSITY OF CALIFORNIA PRESS   Berkeley Los Angeles London

Communication and the

Politics of Representation in a

Photographic Exhibition

ARE WANTED

Corinne A. Kratz

THE PUBLISHER GRATEFULLY ACKNOWLEDGES
THE CONTRIBUTIONS TO THIS BOOK PROVIDED
BY THE JOHN SIMON GUGGENHEIM FOUNDATION,
EMORY UNIVERSITY, AND THE ASSOCIATES OF
THE UNIVERSITY OF CALIFORNIA PRESS.

University of California Press
Berkeley and Los Angeles, California

University of California Press, Ltd.
London, England

Library of Congress Cataloging-in-Publication Data

Kratz, Corinne Ann
    The ones that are wanted : communication and the
politics of representation in a photographic exhibition /
Corinne A. Kratz.
        p.   cm.
    Includes bibliographical references and index.
    ISBN 0-520-22281-4 (cloth : alk. paper)—
    ISBN 0-520-22282-2 (pbk. : alk. paper)
        1. Dorobo (African people)—Portraits—Exhibitions.
    2. Dorobo (African people)—Portraits—Public opinion—
    Exhibitions.   3. Public opinion—United States.
    4. Dorobo (African people)—Attitudes—Exhibitions.
    5. Photography in ethnology.   I. Title.
    DT433.545.D67 K75   2002
    305.896′5—DC21   2001003098

Manufactured in the United States of America
10   09   08   07   06   05   04   03   02
10   9   8   7   6   5   4   3   2   1

The paper used in this publication meets the minimum requirements of ANSI/NISO Z39.48–1992(R 1997) (*Permanence of Paper*).

CONTENTS

ACKNOWLEDGMENTS

I BEGAN WORKING on *Okiek Portraits* in 1989, never suspecting that it would end in a book about the exhibition or that it would occupy me for over ten years. It is a pleasure now to trace this process in personal terms by recognizing and thanking the many people who have given guidance and support along the way, from exhibition through book. My appreciation goes first of all to those who offered early advice on producing the exhibition and who helped shepherd *Okiek Portraits* through its various venues. In Nairobi: Omar Bwana, David Court, Bruce Davidson, Mohamed Isahakia, Richard Leakey, James Maikweki, Dismas Masolo, Eva Ndavu, Anthony Njogu, Donna Pido, Odoch Pido, Inez Sutton, Ros Trail, and Thaddeus Wamuny'u. In the United States: Larry Crook and Sylvia McIntyre Crook, Linda Ellana, James Denbow, Joel Sherzer, Carl Alexander, Tom Harney, Ivan Karp, Sally Parker, Sue Voss, Kris Hardin, Pamela Hearn, Pam Kosty, Juan Alvarez, Carolyn Harford, Ray Silverman, Richard Baker, Joy Bell, Scott Gerson, Julie Green, Tony Hirschel, Elizabeth Horner, Catherine Howett Smith, Lori Iliff, Kipp McIntyre, Nancy Roberts, and Stacy Savatsky. Kris Morrissey deserves special mention for her lively interest and collaboration in the visitor study at Michigan State University Museum. *Okiek Portraits* was first made possible by support from the Rockefeller Foundation (Nairobi), NORAD, Ciba-Geigy, Lufthansa German Airlines, the Kenya Museum Society, and Barclays Bank of Kenya.

I took the photographs for *Okiek Portraits* while doing research with Okiek communities between 1974 and 1989. I am deeply grateful to the people of those communities for their continuing hospitality, friendship, and tolerance. My research has been supported over the years by the Wenner Gren Foundation, the National Science Foundation, the Joint Committee on Africa of the Social Science Research Council and the American Council of Learned Societies, the Fulbright-Hayes program, the University of Texas at Austin, the Anthropology Department of Wesleyan University, the Institute for Intercultural Studies, and the Sigma Xi Foundation. I greatly appreciate this financial assistance and also thank the Sociology Department, University of Nairobi, and the Office of the President, Government of Kenya, for academic affiliation and permission to conduct research. A fellowship from the John Simon Guggenheim Memorial Foundation provided much-needed time later to work on the book manuscript, as did summer support from Emory University's Faculty Development Award program.

Michael Watts and Mary Beth Pudup extended hospitality while I frantically finished a long-ago first essay on the exhibition, also offering inspirational references. I presented portions of that early essay to the Visual Anthropology conference in San Francisco in 1992 and benefited from discussion there. Since then, many colleagues and friends have read sections of the manuscript as it developed and been generous with encouragement and thought-provoking comments: Kwame Anthony Appiah, Mark Auslander, Homi Bhabha, Roderic Blackburn, Micaela di Leonardo, Donald Donham, Carla Freeman, Angelique Haugerud, Bogumil Jewsiewicki, Stephanie Kane, Sidney Kasfir, Bruce Knauft, Robert Paul, Andrew Pekarik, Brett Pyper, Philip Ravenhill, Adolph Reed, Jr., Ellen Schattschneider, Barbara Schneider, Joel Sherzer, Bradd Shore, Ray Silverman, John Wood. Other friends and colleagues gave guidance on particular points: Mary Jo Arnoldi, Bruce Berman, John Falk, Margot Finn, Christraud Geary, Marc Gottlieb, Tony Hirschel, Connie Kratz, John Lonsdale, Catherine Lutz, Joseph Petraglia, Neal Sobania, Enid Schildkrout, Catherine Howett Smith, Pauline Strong, Susan Vogel, Luise White. Rob Gordon and Barbara Kirshenblatt-Gimblett were astute and generous readers for the penultimate draft of the entire book. Ivan Karp read far too many versions of everything but always offered incisive comments and useful suggestions.

I also extend my appreciation to colleagues at Emory University who incorporated the *Okiek Portraits* exhibition or portions of the manuscript into their classes and thank their students for comments. Students in the 1997 graduate seminar on "The Ethnographic Object: Issues of Collection and Display" discussed a version of the manuscript with particular insight, and I give special thanks to Peggy Barlett for including an extra-credit exercise on *Okiek Portraits* in her undergraduate class that year.

When the book finally began to take shape, Monica McCormick was an enthusiastic supporter at the University of California Press; Sue Heinemann helped guide it through production with Edith Gladstone's sensitive editing and Nicole Hayward's design talent. It has been a pleasure to work on maps and figures for the exhibition and the book with delightful and talented artists: Marcia Bakry, Robert Evans, Laura Tindamubona, and Sarah Zingarelli. Color plates were made possible by subvention support from the John Simon Guggenheim Memorial Foundation, the Graduate School of Arts and Sciences and the Anthropology Department of Emory University, Emory

College, and the University of California Press. The Institute of African Studies at Emory University supported work on the final diagrams. My thanks to Eleanor C. Main, Kristin Mann, Robert A. Paul, Shirley Sabo, Steven E. Sanderson, and Carol Worthman for their part in the Emory support.

Portions of chapters 1 and 3 appeared in "Okiek Portraits: Representation, Mediation, and Interpretation in a Photographic Exhibition," *Cahiers d'Études africaines* 141–42, XXXVI–1–2, 1996:51–79. Epilogues used in chapter headings come from the following sources: prologue: Dening (1996, 111); chapter 1: Beckwith and Saitoti (1980, inside front cover); chapter 2: Whitman quoted in Trachtenberg (1989, 64), Theroux (1978, 85 and 117); chapter 3: Beidelman (1986, 3 and 8); chapter 4: Samuel (1994, 357), Trachtenberg (1989, xvi); chapter 5: Stokes (1992, 193); appendix A: Reed (2000, xxvi and 137). The image of Walt Whitman in figure 6 originally appeared in the 1855 edition of *Leaves of Grass;* it was reproduced here from a copy held by the Special Collections Department, Robert W. Woodruff Library, Emory University. The Calvin and Hobbes comic strip (figure 11) and floor plans from the National Museum of Natural History, Smithsonian Institution (figure 13), and the Michael C. Carlos Museum (figure 14) are all used with permission. The Michael C. Carlos Museum also provided the installation shot for figure 17.

Finally, I want to recognize and salute those whose assistance and support have been pervasive, but less easily summarized. When I first went to Kenya in 1974, my parents gave me a professional-quality camera to help with my research. That gift eventually led to the photographs in *Okiek Portraits,* and my family has provided steady, loving support in countless ways over the years. Philip Ennis nurtured my photographic confidence and never let me forget that "the eye is part of the brain." Alas, he did not live to see this book. My friendships with Carla Freeman, Margot Finn, Deepika Bahri, and Joseph Petraglia created an oasis of humanity and humor in circumstances that have been sometimes absurd and often outrageous. I have also had the wondrous benefit of Eleanor Main's support and advice on this and other projects. Mona Moore's cyber-kicks helped move the manuscript and brighten my days. A grateful bow as well to Cheryl Wardlaw, physical therapist extraordinaire, who has helped me maintain flexibility and a modicum of sanity.

I met Ivan Karp in Kenya shortly before I began working on the *Okiek Portraits* exhibition. Since then he has become an ever more cherished friend, colleague, and partner. I dedicate this book to him.

PROLOGUE: FROM EXHIBITION TO BOOK

Prologues are more than just beginnings…. The prologue… educates the audience to its own role, blinkers the audience to its different way of thinking, prepares it for reflexivity and criticism, and most dangerously, liberates the audience's interpretive skills. **GREG DENING,** *PERFORMANCES*

"THESE ARE THE ONES THAT ARE WANTED," an Okiot man told me one day as he looked at photographs from the *Okiek Portraits* exhibition.[1] Photographs of people in "traditional" dress would best please and fulfill the expectations of European viewers, he said, while Okiek also liked to see pictures of themselves in other kinds of clothing. *Okiek Portraits* was shown in Kenya and the United States between 1989 and 1997. It placed color photographs taken during my years of research with Okiek communities in Kenya alongside two sets of multilingual captions that described what was happening in the images and gave conversational Okiek commentary. Captions used three languages: Kiswahili, Okiek, and English. The phrase "the ones that are wanted" highlights the different people, expectations, and meanings that come together in an exhibition and the complicated interrelations among them. Other reactions reflect the range of interests and expectations associated with the exhibition:

> Don't you think those people looking at the pictures were astonished by this? They must have said, "These people eat people!"
>
> LAATO EN OLE LEBOO, OLKEREI, KENYA, 1989

> I expected them to be all skinny, but they are really beautiful. I never really have seen this side of the people.[2]
>
> AFRICAN AMERICAN HIGH SCHOOL STUDENT, ATLANTA, GEORGIA, 1997

How would you describe the Okiek people?

· Primitive, spiritual.

· Not primitive, but they're not modern either.

· Very similar in ways of feelings as ours.

· Very wise and resourceful, self-contained.

RESPONSES TO A VISITOR SURVEY AT
MICHIGAN STATE UNIVERSITY MUSEUM, 1993

Once again, I thank you for introducing me to this tribe. . . . I am trying to study my own Kikuyu people and do my own finding.

LETTER FROM FREDRICK MBURU MUREITHI,
ELDORET, KENYA, 1990

I've seen so many photographs of traditional communities in which the subjects are treated sort of as objects. For example, you see a picture of an old woman, lined and wrinkled, looking perhaps "wise" or "deep" in some way. But the truth is that the photographer has made her mute, and one has no idea what she's thinking about, or who she is or why she is wearing her expression. You have really given voices to the people in your photos, with your captions and their comments.

E-MAIL FROM PAUL GOLDSMAN,
ATLANTA, GEORGIA, 1997

These are not glamour pics: They would never make *Life* magazine, or even *Ebony*. They would also not suit *National Geographic;* there is only one native breast in sight, and it is seen very casually and discreetly performing the function for which it was intended. . . . In fact, technically and visually they are not very good photographs at all. . . . And yet, it is this very gauche handling of the production which makes the exhibition important.

REVIEW BY DONALD LOCKE IN *CREATIVE LOAFING*,
ATLANTA, GEORGIA, NOVEMBER 1997

People who visit a museum exhibition hold many expectations and hopes about what they will see and hear, how the exhibition should and will be presented, and what the experience will be like. Similarly, those who produce an exhibition have varied notions about what it should convey, how to put it together, and who will visit the exhibition. The people and communities represented in an exhibition may add yet another layer of hopes and expectations—about how they should be represented, what visitors will expect, and how visitors will understand what they see and hear in the exhibition. People in these three positions may not be fully aware of one another's wishes and expectations, even though all are significantly involved in the exhibition.[3] The expectations, understandings, and interests that an exhibition inspires are embedded in specific histories and shaped through a number of cultural conventions and institutions. When, in addition, the cultural and historical understandings of the visitors, exhibition organizers, and people represented differ substantially, the meanings and expectations associated with the exhibition become yet more diverse. Such multiple differences in outlook may even produce political contention.

This book examines these complicated interrelations by considering *Okiek Portraits* as a case study. The first part of the book replicates the exhibition. The second part explores questions related to museum exhibitions by following *Okiek Portraits* from its inception through its Kenyan and American showings. There I consider choices about images, labels, and design that shaped the exhibition, how different kinds of museums and galleries select the exhibitions they show, and how visitors in Kenya and the United States understood the *Okiek Portraits* exhibition and the Okiek people portrayed. Thus, the second section sketches the spectrum of expectations, interests, and desires that surrounded *Okiek Portraits,* how they related to different aspects of the exhibition (e.g., photographic form, subject matter, overall organization), how they related to the diverse identities and experiences of those involved, and how people conceived of others involved in the exhibition, attributing desires and interests to one another as well. To summarize with that apt aphorism, then, this book is about "the ones that are wanted."

Two themes guide my discussion of the *Okiek Portraits* case study. The first concerns the kinds of communication involved in exhibitions and the communicative practice through which people negotiate understandings of them. As people with different interests, backgrounds, and expectations engage with exhibitions, and with one another through exhibitions, these negotiations become part of various politics of representation—my second theme. An exhibition might relate to multiple issues and be caught up in several debates over representational forms, meanings, and uses. These diverse politics of representation involve people with different kinds and degrees of knowledge, engagement, power, and influence; they are inherently uneven. Communication and politics of representation are conditions of possibility for exhibitions and interconnected as analytical themes. I discuss both more fully in chapter 1.

Questions of identity and cultural difference figure centrally in both the communicative practice and the politics of representation associated with exhibitions, and they are a recurrent topic in my analysis. "Exhibitions represent identity, either directly, through assertion, or indirectly, by implication" (Karp 1991, 15). How do we know and show who we are and who others are?[4] How do others know us and how might such impressions be changed? Cultural values and evaluations arise in tandem with questions of identity and difference. In *Okiek Portraits,* stereotypes of Okiek in Kenya and of Africans in the United States were part of these dynamics. If exhibitions are occasions and means through which such issues are explored, they might also become opportunities both to recreate and to reformulate identities, values, and social or political priorities and allegiances. In creating *Okiek Portraits,* I sought to foster possibilities for visitors to encounter Okiek as interconnected individuals, and to encourage contact and interaction across differences in ways that acknowledged contemporary Okiek life in Kenya. Such encounters and interactions, I hoped, would entail recognition "based on the kind of knowledge that changes the knower and that by the same token reconstitutes his or her identity" (Fabian 1999, 68).[5]

Issues relating to communication and the politics of representation are fundamental to small-scale exhibitions and blockbusters alike. *Okiek Portraits* was a modest exhibition, just thirty-one photographs plus map and texts. It did not have all the complications of a blockbuster exhibition mounted by a major institution, created by several curatorial, design, education, and production teams, and widely advertised, traveled, visited, and reviewed. *Okiek Portraits* opened at the National Museum in Nairobi, Kenya, in 1989 and was shown at six venues in the United States between 1989 and 1997 (Austin, Texas; Fairbanks, Alaska; Washington, D.C.; Philadelphia, Pennsylvania; East Lansing, Michigan; Atlanta, Georgia). The venues included university galleries, museums of natural history, and an art museum. I was the main organizer and coordinator from start to finish and visited all but one site while it was on display.

As a case study, *Okiek Portraits* is manageable because of its modest size and organization, yet its crossnational and multisited tour also provides interesting opportunities to consider important questions related to exhibitions. Assumptions and practices that are otherwise taken for granted can be thrown into sharp relief by cultural and historical contrasts. In this case these contrasts focus on exhibitions, photography, and portraiture, and on specifically situated politics of representation. Following a traveling exhibition presents opportunities for comparative analysis as well. It is possible to consider how different kinds of museums might handle the same exhibition and how design differences in installation might influence visitors' understandings. These are all important facets of the communication and politics of representation involved in an exhibition.

When I began working on *Okiek Portraits,* I did not intend to write a book about the exhibition. My involvement in producing, presenting, and traveling it, however, led me to think about issues at the heart of how culture is represented through exhibitions. As the exhibition developed and toured, my thinking also changed. I incorporate these shifts and my own involvement in the account given in the second half of the book. I was not a distant observer and had not planned in advance to control or compare the venues (indeed, available evidence about the venues is quite variable). This is not a case study in any scientific or experimental sense, then. Rather, it is a case history that traces an exhibition from first formulations through multiple venues with diverse encounters and understandings. It traces simultaneously how my own inquiry and understanding developed in the process. My hope in writing this book is that it will spur further critical reflection on exhibitions, the communication and politics of representation fundamental to them, and how understandings of identity and difference might be formed and changed through these processes.

Just as exhibition visitors vary in their interests and experience, so too do readers. I have tried to address this book to several audiences, including scholars and museum professionals as well as students and others interested in exhibitions, museums, photography, visual anthropology, and eastern Africa. The needs and interests of these different readers, however, cannot always be balanced easily. Students might need background explanation of concepts, debates, and issues that would bore professional readers already familiar with them, while scholars might be more interested in detailed engagement with such matters and their theoretical implications, matters that might seem esoteric or pedantic to others.

The first part of the book is designed to interest all readers; it reproduces the *Okiek Portraits* exhibition and provides grounding for the second part, Exploring the Exhibition. The account of the exhibition in that part is both narrative and analytical. Chapter 1 outlines my approach to exhibitions and discusses exhibition communication and the politics of representation. Chapters 2 through 5 then follow *Okiek Portraits* from production (chapter 2) through viewings in Kenya (chapter 3) and the United States (chapters 4 and 5). To help make this account accessible to general readers, I explain any specialized terms and references introduced and have included some initial background on the politics of representation and recent scholarship on exhibitions (see also appendix A). I maintain scholarly engagement and commentary in my account but have relegated more detailed and specialized aspects to footnotes, assuming that interested professional readers will pursue the discussion there. As a result, footnotes are somewhat more extensive than usual. In three cases where the topics are central to understanding *Okiek Portraits,* I examine important issues and literature related to them in the main text. These clearly marked sections are on stereotypes, portraits (both in chapter 2), and the history of photography in Kenya (chapter 3). Though I hope this organization enables different readers to find appropriate entrée to the *Okiek Portraits* case study, to return to the account for different purposes and modes of engagement, and to think about the diversity of readers and exhibition visitors, it also provides guidance for readers seeking an account at either end of the spectrum from general to scholarly reader. Professionals familiar with the literature and issues addressed might want to skim or skip orienting sections within chapter 1. Those interested chiefly in the story of the exhibition or leery of detailed scholarly discussions might forgo the sections in chapters 2 and 3 on stereotypes, portraits, or photography in Kenya and the longer, more involved footnotes.

With this prelude to the *Okiek Portraits* exhibition and the concerns of this book, what remains is to introduce Kaplelach and Kipchornwonek Okiek, the communities and people who are the subjects of the exhibition as well as its commentators, and to provide a brief account of our shared history. This presentation accentuates certain contrasts between book and exhibition format. As you will see in the first part of the book, the introductory exhibition text for *Okiek Portraits* uses roughly four paragraphs per language to introduce the Okiek, a fairly standard total length but insufficient for anything but the most cursory statement. Exhibition visitors had to rely more on inference and interpretive readings of visual and material details in the photographs (which were 16×20 inches and 20×26 inches), along with individual labels. The book format allows far more development and detail in verbal presentation, but photographs are smaller and reproduction quality may not be as good. The opening material in the exhibition also had to be reordered slightly to accommodate the printing signatures in this book.[6] Okiek saw the exhibition photographs in small format, as discussed in chapter 3.[7] Kirutari Meitukut, the same man whose observation provided the title of this book, commented on the effect of photographs of different sizes: "This is a small picture. If you look at it in a big picture, a big one, your stomach will cry with the beauty!" It might be useful to keep his caveat in mind when looking at the first part of this book, the *Okiek Portraits* exhibition presented in book format.

AN INTRODUCTION TO KAPLELACH AND KIPCHORNWONEK OKIEK

Kaplelach and Kipchornwonek Okiek live in west-central Kenya on the forested western Mau Escarpment in Narok District; they are the southernmost of roughly two dozen Okiek groups in the country (see map included in the exhibition). Like most other Okiek, Kipchornwonek and Kaplelach long maintained a forest-based livelihood through hunting, making beehives, and collecting honey. Until three or four decades ago, Okiek families moved several times each year, following honey seasons in forests of different altitudes. Forest products provided food (mainly meat and honey) and materials for housing, tools, clothing, and other needs. Okiek also traded products such as honey, ivory, medicinal herbs, pottery and other crafts with others in the region. This economy was the basis of Okiek life for generations, from at least the late 1800s (the earliest period documented by oral history and early written sources). Their forested highland home and hunting and honey-gathering history remain critical features of Okiek heritage and identity, though the lives of Kaplelach and Kipchornwonek Okiek are very different today.

Kenya's population of 25 million includes over 40 indigenous ethnic communities, several "Asian" communities, and "European" settler and expatriate communities. The Okiek people are one of Kenya's smallest ethnic groups, now numbering between 15,000 and 25,000.[8] They seem to be even smaller, however, because they live in local groups dispersed throughout Kenya's highlands, not concentrated in a single continuous area. Each local group is named (e.g., Kaplelach, Kipchornwonek, Maresionik) and includes a number of patrilineages that held adjacent tracts of forest land. Several Okiek groups live in each highland forest area, but Okiek also interact regularly with neighbors of other, more populous ethnic groups whose histories and values emphasize agricultural and pastoral lifestyles.

In some areas these non-Okiek neighbors are Maasai, in others Kipsigis, Kikuyu, or Nandi; over time, the makeup and distribution of these neighbors have also changed. To facilitate communication and interaction, many Okiek learn their neighbors' language in addition to their own Okiek language.[9] Kaplelach Okiek, for instance, have long had Maasai neighbors on the savanna to their south, while Kipchornwonek have interacted closely both with Maasai and with Kipsigis living in the rolling hills to their west. Okiek groups thus have distinctive histories of interaction with one another, with their neighbors, as well as with local government administration. They are a minority relative to their neighbors in every case, however, and their neighbors have generally looked down on Okiek and considered them primitive, polluted, amoral, and inferior.

These denigrating judgments were based on the very aspects of Okiek life that have been central to Okiek identity and history—their forest home and hunting and honey-gathering life—and augmented by the less powerful status of the Okiek minority. While Okiek place pride and value in their forest economy and way of life, their pastoral and agricultural neighbors judge them very differently. In fact, Okiek are more widely known in Kenya by some version of the name used for them in the Maasai language, *il Torrobo,* a term meaning poor people without cattle.[10] In the last decade or so, the name Okiek has become more widely recognized, but many Kenyans still know little or nothing about the Okiek people. The specific shape of stereotypes about Okiek has also shifted some-what as Kenyan society transformed during colonial and postcolonial times. Negative evaluations based on Okiek economic and social practices continue, but they have been subtly recast to include nationally sanctioned values related to "modernity" and "devel-opment" as well.

Okiek areas were never a real focus for infrastructural or institutional development, apart from intermittent efforts by the colonial administration and by Kenya's postin-dependence government to remove certain Okiek groups from their forests when the government declared them forest reserves (these efforts were often unsuccessful, since Okiek would return).[11] Kaplelach and Kipchornwonek areas experienced relatively lit-tle direct administrative intervention in colonial and early postcolonial decades. Roads, schools, and health centers were established largely in neighboring savanna areas, ac-companied over time by commercial expansion and administrative extension.

Even after 1980, when roads, schools, and health centers were beginning to be built nearer the communities where I took the *Okiek Portraits* photographs, most people there walked for hours to reach a market, administrative, or commercial center. Thus Kip-chornwonek and Kaplelach continued their forest-based lives with a degree of relative autonomy until well beyond independence, unlike Kenyans in areas of major agricul-tural production where land was taken over for colonial settlement, or even unlike other Okiek elsewhere who were evicted from their highland forest homes. Yet their auton-omy also meant that, unlike many other Kenyans, Kaplelach and Kipchornwonek did not begin to participate significantly in national educational programs, institutions, or politics until relatively late. Their minority status only magnifies this legacy of mar-ginality and relative disadvantage in influence, power, and access to resources and op-portunities both in Narok District and nationally. Such historically produced struc-tural disadvantages feed into and reinforce long-held stereotypes of Okiek, making them indicators that seem to "demonstrate" the nature of Okiek character, morality, and ca-pacity as "backward."

The various Okiek groups live in a number of different administrative districts and their contemporary circumstances and histories vary considerably. Kaplelach and Kip-chornwonek experienced comparatively little direct or sustained government inter-vention until the 1970s but were not untouched or unchanged by colonial or postcolonial policies. Both groups talk about the caution they learned to practice periodically in re-sponse to new anti-poaching laws; some young men were drafted to construct the Narok-Nakuru road in the 1910s; the first handful of Okiek boys went to primary school for several years in the 1950s; Kaplelach were rounded up and temporarily taken to a holding camp in the 1950s when Mau Mau independence fighters based themselves in highland forests further east. Many Okiek (especially men) also visited Olololunga, Narok, or other trading centers and towns; at times, some lived near such centers. Some of the most far-reaching effects, however, were not direct but mediated through others and sometimes experienced incrementally.

For instance, when the colonial government relocated Maasai into a native reserve after the Masai Treaties of 1904 and 1912, a different group of Maasai (Purko) moved into the savanna area neighboring Kaplelach and Kipchornwonek to the south. Relations between Okiek and il Damat Maasai, their former neighbors, were disrupted as il Damat settlements moved further away; Okiek developed similar relationships with their new Maasai neighbors. Further west, in the area around Kericho and south to the Amala River, Kipsigis were also confined to a colonial native reserve whose southern part was west of Kipchornwonek. A set of linked transformations occurred in the northern Kipsigis area over the next few decades that included the introduction of maize, establishment of tea estates with labor needs, and the formation of a network of markets and communication. Over time, as many of these transformations spread south, the fertile Kipsigis reserve was also reduced to make way for European farms and increasing restrictions were put on Kipsigis grazing on their former lands. To compensate for these constraints, Kipsigis living in the southern area expanded east over the Amala River, into the lower regions of Kipchornwonek forests. The history is complex, but I have argued elsewhere that all these changes in patterns of settlement and interaction became critical factors that contributed to significant alterations in Okiek life (Kratz 1990; 1994a, 64–83).

Beginning about a decade apart, Kipchornwonek and Kaplelach Okiek began a series of parallel changes that has diversified their economy to include farming and herding, replaced seasonal movement with settled life, and shifted gendered patterns of labor. Economic and demographic shifts were accompanied by changes in social relations, dress, ceremonial celebrations, and other aspects of the texture and tenor of Okiek life as well. These changes and their ramifications combined with other factors to produce a profound transformation in Okiek life between the 1950s and the 1990s. Kipchornwonek planted small millet gardens in the late 1930s–40s; Kaplelach began gardening later with maize. Initially this made little difference in living patterns. Over the next twenty years, however, agriculture became more important. Okiek began to settle more permanently in mid-altitude forest and to keep their few domestic animals at home. During these decades, men continued to hunt and collect honey regularly, traveling out from these settlements. By the 1990s both Kaplelach and Kipchornwonek were well established as farmers and herders and relied very little on hunting and honey gathering. As these communities created their own primary schools in the 1980s, school attendance grew steadily. That decade also saw a proliferation of land sales in the area as changing national land policies began to produce new opportunities for cash that are having adverse consequences for the future of Okiek and their children.[12] While

Kipchornwonek and Kaplelach did not face sudden, cataclysmic changes in the past century, then, the cumulative effect of their choices, various governmental actions, and a range of mediated influences has been momentous.

I first met Kaplelach and Kipchornwonek Okiek in 1974, when I went to Kenya as a college student to do ethnographic research. Since then I have continued to live and work with Okiek communities, so we have shared several decades of the shifts and history that I have described.[13] In the preceding pages, I talked about Kipchornwonek and Kaplelach as groups, outlining their general life circumstances and history. That account is the result of research in which documenting and participating in Okiek life were pivotal, including many discussions, daily interactions, and participation in various events. The knowledge produced through this research is thus grounded in the experience and history that I share with Okiek. Documenting Okiek life through photography was part of my research, producing a collection of over five thousand images to date. Most of the photographs displayed in *Okiek Portraits* were taken in the 1980s.[14]

Though I traveled widely in Kaplelach and Kipchornwonek areas to visit people, conduct interviews, attend ceremonies, and learn about Okiek life, that shared experience is denser and more intensely based in the communities where I lived. Similarly, I came to know some families and individuals better than others. Since I wanted to convey a sense of Okiek social life and personal relations in *Okiek Portraits,* these communities and families were well represented in the exhibition. In the Kaplelach area, I lived at Sukumeriet in the 1970s and Ng'aapng'eenta in the 1980s–90s (see map on page 10). My homes in the Kipchornwonek area, roughly two hours away by foot, have been at Olkerei in the 1970s, Nkaroni until mid-1984, and Cumpeek from 1984 to the 1990s. All these communities are spread across the area where what were once Kaplelach and Kipchornwonek lineage forests met, divided by the Ewaso Ng'iro River.[15]

Some people included in *Okiek Portraits* are acquaintances familiar from visits, interviews, market encounters, and ceremonial occasions; others are dear friends and relatives with whom I have shared years of daily life. Anthropologists who do ethnographic research are frequently incorporated into the structure of family life in communities where they live, often given fictive kin relations as a daughter or son of a particular family. I was incorporated as "second wife" to Mentegai Leboo, maintaining my own house as a cooperating and contributing part of the family (though without the constraints that would apply to a true second wife). I also assumed the family relations associated with that role, so the children of Laato Leboo, my friend and co-wife, were my children as well. Many Okiek whose conversations became captions for the photographs are among those I know best. A series of photographs may best convey the shared time and personal changes that imbue the photographs in *Okiek Portraits.* My "daughter," Margaret Nampet Leboo, is a young Kaplelach woman whom I first met when she was a child in 1974. I have lived near or with her family throughout my research with Okiek. In figure 1, she is shown as a young girl in 1975 (third from left), in plate 3 (included in the exhibition) as a young woman soon after her initiation into adulthood in 1983, and in figure 2 as a mature young woman in 1994. Like many of us,

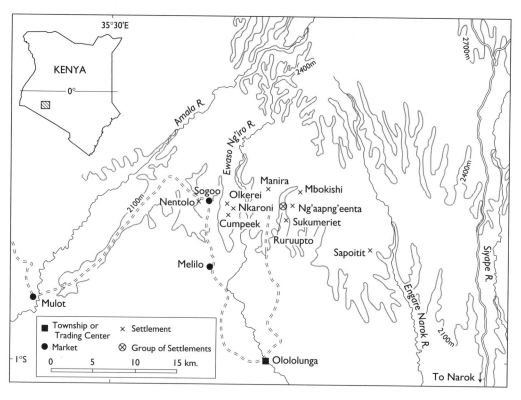

Map of Central Research Area

Nampet is sometimes embarrassed at photographs of her younger self. It seems only fair, then, that I join her and use photographs of myself taken in the same years to illustrate changes through which Okiek have known me as well. In figure 3, I am a twenty-one-year-old student in 1975; figure 4 shows me as a graduate student in 1983. Finally, figure 5 was taken in 1994. Nampet's brother Kishuayon also appears in the exhibition (plate 20) and comments on photographs in captions. He is the tallest child shown in figure 1.

Similar relationships and life changes are associated with other photographs and commentators in *Okiek Portraits.* They were resonant with personal and historical changes for Okiek and for me, though exhibition visitors could not know all this. The exhibition was organized according to the life cycle, going from children to elders. This structure provided a way to show the social range of Okiek communities, but it also hinted at the passage of time that infused each image—a combined overlay of personal, social, and historical time that would enrich the exhibition's texture more for some viewers than others. Life cycle changes related to growth and maturation characterize all human life, so this arrangement also offered initial ways for many visitors to relate to Okiek. The humanism that enables and underlies such connections can lead toward serious engagement with the social, cultural, and political economic differences that also

Figure 1. Margaret Nampet Leboo (*second from right*) with her brother Kishuayon (*second from left*), sister Damat (*far right*), and mother's sister's son Ntekwa (*far left*). Sukumeriet, January 1975.

Figure 2. Margaret Nampet Leboo in January 1994.

Figure 3. The author with guests who came to a ceremony at Olkerei, May 1975.

Figure 4. The author with initiates Sibilo (*left*), Kironwa (*right*), and guests at their initiation ceremony. Nkaroni, December 1983.

Figure 5. The author with co-wife Laato. The boy at left is Laato's son Tutuna, also shown in plates 3, 6, and 7. Ng'aapng'eenta, February 1994.

characterize all human life. But it can also suggest a false or sentimental universalism that effaces significant differences in meaning, history, and life circumstances.[16] In visiting exhibitions, as in other domains of representation, every viewer needs to maintain an interpretive stance that is open yet critically aware of these possibilities and problems.

We all experience biological and social maturation, but people in different times and places understand those processes in diverse ways. Contemporary Kaplelach and Kipchornwonek identify people through social categories based on stages of maturation that differ somewhat from Euro-American definitions. The most basic distinctions are child (*laakweet*), initiate (*taarusyaat*), and adult (*ciita inka oo*).[17] Each age grade is defined through social and cultural expectations about how people will look and act and what rights and responsibilities they hold. Major Okiek ceremonies celebrate stages of social maturation: a head-shaving ceremony where a child receives a new name; an ear-piercing ceremony at age twelve to fourteen (now rarely practiced); and initiation into adulthood at around age fifteen. Becoming an adult is the most significant transformation of personhood and social status for Okiek. The change is accomplished and marked through an elaborate and dramatic initiation that includes a sequence of four ceremonies (Kratz 1994a). The change is also shown and marked physically in the first ceremony when initiates are circumcised at dawn. After the operation they begin a period of seclusion from adult members of the opposite sex. During seclusion they receive instruction in Okiek values, appropriate adult behavior, and gender-specific ritual knowledge. The term *taarusyaat* refers to an initiate during this seclusion period, no longer a child but not yet an adult. Considered a high point for individuals and families alike, initiation defines a touchstone experience for Okiek. Completing initiation bravely is a matter of pride.[18]

The life cycle arrangement of *Okiek Portraits* was based on Okiek social categories,[19] though I did not spell out all their specific names and meanings in the brief exhibition texts. This left ambiguous the similarities and differences between exhibition visitors' diverse assumptions and understandings and those of Kipchornwonek and Kaplelach. The ambiguity opened one of the possible spaces of encounter and engagement between visitors and Okiek. Yet it also illustrates how questions of identity, communication, and cultural difference come together in exhibitions and highlights the sometimes delicate mediating role of those creating exhibitions and other such representations. The second part of this book will explore these spaces, engagements, and issues more fully in its account of the *Okiek Portraits* exhibition. But now, it is time to turn to the exhibition.

THE EXHIBITION

OKIEK PORTRAITS
A Kenyan People Look at Themselves

PHOTOGRAPHY BY CORINNE KRATZ

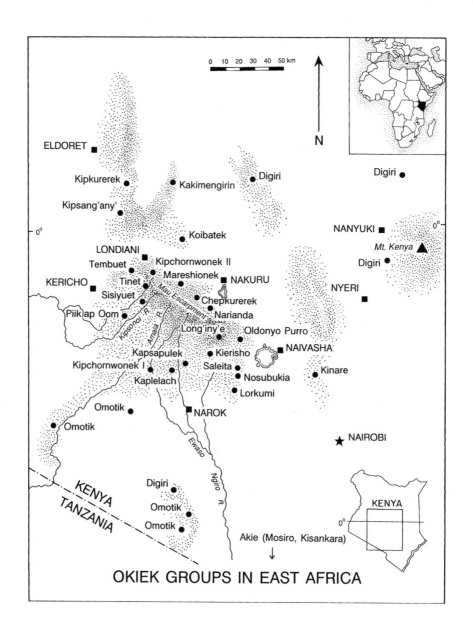

OKIEK GROUPS IN EAST AFRICA

OKIEK PORTRAITS

The photographs in this exhibition are portraits of Kaplelach and Kipchornwonek Okiek, the southernmost of several dozen groups of Okiek who live on the western Mau Escarpment in Kenya (see map at left). Most of the pictures were taken between 1982 and 1989.

FOREST PEOPLE

In eastern Africa, in the deep green forests of Kenya's highlands, dwell the people who call themselves Okiek. Honey and the meat of wild animals have long been important foods and trade products for Okiek. They hunt animals such as giant forest hog and bushbuck; their honey comes from beehives and trees. Much Okiek trade in forest honey has been with cattle-keeping Maasai, who live nearby on savanna grasslands. Okiek are at ease in the forest, at home in a place others dare not tread. Mysterious to outsiders, feared and scorned by their Maasai neighbors, Kalenjin-speaking Okiek seem unconcerned that others know them only as *il Torrobo* (Dorobo). *Il Torrobo* is what Maasai call them, not their own name; it means "poor people without cattle."

TRADE AND DEVELOPMENT

Okiek have never lived a life of isolation in the forest; they have always visited and traded with their neighbors. Today, like other Kenyans, Okiek are involved in many forms of economic development. Nowadays they grow crops and keep domestic animals. Some have opened small shops or purchased trucks to use as public transport vehicles.

PICHA ZA OKIEK

Picha hizi zinaonyesha watu wa Okiek wa kundi la Kaplelach na la Kipchornwonek. Kaplelach na Kipchornwonek ni makundi mawili ya Okiek kati ya mengi yanaokaa huko Mau Escarpment (taz. ramani). Karibu picha zote zilipigwa baina ya mwaka wa 1982 na 1989.

WATU WANAOKAA MISITUNI

Watu wanaojiita Okiek wanakaa ndani ya misitu mikubwa ya sehemu za milimani za Kenya, katika Afrika ya mashiriki. Wanaongea lugha ya Kikalenjin na hutafuta asali katika mizinga yao. Pia, walikuwa wakiwinda sana wanyama wa porini, kama nguruwe wa msitu. Asali na nyama vilikuwa vyakula vyao muhimu; vilevile vitu hivi vilikuwa ni bidhaa vikubwa vya biashara. Watu wa Okiek wako nyumbani msituni, mahali ambapo watu wengine wanaogopa kuingia. Watu wengi hawajaelewa sana desturi za watu wa Okiek. Hata jina lao watu wengi hawajajua; wanatambua tu jina la KiMaasai, *il Torrobo* (Dorobo). Maasai, ambao ni majirani yao, wanawadharau watu wa Okiek na kuwaogopa. Lakini Okiek wenyewe hawajali sana; wanaendelea tu na maisha yao msituni.

BIASHARA NA MAENDELEO

Tangu zamani watu wa Okiek walikuwa wanatembeleana na majirani yao na kufanya biashara nao. Ingawa mambo ya maendeleo yalichelewa kidogo kuwafikia, leo watu wa Okiek ni kama Wakenya wengine. Wanafuata nyayo na kujishughulisha sana na mambo ya maendeleo. Siku hizi wanalima mashamba na kufuga mifugo. Wengine ni wenye maduka na wenye matatu.

CULTURAL CHANGE

People change in many ways, as seen in these pictures. The leather clothes and fur capes Okiek once wore have been largely replaced by dresses and trousers, and the forest home of Okiek is today endangered. Others who have come to live with Okiek in the forest now use it in different ways. The forest is dwindling quickly from extensive clearing, logging, and charcoal burning. Destruction of Kenya's highland forests affects the Okiek and many other people because it affects important water catchment areas. Forest-dwelling animals and unique forest plant species also suffer.

LIFE CYCLES

These pictures take us through some important stages of Okiek life, starting with young children and ending with wise elders. They focus on what Okiek see as a high point in their lives: initiation ceremonies that make girls and boys into women and men.

INITIATION INTO ADULTHOOD

Girls and boys are both initiated into adulthood at the same age, about fourteen, but in separate ceremonies. Four ceremonies mark the different stages of initiation. The first ceremony is the largest and most dramatic. Its climax is circumcision for boys and excision for girls. After that, initiates are secluded from the opposite sex for several months and taught the secret knowledge of adult women or men. The final ceremony brings them out of seclusion again, ready to start new lives as young adults.

MABADILIKO MENGINE

Maisha inaendelea na mabadiliko yanatokea, kama picha hizi zinaonyesha. Watu waliacha nguo za ngozi; suruali na marinda ziliingia. Tena, siku hizi misitu wanapokaa Okiek inazidi kuwa midogo. Leo watu wengine wamekuja kukaa msituni pamoja na Okiek. Wengine wanafyeka msitu, wanakatakata miti ili kuyauza, na kuyachoma ili wapate makaa. Hawajali kama wanamaliza misitu hiyo. Tamaa mbele, mauti nyuma. Lakini kifo cha msitu kitaharibu mazingira yetu na kudhuru maisha ya watu na wanyama wengi.

HATUA MUHIMU YA MAISHA

Picha hizi zinafuata hatua muhimu katika maisha ya Okiek, kuanzia utotoni mpaka uzeeni. Zinasisitiza sherehe za kutahiri, hatua kuu ya kubadili wasichana na vijana kuwa wanawake na wanaume.

SHEREHE ZA KUTAHIRI

Wasichana na wavulana hutahiriwa wakiwa na umri wa miaka kumi na minne hivi. Wasichana wana sherehe zao na wavulana pia wanazo zao tofauti. Kutoka mwanzo mpaka mwisho, kuna sherehe nne za unyago. Sherehe ya kwanza ndiyo kubwa kuliko zote; inapokwisha watoto hutahiriwa. Baadaye watoto wanaingia unyago kwa miezi michache. Wale wa kike wanakaa na wanawake tu; hujificha ili wanaume wasiwaone. Vilevile watoto wa kiume wanakaa na wanaume wenzao; hujificha wanawake wanapowakaribia. Watoto hao hufundishwa ujuzi maalum ya mambo ya kike au kiume wakati huo wa unyago wao au wa jando lao. Sherehe ya mwisho huwatowa kutoka unyago. Wanapotoka wanakuwa wanawake au wanaume, yaani wameacha maisha ya utoto na kuingia katika maisha ya watu wazima.

KEY TO CAPTIONS

Different Languages and Different Points of View

There are two sets of captions for each photograph in this exhibition:

TOP SET in KISWAHILI and ENGLISH, the national languages of Kenya. These labels describe the people in the pictures and what they are doing.

BOTTOM SET in OKIEK with ENGLISH translation. These labels are composed from comments made by Okiek (Oh-key-ek) people looking at the photographs.

The Okiek comments begin with the names of the speakers and tell how the people talking are related to the people in the picture. Initials show who is speaking; CK shows comments by Cory Kratz (the photographer) during the conversations. The Okiek people use their kinship terms to refer to a different range of relatives than Americans do. The Okiek term for "brother," for example, *weeriit kituupce,* includes relatives Americans call "cousin," such as a first cousin on the father's side. The Okiek system may be pictured as follows:

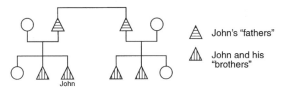

John's "fathers"

John and his "brothers"

Okiek name people in several ways. As a person grows up, he or she acquires new names during different ceremonies that mark stages of maturity. Everyone has nicknames as well. Finally, people are often named by their relations to other people, just as Americans are: mother of so-and-so, brother of Parkesui, etc.

Languages Spoken by Okiek

OKIEK is a Kalenjin language. Several other Kenyan peoples (such as Kipsigis, Nandi, and Tuken) also speak Kalenjin languages. In addition to their own language, the Okiek people also speak the language of their Maasai neighbors and Kiswahili. Okiek who have been to school speak English as well.

Plate 1. Poster from *Okiek Portraits* exhibition in Nairobi, 1989.

Kirorua is definitely up to something. Somewhere in his usual playful mischief, a surprise is in store for us.

Kirorua anashinda wote kwa vituko vyake. Nani ajuae vile atakavyotushangaza hivi karibuni?

LAATO, KIRORUA'S MOTHER

L: You'd think that's Kirorua! Usho! With those clothes of his all full of holes! Aish, that's Longisa all right.

LAATO, KAAMEET AAP KIRORUA

L: Aale ipare Kirorua naan! Usho! Arkoriyaani! Aish, Longisa naan.

Plate 2. Ng'aapng'eenta, 1983.

Dressing up is part of any child's life. Kirorua and his nephew Malaika clown with sisters' scarves while big sister Nampet holds baby Tutuna.

Watoto wote duniani hucheza na nguo za watu wakubwa. Kirorua na mjombake Malaika wanacheza na vitambaa vya akina dada. Dada Nampet anambeba mtoto mchanga, Tutuna.

NAMPET AND HER MOTHER, LAATO

N: I hate that picture! Why don't we tear it up?
L: And so what if you hate it? What are you going to do to yourself [because the picture looks like that]?

NAMPET AK KAAMEENY'IIN

N: Awece piicainaan! An mankemeret.
L: Ai ng'ap ainy'un iwece. Ko ta tuun itaykee nee?

Plate 3. Ng'aapng'eenta, 1983.

With a single turn of her arm, Katais brings her firstborn from back to breast.

Kurahisisha mambo, Katais anamtoa kifungua mimba wake mgongoni ili aweze kumnyonyesha.

KIRUTARI AND MOSEITI, WHO WAS MARRIED TO KATAIS BRIEFLY

K: This is your bride, my friend. . . .
CK: She was yours? . . . You married her?
M: Yes.
K: Yes indeed, a wedding procession even took her to his home.
CK: . . . Did she dislike you? (M: mmm)
K: He chased her away.

KIRUTARI AK MOSEITI. KIMUT MOSEITI KATAIS.

K: Murereeng'uung' toi ni. . . .
CK: Kii inkang'uung'? . . . Kiimut iny'ee?
M: Oo.
K: Oo komyee. Ot kowo kaa.
CK: . . . Ko kiiwecin? (M: mmm)
K: Kiikopiraati.

Plate 4. Sapoitit, 1989.

In fatherly fashion, Temgoi reassures his little daughter that picture-taking is okay.

Kama baba mwema, Temgoi anamtuliza msichana wake mdogo, akimwambia ni vizuri kupigwa picha.

LUTIA AND HER DAUGHTER SELENA, NEIGHBORS TO KIMNY'ALUL

L: It's Kimny'alul.
S: Cory has a lot of pictures of Kimny'alul and his daughter.
L: You'd think it isn't Kimny'alul—it looks too red to be him.

LUTIA AK CEEPINY'IIN SELENA. MENY'E TUKUL AK KIMNY'ALUL

L: Kimny'alul.
S: Caang' piicaisyek aap Cory ce mii Kimny'alul ak ceepiny'iin.
L: Ipare ma pa Kimny'alul. Kipiriiriit.

Plate 5. Nentolo, 1983.

Tutuna and his nephew Parkin, inseparable friends, love to play near the door of the new *mabati* house (roofed with corrugated iron).

Tutuna na mjomba wake Parkin ni marafiki wa pete na kidole. Wanapenda sana kucheza karibu na mlango wa nyumba mpya ya mabati.

LUTIA

L: Ehee! These children never separate from each other! [*laughs*]

LUTIA

L: Ehee! Maipceykee laakookcu! [*laughs*]

Plate 6. Ng'aapng'eenta, 1989.

Growing up means helping in the garden. Tutuna is
determined to succeed with his grown-up-sized hoe.

Hapa Tutuna anaanza kuigiza kazi za siku za mbeleni.
Anajaribu kwa bidii kutumia jembe lake kubwa.

LUTIA AND HER DAUGHTER CHEPOSO

C: Haa! There's someone cultivating!
L: He's not cultivating. Or is he cultivating?
    Who is this, Cory?
CK: It's Tutuna.
L: Tutuna. So this is the last-born child of
    Kopot—oooo.

LUTIA AK CEEPINY'IIN CEPOSO

C: Haa! Inkoraan ne seemperiisyei!
L: Maseemperiisyei. Anaan seemperiisyei?
    Ng'aa ni-o, Cory?
CK: Tutuna.
L: Tutuna. Towaani pa Kopot—oooo.

Plate 7. Ng'aapng'eenta, 1989.

The kids snack on lumps of roasted mash while Kopot Nakwiaki, Rontaini, and Kopot Cheepto chat about the beer they are making.

Watoto wanakula unga wa mahindi uliochachuka wakati Mama Nakwiaki, Rontaini, na Mama Cheepto wanazungumzia vile watakavyotengeneza pombe yao.

LUTIA

L: Is that Cheepto's mother? Who married the daughter of Kopot Nini? Was it Cheepto's mother?

CK: Yes it was.

L: So she's roasting the mash to make the liquor for initiating the child for her son to marry [*laughs*].

LUTIA

L: Kopot Cheepto-i? Kiimut ng'aa ceeptaap Kopot Nini-o? Kopot Cheepto?

CK: Oo.

L: Keelei mayueek ce weeen laakwaani muti [*laughs*].

Plate 8. Sukustosyek, 1983.

The first morning of initiation dawns on Nini and Seraset, ready in their beaded capes and crescent head ornaments.

Siku ya kwanza ya sherehe yao imefika na Nini na Seraset wako tayari, wakivaa nguo za ngozi zenye shanga na mapambo mengine ya kichwa yaliotengenezwa na mbao.

KISHUAYON, SERASET'S COUSIN AND NINI'S FORMER SUITOR, TO HIS SECOND WIFE, A KISII WOMAN

K: That one is the daughter of Saygor. The one that Krismat married. And this one is Jeni [Seraset]. It's when they were children, going to be initiated. See the clothes that Okiek wear when they're being initiated? Kisii don't know about them.

KISHUAYON, IMAAMET AAP SERASET. KIIPA KAAITAAP NINI KORA. MWAICINI CEEPYOOSEENY'IIN NE PA KISIIEEK.

K: Ceeptaap Saigor. Ne kiimut Krismat. Ai ni kile ko Jeni ni. Ko laakook, peentin tuumta. Suen arkoroiikcaan laacei ko pa Okiek ce peentin tuumta. Menken il Kisii.

Plate 9. Sukustosyek, 1983.

Saidimu and his cousin Murureet share a moment during his initiation ceremony. He wears the beaded leather cape of an initiate over his shoulder. Too young to be initiated, Murureet wears a headpiece borrowed from an older girl.

Saidimu na rafiki yake wanafurahia sherehe yake ya kutahiriwa. Kama wali wengine, Saidimu amevaa nguo ya ngozi yenye shanga. Kwa vile bado ni mdogo, ilimbidi msichana huyo aombe mapambo ya kichwa kutoka kwa mwanawali.

KIRUTARI AND MOSEITI

M: This girl is from Parkesui's family. . . . It's Murureet.

CK: She just put a headdress on herself.

M: She just put it on for nothing.

K: She just decided she wanted it.

M: The day that boys were being initiated, when Saidimu was being initiated.

K: . . . I've never seen such a woman! Such beauty in the Meng'ware family. This is the kind you chase after, my friend.

KIRUTARI AK MOSEITI

M: Pa akot Parkesui ceepi. . . . Murureet.

CK: Kiintecikee kityo keelteet.

M: Kiinteci kityo ko len.

K: Kiimuucikee kityo.

M: Peesio ne weentin weeriik. Weentin Saidimu.

K: . . . Toom asue kaarkaani sing'ointo aap Kap Meng'ware! Inko kioonaati wei.

Plate 10. Sapoitit, 1989.

The big moment has come and the costumed girls dance their last good-bye before going into seclusion during initiation. Family and friends gather round the fire to see them off.

Mwishowe, siku kuu imefika. Wasichana ambao watatahiriwa wamevaa nguo za ajabu. Wanacheza usiku mzima, wakiagana na watu wote kabla ya kuingia unyagoni. Marafiki na jamaa wanaota moto wakiwaangalia.

MOSEITI AND KIRUTARI

K: Hehehe! These are truly Kaplelach! No one else! . . . It's a ceremony they're at. . . .

M: You see the colobus monkey skins?

K: Don't you see their legs?

M: Yes—they've got socks. . . . They've been decorated. They have dance costumes.

MOSEITI AK KIRUTARI

K: Hehehe! Kaplelach ainy'un cu! Mainte ake! . . . Tuumta ne inte. . . .

M: Isue karaaiitik?

K: Maisua iny'ee keelyeek?

M: Oo—soksisyek. . . . Akerat. Tiny'e muunkeenik.

Plate 11. Sapoitit, 1989.

Bonds of sisterhood are forged during girls' period of seclusion during initiation. Tinkili and Laakwaani help each other by applying fine decoration on the white body paint so important during seclusion.

Wasichana wanaokaa pamoja unyagoni ni kama dada. Tinkili na Laakwaani wanasaidiana kujichora kwa rangi nyeupe ya watoto waliomo unyagoni.

LAATO, MOTHER-IN-LAW TO TINKILI

L: Ai! Is it initiates in seclusion that you thought you would go show for us, Cory? Don't you think those people looking at the pictures were astonished by this? They must have said "These people eat people!" And then you told them, "They don't eat people."

LAATO, PAKISHU NE PA TINKILI

L: Ai! Taarusyeek ne ipare iwe ipoorueec-a, Cory? Ipare ma kikoing'asyan piikcaan? Koparei "Amei piik piikcu!" Ileici "Maamei piik."

Plate 12. Ororuet, 1983.

Her white and black body painting completed, Laakwaani poses before putting on the outer cape of her seclusion costume.

Baada ya kujipaka rangi nyeupe na nyeusi, Laakwaani anasimama akijitayarisha kuvaa nguo ya pili ya ngozi kama ishara ya mtoto aliye unyagoni.

MOSEITI AND KIRUTARI, FATHER OF LAAKWAANI

K: Here's one that has hidden in seclusion!

M: This is a monster!

K: These are indeed secluded initiates! . . . It's dark. It's not clear who it is. *Cumpeek* [Americans and Europeans] like this kind of picture!

MOSEITI AK KIRUTARI, KWAANTAAP LAAKWAANI

K: Inkiri-ai ce kauny'!

M: Ceemaasiit ni!

K: Taarusyaat ainy'un cu! . . . Uuraat. Mataaku. Ake camei cumpeek kapilani pa piik!

Plate 13. Ororuet, 1983.

Just out of seclusion, Keleges huddles under a ceremonial cape of lush hyrax fur. No one could know at this moment that he would die tragically a few years later while still in secondary school.

Siku ya mwisho wa jando lake, Keleges anajikunja ndani ya nguo nzuri ya ngozi za pelele. Hakuna aliyejua wakati ule kwamba, kwa bahati mbaya, Keleges ataaga dunia baada ya miaka michache tu, kabla ya kumaliza shule ya sekondari.

SIMION, KELEGES'S BROTHER-IN-LAW

S: Oi, death is truly horrible! Where is the other initiate that was with him? This is the other one [the edge of his ceremonial cape is visible]. Aiaiaiai! Emuro! It's difficult to look at this, my goodness! Death is awful!

SIMION, SAANTET AAP KELEGES

S: Oi, ya meet ak inee! Ko inkoro ne pa aeeng'? Ne pa aeeng'-is-o ni. Aiaiaiai! Emuro! Makeerakse otiagi! Ya meet!

Plate 14. Sinentaaik, 1983.

In the final procession of initiation, each young woman publicly dons women's ornaments for the first time. Stopping at each initiate's home, one by one they receive the *enkishilit* headband, their crowning glory. Here Nini follows the others to her mother's house.

Wakati wa kutoka unyagoni, wanawali wanajipamba kwa mara ya kwanza na shanga za kike. Wanaandamana wakielekea nyumbani kwa kila mmoja wao. Kufika kwao, kila mmoja anavaa *enkishilit* kichwani mwake. Hapa, Nini anafuata wanawali wenzake wakielekea nyumbani kwa mamake.

MOSEITI, BROTHER TO ALL THREE INITIATES, AND KIRUTARI, THEIR FATHER

K: Hee! They're all my children! . . . The girls of the Araapkiplet family are sexy! Terree! It's not for nothing that she was driven—One of them was pursued in a car when she ran away with someone. . . . Ai, these awful things were healthy and looked good.

M: What do you mean, they're thin!

K: They must have eaten bewitching medicines to draw men to them.

MOSEITI, TUUPCAK LAAKOOKCAAN TUKUL, AK KIRUTARI, KWAANTAAP LAAKOOK

K: Hee! Laakookcyaak tukul! . . . Suuriaaten simparaakoonik aap Araapkiplet! Teree! Ma ko len kiioonu—Akioonu ake en matatu. . . . Ai, ko neraati arakaik.

M: Cepepaisyek caan.

K: Kooam paaneetwokik.

Plate 15. Mbokishi, 1983.

Emerging as young women from the rigors of initiation, Chepopoo, Tinkili, and Laakwaani proudly show off their finery before retiring, each to her parents' home, to await marriage.

Baada ya kumaliza kazi ngumu ya unyagoni, Chepopoo, Tinkili, na Laakwaani wanafaharisha shanga zao. Wamekaa pamoja unyagoni kwa miezi mingi, lakini sasa kila mmoja atarudi kwa wazazi wake mpaka atakapoolewa.

KIRUTARI, THE YOUNG WOMEN'S FATHER

K: This is the thing we were born with, these decorations for the children. . . . This is a small picture. If you look at it in a big picture, a big one, your stomach will cry with the beauty! And this child of mine [*on the right end*]! Truly, she was burning people with her beauty.

KIRUTARI, KWAANTAAP LAAKOOKCU

K: Kitu tunazaliwa sisi ndiyo hii maridadi ya watoto. . . . Hii kidogo. Kuangalia kwa ile kubwa, ile kubwa, tumbo italia! Na hii mtoto yangu kweli alikuwa anachoma watu.

Plate 16. Ororuet, 1983.

Obviously pleased with herself, Rusi contemplates her achievements and her future as her initiation comes to an end.

Akimaliza unyago wake, Rusi amejipamba akifikiria yale yaliopita na mengine mengi katika maisha yake ya usoni.

LAATO, SISTER TO RUSI

L: What is she holding? She's holding the projection on her necklace. She'll hold it forever. She'll hold it forever and ever and ever in the picture.

LAATO, TUUPCAK RUSI

L: Nee-o ne kiinam? Kiinam enkotooit aap kaatit. Namei kai. Konam ot kai ot kai ot kai.

Plate 17. Mbokishi, 1983.

Like a butterfly emerging from a cocoon, Nini faces her new life as an adult with determination. Many of her beaded ornaments are like those of Purko Maasai, but her headband shows she is not Maasai.

Kama kipepeo anayetoka kwa kifukofuko, Nini anatazamia kwa hamu maisha yake mapya kama mwanamke. Shanga zake nyingi zinafanana na shanga za Purko Maasai, lakini shanga zake za kichwa zinaonyesha wazi ya kuwa yeye sio Maasai.

LUTIA, A KIPCHORNWONEK WOMAN

L: Are all of these Kaplelach? (CK: mm) And which one is this?

CK: It's the child of Saygor again.

L: Saygor's child? Saygor's daughter is very pretty.

LUTIA, KIPCHORNWONINTET

L: Ko Kaplelach cu tukul? (CK: mm) Ko ainoon ni?

CK: Naan pa Saigor kora.

L: Laakweet aap Saigor? Sing'oi-a utko ceep-taap Saigor.

Plate 18. Mbokishi, 1983.

A bride must keep her pace slow and her head down, but Tinkili sneaks a look as her wedding procession approaches her new husband's home.

Lazima bibi arusi aende pole pole, akiangalia chini. Lakini Tinkili anachungulia upesi wanapokaribia nyumba ya bwanake.

MOSEITI AND KIRUTARI, BROTHER AND FATHER TO TINKILI

M: You'd think she was being married or what? (CK: mm) Kishuayon was marrying her. . . .

K: That day she was taken to her husband's place. Tinkili. . . .

M: And the ritual bamboo pole. Don't you see? She's covering her eyes. This is a woman acting as she should!

(IN ANOTHER DISCUSSION, YOUNG CHEPOSO ALSO COMMENTED)

C: And she's put a piece of grass on her head! Ai, what's done in ceremonies is really something!

MOSEITI AK KIRUTARI. TUUPCA MOSEITI AK TINKILI. KO KWAANTA KIRUTARI.

M: Ipare kiiiltai anaan nee? (CK: mm) Kiiiltai Kishuayonin. . . .

K: Siku ile anapelekwa kwa bwana. Tinkili. . . .

M: Ak olartatini. Meisue? Tucei koony'eek. Ceepyoosa ni.

(KIILE KORA CHEPOSO)

C: Kointo suuswaat metit! Ai, ma tukun ce yayei tuumwek-aa!

Plate 19. Ng'aapng'eenta, 1983.

Red-eyed from a night of revelry, Tinkili's husband,
Kishuayon, has enjoyed celebrating the ceremony for
Saidimu.

Macho yake ni mekundu kwa sababu Kishuayon, bwanake
Tinkili, amekesha kwenye sherehe ya Saidimu.

LUTIA AND HER DAUGHTER CHEEPEET

L: This could only be Michael! Is he drunk?
(CK: mm) He's drunk but just a little drunk.
Or is he really drunk?

C: He's drunk. Just look at the eyes.

L: And the mouth—it's whitish.

LUTIA AK CHEEPINY'IIN CHEEPEET

L: Michael ni kityo! Pookiti-a? (CK: mm)
Pookiti-is ko pookiti peny'o. Anaan pookiti?

C: Pookiti. Konto keer koony'eek-o.

L: Aine kuutiit-o—kaleeliit.

Plate 20. Sapoitit, 1989.

Cheepto is absorbed in Saidimu's initiation ceremony while
her little daughter nurses unperturbed.

Cheepto anajishughulisha sana na sherehe ya ndugu yake,
Saidimu. Mtoto wake hajali; yeye ananyonya tu, bila wasiwasi.

KIRUTARI AND MOSEITI

K: It's Cheepto!

M: Cheepto! That's her, my friend. Hehee!
The Leboo family, friend!

K: But they're attractive in their own way. . . .
Ee, that child was lovely!

KIRUTARI AK MOSEITI

K: Cheepto!

M: Cheepto! Inee wei! Hehee! Kap Leboo wei!

K: Ake singoi en oriiny'uaan. . . . Ee, kii singoi
laakweet leyye!

Plate 21. Sapoitit, 1989.

The life of a mother is similar in some ways everywhere. Kopot Yaya prepares lunch for her hungry family.

Maisha ya akina mama ni sawa kila mahali. Mama Yaya anaandalia jamii yake chakula.

LUTIA AND HER DAUGHTERS SELENA AND CHEEPEET

L: There's cooking going on here! [*laughs*] . . .

S: Ai! Cory photographs anything! . . .

L: Where is Kopot Yaya here? Did you photograph her in her house? (CK: yes) Is she making tea? Or what is she cooking?

CK: She's making *ugali* [stiff maize porridge]. . . .

C: Don't you see? That's a wooden cooking spoon. . . .

L: Oh yes, she was making *ugali.* My goodness, Kopot Yaya was pretty.

LUTIA AK TIIPIIKYIIK SELENA AK CHEEPEET

L: Kiyayisyei en iyu! [*laughs*] . . .

S: Ai ma tukun ce pirei Cory! . . .

L: Mii ano Kopot Yaya en iyu? Kale kiipir en kaany'iin? (CK: oo) Iyoei caaiik? Anaan iyoei nee?

CK: Kwany'sei. . . .

C: Maikeer-o? Mukaang'ket. . . .

L: Oooo, kokwany'e. Oi eceekee, kii sing'oi Kopot Yaya kaany'uun.

Plate 22. Ororuet, 1983.

Kopot Nabaru comes home with grass to help roof her daughter's new house and a broom of leafy branches to sweep it out.

Mama Nabaru anarudi na nyasi za kuezeka paa ya mwanae. Tena, anashika ufagio wa majani.

LUTIA AND CHEEPEET

L: This is really an old lady.

C: What's she wearing, Mom? Clothes?

L: Mm. You'd think the old woman who already died [Lutia's grandmother] was stronger than this one is. No, Grandma was older than this one. Or which one, Cory?

CK: I don't know which was older.

L: The older one died. I think this one is still strong. Don't you see she still puts leather earrings in her ears?

LUTIA AK CHEEPEET

L: Intasatat ni kabisa.

C: Kiilaacei nee ee-ee? Arkoroiik?

L: Mm. Ipare kiikowo ne kii tako uuyuuy en ni. E-e kiiyoos kooko en ni. Anaan ainoon-a, Cory?

CK: Manken.

L: Kiikopek ne kiiyoos. Ale ipare uuyuuy ni. Maikeere tako intai muuenik aap iitiik iitiik?

Plate 23. Sukumeriet, 1975.

Preparing to climb a tree to his beehive, Kasana blows on a smudge, nursing its burning ember. The bees will flee the smoke, allowing him to fill his leather bag with honey.

Kabla ya kupanda mti ulipo mzinga wake, Kasana anavivia moto usizimike. Moshi utafukuza nyuki ili apate nafasi ya kuchota asali na kuiweka kwa mfuko wake wa ngozi.

KASANA'S GRANDCHILDREN SELENA, CHEEPEET, AND CHEPOSO, WITH THEIR MOTHER, LUTIA

S: Oiye! It's Grandpa! He's eating honey!

L: Oiye, when Selena sees her grandfather she has a fit. . . .

Cpt: He's blowing on the fire, Mom. You'd think he wants to climb a hive.

L: Is this father-in-law? . . . Was he in the forest? (CK: mm)

Cps: Look at the smoke.

L: Ehee! Is that smoke? My goodness, Cory! You really and truly took his picture.

KASANA KO INKUUKET AAP SELENA, CHEEPEET AK CHEPOSO. NG'ALANI LAAKOOK AK KAAMEENY'UAAN, LUTIA

S: Oiye kuuka! Amei kuumiik!

L: Oiye, inkokeer Selena inkuuket sikopeng'cin. . . .

Cpt: Kuutei maat ee-ee. Ipare macei kolaany' mwaiinket.

L: Pakiteng'-o ni? . . . Kiimii timta-a? (CK: mm) Emuro.

Cps: Sue iyieet-o.

L: Ehee! Iyieet-o niin? Oi eceekee, Cory! Oiye kiipir-ayn iman.

Plate 24. Ng'aapng'eenta, 1983.

Farming in the forest is not easy, but Kopot Mbosholo has a good harvest of finger millet.

Si rahisi kulima msituni, lakini Mama Mbosholo anavuna mtama mwingi.

KIRUTARI AND MOSEITI

K: What is she gathering? Millet?

M: Yes, she's harvesting millet.

K: She's harvesting millet. Ai, these people are strange . . . these *cumpeek* [white people] are hard to understand. So these are the things you go around doing?

KIRUTARI AK MOSEITI

K: Putei nee? Paeek?

M: Oo, kesei paeek.

K: Kesei paeek. Ai, ng'waan piikcu . . . ng'waan cumpeekcu. Aa cu tukcu iyayaati?

Plate 25. Cumpeek, 1984.

Kopot Araap Meriki shapes wet clay into the base of a pot. She will coil the clay "sausages" at right onto the base to form sides for her pot.

Mama Araap Meriki anatengeneza msingi wa chungu kwa uangalifu. Akimaliza, towe nyingine ya kuendelea iko huko tayari.

KIRUTARI AND MOSEITI, WHO IS MARRIED TO THIS WOMAN'S GRANDDAUGHTER

K: It's John's mother-in-law.

M: The mother of Araap Meriki?

K: Yes, it's Araap Meriki's mother. . . . Ai!
   So it's your mother-in-law—no.

M: She's not my mother-in-law. She's not my
   mother-in-law. What would I call her?

K: You call her Grandmother. Or would
   it be Mother?

KIRUTARI AK MOSEITI. TINY'E MOSEITI INKOOKET AAP INTASATANI.

K: Pookerit aap John.

M: Kaameet aap Araap Meriki?

K: Oo, Kopot Araap Meriki. . . . Ai!
   Pookering'uung'—aa-aa.

M: Ma pookeriny'uun anee. Ma pookeriny'uun
   anee. Akuurene nee?

K: Ikuurene kooko. Ee-ee.

Plate 26. Nkaroni, 1983.

Kokeny'in sits wrapped in her hyrax cape, the clothing of
her youth. She was one of the oldest Okiek alive.

Kokeny'in anajifunika na nguo yake ya ngozi za pelele,
kama watu wengi walivyokuwa wakivaa siku za zamani.
Kokeny'in alikuwa mzee kuliko karibu Okiek wengine wote.

LUTIA, KOKENY'IN'S GRANDCHILD, AND LUTIA'S DAUGHTERS CHEEPEET AND CHEPOSO

L: I told you Grandma was old! . . . Oi, Grandma! When I see it, I remember her. . . . Oi I wish I could see Grandma. Oo-aa! She was very old in this picture. She was hardly there still.

Cpt: She wore a hide cape.

Cps: And a few small beads on her neck.

L: Did you photograph her in the place where Mom and them live today?

CK: Yes.

L: She was already going downhill then, when they moved there.

LUTIA, INKOOKET AAP KOKENY'IN. NG'ALANI AK TIIPIIKCYIIK, CHEEPEET AK CHEPOSO

L: Ko kaaalein yoos kooko! . . . Oi, kooko ee-aa! Inakeer-i, apwaati. . . . Oi ton akeer kooko. Oo-aa! Kiikoyoosiit-ayn manko mii.

Cpt: Kiilaac injorupayt.

Cps: Ak kariik tupatukun en kaatit.

L: Kiiipir en iyaan meny'e ra akot ee-ee?

CK: Oo.

L: Kiiaikoreekta peesionaan en iyaan.

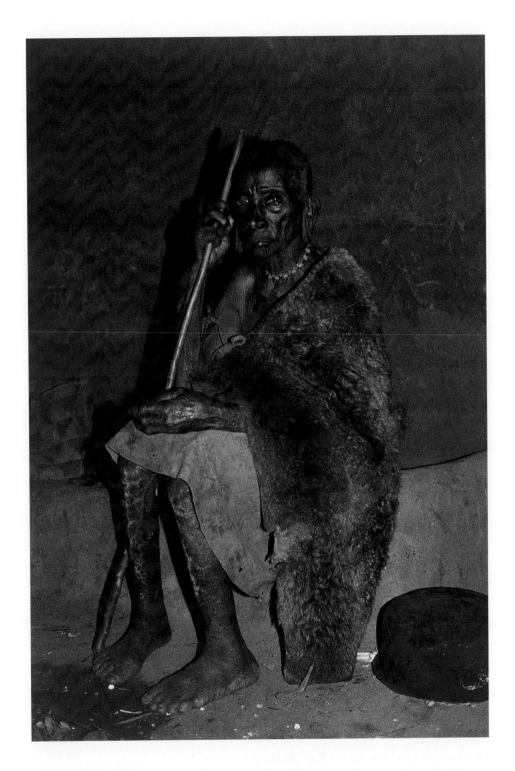

Plate 27. Sinentaaik, 1984.

In high spirits, Kasana brings branches and vines to build the ceremonial shrine that starts initiation.

Akitabasamu, Kasana analeta vitu vya kutengeneza mahali patakatifu na kuanzisha sherehe ya kutahiri watoto.

KASANA'S GRANDCHILDREN SELENA AND CHEEPEET, WITH THEIR MOTHER, LUTIA

S: Oiyee! Grandpa is laaaaaaughing!

C: Where was he? You'd think he was bringing things to build a ceremonial shrine or what? . . . He has—branches from *tepeeng'wet* bushes. And he also has—

L: So he can tie it. I wonder whose ceremonial shrine? Or what was he doing?

CK: It was for those children that were initiated at Kap Sembui.

L: That's right. Don't you see that these things are for a ceremonial shrine?

LAAKOOK AAP LUTIA, SELENA AK CHEEPEET. INKUUKETNY'WAAN KASANA.

S: Oiyee kuuka kaaraaraaaaariyei!

C: Kii mii ano? Ipare akeip ne kilumtaiene mabwaita anaan nee? . . . Tiny'e-i— tepeeng'wet-i, es ko tiny'—

L: Asi korat in—mabwaita aap ng'aa ara? Anaan nee?

CK: Laakookcaan kiipeentin en Kap Sembui.

L: Ooi iny'ee. Maikeer ile pa mabwaita tukcu?

Plate 28. Nkaroni, 1983.

Kwaampat Koipitat has just blessed the ceremonial shrine by spitting honey wine on it. He holds the calabash with the remaining wine, knowing that many people will want to share it.

Baba Koipitat amebariki mahali patakatifu pa sherehe kwa kupatemea muratina. Anashika kibuyu chenye muratina iliyobaki. Anajua watu wengi watataka kuionja.

LOLO AND HER MOTHER, LUTIA, DAUGHTER-IN-LAW TO KWAAMPAT KOIPITAT

L: Is that John's father?

LI: Yes [*laughs*]. He's looking at Cory and laughing.

LUTIA, PAKITENG' EN KWAAMPAT KOIPITAT, AK LOLO

L: Kwaampat John-a?

LI: Oo [*laughs*]. Sue toi Cory koraari.

Plate 29. Sapoitit, 1989.

Heavy responsibility falls on Kibarua, the initiates' senior teacher. With knitted brow, she discusses the next procedure for her girls.

Kazi ya mwalimu wa wanawali unyagoni ni ngumu. Kibarua anafikiri sana akieleza vile sherehe ya watoto itaendelea.

KIRUTARI

K: It's Kibarua.

CK: The one from Nentolo. Isn't she for the Tanki family?

K: Yes, now I know her. Now I know her. The one that was married to the Sonoya family. Ai! Was it the Sonoya family that had her? She's Edilati's sister.

KIRUTARI

K: Kibarua.

CK: Pa Nentolo. Ma pa Kap Tanki?

K: Oo, kaanai. Oo, kaanai. Ne kiitiny'e Kap Sonoya. Ai! Kii Kap Sonoya ocei ne kiitiny'e? Tuupca toi ak Edilati.

Plate 30. Inkipeuit, 1985.

Ndururu listens intently to the discussion as he and other elders plan the boys' initiation ceremony.

Ndururu anasikiliza kwa makini wakati anapozungumza na wazee wenzake jinsi ya kufanya sherehe ya vijana.

MOSEITI AND KIRUTARI, AN OLD FRIEND OF NDURURU

K: Heeheehee! This one is so awful that it must be an enemy! . . . It's Ndururu! It's Ndururu, my friend.

M: Ndururu, the one from Sapoitit. Ndururu who says "hehehe . . . " [*M. imitates him*].

K: But this person is very nice indeed.

MOSEITI AK KIRUTARI, COORUEET AAP NDURURU

K: Heeheehee! O-o-o puuny'aat! . . . Ndururu! Ndururu toi.

M: Ndururu pa Sapoitit. Ndururu keleinci "hehehe . . . " [*M. imitates him*].

K: Ake parapwaat ciici leyye.

Plate 31. Sapoitit, 1989.

Her impish smile cannot disguise the wisdom of old age.
Naoroy is my kind and understanding friend.

Ucheshi wake hauwezi kuficha hekima ya uzee. Naoroy
ni nyanya mwema sana na rafiki yangu mkubwa.

**MOSEITI AND KIRUTARI, WHO WAS INITIATED
WITH NAOROY'S SON**

K: Who is this? Wait, let me look. . . . Hee! It's
the mother of my co-initiate! Mother of my
co-initiate! . . . That old lady that was married to
Orkankait. Torr! Araap Semeri's mother. Usho!
Ai, she's gotten old. I wonder if she's still alive?
Ai, but this old lady is a very kind person.

M: Yes, very much so. . . . That's the end there.
That's really the end.

**MOSEITI AK KIRUTARI (NE KIIPA TUWAI AK
WEERIIT AAP NAOROY)**

K: Ng'aa ira ni? Oo-oo aceeng'. . . . Hee! Kopot
pakule! Kopot pakule! . . . Intasatat ne kiitiny'e
Orkankait. Torr! Kopot Araap Semeri. Usho!
Ai, kiikoyoosiit. Ara takosapei? Ake parapwaat
intasatani.

M: Oo, komyee. . . . Mwisho iyaan. Mwisho pi.

Plate 32. Nkaroni, 1983.

The photographs in this exhibit were taken by Corinne Kratz, who teaches African Studies and Anthropology at Emory University. She is also Research Associate in the Sociology Department of the University of Nairobi. Dr. Kratz has been living with Okiek and doing research in Kenya since 1974. She has published many articles about Okiek life and a book about Okiek initiation entitled *Affecting Performance: Meaning, Movement, and Experience in Okiek Women's Initiation* (Smithsonian Institution Press). Her photographs have been shown and published in Kenya and the United States.

This exhibition was made possible through the generous sponsorship of the following organizations, to whom we express our gratitude.

Picha zinazoonyeshwa hapa zilipigwa na Corinne Kratz, ambaye anafundisha katika Idara ya Elimu ya Kiafrika na Idara ya Anthropologia ya Chuo Kikuu cha Emory. Pia, Daktari Kratz ni Mtafiti katika Elimu ya Jamii ya Chuo Kikuu cha Nairobi. Dr. Kratz amekuwa akifanya utafiti kuhusu maisha ya watu wa Okiek tangu 1974. Utafiti wake unachunguza zaidi mambo ya utamaduni, lugha, na historia ya watu wa Okiek. Ameshaandika nakala nyingi juu ya maisha yao. Kitabu chake kuhusu sherehe zao kinaitwa *Affecting Performance: Meaning, Movement, and Experience in Okiek Women's Initiation* (Smithsonian Institution Press). Picha zake zingine zishaonyeshwa mahala pengi nchini Kenya na pia katika miji kadhaa nchini Amerika.

Maonyesho haya yamewezekana kutokana na udhamini na usaidizi wa wafuatayo. Tunawashukuru wote.

BARCLAYS BANK OF KENYA

CIBA-GEIGY

KENYA MUSEUM SOCIETY

LUFTHANSA GERMAN AIRLINES

NORAD

THE ROCKEFELLER FOUNDATION, NAIROBI

EXPLORING THE EXHIBITION

Kirutari Meitukut and Moseiti Oldio in 1989, looking at a 1984 photograph of Kokeny'in, a very old Okiot woman wearing a hyrax fur cape (plate 27).

KIRUTARI: These are the people of long ago. These are the [pictures] that are wanted, friend.

MOSEITI: Those colonial ones.

KIRUTARI: Yes. These are the ones that are wanted, not the fancy ones [with people in modern clothes]. These. This is the kind that is wanted.... And this thing will continue forever and ever until the country is overturned. They [Europeans] will come to search and say, "Where are those people from long ago?" This is the one that is wanted.

Named for the language they speak—Maa, a distinct but unwritten African tongue—the Maasai of Kenya and Tanzania still live much as they did thousands of years ago, herding cattle, sheep, and goats and existing in harmony with their peaceful environment in and around the Great Rift Valley. Tall, proud, aristocratic in bearing and manner, these handsome people have made their way into the twentieth century with their ancient customs and the structure of their society preserved to an unusual extent.

CAROL BECKWITH AND TEPILIT OLE SAITOTI, *MAASAI*

TRACING OKIEK PORTRAITS

Images, Exhibitions, and the
Politics of Representation

THE OKIEK MEN QUOTED opposite are neighbors to Maasai in Narok District, Kenya. As their discussion makes clear, they have a keen sense of the images that different people hold of them and how dress can visually confirm these expectations and serve as a marker of authenticity. They also recognize how difficult such representations can be to change, no matter how inaccurate or damaging. Beckwith's Maasai photographs were taken south of where Okiek live, but her description here seems to place them in a different world, or at least in a kind of time capsule.[1] It depicts late-twentieth-century Maasai as "people of long ago," another version of what Kirutari called "the ones that are wanted."

These epigraphs highlight issues that are central to almost any politics of representation—differences of communication, inequalities of power, control of knowledge, and intercultural translation. They indicate that questions about representation are ubiquitous but surprisingly varied. Degrees of knowledge or engagement in these issues are uneven and cannot be predicted simply from social identities. Some people of every nationality, ethnicity, race, class, and gender are exquisitely aware of them, while others are blithely oblivious. Most are likely to be somewhere in between.[2] This uneven engagement contributes to the disagreements and misconceptions endemic to the politics of representation. As the epigraphs reveal, debates about representation are multiple and may intersect in complicated ways.

The epigraphs draw attention to European representations of African people,[3] but Okiek and Maasai also have a long history of interaction with one another and involvement in other politics of representation prominent in this region. Different portrayals of ethnic identities and histories have been central in their relations and in the ways they imagine themselves and one another (Kratz 1981, 1993, 1994a; Klumpp and Kratz 1993; Kratz and Pido 2000). The range of representations and social positions involved in those politics is as wide as the one that includes Kirutari and Beckwith.

Kaplelach and Kipchornwonek Okiek live on the Mau Escarpment in Narok District. From there it is a four- to five-hour journey (by foot and vehicle) to Nairobi, the national capital. When I introduced the Okiek in the prologue, I noted that many Kenyans, including their neighbors, the Maasai and Kipsigis peoples, know little about Okiek except that they live in highland forest, hunt wild game, and make hives to collect honey. In this Okiek differ from most other Kenyans, whose heritage is based on agriculture or pastoralism, set in more open savanna, rolling hills, or semiarid areas. Even the name Okiek is foreign to many; Okiek are more widely known by the deprecatory name Torrobo (or Dorobo). Other Kenyans base their notions about Okiek on their own sense of appropriate, respectable livelihoods and their own understandings of hospitable, inhabitable landscapes (Kratz 1981, 1994a; Galaty 1979, 1982). Thus Okiek become an "Other" in opposition to which their neighbors define their own ideal selves, what Michael Kenny calls a "mirror in the forest" (1981). Stereotypes of Okiek cast them as selfish, wild, incestuous, backward, and polluted through hunting, people who live in trees and have tails (Kratz 1994a, 64–70; Blackburn 1976, 61–63). These stereotypes are part of the local politics of representation, framed simultaneously in ethnic, economic, and moral terms that bear heavily on a minority group like Okiek.[4] In creating the *Okiek Portraits* exhibition, I hoped to subvert the stereotypical images and disseminate information from my research to a general Kenyan audience, complementing my written reports on Okiek with a visual record.

As images embedded in politics of representation, the Okiek-Maasai and European-African examples may engage different spheres and concerns, but they are not as separate as they sometimes seem. African representations of one another—in this case Okiek and Maasai—and European representations of Africans have interacted in many ways over the years, sometimes through oblique connections and influences. For instance, European explorers and colonial officers in Kenya first learned about Okiek through Maasai, so they accepted Maasai portrayals and called them by the derogatory Maasai name, Torrobo. Over time, social interaction, cultural interpretation, and political-economic relations have intersected and mediated these representations, changing both their contours and the politics of representation in which they are embedded. One way to understand these processes is to map the contours of a particular case of representation and follow it through different settings, interactions, and interpretations. To return to the photographic examples in the epigraphs, we might begin by asking how Okiek understand wider arenas into which their photographs are incorporated, and how people unfamiliar with Okiek situations and lives interpret their photographs.

This section of the book examines the *Okiek Portraits* exhibition as such a case, looking at it as a process over time. It traces the development of the *Okiek Portraits* exhibition and its display at different venues in Kenya and the United States. The case provides a way to consider questions about exhibitions themselves and about representations of cultural diversity, though the focus of the questions will change as the book follows the exhibition into different phases. Two concerns are prominent throughout, however, as analytical themes: exhibitionary communication and the politics of representation. In combination these themes offer critical avenues for examining the multifaceted processes through which exhibitions are created, circulated, and understood. I will say more about each theme below, but first I outline my general approach to exhibitions.[5]

PROCESS, MEDIATION, AND VALUE IN EXHIBITIONS

An exhibition is event, object, *and* interactive process at one and the same time. The exhibition's production, its travel to other venues, the ways information and impressions about it circulate, the ways people experience and understand it—all these are complex processes. They take place at different moments, in varied settings, and bring into play diverse fields of social relations, but all are connected through the exhibition.[6] To understand exhibitions and what people do through exhibitions, it is essential to understand how such processes unfold over time. It is equally important to understand how they unfold *in* time, that is, how they are situated in broader historical, social, and political terms. Communicative action is fundamental to all the relations, actions, events, and outcomes involved; communicative practice is thus central to understanding exhibitions.

Looking at communicative practice highlights the way exhibitions mediate in all these processes. In the broadest sense, exhibitions mediate between those who create exhibitions and exhibition visitors. However, there is far more going on at each moment in this general process. Exhibitions become an occasion and a medium through which people carry on social relations and through which they formulate particular cultural and political positions and understandings. This is as true of people planning exhibitions and deciding what should be included in them as it is for visitors who come to an exhibition. Exhibitions are further involved in mediations among individuals, social groups, and social institutions. They provide particular, concrete occasions and means through which people experience and engage with public institutions concerned with knowledge, aesthetics, and cultural values (such as museums, libraries, or universities).

Through such mediation, exhibitions are involved in creating, disseminating, and debating cultural values, identities, and cultural knowledge. The very existence of an exhibition assumes an initial judgment of value: it is important to show and know about this. Choices made as an exhibition develops entail many similar appraisals and judgments, formulated and incorporated in various settings and interactions. Cultural values, then, are always part of what exhibitions communicate, though they are not always or only conveyed through words (Kratz n.d.). Hence exhibitions always present particular perspectives on materials shown or sometimes explicitly include several perspectives.

One corollary is that exhibitions are also potential sparks to disagreement or controversy, as people with other perspectives, interests, and values object to or oppose those conveyed. Disagreements do not necessarily create public outcries or vehement arguments, though the past decade has been punctuated by widely reported and highly politicized controversies over exhibitions.[7] Planning discussions can be equally heated; exhibition funders may also insist on particular interpretations. Likewise, visitors vote with their feet, frequenting exhibitions whose perspectives and values they find congenial, interesting, or challenging. Cultural values and perspectives are always grounded in historical experience and specific political economies; they are not a smorgasbord of free selection.

An exhibition's institutional setting also figures in these issues. Where exhibitions are shown can affect how their representations are understood and created. Institutional approval and investment of space, personnel, and other resources lend certain kinds of legitimacy, expertise, and associations to the values and perspectives formulated through exhibitions. The very notion of "museum exhibition" conveys authority; images and interpretations presented are often assumed to be true and incontestable because museums are seen as important educational institutions.[8]

When I created *Okiek Portraits,* I wanted to raise questions about that authority by bending exhibition conventions and making more evident the selections and assumptions implicit in exhibitions. As it was intended for a popular audience, many visitors would have little experience with material shown and would otherwise accept that authority without question. There was a tension between my two goals, however, because exhibitionary authority underwrote the exhibition's challenge of stereotypes at the same time that I sought to question it.[9]

In a recent book about anthropology and popular culture, Johannes Fabian describes ethnography as "communication in a field of power relations" (1998, 56). The same might be said of exhibitions. The communication and fields of relations at issue change over the life of an exhibition, at different moments, and during various processes involved. The communication involves a range of topics; power is rarely the actual, overt content at stake, but the field of power relations influences what is conveyed and how. When Fabian's observation is reformulated for exhibitions, then, the twin themes of exhibitionary communication and the politics of representation come into particular focus.

TWIN EXHIBITION CONDITIONS

Communication and the politics of representation are central themes in this book because they identify fundamental conditions of exhibitions. Like Siamese twins, they are inextricably linked and exist through each other. The circumstances and forms of exhibition communication are themselves defined through various histories and politics of representation. These politics may concern power, knowledge, and resources but they are carried out through communicative forms, with exhibition representations as one explicit topic. Communicative practice and politics of representation are conditions of every exhibition, but the specific patterns and directions they take in particular exhibitions and situations vary. It is always necessary to establish and explore what relations hold among communicative practice and the politics of representation in particular exhibitions. In the process, we can learn much about an exhibition's broader situation and effects and more about such communication and cultural politics more generally.

Exhibitions themselves are multilayered, multimedia communication (cf. Kratz 1994, 15). They combine visual and verbal media into spatial arrangements; material objects, texts, pictures, music, and other multimedia forms such as video might all be included. Each medium included has its own possibilities and constraints. Visitors experience exhibitions as a temporal flow as they move through them.[10] Juxtaposition, spatial design, and movement through exhibitions often contribute to the intended or implied narratives that exhibitions convey (cf. Berger 1982). Space and time are thus also significant means of communication in exhibitions. With multiple components and media, exhibitions incorporate many kinds and layers of meaning.[11] Particular pieces, photographs, and labels might be considered on their own, individually, in pairs, in groupings as part of a thematic section, or as a formal arrangement in a case. Exhibitions also belong to different genres, each characterized by conventions in the styles and expected uses of language and other media combined in exhibitions (Karp and Kratz 2000).[12]

Exhibitions incorporate modularity. Parts might be interesting and effective on their own, but they can also be the basis for larger synergetic and synthetic wholes that are more than the sum of their parts. Juxtapositions, contrasts, unspoken assumptions, and spatiotemporal flows—aspects of exhibitions that defy modular analysis—are also part of exhibition communication and the ways that visitors engage with them. Visitors might learn about particular topics in an exhibition, but exhibitions are not only about learning information. Visitors experience exhibitions socially, often as part of a group. Exhibitions communicate more than referential content and are occasions for other kinds of experience as well.

Exhibitions communicate about what exhibitions are, and how they should be understood and experienced. These aspects are metacommunicative (i.e., they communicate about exhibition communication itself and its interpretative conventions), and are often part of the framing that defines exhibition structure and sets exhibitions apart from other experiences. Thresholds, for example, signal beginning and end with titles, changes of wall color, signature objects or logos, and entrance narratives where visitors often cluster for initial orientation to an exhibition's topic, the kind of exhibition being presented, and so forth. Variations in label and font sizes also indicate different topics or hierarchies of importance. As discussed in chapter 4, different kinds of museums are distinguished by the exhibitions they show, just as different exhibition genres are recognized by the museums where they are shown. Mutually implicating, these differentiations and categories also shape the production of exhibitions and visitors' expectations and understandings. Particular forms of display or genres of representation within exhibitions might evoke their own histories and interpretive conventions (see chapter 2 on photographic portraiture). For instance, the current practice of displaying art in historical progressions according to periods and schools developed in the late eighteenth century, replacing a mode of display that was more decorative and formally motivated. The art historian Carol Duncan characterizes this shift as a transition from the connoisseur's or gentlemanly hang to the art-historical hang (Duncan 1995, 24–25; Bennett 1995, 35–36).

As people visit an exhibition, with all its parts and communicative possibilities, they might take off from any number of details, devise their own questions and answers, focus on particular portions or pieces, skip labels altogether, and see an exhibition through interests and experiences not anticipated by exhibition developers. All these scenarios applied to *Okiek Portraits*. A number of people drew heavily on conversational captions to engage the people pictured; many were arrested by the various kinds of clothing Okiek wear. Some U.S. visitors shaped their understanding through a brief phrase on one text panel, while certain Kenyan visitors concentrated on the exhibition itself as an event and what it meant (chapters 3–5). Exhibition responses and interpretations are never entirely predictable because exhibitions contain so many communicative possibilities and because visitors bring their own varied backgrounds and interests to them. Exhibitions are settings where contradictions, disjunctions, and synergetic interactions among media are all possible, shaping the way exhibitions take form and are understood. This means that exhibitions are always interpretively in process, though the cast of people most engaged in these processes changes over the life of each exhibition (from those who first plan and create it, to those who travel, install, visit, and talk about it). When visitors discuss exhibitions, their remarks represent certain interpretive moments in a continuing process that might encompass other understandings and questions as well. Neither static nor entirely predictable, visitor interpretations and experience may nonetheless be patterned.

In each example above, the mediating role of exhibitions themselves was central. The double-sided nature of exhibition experience, based on this mediation, is stressed throughout this book: exhibition experience relies both on what visitors bring to exhibitions and on what exhibitions bring to visitors (already the outcome of the complex processes and decisions that shaped the exhibition). Visitors have diverse interests and orientations and relate to an exhibition in different ways.[13] The material they encounter there provides resources through which they may experience and formulate various aspects of their own identities and values, whether as individuals or members of social groups. People produce senses of identity in relation to objects and subjects on display, in relation to experience they bring to the exhibition, as well as in relation to particular politics of representation. Recognizing similarities and contrasts with other people and situations is an essential and ongoing aspect of such subject formation. Situating ourselves entails imagining other lives and places even as it brings particular aspects of our own lives and identities into focus. At times exhibition visitors emphasize commonalities, assimilating what is depicted to their own experience; at others, they accentuate differences, exoticizing the people or places featured. Most commonly, visitors relate to an exhibition in ways that combine both assimilating and exoticizing interpretations, as circumstances and identities they bring to the exhibition engage with the material shown (chapters 3–5 take up this point).

Several sources of diversity and complexity converge and interact in exhibitions, then: the multiple forms, functions, and layers of exhibition communication; the various processes and people involved—with diverse expectations and backgrounds—in producing, presenting, and visiting exhibitions. Together, these lay the groundwork for the politics of representation that permeate exhibitions, whether or not they give rise to contentious disputes. Politics of representation are ways that issues of power and control are formulated and contested through cultural forms.[14] Analysis of these politics of representation accentuates the pragmatic dimensions of exhibitions, that is, the occasions and means they provide for social action and for negotiation of the differences produced by such complexity. It also recasts our concern with cultural experience and communication in exhibitions to explicitly take into account questions of political economy.[15]

I noted above that exhibitions always have the potential to spark disagreement through the particular perspectives and cultural values they present and communicate. The different forms and media combined in exhibition communication provide avenues for people to understand and experience exhibitions in different ways. Further, a wide range of people are involved with an exhibition over its life course. Beyond this, an exhibition will touch on different issues defined by its topics, perspectives, genre of exhibition, particular objects included, and more. For instance, *Okiek Portraits* touched on issues related to the Okiek themselves, representations of them and of Africans, ethnographic photography, and other issues raised by particular details in the photographs, captions, and installations. Any of the issues an exhibition raises might be the prism through which different stances refract. Multiple politics of representation always intersect in exhibitions.

These politics are not only multiple, they are also uneven. Those joined in a particular politics of representation are characterized by differences of knowledge, engagement, and commitment as well as differences of position and power. These uneven contours raise questions that again merge political-economic and communicative concerns: how are issues defined, who raises them, who knows about and is concerned with which issues and why, where, and how they are debated? These questions relate to the way disputes in the politics of representation are carried on.[16] Whatever the central issues, any politics of representation is structured by the way information, images, and other resources circulate. Patterns of circulation and interaction help explain whether the constituency for a politics of representation remains local or develops across a wider area, through regional or even global links. Exhibitions themselves can constitute such connections when they are shown in multiple sites.

Paths of circulation are rarely completely direct or smooth, however; exchanges along these paths are typically directional as well. In tracing these paths, it is important to determine what barriers, detours, and facilitating factors shape routes taken and not taken. The political economy of cultural production includes relations and values that favor connections between some locales more than others, and wider distribution for some cultural forms and genres than others. Tourist links from the United States to Kenya, for instance, are particularly strong, emphasizing certain places in Kenya for visiting and particular images in marketing. Kenyans are probably more likely to come to the United States, in contrast, through business, education, and religious connections rather than tourism.[17] Economic realities and the complications of international boundaries also limit the number of exhibitions that travel between these countries.

Yet when images, cultural forms, or political issues do span sites, becoming regional or global in reach, they are not perceived and experienced everywhere in the same way (Hannerz 1987; Cosentino 1989; Tomlinson 1991; Miller 1995). People always draw on the particular histories and backgrounds relevant to their own lives. For instance, visitors to *Okiek Portraits* everywhere recognized initiation as an important topic, but they understood it very differently—from Okiek viewers' personal reminiscence to Americans for whom it was an exotic rite. This should not be surprising when people at a single venue interpret an exhibition differently, but contemporary enthusiasts of global studies sometimes neglect these diverse localizations.

This discussion indicates that in exhibitions, the politics of representation and interpretive, communicative processes are often in tension. The difficulty of defining and delimiting visitors' exhibition experience is one source of this tension. The communicative structure of exhibitions incorporates a range of possible emphases, meanings, and experiences; it necessarily includes some degree of openness and unpredictability. Yet the various politics of representation that intersect in exhibitions each emphasize a particular set of meanings. The tension between these twin conditions again accentuates the mediating role of exhibitions, as both occasions and means through which people produce social relations, social action, and particular positioned understandings.[18] Exhibits are not only sites where politics of representation can be debated, but places where they are also developed and disseminated—through visitor interactions, conversations, press reviews, influences on future exhibitions, and other traces that stretch far beyond the exhibition itself. Such development and dissemination can transform the politics of representation and their uneven terrains.

Case study analyses are essential for understanding how these twin conditions play out and how visitors work within and around them. Specific situated cases also foreground questions about interpretive process and visitors' exhibition experience, questions that thread through this book and—in their reciprocal constitution—reveal how visitors' exhibition experience draws simultaneously on what they bring to exhibitions as well as what exhibitions bring to them.

Several features of the *Okiek Portraits* exhibition make it an illuminating case through which to consider exhibition communication and politics of representation. First, *Okiek Portraits* embodied two ambiguities that unsettle clear definitions of exhibition types: photography and ethnography. Photography has long raised questions about the boundaries between artistry and technical skill, art and science, fiction and reality. Photography is shown as art in many museums and galleries today, but in exhibitions and elsewhere it is also used as documentation, illustration, scene-setting, and in other capacities. Photography's many uses as a medium of representation keep these boundary questions alive, just as some artists do intentionally by their practice.[19] An ethnographic exhibition can blur boundaries between art, science, and history, appearing in museums and galleries devoted to each of these. And an ethnographic exhibition need not be about distant, exotic-seeming places to bring into play fundamental questions about cultural difference, boundaries between Self and Other. Ethnographic photography combines both these ambiguities and highlights the dynamics of assimilating and exoticizing in exhibition interpretation.

Okiek Portraits was both a transnational exhibition and a traveling exhibition; these facets make it an interesting case. Okiek life was unfamiliar for most visitors,[20] but crosscultural questions were not confined to the exhibition's explicit subject matter. With venues in two countries, questions also arose about conventions of display and exhibitions and photography in general. Its multiple display sites highlighted differences in institutional settings, in social and political arenas, and suggested how different installations could subtly shift the sense and feeling of the exhibition.[21] "The traveling exhibition is probably the ultimate expression of the non-linear, polysequential characteristics of the exhibition medium. It can never—by definition—be exactly the same twice" (Ruffins 1985, 57).

The concepts introduced in this chapter will help us explore *Okiek Portraits* and illuminate exhibition experience and interpretation from a number of crosscutting angles. In addition to exhibition communication and the politics of representation, the exoticizing/assimilating contrast can clarify interpretive processes involved in understanding cultural and historical difference in exhibitions. As we delve into exhibition experience, we also need to recognize the interpretive dialectic between what exhibitions bring to visitors and what visitors bring to exhibitions. Thinking about how exhibitions are made, experienced, and understood involves considering conditions that shape an exhibition, different actors involved at various moments, interpretive processes, the ways people produce and invoke multiple identities through exhibitions, and more. *Okiek Portraits* serves as the vehicle for exploring these topics in a particular, situated way.

In tracing *Okiek Portraits* in the following chapters, I also discuss the way my own reflections about the project developed. The process of producing an exhibition raised questions—practical, political, and epistemological—which changed as the exhibition took shape and traveled. Initially these questions and reflections shaped the exhibition's form and content: images included, languages used, perspectives presented in texts. Later, when exhibition components were finalized, they were concerned more with display sites and how visitors experience and understand exhibitions. Instead of changing the exhibition itself, I began writing about it, eventually producing this book. The next chapter considers how the exhibition was originally produced and the selections that shaped it. Chapters 3 through 5 go on to discuss how different people interpreted *Okiek Portraits,* including Okiek themselves, viewers in Nairobi, and visitors at venues in the United States.

There is always, to us, a strange fascination in portraits. We love to dwell long upon them—to infer many things, from the text they preach—to pursue the current of thoughts running riot about them.

WALT WHITMAN (1846)

A great portrait to me was intimate knowledge.... A face was more than an inner state—it was a history of the person's life, some of it yet to be lived.

PAUL THEROUX, *PICTURE PALACE*

PRODUCING OKIEK PORTRAITS

Collaboration, Negotiation, and Exhibitionary Authority

FIRST FORMULATIONS

Okiek Portraits originated in my plans and discussions with Okiek in early 1989, but it continued to change even after opening at the National Museum in Nairobi that August. It reached final form only the following year, in the United States, when captions with Okiek commentaries were included to make the exhibition richer and more multi-layered. Even after exhibition components were finalized, however, each venue meant a new installation, slight adjustments, and different visitors. From these beginnings, *Okiek Portraits* spawned other conversations in places where the exhibition was shown. Visitor interactions with Okiek were enabled by, but always mediated through, the photographs and comments that I selected. This chapter describes how *Okiek Portraits* came into being and the decisions and concerns that shaped the exhibition. As with most exhibitions, the first conception of *Okiek Portraits* differed from the final product. "A great deal of effort often goes into maintaining the illusion that the form the finished exhibition takes is exactly what was intended all along, unmarred by compromise or indecision" (Müller 1994, 14). The final design of *Okiek Portraits* included alternative perspectives meant to foil such an illusion, though these challenges were themselves mediated through the authority conferred through exhibition format and its museum locations.

Twelve years earlier when writing the thesis based on my first research with Okiek (Kratz 1977), I wanted it to include a photographic exhibition that would convey visual, personal, and experiential aspects of Okiek life, so hard to portray adequately in writing. I was also intrigued with the possibilities and problems of visual representation, a concern fostered by courses in film studies, an interest in visual anthropology, and discussions with colleagues about my own photography.[1] Time and resources were limited, so I eventually abandoned the exhibition part of the thesis, but the idea stayed with me. In 1988 I was living in Nairobi and writing again. The end of my doctoral dissertation was finally in sight, and I began to think again about the possibility of an exhibition. I discussed the idea with a few Nairobi-based photographers and journalists and showed them sample photographs. They encouraged me and provided initial advice about how to mount a photographic exhibition in Nairobi.

In early January 1989 I returned from a visit to the United States and began to follow up their suggestions and explore the feasibility of a modest exhibition, that is, whether I could find a venue and financing. With my Ph.D. just completed, I now wanted to present my research in ways that would go beyond the usual audience for academic research, and particularly reach more Kenyans. An exhibition seemed one way to do this; it would also be a much-needed change of pace.[2] Originally I envisioned the exhibition as a Kenyan project. My aims were to introduce my research to a general Kenyan audience and to question—perhaps even change—Kenyan stereotypes of Okiek. Contesting stereotypes meant paying close attention to exhibition form and the conventions and practices through which such stereotypes are formed and perpetuated.[3] Finally, I planned to donate the photographs to the National Museums of Kenya, leaving a visual record to complement the written works I deposited in the National Archives and university libraries.

I added a possible U.S. showing while fund-raising. As most potential funders would be international corporate sponsors, I assumed the project would be more attractive if it traveled, taking their names to another country. In fact, that made little difference to the Kenyan branches of these companies. They were most concerned with their local image, standing, and market. I had not realized how significant support for small-scale cultural projects was for businesses in Kenya. Such support shows their commitment to development, a national value often understood in terms of giving aid. Sponsors wanted their names displayed, but the opportunity to demonstrate civic-mindedness seemed more important than actual advertising capacity. Involvement with local activities through advertising and sponsorship is important in a country where business success can be closely linked to political connections and where foreign organizations are ever open to suspicion.[4]

Though born of pragmatic efforts to encourage support in Kenya, the idea of taking the exhibition to the United States was an appealing extension of my goals. Americans knew almost nothing about Okiek and might well stereotype these hunting-gathering people as "primitive" or "traditional." If the exhibition could question Kenyan stereotypes of Okiek, perhaps it could also help challenge American images of Africans. Both hopes were based on a view of museums and exhibitions "as places for defining who people are and how they should act and as places for challenging those definitions" (Karp 1992, 4).

Initial meetings with potential funders and museum officials suggested that the exhibition might indeed be viable. I met with Richard Leakey, then director of the National Museums of Kenya (NMK), to ask whether the photograph collection could be archived there, as well as others who advised me about producing and storing archival-quality photographs. Leakey was happy to accept the collection at NMK and gave me a letter of support to help in fund-raising; NMK backing was essential for the sponsorship eventually obtained. I also investigated possible exhibition venues and planned to mount it at the French Cultural Centre, which hosted many of Nairobi's art exhibitions. Its gallery could be used for a fee once work was approved. However, the Kenya Museum Society, one potential source of support, would not contribute to a budget that included a site fee. Its review committee suggested I seek special permission from Leakey to hold the exhibition at the Nairobi Museum. The museum was a much better venue. An exhibition there would draw far more Kenyan visitors, but I had not considered the museum because temporary exhibitions there were relatively rare.

At this point, I needed to discuss the exhibition with Kaplelach and Kipchornwonek Okiek and see if they thought it worthwhile. Leaving the venue under discussion and many funding requests pending, I returned to the Okiek communities where I had been working since 1974. I talked about the plan with people in the area over the next few months, as I continued other research. Our initial conversations simply raised the possibility of a Nairobi exhibition to see if people liked the idea or objected to having their pictures displayed. I proposed showing contemporary Okiek life in a range of settings, focusing on portraits to introduce Okiek individuals to viewers. I hoped this would encourage personal engagement and help viewers make connections between Okiek and themselves. At that time, our discussions remained general and hypothetical; financial backing was uncertain. No one opposed the exhibition. Some people were indifferent, but many were pleased that people would learn about Okiek.

We did talk about types of images to include. I felt that certain sensitive images could not be shown without discussion and agreement. In particular, there were pictures of secluded initiates (*taarusyeek*), who are ordinarily hidden from adults of the opposite sex. Since the photographs in question showed female initiates, I posed the matter to several senior women, including some ritual leaders. To my surprise, there was no objection. What mattered, they explained, was for initiates to remain hidden while actually secluded. The initiates pictured had finished their seclusion years earlier, in 1983, so their photographs could be shown. Photographs of secluded initiates were very unusual, so I suspect this was a novel determination made by women consulted as we discussed the issue. This consultation also taught me about the limits of some kinds of secrecy in Okiek initiation.

Exhibitions developed in the past fifteen years put increasing emphasis on consultation and collaboration with communities involved, as museums paid greater attention to the diversity of potential constituencies and as public sphere politics of representation simultaneously became more prominent and fraught. The consultative trend seeks to respond to questions about how representations and knowledge are produced in exhibitions and the institutional authority that imbues them. It broadens the basis of knowledge and participation in exhibition development, creating new grounds for institutional authority. Such consultation can follow many models, ranging from elaborate administrative frameworks with advisory council, working groups, and task forces (Gonzalez and Tonelli 1992; Gaspar de Alba 1998, 239) to continuing community involvement in "dialog-driven exhibits" (Tchen 1992). In planning *Okiek Portraits,* I presented proposals to Okiek for discussion rather than formulating them jointly at every step. The process was more dialogic editing (Feld 1990, 241) than joint development per se and fit into our long-term, ongoing relations.[5]

But our relations also shifted as we planned the exhibition. Not only would it be the first presentation of Okiek communities and my research for a general public, but the exhibition's visual emphasis, Kenyan venue, and relatively quick timetable all made questions about its shape significant and pressing. Our discussions highlighted my role in initiating the project and mediating the representations of Okiek that would be shown. Museums and galleries were far from the experience of ordinary Okiek; I had to explain an exhibition's unfamiliar formats, conventions, and settings. Yet general explanations could not address many subtle assumptions that would shape the exhibition. For instance, the exhibition had to mediate aesthetic notions of a "good picture" that visitors would bring with Okiek ideas about which occasions and people to show (which might have included each family in the community and many posed, formal portraits). A "good picture" might mean many things—interesting, striking, beautiful, informative, different—and the judgment may refer to different formal and thematic aspects of an image (see the discussion of photographic archives and aesthetics below). Collaborative exhibition development often brings to light certain disjunctions in assumptions about what an exhibition should include, its goals, and aesthetics, but others may remain inchoate and unspoken.[6]

Okiek Portraits was a small, independent project, not produced by an institution. My impetus to consult Okiek while developing it came from our long-term relations and from debates in anthropology rather than from the consultative trend in exhibitions, which was not prominent in Kenya in 1989. My discussions with Okiek focused more on content, themes, and overall goals than on aesthetics and design. The final product explicitly juxtaposed Okiek voices and perspectives and my own. These multiple layers became part of an attempt to represent the rich texture and social interconnections in the lives of Okiek that appeared in the photographs. They also allowed me to incorporate into the exhibition's design other choices that could have been made and other ways of viewing the images and exhibition.

FURTHER DEVELOPMENTS

When I moved back to Nairobi in early April 1989, some exhibition funding was confirmed and I had a go-ahead from Okiek. The museum venue was approved in late April. I went to the United States in May to have Cibachromes printed and matted.[7] Nairobi preparations accelerated in June. In late July I returned to Okiek with a progress report. I had finally secured enough backing to include an opening and to hire two vehicles to bring Okiek to see the exhibition. Much of my visit was spent arranging this transportation. With one vehicle for each area (Kaplelach and Kipchornwonek), we spent more time discussing who would go to Nairobi than what would be in the show. The exhibit opened on 15 August; Okiek visitors were to arrive that weekend. Realizing how unusual, perhaps even historic, this occasion would be for Okiek, I decided to record Okiek comments as they toured the exhibition and the museum.

On the appointed day, I assembled a greeting party in Nairobi and had a festive lunch prepared.[8] We waited for hours, but the Okiek never arrived. As people recounted later, other factors had intervened. Some cited the national census, scheduled for the preceding two days, as the main impediment. We had planned the trip to follow the census, but counting took longer than anticipated. Some people in rural areas were uncertain if they could travel, and the few Okiek enumerators had to finish their job. Other problems were also reported: the money for hiring trucks had disappeared; people wrangled over who would go; rains had made roads impassable.[9] Whatever the many reasons, Okiek never saw their pictures in the National Museum. When I visited again several months later, I brought small copies of the photographs, arranged in the exhibition order. I sometimes recorded the conversation as we looked at them; excerpts from these discussions became the second set of captions.

I added the new captions when the exhibit was shown again, this time in the United States at the University of Alaska, Fairbanks. From there, it traveled to the Smithsonian's National Museum of Natural History in Washington, D.C., where a slight title change brought the show to its final form. In Kenya, the full title was *Okiek Portraits: Photography by Corinne Kratz.* The U.S. subtitle, *A Kenyan People Look at Themselves,* indicates a first change engendered by transplanting the exhibition. In American venues, it had to be situated more broadly, the unfamiliar ethnic name linked to a larger, recognizable location.

This renaming also highlights the way circulation and interaction shape representations. When I produced *Okiek Portraits,* I tried to take visitor perceptions of the exhibition into account by thinking about how to challenge stereotypes. As the exhibition traveled, I realized increasingly that I also had to think about the different forms and forums in which representations appear, how they come to be in some places and not others, who encounters them where, and so on. These questions were fundamental to understanding how stereotypes are formed and how they might be challenged, for *Okiek Portraits* would be seen in relation to representations and ideologies already in circulation. This background influenced decisions others made about *Okiek Portraits* and even my own presentations when I sought exhibition support and later, when arranging venues in the United States (see chapter 4). The exhibition played against what might be seen as local and "world markets . . . for life styles and experiences associated with different cultures" (Ebron 1991, 1). In these markets, such as those defined by tourism, cultures and identities are effectively "packaged," often—but not only—for Euro-American tastes; circulation flows are not characterized by equal access and influence.

At the time, I did not think of myself as engaged in markets for identities, presenting a "commodity," but of course I was.[10] The exhibition had to be "sold" in order to be seen. My pitch to funders in Kenya combined arguments based on ethnic equity in representation and learning about national heritage and diversity. Implicit in both was the lure of the obscure ethnic group. The identity dynamics of these encounters were themselves intriguing: a white American woman raising money from foundations and corporations to present photographs of a Kenyan minority group in Kenya.[11] In many cases (and most where I was successful) the people to whom I made the pitch were also expatriates. Ethnic, national, and racial identities figured in the way the exhibit was received at each venue, becoming entwined with different audiences in a variety of ways I may never fully trace.

The geographies and topographies of such markets and flows are complex, easier to map at their centers and junctures than in all their ramifying eddies. To begin such mapping for *Okiek Portraits,* we might note the background against which sponsors and visitors in Kenya and the United States saw *Okiek Portraits.* In both settings there was a profusion of coffee-table books about East Africa, with comparable photographic exhibitions, and other media images.[12] In the United States, *National Geographic* images are also part of the background image bank (Lutz and Collins 1991; Collins and Lutz 1992). Connections, influences, and interrelations among images are contingent and difficult to trace, their meanings shaped through the interpretive transmutations of memory and diverse biographical experiences. Nonetheless, such interconnections and resonances were part of the context for interpreting *Okiek Portraits* in every case.[13]

I wanted to challenge stereotypes prominent in that background less by explicit critique than by offering alternative images, framed somewhat differently than other exhibitions and picture books. But what does it mean "to challenge stereotypes"? When I was producing and traveling the exhibition, I used phrases like this to describe one effect that I hoped it might have. Yet I did not really examine the notion of "stereotypes" at the time, or how they are formed, perpetuated, questioned, or challenged. That goal was, in fact, less an analysis of the situation than a wish that relied on intuition. Could a small photographic exhibition make a difference, or was I engaged in one of "the efforts of a few marginal academics to try to change the terms of discourse" (Gordon 1997, 121)?

RETROSPECTIVE REFLECTIONS
ON STEREOTYPES

Over time, as I worked on *Okiek Portraits,* I came to understand how naive (though not uncommon) a plan to change stereotypes merely by presenting more credible and realistic alternatives actually was. The social, political, and psychological processes involved in stereotyping make any such endeavor far more demanding than this would suggest, as do the complex histories of stereotypes. But I turned to literature on stereotypes only after the fact, while writing this book, in an effort to probe stereotypes in relation to *Okiek Portraits.*

Social stereotypes categorize and characterize people as types, whether focused on ethnicity, gender, class, race, or other social groups and identities. They summarize and generalize but are never neutral. Comparative evaluations are always part of the characterization, even if implicit. One social psychologist calls them "a way of thinking about nationalities and religions and races other than our own with reference to our own standards" (Brown 1965, 183). Stereotypes can present exaggeratedly favorable images as well as overly negative ones, but the latter are more likely to be challenged and condemned.

If the simplistic and inaccurate representation of stereotypes was only a matter of mistaken or inadequate information, they could be easily disproved, countered, and corrected by additional knowledge and counterevidence. But stereotypes are vexingly resilient and unresponsive to empirical disproof and experience.[14] In fact, assumptions and narratives associated with persistent stereotypes often provide the framework for understanding additional information. This means that attention focuses on elements that support stereotypes rather than those that might undermine or destabilize them. Such cognitive tenacity is a persistent conundrum for people who write about stereotypes (Paul 1995).[15]

Opposition to stereotypes strives to counter negative evaluations and their effects as much as to correct factual misrepresentation. At times the goal is simply to reverse rankings, to show that those considered inferior are actually superior. The categories, terms of representation, and criteria of evaluation do not change significantly, though the hierarchy may be shuffled. Whether people are considered noble savages or brute savages, they are seen as savages nonetheless.[16] As one of the Guerrilla Girls said in describing their feminist agenda for the art world, "to actually change the system is so unbelievably complex that at this point, our interest is in getting women more access to it. So that's our attitude about change, as opposed to breaking down the system" (quoted in Barrett 1990, 153).

When I began planning *Okiek Portraits,* I hoped to challenge stereotypes of "Torrobo" (as Okiek are often called) and address the lack of knowledge about them, so other Kenyans might regard Okiek more favorably and less dismissively. The exhibition certainly would not eliminate the politics of ethnicity from Kenya's socioeconomic structure and did not question their premises.[17] I had no illusion that Okiek would move to the top of Kenya's ethnic hierarchy (though Kalenjin-speakers are "in power" while President Moi holds office). Rather, I simply hoped the exhibition might help place Okiek more advantageously in national dialogues, bring some recognition of Okiek rights and interests, and make the sociopolitical field marginally more level. To the extent that I thought about stereotypes, then, I focused on the Kenyan context.

A double set of stereotypes was in play, however, once U.S. venues were added. The extension was an afterthought, just a supplement to the Kenyan exhibition at first. I also extended my hopes about challenging stereotypes to the United States unthinkingly, giving little heed to the different configurations and histories of stereotypes in the two places. Different systems and situations of inequality do not operate in the same way, however, though their representations and workings may interconnect. We cannot assume that analyses of class and gender, for instance, apply directly to cultural, racial, or religious differences (Bhabha 1986, 148). Likewise we cannot transfer analyses of one place and time directly to another without taking account of historical, social, and cultural differences. Yet by assimilating American stereotypes of Africans to Kenyan notions of Okiek, I did just that: both were stigmatizing stereotypes. So what did my unmindful inclination to lump them together overlook and what did it capture?

In Kenya, stereotypes of Torrobo/Okiek are based on ethnic distinctions and especially widespread among ethnic groups who are neighbors of Okiek.[18] Ethnicity is a critical factor in Kenyan politics—defining patronage networks for investing national resources, opportunities for education and employment, and bases for political support—but Okiek have little visibility or clout on the national scene in most circumstances. They typically fare only slightly better at regional and district levels. Unlike larger ethnic groups who dominate Kenyan politics (e.g., Kikuyu and Luo) or those widely known for other reasons (e.g., Maasai), the Okiek minority can be easily overlooked or ignored.[19] If the exhibition could address Kenyan stereotypes of Okiek as backward, primitive, or bestial, Okiek themselves would be affected, for example, if specifically considered in development programs or government policies. Both Okiek and stereotypes about them are unknown to some Kenyans; *Okiek Portraits* would be an introduction for such visitors.

In the United States, Okiek are virtually unknown; the Kenyan stereotypes are largely irrelevant. Exhibition visitors there would more likely relate to the material through concepts and stereotypes about Africans, based more on race than ethnicity.[20] This difference was important. First, it meant that most visitors would approach the exhibition through more general categories. Okiek might be seen as standing for their country, or even the continent, a curious inversion of their Kenyan image and minority status.[21] If the exhibition did affect U.S. visitors' thinking about Africans, Okiek would never know. Challenging U.S. stereotypes would have only indirect effects, as diffuse as visitors' concepts were general. Second, it also meant that initial responses relied more on visual signs of race that tacitly evoked the complex history of race in the United States. These modes of interpretation recontextualized *Okiek Portraits*, relating the exhibition to American circumstances and concerns, incorporating it into categories and issues more relevant and pervasive there.

European images of Africans have a history stretching from at least the sixteenth century. Those images changed over the years in relation to growing knowledge, interaction, experience, and shifting political engagements, but "the later image of Africa was very largely drawn from Europe's first impressions" (Curtin 1964, xii–xiii) and mostly set by 1850. The popular conception was that "Africa is largely homogeneous and static" (Hammond and Jablow [1970] 1992, 13).[22] American understandings of Africans share these roots but also became entwined over those four centuries with understandings of Native Americans and with the social, political, and ideological developments of slavery and its aftermath in the American setting (Jordan 1968). The notion of African culture as a general, unitary category also builds on nineteenth-century African American ideas that elevated race as the basis of common heritage and joint political action, part of the history of pan-Africanist ideas (Appiah 1992, 3–47).[23] As Appiah notes, "this view that Africa is culturally homogeneous" (which the philosopher Hountondji calls "unanimism") relies on a psychology of race and overlooks the extraordinary diversity of African history and culture (24–25). Yet this is the prototype for many American ideas and stereotypes about Africa, held by African and European Americans alike. The multiple histories and influences combined in those ideas show how inseparable the politics of race have been from American ideas about Africa.

This outline begins to suggest the different categories, stereotypes, and histories that *Okiek Portraits* engaged in Kenya and the United States. Visitors were diverse in both countries and approached the exhibition in various ways. For instance, pan-Africanist connections just noted provided one avenue for understanding it in the United States (see chapter 4).[24] And they remind us that stereotypes can present both positive and negative images; they can be used to promote solidarity as well as to disparage. In Kenya, ideas about Okiek as Kenya's original inhabitants cast them more positively but do not obviate or revalue their characterization.[25]

Some strikingly similar negative evaluations are used in Kenyan stereotypes of Okiek and American stereotypes of Africans: uncivilized, backward, primitive. The reasoning behind these judgments may differ,[26] but the correspondence points toward the wider range of categories used and historical links between the two countries. Evaluative social (and political) categories were certainly used in eastern Africa before Europeans arrived, but contemporary Kenyan categories are also the product of a century of varied interaction with European ideologies of race, ethnicity, class, and gender—decades of intermittent early association with European travelers, seventy years of colonial administration, forty years of postcolonial engagement, and missionary activity throughout. For instance, colonial and postcolonial ideologies converge in notions of "development" (*maendeleo* in Kiswahili) that often incorporate the same evaluative terms, contrasting them with "progress" or "modernity." "Development" notions link religious, economic, and political realms in Kenya and in Euro-American nations, shaping interchanges between them as well (Cowen and Shenton 1996; Karp 1993; Escobar 1995; Cooper and Packard 1997).

"Okiek" has little meaning as an ethnic identity in the United States, but ethnicity is clearly recognized and used as a way to characterize and categorize people there. Similarly, while Kenyan notions of Okiek emphasize ethnicity, racial distinctions are very much part of the broader Kenyan landscape of social identities. Ethnicity and race are both relevant in Kenya and the United States, but their specific meanings and the history of connections *between* ethnicity and race differ (even if they intersect). Though they often seem like facts of nature, ethnic and racial categories relevant in each situation are products of different histories and social relations; their definitions also change over time.[27]

In the United States, for instance, changing definitions of race and ethnicity meant that people of Mediterranean origin were considered "black" in the early 1900s. By the

1930s, they were increasingly classified as "white" instead and ethnicity became the primary way to identify people from southern Europe living in the United States (Hirschfeld 1997, 72; Reed 1996a). U.S. history in the past century also shows a changing hierarchy of ethnic group evaluation, with different groups promoted as "model minority" at different times (di Leonardo 1994). In Kenya, the dominant racial triad is African, Asian (i.e., Indian), and European. This contemporary configuration is a product of history since the late 1800s, when Europeans and Indians began to settle there.[28] African Americans who visit Kenya confound these categories and are often perturbed when Kenyans identify them as *wazungu,* like white people (cf. Ebron 1997, 238–40; Clarke 1999, 229). As for ethnicity, many studies show how contemporary Kenyan ethnic groups have taken their present names, shapes, and meanings since the mid- to late 1800s.[29]

When I extended my hopes about challenging stereotypes to the United States, I took little account of these differences in the two settings. Rather, I generalized from one basic commonality: evaluative social categories structure political-economic life and configure and identify groups in terms of both ethnicity and race. Stereotypes of Okiek/Africans both bind together a "range of differences and discriminations," though one emphasizes ethnicity and the other race.[30] Consideration of the counterpoint between the two, however, underlines the importance of examining how different configurations of categories are formed and change over time, and how they shape the ways people understand themselves as well as others.[31]

In considering these two situations, I touched on issues prominent in scholarly writing about stereotypes. That work has two main strands: one considers stereotypes in terms of cognitive psychology, the other focuses on their social and political aspects. Both struggle to define the concept of stereotype and to identify the processes and effects of stereotyping. These approaches converge in efforts to understand the role of stereotyping in people's self-understanding (subject formation), efforts that often draw on psychoanalytic and postcolonial concerns (Bhabha 1986; Fanon 1967).[32]

It is surprisingly hard to distinguish stereotypes from other general categories on a cognitive basis.[33] Stereotypes, archetypes, prototypes, and other general categories are all ways of knowing that generalize and differentiate kinds of things (Ruffins 1998, i.p.; Hirschfeld 1997, 65).[34] They are abstractions that highlight a narrow range of features for "cognitive economy" (cf. Brown 1965, 176–77). Stereotyping, however, always ties categorization to hierarchical evaluation. The ranking emphasizes differences among types of people, but all are nonetheless included in the larger category of "people."[35] Stereotypes thus include an interplay between difference and similarity, creating room for both positive and negative stereotypes and shifts in ranking. (Chapter 3 discusses a similar interplay between exoticizing and assimilating in exhibition interpretation.)

A narrow range of features is used to create and rank social categories (e.g., economic pursuit, skin color, place of origin), but the rankings of stereotypes are also projected onto other domains, totalized, and taken as signs of inherent, unchanging character. For instance, societies that use simple technology have been called "primitive," but "primitive" is then projected onto cultural and intellectual capacity as a totalized judgment. Stereotypes essentialize a social group by fixing the identity of all its members in terms of a few properties (themselves perhaps problematic).[36] Group features are represented as fundamental and unchanging; the present is taken as eternal (cf. Said cited in Bhabha 1986, 157).[37]

Stereotypes can also reflect superficial knowledge, whether from brief acquaintance or limited access and interaction with those portrayed (Gordon 1997, 91; Cohen et al. 1992, 217).[38] But as noted above, few stereotypes change when more information or factual errors undercut them. They combine "fixity and fluidity in ways that make them both resilient and impervious to empirical, experiential counterclaims" (Stoler 1997, 104). One kind of fixity-fluidity is historical: characteristics attributed to those stereotyped may shift over time without changing the evaluative hierarchy (cf. Goldberg 1990, xii–xiii). Another kind is situational and "depends on defining the situation in such a way that any possible empirical situation can be interpreted in accord with . . . a repertoire of available models so as to sustain, rather than contradict, the fundamental premise that there are different kinds of people, and that 'we' are the best kind" (Paul 1995, 15; cf. Kratz 1994b, 180–84). Paul illustrates by describing how casual observers might interpret an interracial male trucking crew. If the white man drives, it can be seen as preventing the black one from being in charge; if the black one drives, it can be seen as making him chauffeur. Multiple interpretive frameworks can be invoked, but the common premises of racial inequality and evaluative ranking remain.[39]

The resilience of stereotypes might suggest "cognitive incapacity" for using empirical evidence and logical reasoning (Appiah 1990, 8; 1992, 13–15), but it also demonstrates the cognitive agility typical of ideological positioning. Such agility helps maintain a particular status quo by protecting from question its unequal access to resources, opportunities, and power. The classificatory criteria and justifications associated with stereotypes are thus part of broader ideologies, grounded in sociopolitical relations and cultural history (Dominguez 1997; Appiah 1990, 8; Appiah 1992, 14–15, 38). These observations return the focus to the uses and effects of stereotypes, the processes through which they are formed and supported, and their role in constituting identities.

These interlocking issues show why the simple aim of challenging stereotypes is so difficult to achieve in practice. Most attempts to confront derogatory images target a particular stereotype, as I did, or perhaps select a contrasting pair (e.g., African vs. European). But any stereotype is part of a larger set of contrasting categories or types, tied together as a conceptual domain and connected through common criteria of evaluation.[40] As a whole, those premises and broader schemes of categories are ubiquitous.[41] Trying to "correct" or change one among many is like pulling one thread from a densely woven fabric. Contrasts between Kenya and the United States showed how configurations of categories vary, yet they also showed how similar their effects can be.

Bound within a broader set of categories and integrally linked to other domains of action and understanding, stereotypes are also paradoxically difficult to locate in a clear, complete way. They are widespread, found in many forms, genres, and media; their premises are pervasive. If addressing a particular stereotype is like pulling a single thread from the sociopolitical tapestry, then that thread is a discontinuous one, changing color and shape, disappearing and reappearing. Dispersal and repetition are integral to the formation, communication, and perpetuation of stereotypes. These features also make them difficult to isolate and challenge. As Frantz Fanon said in trying to manage the distortion, misrecognition, and discrimination of being stereotyped, they "had woven me out of a thousand details, anecdotes, stories" (1967, 111).[42]

Stereotypes of Africans in the United States, for instance, draw on descriptions and images dispersed in travelogues, fiction writing, journalism, school textbooks, scholarly writing, foreign policy debates, photography, Hollywood film, documentaries, television, museum exhibitions, theme parks, cartoons and comics, home and fashion magazines, tourism, and international development programs. Their formulations are transformed and adapted for specific uses, but they still repeat and echo one another. Widespread but disparate, they seem to confirm one another; this is one way stereotypes come to seem "natural." In each of these realms, the representation of Africa differs in particulars but has many common influences and intersections.[43] "[F]or example, why in the last five years of the Pulitzer prize in photography have six of ten images been of distress in Africa or Haiti. . . . However only three of a possible fifty categories of written journalism concerned Africa" (Ritchkin 1999, xviii).

The hydra-headed resilience of stereotypes has several sources, then, which together make challenging any single stereotype a formidable task. They are communicated and encountered in diverse, dispersed, and reiterative ways, making a stereotype difficult to locate or isolate. Stereotypes are also difficult to refute because they not only draw on empirical information but rely on sets of basic categories and understandings about human difference. And they are difficult to "disprove" because the cognitive agility of an ideology supports them, whereby multiple interpretive models are available that confirm existing social and political arrangements.

Nonetheless, harmful stereotypes can and should be questioned and resisted. There *can* be movement and change in the way social groups are understood and their members treated, even if much grounding for the broader ideology and system of categories persists. Brown documents shifts in American stereotypes; for example, how national images change in relation to military alliances (1965, 175–76, 183). Small actions and ideological shifts can be critical to more comprehensive or cumulative movement. Every question and challenge is a reminder that "it could *always* be *otherwise*" (Gupta 1995, 394 [original emphasis]; cf. Appiah 1990, 8).

One lesson here is that stereotypes cannot be effectively challenged or changed through a single site or instance. Rather, challenges must be carried on in many sites and many ways. They must address cultural representations and institutional structures alike. Exhibitions can certainly be among those sites. Some might even be catalysts to synthesis, providing settings and experiences through which visitors connect a range of other sites and experiences.[44] Challenges need to be as persistent, recurrent, and widespread as stereotypes themselves if they are to alter the terms of debate and produce different shared understandings. Dispersal contributes to the resilience of stereotypes, but this scattered circulation also provides diverse opportunities for engagement and room for maneuver. Understanding patterns of circulation, social embeddings, and rhetorical/communicative structures that help constitute resilience through dispersal might also suggest models for more effective challenges.

In the end, my small effort to question stereotypes with *Okiek Portraits* may have been quixotic jousting with windmills. One minor exhibition was unlikely to make a discernible difference in stereotypes of Okiek or Africans in Kenya or the United States, especially when visitors might understand it in disparate ways (see chapters 3–5). In any case, its influence would be difficult to recognize and may have been delayed and diffuse. Still, my hope remains that the exhibition encouraged some individuals to think twice about these stereotypes and that it has contributed to similar efforts that together continue to raise such questions in many settings.

When first producing *Okiek Portraits*, I left largely unexamined questions of how stereotypes work and how those known or held by exhibition visitors could be affected. This discussion has highlighted issues and difficulties involved, with the benefit of hindsight. Yet even without this broader, more analytical understanding, I did explicitly try to use Okiek portraits (particular images of actual persons) to counter and speak to the visual icons of stereotypes (generic types of people). I tried to create conditions for "recognition," a kind of engagement that can move beyond exoticizing and assimilating (Fabian 1996b, 1999). Recognition of cultural others "entails some form of reaching out," moving beyond cultural constraints to learn about other experiences, appreciate commonalities, and acknowledge others as co-present (Fabian 1999, 59).[45] Communicative exchange and engagement are fundamental for such recognition, so questions of language and the exhibition's overall impression were also important. The rest of this chapter considers decisions that shaped the exhibition and how *Okiek Portraits* tried to destabilize conventional images of Okiek and of Africans. Later chapters turn to the exhibition's reception.

REPRESENTING THROUGH SELECTION: BREAKING AND CREATING SILENCES

An exhibition's shape, content, and viewpoints—its representations—begin to crystallize with decisions about what images or objects to use, how to write labels, and how to combine and arrange them. All representation is selective. Selections inevitably create certain silences, even while they may break others. Those silences—gaps between viewers and viewed—are not simple voids, but spaces of imagination and mediation. "The discontinuities within the arrangement will be far more evident than those in a verbal story. . . . The spectator (listener) becomes more active because the assumptions behind the discontinuities (the unspoken which bridges them) are more far-reaching" (Berger 1982, 287). In creating exhibitions the question is how selections can shape those spaces yet also encourage viewers to recognize and question both shaping and silences alike.

For *Okiek Portraits,* I began with the photographs. Before I even considered exhibition texts and design, I thought about potential audiences for the visual images. Since I wanted the exhibition to undercut stereotypes of Okiek/Torrobo (in Kenya) and Africans (in the United States), my primary sense of visitors had to do with the interpretive background of images and identities they would bring to the exhibition: for example, popular American images of Africa as a continent of primitive natives, drought-stricken poverty, and wild animals.[46] Most of the daily activities, events, and sociality of contemporary Okiek life were missing in these stereotypes; I wanted images and texts for *Okiek Portraits* to break those silences.[47]

There were several ways to challenge the misleading clichés. A historical approach could undercut their seemingly natural, essential, universal truth by showing the changing complexity of particular situations over time and diverse ways stereotypes are produced. But historical images of Okiek are very few, and I know of none from Kaplelach and Kipchornwonek areas.[48] Even if there were historical images to combine with recent ones, selective attention to older images might reinforce preconceived notions and inadvertently emphasize temporal and personal distance. That was not the kind of visitor relationship I hoped to encourage. The first decision, largely pragmatic, was to use only my own photographs.

I thought that giving visitors a sense of personal connection with people shown might incline them to embrace alternative images. To create conditions where visitors could think of Okiek in relation to themselves, showing contemporary Okiek life was fundamental. An implicit evolutionary framework underlies the primitive/modern scale in Kenyan ideas about Okiek and American understandings of Africans. This places Okiek/Africans in the past, distancing and differentiating them temporally. The exhibition had to convey a sense of Okiek as *contemporaneous* with visitors, sharing time and history though in another place, creating a sense of coevality (Fabian 1983). This was one reason I included only color photographs. Black and white photographs are typically read in one of two ways, each in relation to color photographs. Either they are seen as old, compared to newer color technology, or they are seen as art photography, contrasting with the color of fashion, mass media, and commercial photography (Clifford 1997, 157–59; Barrett 1990, 149; Clarke 1997, 23–24; Lutz and Collins 1993, 31–33). Given the ambiguous artistic status of ethnographic photography, black and white photographs were likely to be interpreted as remote and historic.[49] I decided on Cibachrome prints because they have better archival qualities, but their rich, vibrant colors also enhanced the photographs' vividness and immediacy.

As the exhibition took shape, portraits became the central focus. Portraits provided a compelling way to represent Okiek life, but I also hoped they would touch chords with visitors, rouse curiosity, and create a sense of engagement.[50] I thought of the way photographs can affect viewers, described by Roland Barthes: "suddenly, a specific photograph reaches me; it animates me, and I animate it" (1981, 20). Fostering personal connections and interaction with the exhibition thus became one tactic in trying to counter stereotypes. I made these decisions only as exhibition plans developed, influenced by various pragmatic, aesthetic, and philosophical reasons discussed below.

My efforts to counter stereotypes were also bound to my concern to foreground the selection processes of an exhibition and encourage critical engagement with the way representations are produced. Photographic juxtapositions were one way to highlight gaps common in popular representations. For instance, I combined photographs resembling popularized African scenes with others showing aspects of daily life usually absent from stereotypical images. "Such images, which challenge the existing set of codes rather than recycle and reinforce them, are impertinent or politicizing inasmuch as they pose questions to what is regarded as appropriate and authoritative" (Shapiro 1988, 150). Such contextualizing juxtapositions could raise questions about selective gaps. Their fuller depiction might also help visitors relate the visually exotic to their own experience and understandings of daily life.

Incorporating multiple perspectives into an exhibition can also help expose selective processes and problematize stereotypes. For instance, the different captions and languages in the texts of *Okiek Portraits* presented different perspectives, accentuating some of the exhibition's "seams." Okiek comments disclosed their imagined audiences and understandings of photographic form, offering contrasts with my own ideas and those that visitors would hold. These different juxtapositions highlighted only some seams and choices but might encourage visitors to ask where others lie.

Okiek Portraits was not directly "about" either stereotypes or exhibitions. It manifested the constructed nature of exhibitions and stereotypical representations through exhibition devices, not by explicitly referring to these issues. Fostering critical awareness was an important goal, but more implied than proclaimed, introduced in the ways images and information about Okiek were presented. Through their multiple media, exhibitions convey far more than their explicit topics might suggest. Implicit and non-referential aspects of exhibition communication can be vital to overall effect, interpretation, and to the way an exhibition engages with various politics of representation.

These multiple goals meant that image selections were significant within several different calculi at once: what individual images and the full combination of photographs would convey, what kinds of coverage they provided (particularly in relation to popular representations and stereotypes), and how various formats and framings (e.g., landscapes, individual portraits, groups, close-ups, wide-angles) might affect visitors' reactions, interpretations, and engagement. I deliberately tried to cover the social range and variety of contexts and activities in Okiek life. There are pictures of young and old, male and female, people working in garden and forest, cooking lunch, at shops, at home, and during ceremonies. People wear ritual costume and blue jeans, blankets and flowered dresses.

Selecting exhibition images meant approaching my research photographs in a different way. The photographic archive from my research had been produced primarily as documentation. It emphasized photographic sequences, broad coverage, and systematic comparisons (e.g., building houses, making beehives, special occasions and quotidian activities, landscapes at different seasons, market centers growing over time, ceremonies at different times and places). Framing and composition varied to provide different perspectives on the same topics and occasions, including images that showed broad settings and contexts, medium-distance groupings of people, as well as more closely framed details of events and processes. These principles created an information-rich collection (cf. Ben-Ari 1991, 92). Individual photographs took full meaning in relation to other images; even photographs awkwardly framed, soft in focus, or slightly under- or overexposed could be useful.

When I turned to this archive for exhibition photographs, other concerns became equally significant (cf. Becker 1998, 3). Photographs would have to stand on their own. The exhibition would take them out of pairings and sequences that had enriched them as documentation. In the evaluation of their visual interest as images, technical and formal quality were now baseline requirements. I first culled the best photographs, creating a much smaller exhibition archive of interesting and striking images. Portraits were prominent among them. Within the research archive, I had included occasional portraits, many of which were almost asides, created by focusing tightly on individuals within a larger scene or series, or turning to photograph people away from the main event. In the exhibition archive, this gallery of Okiek friends and acquaintances came to the fore and provided a focus that coincided with goals already discussed.[51] Posed portraits that Okiek requested were also important (plates 3, 5, 13, 16–18, 20). In the research archive, they were downplayed amid the unposed realism stressed in documentation. The very co-produced nature of these images—Okiek presented themselves to the camera, I framed the photographs—made them of interest in the exhibition archive. When I assessed the portraits' range, I realized children were underrepresented and took additional portraits during February 1989 (plates 6, 7).

A life cycle arrangement seemed a simple, accessible way to present an exhibition that combined a portrait focus with broad social and contextual range. Pictures followed Okiek ideas about stages of maturation: including children, initiates, young women and men, and mature/old men and women (*laakok, taarusyeek, murureenik* and *murenik, paaiisyaanik,* and *ceepyoosook*) and emphasizing initiation as the most important ceremony. I did not explain these categories in exhibition texts or explicitly discuss cultural differences in defining life cycles and maturation; other topics seemed more important or more likely to obscure visitor understanding if unaddressed.

Though I was less mindful of it, my initial culling and selection of exhibition photographs were also informed by an aesthetic sense, as were the photographs I took. The subtitle in Kenya, "Photography by Corinne Kratz," emphasized my role as photographer/anthropologist, acknowledging that "any photography, whether or not it aspires to the status of art, has a hidden aesthetics" (Samuel 1994, 364). What did I see as "good" photographs? With the exhibition goals and archive described above, a general documentary style was virtually given, stressing subject matter and usually favoring sharp focus (Barrett 1990, 55). The photographs have strong visual foci that always include the people shown, enhancing the portrait emphasis. In many, I accentuated portrait subjects by placing them against rich green or brown backdrops (leaves, walls) and/or through a narrow depth of field that sets their sharp focus against a soft background.

The portrait emphasis brought other social and aesthetic conventions into play as well (see below).[52]

Other formal and stylistic elements vary, but many photographs feature contrasts of light, color, and texture, as the following examples illustrate. Plate 14 foregrounds the young man against a glowing, mistlike background. His intense gaze is framed by the encircling fur cape, amid an interplay of textures among fur, leaves, and skin. Lines of red beads form a second, face-framing point of interest, a counterpoint to predominant browns and greens. Plate 27 also features multiple brown shades and textures. Placing Kokeny'in within a relatively narrow, flat plane, gradations of brown set against one another the smooth light mud bench, darker wall and fur (both variegated, with different textures and tones), deep brown skin, and golden staff. Prominent dark tones are brightened by light from the right reflecting on Kokeny'in's face, hand, and staff. These foci of light run parallel to and contrast with the deep black shadow cast by her arm and staff, a shadow echoed by the black shape at bottom right (an overturned pot). A small red accent—her necklace—also catches the light, countering the somber browns and drawing attention toward her face.[53]

Finally, in plates 10 and 21 reds are more than an accent, with light and line important as well. Areas with different red/pink tones and patterns resonate through the images, contrasting with the other prominent color, brown. Plate 10 sets two red/white/black patterns in the girl's headdress and clothes (right) against the initiate's red-checked shirt at left, with blue accents tying both figures together. Emphasized against the softly blurred background, the two are connected (through her hand) yet separated by their expressions—Saidimu pensive, with downcast eyes; Murureet's direct look reaching the viewer. Her face is the first focus of attention, accentuated by lighting and framed by her headdress. In plate 21 Cheepto's pink/brown dress and red/white/black cloth are central pattern contrasts, with a rectangular patterned edging of similar colors at far right. Light reflections highlight the reddish brown of the two faces. As in plate 10, the figures are closely linked, but attention turned in opposite directions. The chief contrast to the figures lies in strongly vertical, brown fence posts, incorporating color contrast as well as an interplay with the rounded shapes of their glistening faces and Cheepto's horizontal arm, holding the child.

Formal features and relations vary in other exhibition photographs. Some images are more compelling than others in aesthetic terms, for criteria such as representational coverage also mattered. It is clear from these examples, however, that form, color, and composition can affect the way photographic subjects are apprehended and evoke emotional tones. In portraits, facial expressions, posture, stance, background, and angle are also significant in defining relations between viewers and photographic subjects (see below).[54] Would my care in selecting and balancing images work? It might help, but it could not guarantee that visitors would see Okiek the way I hoped they would. The same photographs can be interpreted quite differently, depending on viewers' own positions, assumptions, and attention (cf. Shapiro 1988, 130–31). The portrait focus itself brought diverse interpretive possibilities and ambiguities to the exhibition.

"The portrait is . . . a sign whose purpose is both the description of an individual and the inscription of social identity" (Tagg 1988, 37). The attribution of social identities involves recognizing people as types and so presents an important point where stereotyping can be either reinforced or questioned. Social identities are not always separate and discrete, however, and photographic inscriptions may well show social identities that intersect and overlap. Such conjunctions present interpretive puzzles that unsettle the social categories we use and create moments when problematic assumptions are recognized and articulated. They may become interpretive flash points in an exhibition, signs of contending perspectives, as some visitors see the combinations as contradictory and others find them unproblematic. One Nairobi review illustrates (plate 10):

> Here stands a young boy in a checkered red school shirt and navy blue pullover over which a beaded leather cape is flung. . . . [This] captures the duality of the community, one leg is steepled [sic] in the traditional way while the other straddles, even embraces, the modern. (Wakanyote 1989)

Wakanyote reads this dress as a mixture denoting transition, extrapolating from the moment depicted to a transformative process. His temporal narrative affirms the categories "traditional" and "modern" and implies that their "true" sense entails pure states without such mixtures and temporal residues.[55] The reviewer places himself as modern, looking "back" as the Okiek youngster moves eagerly toward modernity. But dichotomies like traditional/modern and primitive/civilized are the conceptual foundations for contrasting ideal types in popular representations and stereotypes. They distance other times and places as foreign and assign certain identities to those who are "traditional" or "modern." In challenging stereotypes, I wanted to subvert such dichotomies. We could infer a different cultural process from the same image without creating a temporal divide: the costume combination shows how people blend and redefine different cultural resources and "maneuver multiple identities depending on the specific circumstances in which they find themselves" (Ahmadu 2000, 306).

Understandings and expectations formed through notions of traditional/modern are part of the process through which popular representations of Africans are produced, reiterated, and dispersed through many domains, in many forms. They direct attention to certain settings, characters, and activities as visually relevant, interesting, and "characteristic" of Africa, passing over other images and aspects of daily life. This selective attention emphasizes images and interpretations that illustrate the "pure" types and make them almost self-confirming. Hence, images showing juxtapositions and "mixtures," presenting the range of material resources and settings common in contemporary African lives, call for interpretation and explanation. Wakanyote's text fell back on what I felt were ready, familiar terms, sorting seemingly incongruous elements into clear either/or categories: traditional or modern. Alternatively, such striking juxtapositions, pervading the overall exhibition, might give pause to other visitors. They might present an opportunity and means to question and reconsider those very categories, challenging representations that portray Africans as unchanging and "traditional" by ignoring certain aspects of daily life. How different visitors will interpret such exhibition flash points, and why, are among the riddles that audiences present to curators.

These riddles relate to the capacity of exhibitions to engage visitors' own identities and their sense of other social groups and relations. Visitors encounter and apprehend exhibitions through the prism of the self, bringing to an exhibition different expectations, tastes, and experiences. They relate to exhibition material—at least in part—in personal terms, through their own identities and positions in multiple interpretive communities (see Karp 1992). Exhibitions that feature cultural difference can clarify and strengthen visitors' self-definition; displays of foreign peoples create self-defining oppositions for viewers (Bennett 1988; Karp and Kratz 2000; Lutz and Collins 1992, 136). They become means for formulating collective identities that simultaneously accentuate self/other differences and downplay diversity within one's own group (differences of class, gender, etc.).[56]

The people shown in *Okiek Portraits* could be incorporated into several fields of identification, serving as one pole in various intersecting dichotomies. Apart from the traditional/modern contrast already discussed, they could be seen as rural Kenyans (versus town and city dwellers), as Okiek (versus other ethnic groups), as Africans (versus Europeans and Asians), and through other distinctions as well (though few visitors would recognize all signs and details of social identity that Okiek would find relevant).[57] Such categories deal with the social identities portraits seem to convey. Yet portraits also characterize and portray individuals, as Tagg noted above. This was a resource I wanted to emphasize and draw on in resisting stereotypes, but I paid little attention to the different traditions and conventions of portraiture through which visitors might interpret the exhibition.

PORTRAITS: PERSONAL, POLITICAL, PARTICULAR, UNIVERSAL

Portraits were meant to communicate a sense of Okiek personalities and interactions, to invite visitors to imagine and make personal connections. The assumptions behind this idea, unexamined at the time, were that portraits would speak to viewers in all settings, that they provided means for personal connections, and that such personal connections would help deter, or at least interfere with, ready stereotypes. But visitors would come with a variety of aesthetic and interpretive backgrounds; there are many traditions of portraiture whose specific forms and meanings vary considerably over time and space. Several modes of portraiture coexist and interact in most settings, and in some a portrait need not be a likeness that resembles its subject visually. My link between portraits and personal connections was probably related to contemporary American expectations "that, for most people, photography is primarily a means of obtaining pictures of faces they know" (Tagg 1988, 35).[58] Clearly, each of my assumptions needed questioning, closer consideration, and grounding in the various histories and aesthetics of portraiture.[59]

Photographs do not "speak for themselves" or provide a transparent "universal language." The personal connections I sought to facilitate relied on the communicative capacity of human faces but took little account of the many ways that capacity is particularized and realized.[60] The art historian Richard Brilliant talks about "the magical power that portraits have to bring the viewer—wherever present—into a personal, even intimate connection with another being, however remote from him in time [or space] that subject might be" (Brilliant 1991, 82). The question is whether and how this magic operates across cultural settings. There is considerable cultural variation in the meanings of particular facial expressions, gestures, and postures and the extent to which individuals show fleeting emotional states or interactional responses facially. For instance, members of Akan royalty in Ghana "cultivated a facial expression intended to veil individual personality and project an ideal regal character. At an early age, children of royal households learned through mimicry and admonishment to affect a quasi-remote countenance" (Preston 1990, 76).

Precisely how the Okiek portraits would speak to different exhibition visitors, then, might vary significantly. Like Walt Whitman looking at daguerreotypes in the 1840s, I "wanted the portrait[s] to provoke inference, to awaken desire for dialogue" (Trachtenberg 1989, 64), but that dialogue entailed several kinds of translation. Different conventions of facial and bodily expression, different signs of social identity, and different traditions of portraiture all came into play, laying a complex foundation for other questions of exhibitionary communication and politics of representation. Yet portraits are often associated with a dialogic quality and intensity of viewer engagement (Brilliant 1991, 19), characteristics that might lead visitor interactions with Okiek to approximate the kind of recognition of cultural others that changes those involved (Fabian 1999, 53).

All the Okiek portraits were naturalistic. The photographs looked like their subjects, and exhibition visitors could easily tell that particular people were portrayed. Many traditions of portraiture, particularly in Europe and North America, define portraits in terms of close visual correspondence with their subjects, but that is not the only way images can represent and refer to particular individuals.[61] The appearance of great European thinkers and statesmen, in fact, was often adjusted in painted or sculpted portraits to make them look more the part, as envisioned at the time (Brilliant 1991, 36–39, 120–22, 137–38). Greek and Roman artists conventionally represented philosophers in portraits as mature, bearded men (16). As photographic practice developed in the United States in the late 1830s, the extreme lifelike quality of daguerreotypes was seen as a *hindrance* to portraiture. Photographic conventions that distinguished between portrait and mere likeness developed in the 1840s, drawing on portrait conventions in other media (Trachtenberg 1989, 24–26). According to Oguibe (1996), realism is not always photography's most important feature in African settings.[62]

Even portraits that resemble those they portray usually incorporate other references to these individuals as well. Names and characteristic clothing, objects, or gestures are often part of naturalistic portraits, reinforcing their identification with individuals.[63] Used and combined differently in different traditions of portraiture, these modes of identification also provide resources for representing different aspects of their subjects' identities. This returns us to the tension between personal identity and social identity, individual and type, a tension integral to portraiture.[64] Indeed, this may be part of portraits' appeal, a fascination with giving visual form to the ambiguities this tension entails. "[T]he portrait photograph is fraught with ambiguity. For all its literal realism it denotes, above all, the problematics of identity, and exists within a series of cultural codes" and notions of personhood (Clarke 1992, 4; cf. Preston 1990; Brilliant 1991, 8). Viewers looking at unfamiliar portraits may not entirely understand the codes through which they were produced, but they recognize that cultural codes apply and read them through conventions they know.[65]

These dynamics of identity converge with a second, temporal tension that informs photography generally. A tension between past and present arises from what John Berger calls the abyss "between the moment recorded and the present moment of looking" (1982, 87; cf. Barthes 1981).[66] Looking at a portrait raises questions about when it was made, how that past relates to the present of looking and to the present where its subject may be. "The portrait is a metaphor that displaces its subject from a state of action to one of duration . . . and extracts it from time. However, the act of looking reinserts the image in time" (Jewsiewicki 1996, 19, my translation). By freezing time, a portrait might suggest stability of self (Brilliant 1991, 112), yet this temporal tension simultaneously evokes changing biographical trajectories and the complexities of life history (Kratz 2001). The visual signs of identity and the stories with which we fill the abyss all partake of various social, communicative conventions, specific to the times and places where a portrait is made and viewed and to reigning understandings of what is visually interesting, appropriate, and worth photographing (cf. Stokes 1992, 204; Chalfen 1991).[67]

Tracing the nuances of communication and representation these tensions involve in any setting would be complicated, but *Okiek Portraits* intersected several photographic histories and understandings. The following sketch of photographic portraiture in Africa, Europe, and the United States can only suggest what was involved.[68] In each of these settings today, at least three traditions of photographic portraiture coexist and interact: personal portraits, which began in each case with studio portraits; portraits taken as part of social and government control (e.g., identity cards, prison records); and portraits taken as documentary or journalism. These traditions sometimes overlap and photographers often produce pictures in more than one idiom.[69] My overview here focuses on personal portraits.[70]

As personal portraits developed in the United States and Europe in the nineteenth century, photographers and subjects alike drew on conventions for other types of portraits and public presentation, especially portrait miniatures, royal and aristocratic portraits, and theater (Tagg 1988; Trachtenberg 1989; Samuel 1994, 367; Clarke 1997, 103). Particular poses, body postures, and facial expressions became typical ways to suggest a subject's traits and character. Backgrounds, settings, particular objects, material possessions, and other props became ways to convey social roles, affiliations, personal passions, or pastimes. Modes of framing and lighting photographic portraits further modulated the conventions developed. As personal portraiture changed over time, these portrait conventions transformed and became more diversified, particularly after technological developments in the 1880s made photography more broadly accessible. Preferences for "unposed," "candid" photos developed later as well, enabled and promoted by further technical developments and stylistic interactions between personal and documentary portraiture.[71] People continued to draw models for personal portraits from other media, including cinema (Samuel 1994, 369).

In every setting, such influences on portraiture came through photographers and subjects alike. Malian studio photographer Seydou Keita insists in a much-cited 1995 interview, "I've never met any foreign photographers, nor seen their photos. No information ever reached us. French or American books and magazines were very rare" (Magnin 1997, 12). Yet several captions for his portraits (probably from the late 1950s) note poses and dress that identify their subjects as fans of Eddy Constantine, "who played the role of 'Lemmy Caution, Federal Agent Number One' at the cinema" (277). Photographic studios began opening in African countries soon after 1840, but African photographers probably did not begin practicing regularly or open their own studios until the end of the century.[72] A significant African clientele for studio portraits probably began developing about the same time, though some elites had portraits made earlier.

As in western Europe and the United States, people in various parts of Africa adapted the new technology and mode of representation to those already familiar. Sprague, for instance, presents convincing analogies between Yoruba sculptural aesthetics, notions of personhood, and 1970s photographic portraits, as seen in stylized poses and facial expressions, framing, full facial view (both eyes shown), and other details in traditional formal portraits (the most common) (1978a, 54–56).[73] But photography was not introduced into African settings as pure technology, shaped only by indigenous ideas. Those who brought photography also brought their conventions of representation. Some of the earliest portraits of Africans were taken by amateur European photographers. At times they tried to bend African subjects into body postures that Europeans found "natural" and "classical" but that subjects found unnatural and awkward, for instance, a stance with unevenly distributed standing weight (Kramer 1989, 203–7). Such encounters started the development of photographic portrait conventions on the continent.[74]

In each African setting, photographic techniques and conventions of portraiture were learned in tandem, though African photographers and subjects adapted and transformed both and incorporated other influences over the years.[75] Conventions for personal portraits developed particularly in studios, where most were produced. Background setting, posture, expression, and objects held or included were as important here as elsewhere; appropriate photographic signs of status, identity, and demeanor developed in each place. For instance, curtain backgrounds have been common since photographic portraits began; African studio settings also came to include painted backdrop/mural scenes, patterned floors, and other textured environmental features uncommon in European settings.[76] Studios throughout the continent provide props to use; plastic flowers are standard everywhere. Many also have particular stools, chairs, a balconylike grill (Werner 1996, 97), and objects such as radios, watches, or bicycles. Seydou Keita, successful photographer of Bamako elite, describes these practices and the unusually large range of accessories he kept for clients in Mali in the 1950s:[77]

> Some of my customers brought things they wanted to be photographed with. This woman with a sewing machine, or that man with his brand-new bicycle. He wanted a close-up portrait but he also wanted to show off his new bicycle. That's why the bicycle is cut-off in the photo. I had several European suits available in my studio including straight ties, bow ties, breast-pocket handkerchiefs, shirts, hats, and even a beret. I could dress my customers from head to toe. I also had accessories available for them: watches, fountain pens, watch-chains, plastic flowers, a radio, a telephone, a scooter, a bicycle, and an alarm clock. A lot of people liked to be photographed with this kind of thing. For women . . . sometimes they arrived with several changes of clothing. . . . What was important was that their jewels appear in the photos . . . all the accessories that the elegant women in Bamako liked to show. Some "grande dames" used elaborate make-up around their mouths; they were very impressive. All of these details, external signs of wealth, beauty, and elegance, were of great importance. . . . They also liked to show off their hands and slender fingers that were a sign of their high social standing. (Magnin 1997, 12–13)

Not everyone Keita photographed used these props or wanted such images, and many other photographers worked in smaller towns. His description nonetheless shows that some clients were highly self-conscious and discriminating about personal portraits and that portrait conventions in 1950s Bamako were well developed and known. Several photographers working in other capital cities at the time also note that personal portrait clients were often elite, bourgeois, and younger, with some urban connections (Pivin 1994). Personal portraits were associated with social elite and bourgeois in Europe and the United States as well until photography became more widely available.

We know little about African photographers in smaller towns and centers, or just when studios spread further afield in different countries. Nor do we know how portrait conventions have changed over time in particular African settings, though Ouedraogo (1996) demonstrates the need for research on such topics.[78] He looks at shifts in the photographic poses and objects in a Burkina Faso town over a decade, as well as significant postural changes in portraits of couples. Similarly, Werner identifies different portrait conventions in different periods in Côte d'Ivoire, including a recent preference for the more candid "photo-surprise" (1996, 102–4). Fragmentary observations about diverse ways of displaying and using photographic portraits in various parts of Africa further underline the need for careful ethnographic and historical study.[79]

In every tradition, then, photographic portraits are situated through various conventions of composition, representation, interpretation, and use. Small details can be distinctive in social and/or aesthetic terms. Though I realized the *Okiek Portraits* photographs would intersect European, American, and Kenyan traditions of portraiture, I did not try to work this out in detail.[80] Indeed, the complexities could have paralyzed exhibition planning. Yet some details may have been crucial for visitors' interpretations. They were also part of the implicit aesthetic I exercised when choosing portraits to include, influenced by my own middle-class American background. I did not pay conscious attention to questions of posture, orientation, eye contact, or view direction, yet "variation in how and where the other looks . . . most determines the differences in the message a photograph can give about intercultural relations" (Lutz and Collins 1991, 139; cf. Simmel [1901] 1959, 281).

This statement refers to middle-class white Americans that Lutz and Collins interviewed in the late 1980s.[81] Patterns of eye contact and proxemics in interaction are quite different in other places, as Chet Creider has shown for Kalenjin- and Luo-speakers in Kenya (1977, 1978a, 1978b). Kenyans and Americans might read photographic eye contact differently, then, though questions of expression and orientation are important for both.[82] Lutz and Collins's interviews were part of a study of photographs published in *National Geographic* between 1950 and 1986. Focused on an important canon of crosscultural images in the United States, they look at the history and significance of *National Geographic* and consider how Americans view its ethnographic photography. Their *National Geographic* corpus differs from *Okiek Portraits* in many respects,[83] but the study still provides a useful and interesting comparative counterpoint that I will return to several times in chapters that follow. The *Geographic* study illuminates the expectations of many who saw *Okiek Portraits* in the United States,[84] and there are no empirical studies as extensive of how people read ethnographic photography. Further, the demographic profile of the *Geographic's* readership, and their interviewees, generally parallels that of many U.S. museum audiences: white, middle-class people with slightly higher than average education are in the majority (Doering and Bickford 1994, iv–vii; Lutz and Collins 1993, 221–23).[85] The *Geographic* study also discusses patterns of orientation and eye contact that can be compared with those of *Okiek Portraits*.

Lutz and Collins found that a non-Western local looks directly at the camera (and reader) in 24 percent of the *National Geographic* pictures.[86] A smiling person appears in 38 percent overall, but in 55 percent where someone looks directly at the camera. Those who look directly at the camera are often shown in full frontal posture. Following Tagg, Lutz and Collins relate these patterns to the history of portrait conventions that encode class and social hierarchy. In the United States and western Europe, frontal portraits have often been associated with a "code of social inferiority" and documentation of human beings for diverse scientific, legal, and medical purposes (Tagg 1988, 36–37, 76, 80). By contrast, "the 'civilized' classes, at least since the nineteenth century, have traditionally been depicted in Western art turning away from the camera and so symbolize themselves as less available" (Lutz and Collins 1991, 140). Lutz and Collins are concerned with American interpretations and conventions, but we do not know if some international subjects portrayed might themselves consider frontality imperative for proper self-presentation, like Yoruba in Nigeria (Sprague 1978a, 54, 56).

Okiek Portraits' small sample of photographs provides an interesting comparison. Of thirty-one photographs, 61 percent show someone looking directly at the camera. People are in full frontal pose in only 26 percent. Someone smiles in 42 percent of all photographs, while 58 percent with direct eye contact include a smiling person.[87] These smile figures do not differ significantly from the *Geographic* ones. However, the difference in eye contact is statistically significant and surely relates in part to our different orientations and aims.[88] *National Geographic* seeks to portray their representations as objective, informative, and true (which usually also means the photographer should be invisible). When they include portraits, they "can achieve both the goals of intimacy and invisibility by taking portraits . . . where the gaze angles off to the side of the camera" (Lutz and Collins 1991, 140). *Okiek Portraits* wanted to encourage recognition through empathetic connection rather than a detached, scientific-seeming distance. Thus, I sought to maximize eye contact between visitors and those photographed, though I was not fully aware of this choice at the time.[89] This reversed the *National Geographic* pattern but still followed the same conventions for reading photographic images and interpersonal relations. I wanted to communicate with several audiences, but my photographic choices may have been most informed by particularly American conventions.[90]

Those conventions include other ways to read direct eye contact and frontal pose, however. Brilliant describes one in talking about a Botticelli portrait of a young man. As expected for the "civilized classes," the subject's body is "set slightly oblique, but the psychological distance between the youth and the viewer has been closed by the directness of his outward, frontal gaze towards the viewer" (1991, 27). Eye contact here is a way of bridging distance to come into contact.[91]

Other meanings and uses of eye contact and frontality have been forged in direct opposition to the readings of control and submission emphasized by Lutz and Collins. African American photographer Dawoud Bey presents some subjects frontally, a challenge that goes with his explicit discussion of eye contact: "There is tremendous power in the gaze. Black people have been killed for directing their gaze at the wrong person. . . . I wanted the subjects in those photographs to be possessed of the power to look, to assert oneself, to meet the gaze of the viewer" (Walker Art Center 1995, 107). Bey is a contemporary photographer, but political challenges to social meanings encoded in photographic portraits began almost as soon as conventions formed. In 1855, Walt Whitman challenged portrait conventions and social hierarchy in the frontispiece for the first edition of *Leaves of Grass,* an engraving made from a daguerreotype. It showed him standing, casual in dress and posture, facing viewers frontally and looking directly at them, breaking formal conventions of the time (see figure 6) (Trachtenberg 1989, 62–70).

I was somewhat naive about what portraits would evoke and my own assumptions in using them to question stereotypes in *Okiek Portraits.* Nonetheless, the portrait focus

Figure 6. Walt Whitman in the frontispiece to the 1855 edition of *Leaves of Grass*.

capitalized on the curiosity and fascination that faces seem to summon, for various reasons, and the engagement with puzzles of identity and time intrinsic to portraits. Shot through with conventions of representation and self-representation, portraits contribute to the semiotic material from which stereotypes are made. They thus offer means to jar conventions and their associations, within a space that seems at once personal yet sublimely social. The social, the aesthetic, and the political are here deeply entwined (see Jewsiewicki 1996, 17–19).

Taken as a group, the portraits in the exhibition presented a more densely connected and iterative portrayal of Okiek conventions of self-presentation. Together, they also evoked the world of Okiek social communities and kinship (cf. Fisher 1991, 11). Setting individuals shown in conversation could echo and enhance particular portrait-encounters and draw exhibition visitors into participating. Visual reverberations were important in this result, but captions were crucial to its success.

LABELS AND TEXTUAL CHOICES

Initially, when the exhibition had only descriptive captions, the suggestion of "conversation" among images and people shown relied on cross-referencing and tone. Visitors could tell from captions that Saidimu and his cousin (plate 10) were at the same ceremony as Cheepto (plate 21), that Tinkili (plates 19, 12, 16) and Kishuayon (plate 20) were married, and that the children in plates 2, 3, 6, and 7 were all related. When captions with Okiek commentaries were added later, however, conversation was quite literally part of the exhibition. Cross-referencing among photographs and among photographs and labels became much denser, heightening qualities incipient in the descriptive captions.

Exhibition labels are interpretations; they "have a rhetoric, telling us what we are to see and how we are to see it. . . . However spare, they are never purely referential" (Samuel 1994, 364). Texts help direct visitors' attention in particular ways, but visitors have "the task of intentionally, actively, building cultural translations and critical meanings" in the space of meaning and interaction opened between labels and images (Baxandall quoted in Clifford 1988, 239). When I worked on texts for *Okiek Portraits,* I gave explicit consideration to how to communicate effectively with Kenyan visitors. I decided early on to make the exhibition multilingual and use both of Kenya's national languages, but developing an appropriate language, style, and tone entailed many other decisions and details. Together, these constituted the label rhetoric that helped shape visitors' experiences. As with visual selections, certain textual choices were deliberate and considered, while others remained tacit, based on assumptions I held implicitly and on the linguistic structures and possibilities of English and Kiswahili.

Several forms of Kiswahili are spoken in eastern Africa. At the coast, native-speakers use varieties of "standard Swahili" (*Kiswahili sanifu*) with complex systems of morphological agreement and noun classes. Further inland where Kiswahili is a lingua franca but often not a first language, speakers use less agreement, fewer complex tenses, and less Arabic-derived vocabulary.[92] To devise Kiswahili captions that would communicate with the full range of Kenyan visitors but still be considered "proper" and "grammatical," I consulted a variety of Kenyans. Some had better than average command of *Kiswahili sanifu;* others spoke colloquial Kiswahili as a second language. I wrote labels in English, then showed draft translations to Swahili university students from Mombasa, a Kenyan professor of philosophy raised at the coast, and people from other ethnic groups working in Nairobi. They reacted to wordings, made corrections and suggestions, and discussed varieties and nuances of Kiswahili with me.

The initial impetus for multilingual labels was simply to communicate with as many Kenyan visitors as possible. But the use of multiple languages also foregrounded issues of translation, pointing to the multiple perspectives possible on photographs displayed. Their use had the potential to raise questions for all visitors about how exhibitions are created and presented. When conversational captions were added later in Okiek and English, these issues came into focus more clearly. Those labels added information about Okiek and voiced their impressions, but the contrast between the two label types simultaneously problematized textual tone, style, and voice, in addition to perspective and translation.[93]

Settling on an appropriate tone and style for the descriptive English/Kiswahili captions was less straightforward than choosing languages. Captions had to provide contextual information about what was depicted, and Okiek life more generally, yet foster a sense of particular persons and events and disarm stereotypical generalization. I tried to strike this balance by using individual names and descriptions of personal relations and emotions along with information on activities pictured. For instance, the English caption for plate 23 reads, *Kopot Nabaru comes home with grass to help roof her daughter's new house and a broom of leafy branches to sweep it out.* A different kind of descriptive caption might read, *Women are responsible for several aspects of house construction, including bringing grass for thatching.*

Both identify Okiek houses as thatched and women's role in getting roofing material, yet their other connotations and tone differ. The latter states a general social norm, using present tense to convey the habitual and regular, and presents the individual shown as a type of person, exemplifying the social category "women." Its stance is rather distant from the scene shown. A style commonly associated with ethnographic representations, its contextualization emphasizes objectivity and generalization.[94] The overall caption style might be called generalizing or typifying. The first caption, by contrast, names the individual shown, places her socially as a mother helping her daughter, and evokes personal meanings of place by calling her destination "home." The present tense is also used here, but it is a narrative present, indexing the particular action and occasion shown.[95] This is a particularizing style, placing more emphasis on the specific experiences, events, individuals, and occasions shown. In some cases it may also narratively amplify what is shown, providing information not available from the image alone (e.g., that the grass is for the woman's daughter; cf. Edwards 1992, 11).

As much as these two styles differ, however, both are associated with genres of exhibition that stress contextualization (e.g., exhibitions of ethnography, natural history, or cultural history) and could be contrasted with the spare aestheticizing caption style common in art exhibitions (Vogel 1994, 83; 1988). Labels in art exhibitions provide information on media, style, artist, and period, with varying amounts of other information on iconography, technique, genre, and aesthetic quality. An aestheticizing caption for the same photograph might simply read: "Woman carrying grass. Cibachrome print, 1975" or "Kopot Nabaru carrying grass. Cibachrome print, 1975." Contextualization and aestheticization represent two ends of a spectrum in caption style and display; contemporary exhibitions of art, anthropology, and cultural history often combine the two in various ways.[96]

Looking at them now, I can see that my own descriptive captions combined the two contextualizing caption styles. They identified people shown, the multiple relationships linking them with others, and something of the texture of those relations or moments shown. They tried to personalize Okiek, attempting to bridge viewers' distance from them. Yet I also had to provide some general contextual background.[97] When writing them, I drafted and revised until it "felt right," not fully aware of how I was combining styles and balancing such elements as tense, person, and modes of identification and address in creating the captions' rhetoric.[98] How did these patterns work?

The descriptive captions predominantly use the present tense, in both a narrative and generalizing/habitual sense. The narrative present is a way to give immediacy to photographs, placing viewers in the same temporal frame of reference as what is shown. Future and past tenses occur occasionally, mainly to create a flow of events or actions (not seen) in relation to the narrative present shown. The habitual present, less common in the captions, provides broader context. I was well aware of critiques of the "ethnographic present" that regard textual representation in the present tense as a way of "denying history" to those shown, but these critiques do not always take into account the diverse ways tenses are actually used or the way visual and verbal media interact in exhibitions.

Three captions break these general patterns, foregrounding the tension between the present of the moment shown, the present of those looking at the exhibition, and the gap between filled by other significant events. All three signal some emotional intensity or attachment associated with the way that tension plays out for its image. The first, plate 14, describes the scene in narrative present, but then makes this explicit: *Just out of seclusion, Keleges huddles under a ceremonial cape of lush hyrax fur. No one could know at this moment that he would die tragically a few years later while still in secondary school.* Death erupts into the tense of the caption for plate 27 as well, though more subtly: *Kokeny'in sits wrapped in her hyrax cape, the clothing of her youth. She was one of the oldest Okiek alive.* The final example, plate 32, employs the simple present in a straightforward declarative statement. Combined with the only use of first person singular in the descriptive captions, it foregrounds my own ongoing relations with those shown and my role in creating the exhibition: *Her impish smile cannot disguise the wisdom of old age. Naoroy is my kind and understanding friend.* Conversational captions later heightened these aspects in all three cases, with relatives reflecting on death and remembrance in the first two and, in the last, a close friend reinforcing my characterization of Naoroy and wondering whether she, too, had died.

That last caption is one of two exceptions to a consistent use of third person in the descriptive captions. Paired with the final photograph, its first-person reference ("*my friend*") is paralleled in the caption for the first photograph (plate 2): *a surprise is in store for us.* At the start of the exhibition, this first-person plural addresses visitors directly, drawing them into a group along with the caption narrator. The final caption reminds them that I am that narrator. Together, the two occurrences of first person seem to frame the exhibition as a visit during which I introduce Okiek friends and acquaintances to exhibition visitors. Initially these captions were my main overt presence in the exhibition, explicitly acknowledging my curatorial shaping of its representations.[99] With conversational captions later, I was also included in interaction with Okiek and as someone about whom Okiek comment. Those captions also incorporated other pronominal patterns, with usages of first, second, and third person relative to yet another "present," the present of the moment when Okiek were looking at the photographs.

In identifying people and locating photographs, the caption descriptions convey different tones. I referred to people shown by names commonly used in informal conversational reference or address—their first name, common nickname, or teknonymous name (Mother/Father of so-and-so). It might be argued that identifying people more fully, with first and last (lineage) names, would have been more respectful or suggested greater status or dignity. But it would also have conveyed a far more formal, distant stance. I wanted to create a more relaxed atmosphere and familiar tone, as if seeing (potential) friends and acquaintances. Pointing out relations among those shown (parents, cousins, siblings, spouses, friends, co-initiates, grandchildren) was a way to buttress that tone by underlining familial and community networks that bound together those represented. Pragmatically, my choice also meant exhibition visitors had fewer new and unfamiliar names to assimilate. Conversational captions later heightened the informal sense and web of relationships I tried to convey, adding enough names and relations to require a new explanatory panel (see chapter 3).

Recognizing the need to identify when and where the photographs were taken, to specify that the Okiek shown are Kaplelach and Kipchornwonek and place them in time, I noted in the introductory text that most were taken during the 1980s and mapped Okiek groups in East Africa. I must have thought these efforts located the photographs clearly enough, for I did not also identify the place and year of each image. I now think I should have reinforced this information on individual captions; I have included that information in this book as part of the line identifying plate numbers. The addition allows interested readers to work out temporal relations among images and points to the different locations and communities within Kaplelach and Kipchornwonek areas. Those familiar with the area may also appreciate knowing specific locations.

Taken together, these language patterns and modes of identification created a rhetoric and style that were intended to draw visitors into interaction with Okiek shown and create a sense of intimacy and familiarity.[100] Fostering that sense of engagement was one way I thought *Okiek Portraits* might begin to counter stereotypes. The descriptive captions used in Kenya seemed personal and friendly compared to generalizing labels common in ethnographic photography and other museum displays. Yet they seemed detached and artificial after I included Okiek commentary, with verbatim reactions, observations, and reflections. Okiek commentary captions made viewing the photographs more like an experience shared with Okiek and helped maintain a greater measure of local meaning and texture. Could the commentaries have stood alone? Perhaps, but I had not relinquished the pedagogical goal of informing viewers about Okiek life. Any effort to question stereotypes required contextual information provided by descriptive captions. The captions were particularly important in U.S. venues, where most visitors knew little of Okiek or rural Kenyan life.

My portrait selections played to the sense that a viewer "can imagine the other is about to speak" (Lutz and Collins 1991, 139). Captions augmented this sense by naming and describing people in personal terms, but especially by including Okiek comments. Okiek *do* speak to and about one another in the exhibition. Decisions about which comments became captions, then, were important. In my curatorial role as editor, translator, and mediator, I had to consider how visitors might interpret and react to the settings and what might be understandable across settings. But all that happened later, after the exhibition reached the United States.

My hope in including multiple multilingual captions was that visitors would recognize and appreciate the various perspectives and interpretations that can be brought to exhibitions and find a space in which to construct their own photographic encounters with Okiek. In final form, *Okiek Portraits* incorporated multiple viewings into the very exhibition. Exhibition visitors gazed at pictures of Okiek, and Okiek also looked at their own pictures. Okiek saw people they knew and knew that the photographs would be on view elsewhere, before strangers. Their viewings became occasions, then, for Okiek to see themselves as imagined viewers would, and to envision those viewers. Reflections emerging from that returned gaze were presented to exhibition visitors in captions. Okiek saw the photographs in terms of their own experiences and understandings of images, as did other visitors, but those understandings were not always the same. Issues of communication and the politics of representation informed choices I made in producing the exhibition; they took on greater significance as *Okiek Portraits* traveled. The photographs and captions became an interpretive canvas for diverse audiences with different interests, concerns, and expectations.

[I]magination is inextricably linked to the emotions; how could it be otherwise, since imagination is rooted in our deepest convictions, aspirations, and visions of our experiences?… [T]he fantastic quality of imagination takes us outside ourselves in two ways, by presenting a version of experience and things that is both less and more than what we ordinarily encounter.

T. O. BEIDELMAN, *THE MORAL IMAGINATION IN KAGURU MODES OF THOUGHT*

IMAGINING AUDIENCES

Okiek Portraits in Kenya

As the exhibition of *Okiek Portraits* took shape in different sites, visitors themselves began to imagine what Okiek are like and to place themselves in relation to Okiek and the exhibition. The next three chapters follow the exhibition's travels, considering its different venues and how visitors experienced and understood it. In Kenya, *Okiek Portraits* was seen in two very different settings: Okiek homes and the National Museum, Nairobi. Questions about what and how the exhibition would communicate figured in both settings and touched on several politics of representation, as the following two examples show.

> In June 1989, shortly after I had returned from printing exhibition photographs in the United States, a young Okiot man visited me in Nairobi. He was returning to school and brought greetings and news from home. The news included an account of his brother's untimely death, which had called him home. Before he left, I told him about progress on the exhibition and asked his advice on what had suddenly become a dilemma. While in the United States, I had also worked on the exhibition poster. Its design featured a photograph of his brother. Should I abandon that poster or was there some way it could still be used? I was raising funds for printing costs and could just replace it with a simpler, noncolor flier. After seeing the chromoline proof, the brother felt that it could and should be used in Nairobi, but that his parents, particularly his mother, should not see the poster so soon after the loss. Others later confirmed

his judgment, so I never took the poster back home.[1] When I showed the photographs to close relatives, I removed that image. Our discussion that day recognized the evocative power of images, the different contexts of meaning involved, the diverse viewers who would encounter the poster and exhibition, and the volatile meanings and possibilities of particular images.

In Nairobi, local debates about other photographic exhibitions formed part of the larger context for *Okiek Portraits*. *Images of Kenya* was one such exhibition, shown in Nairobi in 1986. Public commentary on that exhibition (discussed further below) paralleled Kirutari Meitukut's description of "the ones that are wanted" and encapsulated similar politics of representation and communication: "The impression given by the work was not, in my opinion, representative of Kenya today, even with its variety of rural and urban life. The images leaned towards the exotic and dramatic and I found many of them romantic, as they did not portray the dynamism of our changing society. . . . On this issue, evidently what pleases the foreign eye and draws the tourist does not necessarily please Kenyans, whose culture is being presented, and often manipulated. This presents a dilemma which is not easily resolved, for it is so often the absence of information rather than the presence of lies that makes propoganda [*sic*] out of essentially valid statements. The 'Images of Kenya' are not bogus (with one important exception) but the picture is incomplete. Yes, many of our people continue to wear traditional dress, but equally, many wear jeans and Bata shoes" (Saitoti 1987, 26).

Every exhibition entails multiple imaginings. Its organizers, visitors, and those portrayed all have ideas about what is shown, what is intended, and one another. They characterize themselves and others involved, forming concepts and making attributions about individuals and social groups. Shaped through the ways exhibitions communicate and the politics of representation they engage, such imagining is a fundamental way of constituting relations between Self and Other and grasping cultural difference.

Those portrayed might be perceived as radically different or very similar to imagined selves, depending on facets emphasized. More likely they are seen as both alike and different, for a dynamic of assimilating and exoticizing informs exhibitions (Karp 1991, 375–80). Displays that foreground cultural difference make this dynamic particularly clear. Many authors note that identity formation involves the interplay of similarity and difference (e.g., Berger [1972] 1987; Barthes 1957; Bhabha 1986). Karp develops this insight further, and in relation to exhibitions specifically, using the terms exoticizing and assimilating to describe both exhibiting strategies and modes of exhibit interpretation. He stresses the way these interpretive modes co-occur and the dialectical tension this simultaneity produces (see Karp and Kratz 2000, 194–99). Exhibitions, then, are part of the moral imagination, relating to "the ways that people construct images of the world in which they live, . . . measure, assess and reflect upon the reality of their experiences . . . picture a world different from that which they actually experience, . . . [and] stand back to scrutinize, contemplate and judge their world" (Beidelman 1986, 1–2). Exhibitionary imaginings are always constructed and expressed in historically and culturally specific ways.

Yet stereotypes also entail an interplay of similarity and difference, as noted in the last chapter;[2] and people may well find means to reinforce essentialist stereotypes in exhibitions.[3] The question is how to encourage people to recognize the variability and subtlety contained in cultural and historical difference and the ongoing social processes through which difference is produced. What kinds of engagement with assimilating and exoticizing might produce this understanding and the kind of recognition of others that moves and changes those involved? This would mean that "human beings everywhere (as individuals as well as collectivities) must be presumed to be engaged in identity-forming (hence identity-changing) activities and processes" and "identity—and its recognition—is thought of not as a property or state but as a process" (Fabian 1999, 68).

Exoticizing and assimilating dynamics figure variously in the imaginings of exhibition planners, visitors, as well as those portrayed. Their interpretations may be grounded, however, in different assumptions and experiences. As I begin considering how audiences interpreted *Okiek Portraits,* it will be important to identify dimensions of assimilating and exoticizing emphasized in each case, explore the idioms through which they were expressed, and consider the tensions and politics of representation they involved for people in Nairobi, in the United States, and for Okiek.[4] I describe the installations and different venues where *Okiek Portraits* was shown to provide a sense of its institutional framing in each case.

Understanding how visitors interpret an exhibition is often an exercise in extrapolation from fragments. "Everyday viewers of art can walk away from . . . an exhibit with minimal responses, unarticulated feelings, and incomplete thoughts" (Barrett 1990, 13), yet the exhibition may still make an impression. Visitor surveys and focus groups increase coverage and offer summary accounts but provide frustratingly little depth or detail. It is particularly difficult to untangle the interpretive processes through which visitors form understandings over the course of their visit and afterward, to illuminate the interplay between what the exhibition brings to visitors and what visitors bring to the exhibition. Much recent scholarly writing about exhibition representation considers the author's impressions alone. Analyzing exhibitions as texts, it treats the author as the "typical"—or perhaps the "critical"—visitor and offers a reading that might result from a particularly attentive visit. Some valuable analyses, insights, and debates have resulted (Harraway 1984; Bal 1996; Schudson 1997; Kirschenblatt-Gimblett 1998), but they tell us little about the variety of visitor interpretations or the communicative and interpretive processes involved.[5]

A variety of sources gave me windows into visitor understandings of *Okiek Portraits.* In Nairobi, there were newspaper reviews and conversations at the exhibition opening and elsewhere. Discussions with Okiek informed my account of Okiek interpretations. For the United States, there were reviews from Washington, Philadelphia, East Lansing, and Atlanta; a comment book from Fairbanks; student papers written in Washington and Atlanta; and docent comments, letters, and a video interview from the Atlanta showing. On various occasions I discussed the exhibition with visitors in Philadelphia, East Lansing, and Atlanta.[6] Soon after the 1989 Austin presentation several people talked with me about it,[7] and I sent the first draft of this book for comment to nine people who were anthropology faculty at the time. Finally, a small visitor survey provided more systematic information from Michigan State University Museum. The remaining chapters use these sources to consider visitor understandings of *Okiek Portraits* at its various venues. I describe them chronologically, beginning with Nairobi.

THE NATIONAL MUSEUM, NAIROBI

The Nairobi Museum grew out of a private natural history museum created in 1910. Today it is the headquarters and flagship museum for National Museums of Kenya (NMK), a body also responsible since 1969 for "all archaeological and paleontological sites and monuments within the country" (NMK 1990, 5, 7). Efforts to extend museum services beyond Nairobi and make them "accessible to more people in Kenya, especially the young" began that same year (NMK 1981, 4). NMK now includes twelve regional museums and seven major sites and monuments, in addition to the Nairobi Museum.[8]

The present Nairobi Museum building opened as the Coryndon Museum in 1930, with major gallery expansions built in the late 1940s and early 1950s while Louis Leakey was director.[9] In 1964, a year after independence, the museum changed its name and became the National Museum (NMK 1990, 6). It maintains the encyclopedic organization of a natural history museum focused on Kenya and eastern Africa, with galleries about mammals, fish and reptiles, geology, and prehistory on the ground floor; exhibits of ornithology, ethnography (including Joy Adamson's "Peoples of Kenya" portraits), and space exploration on the second floor; and an annex wing showing colonial and postcolonial Kenyan history and further mammal and ethnography displays. In 1986 a small corner gallery on the second floor was devoted to contemporary East African art. *Okiek Portraits* was shown on the second floor in a long gallery stretching between the Ethnography Gallery and the Bird Gallery. Once the Insect Gallery, it was converted to temporary exhibition space administered by the Gallery of Contemporary Art in the mid-1980s.

Visitors to the National Museum include local residents and visitors to Nairobi, school groups from throughout the country, resident expatriates, and visiting tourists.[10] Kenyan audiences for *Okiek Portraits* were most important to me, but I hoped to interest the full range of visitors. Many Kenyans have heard of the National Museum and a good number visit as schoolchildren. However, it is not clear how many Kenyans see the museum as a place for repeat visiting. The Nairobi Museum has been notably lax in advertising itself and its programs, whether to tourists or local residents. According to a review committee, local "attendance at the museum seems to occur despite the lack of information to the public. We could find no evidence of any attempt to market the museum to local adults" (External Review Panel 1992, 14). One concern, then, was how to encourage Kenyans to visit while *Okiek Portraits* was on view.[11]

I did not expect many Okiek to come to the museum while the exhibition was on view in 1989, particularly after the failed Nairobi trip for people from communities involved. As far as I knew, few Okiek lived in or near Nairobi.[12] Discussions over the years made it clear that Kenyans generally knew little about Okiek. For instance, one museum employee initially thought Okiek were part of the Luo people because the name begins with "O," like many Dholuo words. I developed promotional material that addressed this lack of knowledge; the exhibition's introductory material also explained the names Okiek and Torrobo. Press releases and posters were the main publicity; funding was insufficient for other advertising.

I sent press releases with photographs to the four national newspapers (three English language, one Kiswahili), resulting in good initial coverage. Barclay's Bank also announced its sponsorship in the newspaper. During October 1989, the exhibition's last month, *Signature* (the Diners Club magazine) profiled the exhibition and my research in an article reaching a narrower audience, largely middle to upper class. Reviews and mentions in three newspapers also continued to spread the word. These newspaper stories also brought information about Okiek to a population beyond Nairobi who would not see the exhibition. One person wrote to me from Eldoret that he "was encouraged to read more about Okiek/Iltorobo," had gone to visit Omotik Okiek, learned of their displacement and land difficulties, and concluded "I am trying to study my own Kikuyu people and do my own finding" (F. M. Mureithi, p.c.). Though the author lived far from the exhibition, his letter brought up issues about ethnic heritage, national unity, personal identity, and economic circumstances in Kenya, issues that also figured in Nairobi.

Other publicity was concentrated in Nairobi itself. Attractive color posters announced the exhibition throughout the city (plate 1), but they disappeared almost as quickly as they went up. Posters often announced events (though they rarely featured color photographs), so I did not anticipate this response. I replaced posters several times; shopkeepers eventually displayed some inside their windows to prevent them from "going missing."[13] The *Okiek Portraits* poster must have decorated dozens of rooms in town in 1989; five years later I still encountered occasional copies in unexpected places and received requests from museum, government, and university staff who remembered it. People clearly liked the posters, but I don't know whether their appearance in these other settings helped bring people to the exhibition or what people there thought of them.

As interpretive background and immediate reference for Nairobi visitors to the exhibition—especially if they were expatriates and relatively wealthy or well-educated Kenyans—there were books and local photographic exhibitions. Kenya features in a raft of coffee-table photo books, many sold in Nairobi though beyond the budget of most Kenyans. At the time, photographic exhibits were mounted in Nairobi once or twice a year at various venues (French Cultural Centre, Goethe Institute, American Cultural Center, and several galleries, but rarely at the museum).

People I spoke with while producing *Okiek Portraits* often recalled another exhibition, *Images of Kenya*, the 1986 display of color photographs by David Coulson, Carol Beckwith, and Angela Fisher mentioned at the start of this chapter. Common setting and product seemed the basis of association (though people did not draw comparisons between actual images or presentation of the two exhibits, which differed). Both were shown at the National Museum, and Coulson produced a handsome *Images of Kenya* poster sold at the museum shop.[14] *Images of Kenya* included scenes from the entire country and began as a government-commissioned Kenya Pavilion display for an international audience at Expo '86 in Vancouver, Canada. As Beckwith described it, "my colleagues and I were provided with a twenty page brief by the ministry of transport and communication identifying what was required picture by picture" (1987, 2–3). Debates about that exhibition illustrate some of the issues and politics of representation that formed the broader context for *Okiek Portraits* as well.

Kenyan reviews appreciated the striking photographs in *Images of Kenya* but questioned its lack of contemporary scenes and emphasis on the "traditional" (Andere 1986; Ciira 1986). Ciira (1986, 24) also criticized the captioning, closing with a sharp reproach:

> The argument against using more pictures of contemporary life is that the audience for whom the exhibition was prepared was more interested in seeing the Masai [*sic*], Samburu, Gabbra, and other peoples regarded as "exotic." But if people in the outside world are only exposed to such and other images of Kenya contained in such films as *Out of Africa*, no wonder some Africans have been asked, on arrival in some western countries, where they got the clothes they were wearing.[15]

Several months later these issues arose again, when *Images of Kenya* became the topic of an acrimonious exchange between Beckwith and Tepilit ole Saitoti in the *Weekly Review*, Kenya's equivalent to *Time* or *Newsweek* (Saitoti 1987; Beckwith 1987). Saitoti, a Tanzanian living in Kenya who co-authored *Maasai* (1980) with Beckwith, was surprised to find a 1978 picture of his Tanzanian mother in the exhibition. This provoked him to write an opinion piece, to which Beckwith responded. The exchange delineated sensitive issues in the Kenyan cultural arena, though Saitoti seemed to be settling an old score, too, when he expanded charges to their own collaboration. Beckwith responded to three sets of accusations, summarized by the magazine's heading "Cultural Exploitation."

The first concerns questions of power, representational authority, and economics common to all documentary projects. Saitoti registers concern over exploitation of those shown in the photographs: they may not realize how their images may be used and receive no (or inadequate) financial compensation. Beckwith argues that she lectures about Maasai internationally and describes her support for them, yet this actually begs the question of who speaks for photographic subjects in what arenas. In the second, Saitoti presents his own collaboration with Beckwith as an example of exploitation. Beckwith points out that they shared royalties equally and Saitoti also went on the international lecture circuit, making his accusation appear rather disingenuous.[16]

To me, much of Saitoti's essay seemed personal, petty complaints about Beckwith and *Images of Kenya;* however, his third set of issues raised the ideological stakes by moving to a broader political arena. He frames his experience as symptomatic of neocolonialism and decries expatriate dominance that hinders promotion of local talent and expertise. Without acknowledging larger sociopolitical relations, Beckwith professes willingness to assist such promotion and pleads, "Please let us try and kill the 'us' and 'they' approach to life and culture. 'Foreigners' come from other planets; on this one we are all human beings and should share the experiences which art and culture take across national boundaries" (1987, 3).

Saitoti's other criticism, quoted earlier in this chapter, concerned the exhibition's visual representations. He saw its narrow range of representations as reproducing stereotypes of Africa as "traditional." Beckwith ignored these remarks, claiming they just followed government orders. Apart from the appearance of Saitoti's mother, there was no discussion of actual images—aesthetic form, poses, framing, relations shown; nor were exhibition texts or design considered.

The Saitoti/Beckwith exchange had relevance only for certain segments of the exhibition's audience. They attended to—or discounted—it in part for the gossipy titillation of former collaborators turning on one another publicly. Still, the fact that these charges could be plausibly raised in Kenya's major news magazine reveals certain tensions in Nairobi's cultural politics that remain part of the backdrop for other photographic exhibitions and cultural endeavors.[17] A glance at other media articles at the time show how pervasive questions about representation and neocolonialism have been: Kenyan author Ngugi wa Thiongo's book *Decolonising the Mind* is reviewed in the *Weekly Review;* letters to the editor discuss Wole Soyinka's recent Nobel prize and whether his style and use of English show that he writes for foreigners; a wildly successful Africa Film Week generates feature articles, government speeches, and editorials about producing films on African themes with positive images, indigenizing the film industry, and discussions of cultural imperialism. As discussed in chapter 2, I considered such issues while planning *Okiek Portraits,* but even the most well-meaning efforts can still go wrong or unwittingly offend (cf. Schildkrout 1991). Regardless of self-critical or collaborative efforts, charges of neocolonialism always remain possible when an expatriate produces an exhibition. Identity politics are no stranger to Kenya, but neither is that idiom always invoked. What did visitors and reviewers think, then, when *Okiek Portraits* was shown three years later?

Two Kenyans who spoke with me suggest the possible range of reactions and interpretations that *Okiek Portraits* evoked. The first (GL) is a Kalenjin man[18] who worked in Nairobi in the Presidential Escort, an elite security corps comparable to the Secret Service in the United States. In his mid- to late forties at the time, he has a home near where I lived with Kipchornwonek Okiek. I invited GL to the Nairobi opening; he came very late. While the reception was cleaned up, he looked carefully at each photograph and slowly read the Kiswahili captions. He examined photographs closely, verbally identifying the activity or kind of occasion shown, picking out details that revealed their specifics. Occasionally he recognized the person shown; with other photographs he asked me to locate people in webs of kinship and place. His entire experience seemed imbued with the delight of recognition (see Gaither 1992; Clifford 1988).

GL's interpretation of the exhibition was mediated by experiences associated with his age, Kalenjin background, and familiarity with the general area depicted. He sought and found associations and commonalities as he looked at images: he, too, had braved initiation and attended ceremonies where girls danced in similar costumes; while not identical, the kitchen and garden scenes might have been his cousins' or neighbors' homes. Other aspects, though not unknown, offered less immediate personal linkages (e.g., certain ritual costumes, jewelry, and honey-gathering activities).

GL might have emphasized experiences that distanced him from Okiek shown; in other contexts, he sometimes does. Living in Nairobi, traveling widely with his job, growing up in a more "developed" area,[19] he built one of the first *mabati* houses (roofed with corrugated iron) in the Sogoo area when he bought land and moved his family there. In October 1984, as master of ceremonies for the first *harambee* (self-help) fund-raising meeting ever held there, GL felt he had to instruct the assembly in conventions of political meetings (e.g., stand and remove your hat for the national anthem). He did so jovially and generously, but it was clear from this and our conversations that he regarded the area and most Okiek native to it as unsophisticated, inexperienced, and in need of development—both economically and socially.

GL's response to *Okiek Portraits* was very much an assimilating gesture, then, but not a simple or totally predictable one. The exhibition setting itself may have contributed to this inclination. It was a matter of pleasure and pride to find scenes and people from an area he knew presented respectfully in the Nairobi Museum, a national institution. Though he already had basic knowledge, GL also learned about Okiek. He took time and was interested enough to look closely; Kiswahili captions made exhibition information accessible for him.

The second person, KK, was a university student at the time, finishing his degree in land economics. A reflective young man from Karatina (a small town in Central Province, southeast of Nyeri), KK was also an aspiring writer, composing poetry and writing short novels. He spoke to me about the exhibition a week or so after it opened. KK's impressions were complex, at times ambivalent, considering the exhibition from several angles. He spoke of individual photographs, their overall effect, as well as the exhibition as a whole. KK appreciated the photographs but felt little immediate connection to his own experience. He found the exhibition valuable for showing Okiek traditions, but his commendation was tinged with resentment. He expressed a certain bitterness that a fine exhibition about Kenyans should be produced by an expatriate, asking, "Why can't we do it for ourselves?"

Of course, Kenyans *do* produce cultural displays for and about themselves and others using many media—for example, in annual shows and festivals. In photography, Mohamed Amin immediately comes to mind: he is an internationally recognized photojournalist and cameraman, with over twenty-five books, photohistories and photobiographies of Kenyan figures, and travel surveys about Africa and Asia.[20] But KK's question was not really about counterexamples or exceptional individuals. Rather, it suggests that, in some ways, he was more concerned with the *Okiek Portraits* exhibition per se—its setting, sponsorship, producers, and capacity to represent Kenyan heritage—than with its content and the people represented.[21] His interpretive stance invoked a national vision, a united national identity vis-à-vis non-Kenyans. This contrasted with GL's general stance, which placed more emphasis on local positions in an internally differentiated national perspective.

Like Saitoti, KK took expatriate involvement as a telling sign for interpreting the exhibition-as-event. Both felt this called for explanation and blame. Unlike Saitoti in his accusations of neocolonial exploitation, KK turned the onus inward. His question simultaneously presumes Kenyan inadequacy and yearns for cultural independence. Still, their views are two sides of the same coin—one phrased as political charge, the other a more personal, self-castigating lament. Considering the political economy of cultural production would suggest that both are too one-sided. The public sphere in contemporary Kenya, including training and opportunities in the arts and the academy, has taken shape through a long history of interaction among diverse people and institutions with specific priorities. These include colonial and postcolonial governments, religious, educational, and commercial enterprises, and international funding agencies. This history has produced an uneven distribution of resources and uneven access to information and opportunities within Kenya for different groups of people, and for cultural endeavors relative to other fields, in addition to striking differences between Kenya and Euro-American countries. Neither Saitoti's "we have no chance" nor KK's "have we no talent?" speaks fully to the complexities of this larger, longer, systemic view, but both personal views convey frustration at constraints and disadvantages with which Kenyan artists and scholars work.

As part of a rhetoric of identity, they also help establish social groups and self-definitions. Saitoti and KK both use the Kenyan/foreigner dichotomy to set one boundary, assimilating all nationals into a "we." In fact, there is often some ambiguity about whether white or Asian Kenyans are included in this imagined "we."[22] As for the exhibition's subjects, Okiek *were* included; KK did not ask "Why can't they do it for themselves?" But KK tended to see Okiek historically, as part of Kenya's past. Individual photographs reminded KK of his grandmother and customs he had only heard about. This orientation was mediated by his own ethnicity (Kikuyu), age, and experience—all rather different than GL's. KK's comments on particular photographs suggest that he saw *Okiek Portraits* from several standpoints, but questions about Kenyans and expatriates were more important to him when we spoke than Okiek identity, their place within Kenya, or other connections he may have felt.

Both GL and KK, however, saw the exhibition and the museum as having a valuable role in recording and preserving Kenyan customs and history. Nairobi newspaper coverage also emphasized this concern. Wakanyote's review, for instance, was headlined "Camera lens snaps a changing society," and commented in closing, "In a generation or so these faces, the modes of dress and all will have changed most drastically. Corine [*sic*] Kratz's legacy will be that she preserved the lifestyle of these people for us all and we are the richer for it" (1989b). Articles also stressed the general lack of knowledge about Okiek: "The Okiek: Just who are they?" (Wakanyote 1989a). Wakanyote reviewed popular misconceptions about Okiek, while Ndavu discussed Okiek history, commerce, and material culture (1989a, 1989b).

Reviews treated the exhibition as documentary, mainly describing and interpreting what was shown.[23] The documentary "rhetoric of immediacy and truth" (Tagg 1988, 8), buttressed here by the photographer's academic/researcher role, was not questioned.[24] Thus exhibition content alone—its "facts"—received comment, though reviews appeared in arts columns. This focus is particularly striking in Ndavu (1989b) because her discussion of a painting exhibition in the same feature emphasizes formal analysis, describing composition, technique, themes, and use of color. Ndavu notes the lifecycle arrangement of *Okiek Portraits,* but otherwise Nairobi reviews did not discuss its installation, portrait focus, or formal and aesthetic aspects of the photographs.

Nonetheless, Wakanyote looked closely at the photographs, reading details to find moments of change, junctures between tradition and modernity. There are other ways to interpret the different kinds of clothing and objects shown (see chapter 2), but in some ways this was an important move away from exoticizing Okiek as unknown and uncivilized. Not totally Other but "contemporary ancestors," Okiek were still kept at a distance, not quite coeval. By interpreting visual signs as historical process, the reviewers assimilated Okiek to other Kenyans through general contrasts and historical changes they had in common. Though these changes took place at different times, in different ways, with different local consequences, the shared national narrative of modernization could be seen as uniting all. Okiek were latecomers to the process, still catching up to others.

Nairobi reviews did not critique the exhibition's modes of representation, then, but rather incorporated Okiek, through the exhibition, directly into the collective Kenyan mosaic of ethnicity. In public interpretation, they went beyond simply imagining affinities and contrasts with Okiek. Their claims were stronger and broader, explicitly assimilating Okiek into Kenyan heritage. The import was less "they are like us" than "they are us," though historicizing twists reimported a sense of distance, difference, and hierarchy at the same time, as in KK's reaction. KK was sensitive to tensions related to power, knowledge, identity, dependence, and exploitation highlighted by expatriate involvement in cultural production. But these issues are also replicated within Kenya in perennial concerns with ethnic inequalities, culture, and identity: who can represent Kenya's diverse cultural traditions, how are minorities appropriated or excluded, how is national, *Kenyan* heritage construed in the context of ethnic diversity?

GL's sense of the exhibition seemed to negotiate these questions as well, perhaps recognizing Okiek in ways that created less distance.

Exhibition interpretations are filtered through visitors' past experiences and related to their definitions of relevant fields of identity. Certain dimensions and idioms of assimilating and exoticizing are made pertinent and prominent by the ways they define those fields and position themselves within them at different times. In Kenyan responses reviewed so far, these ranged from questions of personal identity, to ethnic and national heritage, to international relations. Kenyan visitors found individuals in *Okiek Portraits* who looked like people in many rural parts of Kenya (plates 5–7), but they also saw people with distinctive ornaments and ceremonies (plates 13–16). The exhibition tried to encourage engagement, but such features provided means for both assimilating and exoticizing. For instance, many Kenyans go through initiations like those shown in *Okiek Portraits,* though particulars differ. For visitors so inclined, initiation photographs could be construed in terms of common experience. Others might distance Okiek practice more as "traditional," though not unfamiliar. For European visitors, these same features would more readily make Okiek seem foreign; clear visual parallels would be more difficult to make. When Okiek looked at their own pictures, they recognized the exoticizing-assimilating dynamic that would inform other viewings. Their interpretations combined animated acts of recognition, joyful and wistful memories, and reflections on photographic representation and interpretation.

OKIEK VIEWINGS: BACKGROUND

Okiek Portraits traveled to different exhibition contexts in Kenya and the United States, but it was also seen outside the museum setting within Kenya. When Okiek finally viewed the *Okiek Portraits* photographs, they were at home. Yet the museum was also evoked in Okiek homes. People knew these photographs were shown in Nairobi, and we discussed the National Museum as their place of display.[25] While museums and their visitors were imagined, Okiek viewings were different. Musello's (1980) notion of family viewing context might seem appropriate for these Okiek settings,[26] but "family viewing" is a culturally and historically specific activity, always located in a particular cultural, political, and visual economy. Before turning to Okiek comments, then, I sketch the background of photography in Kenya.

In eastern Africa, photography arrived with European explorers, missionaries, administrators, and settlers in the late 1800s and early 1900s. Europeans began setting up photographic studios on the coast, followed by Indians from Goa (Behrend 1998, 139). In the 1880s, Zanzibar boasted several commercial studios, including the Gomes firm founded around 1868 (Monti 1987, 165).[27] Studios were established somewhat later in mainland ports and farther inland. For instance, William Young, photographer during construction of the Uganda Railway, opened commercial studios in Mombasa (ca. 1899–1904) and Nairobi (ca. 1905–19 [Monti 1987]);[28] H. K. Binks opened a Nairobi studio in 1904 (Bensusan 1966, 81). Europeans and Indians probably provided much of the clientele for the earliest Kenyan studios, but the history of photography in Kenya has yet to be written.[29] Gomes, at least, was making striking portraits of well dressed African women in his Zanzibar studio in the 1890s (Bensusan 1996, 145–46).

Outside the studio, Maasai were a favorite subject for ethnological photographs around the turn of the century (Bensusan 1996, 33, 111, 139, 149). But again, we can only conjecture about the extent to which photographs were given to African subjects and how they may have understood them at the time. In some areas, those who became involved with missions (Strayer 1978, xi–xiv), government work, and settler households may have been among the first to acquire and become familiar with group and individual portraits.[30]

Amateur and professional photography became more widespread in Kenya after World War I, but personal photographs were still uncommon in many African communities.[31] Education, income, employment, proximity to towns, and mission involvement all influenced the extent to which Kenyans experienced and acquired photographs. For instance, early pictures of Jomo Kenyatta suggest considerable involvement and concern with photographs. While Kenyatta was hardly a "typical" Kenyan after his political engagement developed in the mid-1920s and he became a national leader, these early scenes are still revealing for photographic history. A 1910 portrait shows a young barefoot Jomo Kenyatta at sixteen to eighteen years old, standing in a garden against a tall hedge of flowers wearing tie and jacket and holding a walking stick (see figure 7a). Likely taken while Kenyatta was staying at the Church of Scotland Mission at Kikuyu, this was followed by regular photographic portraits: 1914 (the year he was baptized), dressed in a suit, standing on a veranda; 1920, studio portrait with two friends, all in suits, ties, and hats, one smoking a cigarette; early 1920s, studio portrait with his son and a motorbike; 1924, a formal family portrait with his wife, son, brother, and a cousin (see figures 7b–e). Kenyatta and other leaders of the Kikuyu Central Association also made group studio portraits in 1928 and 1930 (Howarth 1967, 45–49; Kenyatta 1968, following page 190).[32] These examples probably illustrate one extreme on a continuum of familiarity and use of photographs by Kenyans during these decades, but they also illustrate conventions concerning dress, posture, settings, and props that continue in various forms to the present.[33]

At the same time, photographs became increasingly commonplace in diverse public settings and uses. In his novel *Master and Servant,* David Mulwa makes one example central to a new schoolboy's first encounter with the headmaster:

> Here I was to sit and wait, so said the headmaster. I was not to touch anything; was not to look at the picture of the woman directly opposite me; was to fold my hands and books on my lap and employ all my faculties in contemplating them. With these directions, Headmaster Mathayo closed the door upon both me and the strange white woman who (much against my will) stared at me through the glass frame. (1979, 24)

Photographs also figured in political controversies. In 1947 African members of the Legislative Council demanded the abolition of the *kipande* registration system for African men, a long-standing grievance.[34] The colonial government responded by extending it to all races but then backed down in response to European protest "by exempting people who could sign their name and provide two photographs of themselves, i.e., virtually all Europeans" (Gordon 1986, 93; cf. Berman 1990, 387). Several years later, mandatory photography of Kikuyu people for new labor records in the 1950s met with massive refusals (Kanogo 1987, 140).

Photography permeates life in Kenya today, especially, but not only, in town and city. Every adult holds an identity card (*kipande*) bearing their photographic likeness. Every shop, down to the smallest tea kiosks in remote rural areas, displays a photograph of the president (see figure 8).[35] Newspapers feature the usual range of current events pictures, photographic death announcements and memorials, and advertising photos. Commercial products use photographs in package design, and posters might publicize events with eye-catching pictures. Even small towns usually have at least one photography studio and larger ones have licensed street photographers as well. In 1994, nearly a dozen surrounded the Nyayo Monument in Nairobi's Uhuru Park, each displaying sample work and the varied backgrounds available nearby, including the Serena Hotel, Nairobi skyscrapers, bougainvillea boughs, and the monument itself.[36] The photo album is a fixture in many middle-class Kenyan homes, perhaps more than in many American homes today. It is part of a protocol of visiting and hospitality in Kenya and figures as well in family reminiscences.

Photo albums have only recently become part of Okiek practice. Among Kaplelach Okiek, they caught on from about 1990; young people were virtually the only ones with albums in the mid-1990s.[37] Most older Kaplelach remember clearly the first time they were photographed; it is such an infrequent experience for some that they can also recount each time since. Men of the *il kalikal* age-set (now in their sixties)[38] reported that they were the first Kaplelach in the area to encounter personal photographs. Kirutari Meitukut, for instance, first had his picture taken as a young man (*muran*), while working for the Game Department in the late 1940s or early 1950s. The District Game Officer photographed him climbing a hive for honey with another Okiot; Kirutari was given a few shillings and, later, a copy of the picture, long since lost. Noting changing Okiek attitudes toward photographs, he told me in 1993:

> We were afraid of it. We would say, "It will finish your blood. It takes your heart out so you will die."[39] Because we didn't know about them. . . . It's people of today who have started to put them away and save them, so they can see them later.

Though a few Kaplelach men encountered photographs and cameras then, personal photographs remained unfamiliar, a phenomenon of towns and Europeans. The first photographic experience of Mentegai Leboo, a man of the following *eseuri* age-set (now in their fifties), parallels that of Kirutari. When Mentegai was grown and married, his first child nursing (i.e., probably in the early 1960s, before Kenyan independence), a European man passed through Ololulunga center one day and photographed him in a group with several other men. The man gave them ten shillings to split. Some

a   b

Figure 7. Early pictures of Jomo Kenyatta
showing some conventions of photographic
portraiture in Kenya: (a) in about 1910 (then
Johnstone Kamau); (b) in about 1914; (c) in
1920 (*at right*) with friends; (d) in the 1920s
with his son Peter Muigai and motorbike; (e)
in about 1924 with family members.

13th October 1926 at Nairobi BE AFRICA.
W. MARTHUR KAMPAINEHAS K.T. JOHNSTONE

c

d

e

Figure 8. President Moi's portrait (*at right*) is hung higher than other pictures, overlooking the shop of Samwel Araap Maasai. Megeny'o, 1993.

time later he returned and gave Mentegai a copy of the photograph. Mentegai, too, noted generational shifts in how Okiek regard photographs:

> People then were foolish, friend. They didn't care. What did they care for photographs? I don't go looking for pictures. If I get one [somehow], then I can come and put it in the house. But young people now go looking for photographs so that they can come and hang them in their houses.

Indeed, the household of Simon Inkutukai Leboo, a young man of the *il kishili* age-set (now in his early thirties), may epitomize this increased interest in and desire for photographs. In 1994, the sitting room of Inkutukai's *mabati* house was hung with twenty-one framed photographs and several posters; his wife had also painted it with designs (see figure 9). In addition, he kept a small album with another seventeen photographs.[40] The earliest pictures on the wall were two I had taken in 1983 and 1984. Most (thirteen) were studio portraits accumulated between 1987 and 1990, taken in Narok town (two to three hours away) at Imani Studio and Narok Studio. Several others

Figure 9. Sitting room in the home of Simon Inkutukai
Leboo and his wife, Grace Chepopoo, in 1993.

posed in outdoor settings belonged to Inkutukai's younger brother. He had paid an
itinerant photographer to take them all on a single day.[41]

These examples suggest the age-stratified nature of Okiek experience with and attitudes toward photographs. Inkutukai's collection is unmatched even among his age-
mates, but they share his enthusiasm for photographs. Young men often have formal
portraits made in Narok's photographic studios. Many older Okiek have also come to
appreciate photographs as reminders of events and people, signs of friendship, and indicators of values associated with development and modernity.[42] Some older people,
too, may try to get photographs to display, or even visit a photographic studio. But
they rarely keep pictures with the same care or regard framing them as the same priority. For Okiek as for many other Kenyans, "These are a luxury." A Nairobi street
photographer used this phrase in 1993 to describe the highly elastic demand for photographs and explain his profession's financial difficulties during a time of rampant

inflation and shrinking real income. "Even you can stay until you die without one of these pictures, and it won't matter. It is a luxury."

Whether they seek out photographs, obtain them casually on occasion and then try to safeguard them, or disregard them entirely, Okiek today recognize photographs as objects that are saved, sometimes prized. They appreciate photographs as entertainment and examine them with interest. Photographs are traded, loaned, saved, framed, and hung in *mabati* houses, especially by younger Okiek. Even those who usually don't care about them borrow framed photographs to decorate their houses on ceremonial occasions. Cameras are coveted possessions, but few Okiek have acquired them.[43]

Okiek "home viewing," then, is a context as likely to involve peers as family. New photographs typically appear singly or in pairs. It is not common for a collection of photographs to arrive, though I always returned from Nairobi trips during my research with a backlog of pictures to give people. When I came with the *Okiek Portraits* photographs in 1989, viewings differed from my other homecomings. Instead of stacks of photographs passed around, these photographs were in an album, showing one picture at a time. Further, I kept them together in the album so everyone could see them, rather than giving them away. The photographs themselves were not quite like "the ones that are wanted" by Okiek themselves. They differed from formal posed portraits produced in studios, by itinerant photographers, or arranged by Okiek when they asked me to take their pictures (see figure 10).[44] Finally, viewings differed because these were the photographs from the Nairobi show; people knew they were seen by many visitors and preserved in the National Museum for future generations. In these viewings, people were not only looking at pictures of themselves but imagining others looking at their pictures.

OKIEK VIEWINGS: COMMENTARIES

People had seen most photographs in the *Okiek Portraits* album previously, when I gave copies away. The album was a kind of retrospective of years we had shared, glimpsed though a few of our common experiences. About ten small groups looked at the photographs during my visit; I recorded five of the sessions.[45] In several, people finished the album, then started over, looking at them all again. Viewings were full of lively interaction and discussion, not structured as formal interviews.[46] Still, the literature on photo interpretation in interview settings includes two observations that characterize these Okiek viewings as well (Collier 1967; Geary 1988; Bravman 1990; Chalfen 1991; Schwartz 1992).

First, the photographs were mnemonics that prompted people to talk about events, people, and social relations, going beyond what was shown. The "metonymic power" of the photograph to "encode the totality of an experience" (Sekula quoted in Musello 1980, 39) extends beyond occasions depicted, evoking the lives and characters of people shown.[47] For Okiek, this metonymy was anchored in knowledge of people, places, and events, producing reminiscence and reflection. Second, many Okiek comments involved "looking through" photographs, that is, focusing on what is shown as if it were present

Figure 10. This photograph of (*from right*) Simon Inkutukai Leboo, his brother Samuel Sanare Leboo, and his mother's brother's son Ben Kintet Senoi was taken at Narok Studio in 1987.

and the photograph itself "transparent." These remarks centered on photographic "content," disregarding questions of framing, form, and their construction as images (Messaris and Gross 1977; Musello 1980; Schwartz 1992, 13; Worth and Gross 1974; Barrett 1990, 142–43).

Yet other comments *did* pertain to formal properties, remarking on perspective, framing, and the realist aesthetic of photographs, as well my own involvement and intentions, and selections made for the exhibition. Compared to viewers elsewhere, all Okiek commentaries were more oriented to specific individuals and places shown, highlighting the indexical nature of photographs. This specificity raised questions later, when I excerpted label copy from Okiek conversations. How could this wealth of information be made accessible and interesting to visitors lacking the interpretive background these discussions assumed? What should be included?

Okiek photographic readings always began with identifications, naming what was shown.[48] Into an initial series of recognitions (specific people, social categories of people, particular places, occasions, objects, and activities), viewers interspersed evaluations, musings, memories, and critiques. People often used different names for the same individual in a photograph, indicating both varied relationships with the person shown and changes in social position since the picture was taken. A few of the photographs had been taken in 1989, but many were six years old, and one was from fourteen years earlier. They portrayed people from several settlements, including some viewers had not seen for years or had never met. Unlike viewers elsewhere, then, for Okiek the photographs were suffused with the passage of time.

> KIRUTARI: Who is this? Wait, let me look. Hee! It's the mother of my co-initiate! . . . There are none of these [people] that I don't know, friend. Mother of my co-initiate. That old lady that was married to Orkankait. Torr! Araap Semeri's mother. Usho! Ai, she's gotten old. I wonder if she is still alive? Ai, but this old lady is a very kind person.

> LUTIA: Is this Kachacha?
> CORY: No, it's Kopot Nabaru.
> LUTIA: I wonder if this one is still alive, Cory, or has she died?
> CORY: I don't know; I took the picture long ago.
> LUTIA: Yes, at Mau. . . . This is really an old lady.

They situated the ambiguity and discontinuity of the photographs through their memories of and continuing relations with those pictured (see Berger 1982). At times this temporal discontinuity created a sense of self-estrangement, familiar to us all. Margaret Nampet Leboo expressed embarrassed distaste at her own picture from six years earlier (plate 3):

> NAMPET: I hate that picture! Why don't we tear it up?
> LAATO: And so what if you hate it? What are you going to do to yourself [because the picture looks like that]?

The same feeling of self-distance is captured by Calvin and Hobbes in figure 11: "Isn't it weird that one's own past can seem unreal? This is like looking at a picture of somebody else." As Roland Barthes observed, "the Photograph is the advent of myself as other" (1981, 12).

Present and past converged at times in the multiple names Okiek used for initiates pictured. When photographed, they were known only by childhood names; in viewings people also used names initiates had acquired after marriage and motherhood. Exclamations over their health and beauty as initiates were edged with nostalgia for some, pride for others. Looking at these pictures, viewers also elaborated further, gossiping about initiates' adventures, asserting the continuity of tradition, and commenting on the permanence of photographs (plates 15–17):

Calvin and Hobbes   by Bill Watterson

Figure 11. Calvin and Hobbes © 1995 Watterson.
Reprinted with permission of Universal Press Syndicate.
All rights reserved.

KIRUTARI: The girls of the Araapkiplet family are sexy! Terree! It's not for nothing that she was driven—One of them was pursued in a car when she ran away with someone. . . . Ai, these awful things were healthy and looked good.

MOSEITI: What do you mean, they're thin!

KIRUTARI: They must have eaten bewitching medicines to draw men to them.

KIRUTARI: This is the thing we were born with, these decorations for the children. It was born here, and it was—This is a small picture. If you look at it in a big picture, a big one, your stomach will cry with the beauty! And this child of mine [*on the right end*]! Truly, she was burning people with her beauty.

LAATO: What is she holding? She's holding the projection on her necklace. She'll hold it forever. She'll hold it forever and ever and ever in the picture.

All Okiek viewers paid particular attention to photographs dealing with initiation. The subject of excited exclamations, reminiscences, and explanations to non-Okiek, these photographs were also prominent in later discussions in other venues. Apart from initiates' youthful beauty, Okiek focused on specific signs of initiation and guests' enjoyment at ceremonies. They found two photographs of secluded initiates especially striking and surprising; secluded initiates are not ordinarily seen (plates 12–13).

LUTIA: Oi my goodness! Oi Kaplelach will still do something! Ehee! Is this Laakwaani again? Muro, muro! We talked about these pictures with Kopot Ntekwa. Did you ever see secluded initiates that show themselves about?

ARAAP NTETE: I say, Cory, when did you go around photographing secluded initiates, otiagi, because we're amazed?

LAATO: Muro!

NAMPET: Initiates in seclusion! Pilini and them! and Kopot Edina! [laughing]

LAATO: They were decorating each other.[. . .]Where were they, Cory?

CORY: We were down at Ruruupto [the settlements in the river valley].

LAATO: And didn't they say, "Call Cory for us [to take our picture]," my goodness.

I had discussed using such photographs with Okiek when planning the exhibition and received permission to include them. Nonetheless, seeing them was still startling. People also recognized that seclusion costume would be strange to other viewers: "Don't you think those people looking at the pictures were astonished by this? They must have said, 'These people eat people!' And then you told them, 'They don't eat people.'"

Photographs of older men also drew extended commentary, marked by affectionate humor rather than nostalgia or remembrance. Notably, when people saw these pictures they began to imitate the man shown (plates 24, 29, 28):

LAATO: Who is this, this one with the bracelets on?

NAMPET: You'd think it's Larusi's father [*laughs*]. He's blowing on the fire, friend.

LAATO [*imitating him*]: Hee hee, let me blow on the fire. Hee!

MOSEITI: Which one is this?

KIRUTARI: Koibitat's father.

MOSEITI: Yes, it's Araap Teepes. . . . Yes, this is that coat of his that he usually has.

KIRUTARI: Don't you see the calabash? He's saying a blessing. Don't you see that it is really him?

MOSEITI [*imitating him*]: Heeheeheehee I swear by my mother-in-law.

KIRUTARI: These are the ones that are wanted. These.

KISHUAYON [*imitating*]: Let's go to that low forest area, *kapatang*. He was at a ceremony, Cory. [*Imitates again, speaking Maa:*] Aiye inkapatak pormora. I say, don't you think this is just like Meja?

Identities, contexts, and activities all figured in these commentaries, but mimicking performance was a primary way to recognize the distinctive characters and personal quirks evoked by these photographs.[49] The passage of time was less obvious in pictures of people already mature, and correspondingly less prominent in Okiek interpretations.

At times Okiek explained photographic scale and representation to one another (plate 4):

NAMPET: Let me take a good look at this child.

LAATO: I think it must be Katais's [child]. Whose do you think it is?

NAMPET: This child, this big?

LAATO: Isn't that what it's like in a picture?

NAMPET: No. Where did you take it?

CORY: At Sapoitit.

NAMPET: Oo. It's hers then.

LAATO: It's the picture, indeed. That's what it's like.

They read details of representation with keen attention, interpreting the states of those shown. Many commented that Kishuayon's eyes showed drunkenness; one person interpreted light reflecting on his mouth the same way (plate 20):

LUTIA: This could only be Michael! Is he drunk? He's drunk, but just a little drunk. Or is he really drunk?

CHEEPEET: He's drunk. Just look at the eyes.

LUTIA: And the mouth—it's whitish.

A number of Okiek commented on my photographic selections and framing, revealing our different assumptions about what photographs should be like and what should be photographed. For instance, my photograph of a woman cooking (plate 22) made Okiek marvel:

LUTIA: There's cooking going on here! [*laughs*] . . .

SELENA: Ai! Cory photographs anything!

MOSEITI: Is she cooking, friend? There are plates.

KIRUTARI: Don't you see the soap? There's nothing this one doesn't take [pictures of]!

This subject, like several others in the exhibition, illustrates the documentary impulse that shaped my research photography, with its emphasis on recording all aspects of daily life (see chapter 2).[50] The cooking photograph and others manifest the documentary preference for candid photographs, too.[51] Okiek ideals and values of photographic self-presentation, however, were not rooted in documentary traditions.[52] In contrast to *Okiek Portraits,* all photographs displayed in Inkutukai's sitting room were posed, including the ones I took.

My portrait framing of the bride in a wedding procession consistently raised questions for Okiek as well (plate 19). In this case, my approach was at variance with Okiek notions of photographic completeness, based on knowledge of the event: why weren't others in the procession shown? These comments suggested Okiek notions of what constitutes adequate documentary:

LAATO: It's Pilini that's being married here. But where are the people who are bringing her? I say, aren't we here, Cory?

Similarly, Simion Sena reframed the picture of his wife's brother (plate 14) in its broader setting: "Where is the other initiate that was with him? This is the other one [the edge of his ceremonial cape is visible]." These comments suggest that Okiek found it odd for me to single out individuals at ritual moments so profoundly implicated in creating social relations.

Okiek also judged the overall array of photographs in *Okiek Portraits,* considering both how comprehensive coverage was and whether their characterization was representative of Okiek life.[53] After looking at all the photographs, several people seemed disappointed at the limited range of individuals shown. "Why aren't all my children here?" "Don't you have any more?" "So what did you do with the others? Did you just skip me? There isn't a single one from my household." Limitations of cost and space were my excuses, readily accepted, but Okiek wanted and expected a more exhaustive portrayal of their communities, given our shared experiences. While some wanted to see more individuals, however, no one found major topics or types of photographs to be missing.

As they thought of the Nairobi showing at the National Museum, Okiek sometimes imagined how visitors would perceive them, musing about what visitors wanted and expected to see.[54] These comments usually accompanied photographs that Nairobi reviewers would label "traditional": an old woman in a hyrax fur cape or secluded initiates in white body paint. The exchange that began chapter 1 is one example (plate 27):

> KIRUTARI: These are the people of long ago. These are the [pictures] that are wanted, friend.
>
> MOSEITI: Those colonial ones.
>
> KIRUTARI: Yes. These are the ones that are wanted, not the fancy ones [with people in modern clothes]. These. . . . And this thing will continue forever and ever until the country is overturned. They [Europeans] will come to search and say, "Where are those people from long ago?" This is the one that is wanted.

All viewers, including Okiek, recognized such photographs as prime means of exoticizing, providing ways to emphasize strangeness, difference, and distance from themselves. Other photographs, however, seemed similarly "exotic" only to some viewers. For instance, many Nairobi (and American) visitors saw pictures of beautifully adorned initiates this way. For them, initiates' Maasai-like ornaments identified them with modes of dress long abandoned in other parts of Kenya. For Okiek, this potential strangeness was overshadowed by initiates' beauty, by delighted recollections of ceremonies, and, perhaps, by routine use of beaded ornaments in their Maasai-dominated district.

Okiek viewers assimilated and engaged *Okiek Portraits* photographs through narratives of remembrance, evocative imitations, and identifications bridging time and place, identifying with them strongly. Their recognition emphasized shared experience and personal relations. These modes of relating to the photographs foregrounded "internal" perspectives and local frames of interpretation, even more so than GL did in Nairobi. This internal stance also highlighted differentiations invisible to viewers less familiar with local concerns and limited to a more distant, "external" perspective. For instance, Okiek noted differences between Kaplelach versus Kipchornwonek groups, attending both to quantitative representation and qualitative differences in appearance. Even differences among particular families were discussed.

At the same time, Okiek recognized some dimensions and idioms that other view-ers might accentuate through exoticizing. In doing so, Okiek simultaneously took a distanced, "external" stance to their own pictures, ironically self-exoticizing and iden-tifying with those who might take an external stance. Yet Okiek also criticized viewers who exoticize persistently, in the face of other evidence and experience, refusing to rec-ognize Okiek except through stereotypes. The main group cited for this were *cumpeek*, an Okiek category that encompasses Europeans and government officials. Okiek read-ily identified "traditional" photographs that *cumpeek* prefer, effectively capturing the images and tropes prominent in Western representations of Africa and Kenyan stereo-types of Okiek. Their comments recognized that such misrepresentation by those with influence and power can have serious ramifications.

Okiek viewings of the *Okiek Portraits* album went far beyond the local associations of "home movies" to reveal sophisticated understandings of the politics of representa-tion. Those understandings emerge from the history of Okiek interactions with oth-ers, including photographic encounters. Okiek photographic history began with brief interchanges with Europeans, associated from the start with both immediate monetary return and later receipt of a self-image, at once foreign and familiar. In part discounted as the strange ways of *cumpeek,* these early encounters and the distanced, frozen like-nesses produced also met with some initial fear and discomfort. Uneasiness might have been fed by other associations with colonial officers, coerced road labor, possible game law enforcement, and other colonial constraints, though this was not noted directly.[55]

Okiek photographic encounters, however, also raised more general questions about self, other, and cross-cultural communication. Why do they photograph us? Over time Okiek noted patterns in what these people photographed, "the ones that are wanted." As the circumstances and practices of Okiek life changed over the years, those patterns remained remarkably the same. "And this thing will continue forever and ever until the country is overturned. They will come to search and say, 'Where are those people from long ago?'" As years passed, Okiek also had greater opportunity to ob-serve, if not always interact with, other white *cumpeek* as Narok town, the district head-quarters, developed into a tourist entrepôt between Nairobi and the popular Maasai Mara Game Reserve.

Okiek ideas about the practices and images accentuated in those photographic pat-terns have also changed, however. Many activities preferred for photographs (e.g., climb-ing hives and hunting) remain part of Okiek life, but to Okiek, too, they are "from long ago" (*pa keny*').[56] This double-edged phrase encompasses two perspectives and two sets of values that might seem incompatible. On one hand, their forest skills are a matter of great pride to Okiek, central indices of their distinct ethnic heritage and his-tory. On the other hand, they contrast markedly with values of modernity, develop-ment, and progress (*maendeleo*) now current among Okiek (especially younger people) and are a sign that Okiek embraced these values more recently than some other Kenyans.

Both perspectives are captured in the photographs in figure 12, taken in the space of a few minutes in 1994 when friends asked me to photograph them. After William

Figure 12. William Nagorum Sirma
poses in 1993 with his family
and with his brother Samson
Kuunku Sirma.

Nagorum Sirma posed with his family, wearing a suit jacket and holding a radio–cassette player, he and his brother Samson Kuunku Sirma disappeared into the house.[57] They quickly emerged with another set of props for the next picture: honey bags, bow and arrows, and a hunting spear. Both photographs capture aspects of Okiek identity and images of themselves. They know themselves to be both progressive and traditional, combining principles and values these imply in different ways according to particular circumstances and domains of practice (Kratz 1993).[58] But they also know full well that others see them through a more limited purview. When looking at the *Okiek Portraits* photographs, Okiek recognized, too, that some viewers would even think they were Maasai, unable to appreciate subtle differences of dress (Kratz and Pido 2000).

Okiek have long brought an analogous double interpretive perspective to their relations with Maasai (Kratz 1993, 1994a, 62–70). Okiek know Maasai have regarded them as contemptible because of their forest life. Yet Okiek pride in that life is undiminished, and they often recast their accommodations to Maasai dominance (such as Okiek multilingualism) to emphasize Okiek skill, graciousness, and pragmatism. Okiek/Maasai relations themselves embody a politics of representation with a long history. Facets of all these perspectives on self/other representations came up in Okiek home viewings of *Okiek Portraits* and the encounters imagined there. When I made additional exhibition captions from the recorded conversations, then, Okiek commentaries provided a wealth of material that could enliven the exhibition, add other perspectives, and help convey a more diverse, nuanced sense of Okiek life.

FURTHER SELECTIONS: CREATING
CAPTIONS FROM CONVERSATION

Because the give-and-take of interpersonal relations, so apparent in Okiek viewings of the *Okiek Portraits* album, is difficult to portray, it is seldom part of ethnographic exhibitions. Equally rare are exhibitions with reflections by people portrayed, their observations and comments on people and occasions shown and the exhibition itself.[59] Yet these are an integral, vital part of the feeling, meaning, and texture of daily life. When I thought of having Okiek comments in *Okiek Portraits,* it was too late to include them in Nairobi. However, they could still be incorporated for U.S. venues. The new captions would bring Okiek home contexts and viewings into the museum, including their imagined visions of metropolitan exhibition contexts and visitors. Evoking the familiarity of home viewings in the museum, they might make the two more alike and offer a bridge between museum visitors and Okiek viewers.

I had tried to capture this informal tone in the multilingual descriptive captions by using personal names, noting relations among those pictured, and suggesting the emotional tenor of some scenes. But they were still third-person descriptions and sought to convey other background information as well. They could not have the spontaneity of conversations or the intimacy of chatting with friends and relatives. The conversational captions gave voice to Okiek and "eavesdropped" on such situations. I thought this would help visitors engage with Okiek, recognize commonalities and connections, and help counter the simplification of stereotypes. Conversational captions were a device to enrich the representation of Okiek and help nudge visitors toward making connections with Okiek despite their differences.

"Giving voice" to Okiek through captions was no simple or transparent process. "The staging of translated, edited 'voices' to produce a 'polyphonic' ethnographic authority has never been an unproblematic exercise. But represented voices can be powerful indices of a living people. . . . And to the extent that quotations are attributed to discrete individuals, they can communicate a sense of indigenous *diversity*" (Clifford 1997, 167 [original emphasis]). Creating these new captions from conversational excerpts raised questions of selectivity and representation again, with additional wrinkles concerning language and translation.[60] How can the spontaneity of conversation translate into written form, in particular into the succinct form of label copy? Informal conversation relies heavily on shared knowledge of social occasions, personal relations, cultural geography, and history—implicit interpretive background that remains largely unspoken.[61] Okiek exchanges had to be translated in ways that would make them accessible to exhibition visitors from very different cultural milieus. Further, words convey only part of the meaning and nuance of conversation. Without the gestures, intonation, voice quality, timing, and stress that accompanied them as speech, words alone might be interpreted in ways quite contrary to their conversational sense. On related problems in film subtitles, David MacDougal remarked:

> Subtitles have their own dynamics. For example, they present us with speech in segments, not in the flow that actually characterizes speech. They also reach into the film and pull out a particular level of meaning. When a dog barks, the subtitles ignore it. . . . They tend to take over, so that even if other things are really more important, such as *how* people speak rather than what they say, you have to keep the subtitles going or the audience will think something has gone wrong. (Barbash and Taylor 1996, 379 [original emphasis]; cf. MacDougal 1998)

The initial question was what to include from Okiek commentary; what would Okiek say in the captions? I included straightforward identifications, extremely common in the full discussions and important in maintaining their interactive, conversational quality. For viewers from outside the community, however, an exhibition full of "Look, there's Jane!" captions would be neither illuminating nor interesting. My first principle of selection was variety. Conversations about initiates' pictures were full of comments on how lovely they were. Rather than repeat this single, simple theme, I selected remarks on a range of topics and facets of youthful beauty (some of them illustrated above). I also emphasized excerpts that reached beyond the immediate Okiek home setting: explanations to non-Okiek present, imagined audience reactions, and comments on the photographic process, my research, and the nature of photographic representation. Such reflections and interpretations, I thought, would be more likely to interest visitors unfamiliar with the specific people and contexts shown. The commentary captions added to *Okiek Portraits,* then, did not reproduce Okiek conversations exactly. They included all recurrent conversational themes and tried to maintain and convey their interactional quality and familiarity, but the captions accentuated the diversity of topics and attitudes in the full discussions. While maintaining the enthusiasm and intimacy of home viewings, I sought to multiply the modes of access and understanding they might provide for visitors.

Like the first descriptive labels, the conversational captions would also be bilingual. This time, however, the languages were Okiek and English. With a third language, the exhibition provided a better sense of the multilingualism of many Kenyans (Whitely 1974, 38–54; Myers-Scotton 1993, 33–38).[62] As with English-Kiswahili translations, I sought an idiomatic flow in Okiek-English translations. At the same time, I wanted to maintain some of the colloquial quality of Okiek expression in English. Each translation entailed decisions about details of phrasing and emphasis, seeking the right balance. My first translations, usually quite literal, often sound wooden and strange in English. I translated again from literal versions to more colloquial language, asked friends to read them and note problems, and then reworked them again. Many decisions were intuitive, based as much on "feel" for the languages as explicit reasoning. As I worked on the captions, however, I noted that questions often arose about how to handle interjections and personal names. These two topics can provide a more detailed sense of the decisions involved.

The "meaning" of exclamations is expressive, indexical, and emotional rather than strictly referential. This makes them difficult to translate, yet it also makes them distinctive and vivid. At first I kept Okiek exclamations simply because they are hard to translate, figuring I would go back to puzzle over them. As I worked on captions, however, I decided to keep exclamations because they are a characteristic feature of Okiek conversations. Maintaining emotional interjections would both show how they peppered the conversations and convey some of the sound of the original language even in translation. In a few cases I found and used a close English equivalent. I translated *oi eceekee* and *oi anee,* exclamations of mild surprise in several captions, as "my goodness" (literally they mean "oi ourselves" and "oi myself").[63] Other exclamations variously call attention to and/or express shades of surprise, sympathy, alarm, protest, or pain, depending on circumstances: *ai, aish, oi,* and its stronger form, *oiye.* I thought these similar enough to English exclamations (like "oh" and Yiddish-derived "oy") to be recognized as Okiek equivalents. More striking to English-speakers would be stronger Okiek exclamations, such as *usho, otiagi,* and *emuro.* These express greater surprise and/or alarm, astonishment. In some situations they show exertion, disbelief, mild reproof, or recognition of an impasse. The affective particle *-toi* also appeared in several conversational captions. *-Toi* is like an exclamation in having primarily emotional and indexical meaning. Unlike interjections, however, which express the speaker's state or attitude, *-toi* generally indexes friendly relations between speaker and interlocutor. In captions, I translated this with the vocative phrase "my friend."

The final example, *kaale-i,* is a very common Okiek phrase that has both referential meaning and other pragmatic, interactional uses. Literally *kaale* means "I said," but the word takes on another role when the final vowel *-i* is added, spoken with the sharp intonational jump characteristic of Okiek interrogatives. Used at the start of a sentence or conversational turn, *kaale-i* becomes an interjection that draws attention, marks a speaker's intent to talk, and in some cases shows surprise or puzzlement. Its referential sense becomes almost incidental in this usage. Since its literal meaning was similar to an exclamation used by British speakers of English, I translated *kaale-i* with "I say." For some American visitors, however, this translation might have suggested associations totally unconnected to the Okiek setting. The British "I say" can also convey class connotations, evoking ideas of upper-class restraint and polite self-control. The American interjection "Say!" functions much like "I say" and *kaale-i,* and might actually have been more appropriate. The literal meaning of the Okiek phrase, however, led me to use "I say" without thinking of these other associations.

Like interjections, personal names and relations are also diacritical signs of linguistic and cultural difference and raised other questions in creating conversational captions. Some descriptive captions already identified relations between people shown in the same or adjacent pictures. The conversational captions added a profusion of new names and relations. People talking used a variety of different names to refer to individuals shown. For example, a mother refers to her young son with different names in quick succession here (plate 2):

> LAATO: You'd think that's Kirorua! Usho! With those clothes of his all full of holes! Aish, that's Longisa all right.

I did not change names in the captions or try to make them consistent with those used in descriptive captions. Similarly, I kept most teknonymous names in Okiek (*Kopot* mother of so-and-so; *Kwaampat* father of so-and-so), leaving intact their sense as proper names. This was potentially very confusing. To help exhibition visitors sort out the names and make clear who was speaking with and about whom, I added headings for each conversational caption. They provided information about social relations among those shown and those speaking. Still, visitors would need orientation to this welter of specific information; another introductory text panel was required.

The new panel, a key to captions, identified all languages used and explained both the exhibition's double caption scheme and the variety of personal names. It also noted and illustrated some differences between Okiek and American ways of defining kinship relations. The kinship information was limited, but with nothing to alert visitors to such differences Americans would read captions through their own assumptions about kinship. At times Okiek themselves struggle to determine precisely what relations hold (plate 26):

> KIRUTARI: It's John's mother-in-law.
> MOSEITI: The mother of Araap Meriki?
> KIRUTARI: Yes, it's Araap Meriki's mother. . . . Ai! So it's your mother-in-law—no?
> MOSEITI: She's not my mother-in-law. She's not my mother-in-law. What would I call her?
> KIRUTARI: You call her Grandmother. Or would it be Mother?

Many other questions and decisions arose before translations were finalized. Particular words proved problematic either because they refer to things unfamiliar to most English-speakers or because Okiek and English categories do not correspond. In two cases, I left words in Okiek with parenthetical explanations: *ugali*[64] (stiff maize porridge, similar to polenta) and *cumpeek*.

Some decisions probably escaped the notice of most American visitors but nonetheless preserved aspects of Okiek conversation. For instance, in Okiek (as in Kiswahili) the verb "to marry" generally takes male agents and female patients. If a young woman is the subject of a sentence, the verb will be passive ("she was married").[65] I retained this pattern in translations, though one caption took several attempts. When speaking of their son's marriage, older women *can* be agents, but this does not carry into English well. In the caption for plate 8, Lutia focuses on one woman in the group shown; her son was to marry the girl for whose initiation they were preparing liquor. Here are some of my successive attempts at translating the last sentence (the Okiek sentence does not mention the woman's son, but it is clear he will be the husband):

> So she's roasting the mash to make the liquor for initiating the child she will marry.
>
> So she's roasting the mash to make the liquor for initiating the child she will marry for her son.
>
> So she's roasting the mash to make the liquor for initiating the child she will marry to her son.
>
> So she's roasting the mash to make the liquor for initiating the child for her son to marry.

None of these sounds quite right in English, but the first three present assumptions so counter to American understandings of agency in marriage that they clearly would not do. The last attempt is the one I used in the end. At the time it seemed as close as I could get, though looking back now I see that I was having my own problems switching to the underlying English assumptions. The major change needed was to make the son the main actor—though the sentence does not even mention him. The last attempt made the main switch, but had I realized it, one further adjustment would have consolidated that perspective and made it sound quite normal in English:

> So she's roasting the mash to make the liquor for initiating the child that her son will marry.

Creating captions from Okiek conversations and commentary involved as many questions and decisions as writing and translating the initial descriptive captions. Visitors might not have noticed details and nuances of phrasing and translation that I worried over, but their experience and impressions would be influenced by their cumulative effect. With the additional captions, the exhibition's representation of Okiek became more diverse and lively. The many cross-references among captions and images suggested an Okiek community of interaction. Visitors who took the time could find not just descriptive information, but a densely interwoven world of social relations, humor, and affection connecting people in the photographs and those who commented on them. Had any visitors actually plotted relations among all those in photographs and captions, they would have discovered many webs of relation linking them.[66]

Okiek were also shown—or rather, overheard—musing about visitors to *Okiek Portraits,* imagining their reactions and, it might seem, inviting them to respond. Such comments broke through the usual exhibitionary frame, crossing the separation between visitors and those depicted and introducing a different tone. The very combination of descriptive and conversational captions juxtaposed different settings, styles, and perspectives in ways that might draw visitor attention to expectations commonly associated with captions and exhibitions. Visitors might be more likely to think carefully and critically about conventions of exhibitionary communication and representation thus thrown into relief through the juxtaposition.

KENYAN ENCOUNTERS
WITH *OKIEK PORTRAITS*

As this chapter followed *Okiek Portraits* into its first display settings, starting to focus on how visitors understood and imagined Okiek and themselves through the exhibition, it did not ignore exhibition production, for the exhibition changed even after its Nairobi showing, adding Okiek commentary captions. The next chapters continue to follow the exhibition on tour to its venues in the United States. Some production-related questions will return again there, though in more muted form, because each installation involved new decisions about presenting the exhibition.

Though the two Kenyan display settings entailed different modes of interaction, Nairobi visitors and Okiek alike interpreted the exhibition at a number of levels, focusing at different moments on what was communicated by particular images, details in certain images, conjunctions between labels and images, the overall array within the exhibition, and the exhibition itself as an event. Likewise, their comments and concerns ranged across issues related to representational content, form, and the meanings and conventions of exhibitions themselves. Each of these communicative levels and sets of concerns might allow visitors to link an exhibition to various issues and politics of representation. Precisely how visitors come to understand an exhibition and forge those connections depends in part on visitors' own identities and interests. As visitors encounter an exhibition, they form interpretations through an interplay between what the exhibition brings to them and what they bring to the exhibition.

In Kenya, interpretations were informed especially by issues related to colonial and neocolonial relations, national and ethnic identities, "tradition" and "heritage," though viewers took varied stances and emphasized different aspects of them. These also provided some of the dimensions and idioms through which Kenyans formed assimilating and exoticizing understandings of Okiek, including ironic self-exoticization by some Okiek. Nairobi visitors and Okiek were both sensitive to photographs that could be associated with stereotypes. Yet those same "colonial" and "exotic" photographs were also among those seen as representing "tradition," "heritage," and signs of distinctive ethnic identity.[67] Their stances toward such representation by "foreigners" (*cumpeck, wazungu* [Sw.]) were often similar, but their perspectives on national debates sometimes differed. *Okiek Portraits* tapped contention within Kenyan national images by magnifying the presence of a minority group commonly disdained or ignored, drawing attention to ethnic stereotypes within Kenya. By recognizing and validating Okiek as a minority group, though, the exhibition also enabled interpretations appropriating

Okiek difference and "heritage" into the national whole through assimilating rhetorics of inclusion. Politics of representation involved in colonial or neocolonial relations can be quite similar to those related to appropriation in the interests of nation-building, as Okiek know. Yet without such recognition and entry into national discourse, Okiek misrepresentation (and *non*representation) would continue.

In Kenya, *Okiek Portraits* became a nexus where different perspectives, interpretive frameworks, and politics of representation intersected, whether in the National Museum, Nairobi, or in Okiek homes. When it went on to the United States, the exhibition would be seen in new settings by visitors likely to understand the exhibition rather differently, in relation to histories, communicative backgrounds, and politics of representation relevant there. The new labels also recast the exhibition itself and the way it represented Okiek. In the next chapters I consider how people in the United States imagined Okiek and *Okiek Portraits*.

Photographs here are not so much kindling memories as creating an allegorical space and allowing us to people it with our imaginings.
RAPHAEL SAMUEL, *THEATRES OF MEMORY*

All photographs have the effect of making their subjects seem at least momentarily strange, capable of meaning several things at once, or nothing at all. Estrangement allows us to see the subject in new and unexpected ways.
ALAN TRACHTENBERG, *READING AMERICAN PHOTOGRAPHS*

4

IMAGINING AUDIENCES

Okiek Portraits
in the United States

As I crossed the Emory University quad that October morning, I noticed a small gathering outside the Michael C. Carlos Museum. Getting closer, I saw it was a school group waiting for a tour; the students were older, not primary schoolchildren. Threading through them, I entered, waved to the guard, and turned right, passing through the Ancient Greek and Roman Galleries. I was headed to the adjacent hinge galleries, where *Okiek Portraits* had been on display since September, to meet undergraduates taking a class on "Culture and Development in Africa." In addition to doing gallery talks and docent training while the exhibition was at the Carlos, I was invited to several of the classes that incorporated *Okiek Portraits* into their syllabi. Colleagues usually advised me of issues they wanted discussion to cover and asked me for readings to help students understand the exhibition. The readings helped instructors focus students' attention on particular topics and questions before my classroom visits.[1] This particular class had little prior consultation, but the instructor was familiar with my work, even my first long essay about *Okiek Portraits*. I was told only that students would interview me about the exhibition and perhaps videotape the discussion.

It was a small class, about eight students. A video camera was set up and running even as I arrived.[2] "You want to just fire away?" the instructor asked the students. I requested some minimal introductions first, so I would at least know a few students' names. The camerawoman—herself a student in the class—began with a warm-up question about how I started working with Okiek, remarking on the close relations evident in the photographs. I hadn't had a chance to take my coat off but managed to do so while answering this first question. As I finished responding, another student declared, "I have a question," and launched into a very different topic: "I was reading in, I guess, one of the panels in the [. . .] called Life Cycles [. . .] here that the men were initiated into the society by circumcision as were the women. How do you feel about that toward the, like, growing debate on international universal human rights and mutilation of, I guess, the woman's body?" Delivered without pause, his question seemed prepared, even rehearsed, almost as well formed as if he were reading it (though with hedges common in adolescent American speech).

Among the various types and contexts of interviews—ranging from job interviews, to exploratory, open-ended, or in-depth interviews conducted in research or journalism, to survey interviews with a set schedule of questions—this student seemed to be imitating a hard-hitting investigative television reporter, with fast delivery and pointed questions. I wondered if the video setup somehow encouraged this style and how these students had been prepared for the class. Having discussed international debates about female circumcision in various situations, I explained that this was a complicated issue, that the debates raise many difficult questions and must be considered from several perspectives. I reviewed various aspects and directed the students to articles I had published about the debates, including one available in the exhibition's reading room. This kind of reply often frustrates sound-bite journalists, but responsible analysis cannot avoid complexities.[3]

The camerawoman continued, following the same model, "So circumcision stands as, I guess, part of the larger paradigm of the human rights issue and Africa. How do you see the duty, I guess, of—or the place of experts like yourself or, um, people involved in anthropological research and such? How do you see that?"

Again, I wanted to ask the students to think first about when and how human rights have been defined, by whom, from what perspectives (see An-Na'im 1992). I also wanted them to step back and think about how female circumcision had become their first focus for a discussion about the exhibition. A few visitors at other U.S. venues also fixed on female circumcision in responding to the exhibition, but this would be my first opportunity to actually ask such people how that focus emerged from their experience of the exhibition itself. The exhibition certainly did not emphasize it; the introductory panels mentioned male circumcision and female excision just once, together, in a single sentence. Did these students become riveted by that phrase? What aspects of the exhibition made it so prominent for them? In this class, they had been learning how cultural assumptions inform development projects in Africa as well as representations of Africa in the United States If portraying Africans chiefly in terms of famine and poverty contributes to reductive stereotypes, how does that differ from reducing Okiek life to one part of one ceremony as experienced by half those participating?

Noise began filtering into the gallery. Looking over my shoulder, I saw the school group approaching. The gallery was soon crowded with about a dozen students from an arts high school in Augusta, Georgia, so I could not finish my comments. These students were largely African American, mostly young women, accompanied by two docents or teachers. The camerawoman asked permission to keep the video running. The docents then asked the students to relate the exhibition to their own experience; for instance, the initiates shown are about their same age, so what comparable milestones or rites of passage do American teenagers go through?

When the students had been in the gallery for about three minutes, the self-possessed young camerawoman began to interview a group of the young women about the exhibition, "Do these images that you're all seeing counter any images that you had in your mind already of what these people may have looked like? How are they different from what you expected?" Although she asked leading questions, the exchange that ensued is interesting:

STUDENT 1: I kinda like expected them to be all, you know, skinny, you know like— but they are really beautiful, you know? I never really have seen this side of the people.

STUDENT 2: They're rich. They are so rich. . . .

STUDENT 3: They're rich in culture and love. They love each other. Like the mother and baby. Or the two friends.

STUDENT 4: I expected them to be, like, unhappy because of the environment they live in but they're smiling and having fun and stuff.

CAMERAWOMAN: How would, how would [you] see them—Do you think the, uh, media in America has built up this idea that Africans aren't happy in their environment?

ALL: Yeah.

CAMERAWOMAN: What mostly do you hear about, what parts of Africa do you mostly hear about?

ALL TALK AT ONCE; A NUMBER SAY: Somalia.

STUDENT 1: Help the children—five cents a day. That's all. Five cents a day. I mean they make it seem like everybody is like—you know, small like that [*she hunches her shoulders up to show emaciation*]. Only five cents a day.

CAMERAWOMAN: So what do you think needs to happen to change that?

STUDENT 5: Pictures like this.

STUDENT 1: They need to see this. They need to see, you know, things like this that, you know, show people that it's—it's not all, you know, poor, you know. . . . These people, they don't have what we have, but what they do have, they—they are very happy with it, you know, and it seems to me like that they really wouldn't need what we have because they're fine. They're doing fine with what they have . . .

CAMERAWOMAN: How do you think, I mean, as predominantly African Americans, not to exclude anybody, but I would like to ask you all how does seeing images like this have a perception on yourself and your ancestry?

STUDENT 2: I think we should really get closer to our cultures because we're so Americanized that we don't get involved with things overseas and everything.

CAMERAWOMAN: Do you see any commonalities, any—any similarities between [Africans and African Americans]?

STUDENT 3: Ah, yes. Like my family and my grandmother and everything, we're all really close, and when I went to Douala, Cameroon [as an exchange student], they were really close. If somebody came up to you and gave you a hug and a kiss on the cheek it wasn't a big deal. And when somebody invited you to dinner and you sat down and you ate a stranger's food it wasn't a big deal but in America it is. That's a difference that I see.

CAMERAWOMAN: I see. Anybody else? . . . Thank you all.

As the group filed out to go see the second half of the exhibition in the other hinge gallery, the camerawoman nabbed two white male students for further questions, asking what they thought of the exhibition. Only one answered, noting his interest in photography and appreciation of color composition in the photographs. Directing him toward the same topics did not produce a similar animated response, so she curtailed the interview quickly, in less than a minute:

CAMERAWOMAN: Do you share some of the opinions that in American culture, um, we're exposed to negative perceptions?

STUDENT: Yeah, it seems like the—it's like just one—the Americans tend to focus on the negative, and the negative seems to weigh down the positive so much that, it's like you can't see the good stuff.

CAMERAWOMAN: Exactly. Well, thank you, I appreciate it.

As she turned the camera back to the Emory class, we all commended the camerawoman for quickly adapting and taking advantage of the group's arrival. My interview did not resume, however, because the camerawoman was leaving early for a midterm exam and the instructor dismissed class. We agreed to reschedule and the camerawoman left, saying, "Definitely we'll talk again." The discussion was not rescheduled, so we never did.

The Carlos Museum was the last U.S. venue for *Okiek Portraits*. The exhibition had shown in five other American settings since it opened in Nairobi, but just fifteen minutes with these two groups of students encapsulated many of the issues *Okiek Portraits* engaged in the United States. The Augusta secondary school students showed considerable familiarity with politics of representation revolving around Africa and African Americans as well as stereotypes of Africa common in the United States. Critically aware of the same topics, the Emory students also introduced an intersecting politics of representation particularly prominent in the United States in the past decade or so, though they did not ask critical questions about how debates about female circumcision frame the issue and represent those involved (Kratz 1994a, 341–47; 1999a).

Fundamental to these politics of representation were questions of communication— how do people experience and understand exhibitions? The young camerawoman asked the Augusta students to formulate their impressions after just a few minutes in the gallery, when they had seen only half of the exhibition but had read none of the texts.

What categories and conventions did they draw on to create that rapid understanding and how did they relate them to the exhibition? Did other visitors look at the exhibition more thoroughly? How did they understand the exhibition? Emory students in a different class wrote papers that showed a variety of responses and identified (often unwittingly) points of misunderstanding (see chapter 5). Finally, this example suggests how exhibition design can influence visitors' experiences and understandings. *Okiek Portraits* was installed at the Carlos in two parallel but nonadjoining galleries. Both were clearly visible on approach and a sign in each room indicated that the exhibition continued in the other gallery. Nonetheless, some visitors didn't notice and saw only half the exhibition without realizing it.

Using the range of U.S. venues and material in chapters 4 and 5, I trace the interpretive interaction between visitors and exhibition and consider various ways of learning about visitors' experiences and understandings. I explore how visitors negotiate relations of cultural difference and ask what circumstances might enable and facilitate engaged recognition across cultural difference.

The multiple U.S. venues accentuate differences in installation and the role of "designed space" in exhibition communication. Fred Wilson, an installation artist, uses the notion of "designed space" to emphasize its communicative role. Wilson uses all aspects of exhibition design—wall color, lighting, orientation, exhibition furniture and cases, paths through a display space, as well as arrangements and juxtapositions of objects and texts—to draw attention to the conventions of display, their influence on expectations, judgments, and interpretations, and to offer trenchantly witty social and political commentary (1994).

> The seemingly neutral environment in which works of art are displayed plays a significant role in our experience of art. The museum space often tells us what we should think about a work of art and the artist before we can grasp the significance of the work for ourselves. The wall text, the lighting, and the overall design of the space can tell us more about the society of the curator and the exhibition designer than any cultural information that we may be getting about the art. (Wilson quoted in Sims 1993, 8; cf. O'Doherty 1986; Vogel 1994)

I discuss different installations of *Okiek Portraits* as part of what the exhibition brought to visitors at each venue, contributing to their understandings.

To attract any U.S. visitors at all, *Okiek Portraits* first had to appeal to those who select exhibitions for various venues. They would consider how it related to exhibition genres, styles, and expectations at the institutional level, and decide whether it was right for them. Cumulatively, such processes help shape the paths through which cultural representations circulate and influence the very kinds of exhibitions produced. Defining and redefining differences among types of museums and galleries, they reveal important features of the political economy of cultural production and representation. I learned more about these questions as I sought venues for *Okiek Portraits* and traveled it in the United States.

WHERE DOES ETHNOGRAPHIC
PHOTOGRAPHY FIT?

As recounted earlier, I added a U.S. showing of *Okiek Portraits* while seeking support in Kenya.[4] Though no specifics were worked out then, I thought a university venue would be suitable and most likely because *Okiek Portraits* was a small exhibition: it could be coordinated with courses, and my contacts would be best in university settings. An exhibition's venue helps determine who will see it, so this intuitive supposition was, in fact, a first step in imagining U.S. audiences.[5] But my attention then was focused on the Nairobi exhibition, not future U.S. visitors. After the Nairobi opening, I began working on U.S. venues more seriously. I sent information to colleagues in October and made contacts during a November 1989 trip to the United States. By April–May 1990, when I edited the new conversational captions, *Okiek Portraits* had two confirmed venues: in late May at the University of Alaska, Fairbanks, during the Sixth International Conference on Hunting and Gathering Societies, and shortly after at the Smithsonian Institution's National Museum of Natural History in Washington, D.C.

These two early venues represented the types of sites where *Okiek Portraits* was eventually shown: ethnographic, natural history, or culture history museums and university museums or galleries.[6] Arranging venues provided lessons in how display institutions are organized and how exhibitions are differentiated and marketed. Most museums and galleries have committees that consider proposals for traveling exhibitions and choose or recommend those to be shown. Decisions are based on exhibition quality, schedule, cost, fit with the institution's definition and audiences, and similar matters. It is unlikely, for instance, that the Museum of Modern Art's Matisse exhibition would be shown at the Boston Children's Museum. This selection procedure—from the way exhibitions are described and presented, to decisions about where to send different proposals, to the actual committee discussions and decisions—is itself one process through which exhibition genres are defined and redefined.

Though *Okiek Portraits* tried to problematize some exhibition conventions and common stereotypes, people readily categorized it as an ethnographic exhibition. Indeed, it had to be recognizable and fit exhibition conventions in many ways to communicate with visitors and be acceptable to museums in the first place. The categories and concerns that would be prominent in the United States were clarified for me at a helpful meeting with the registrar of the Smithsonian Institution Traveling Exhibition Service (SITES) in November 1989.[7] Touring an exhibition in the United States meant considering market segmentation by exhibition size and genre and cross-cutting segmentation by institutional type, creating a "total package" that included exhibition programming, and filling institutional needs for topically varied exhibitions. Summarizing how these would apply to *Okiek Portraits,* I noted at the time:

> Emphasize theme of life cycle and information, not just nice pictures. They would
> try to package me as part of the programs that could go with the show. They have

nothing in the catalog on Africa at the moment, and little of this small size that could go to smaller institutions.

That succinct first sentence underlines the distinction between ethnographic and art exhibitions and venues that would show each, drawing the usual contrast between content and context versus form and aesthetics. Multiple, multilingual labels were a slightly different twist that made *Okiek Portraits* interesting, but SITES wanted proposals that identified an exhibition's genre clearly and unambiguously.

The U.S. market for ethnographic displays was more differentiated than the Kenyan one, with many potential venues. But it was also far more saturated. In the United States, the ethnographic "slot" is filled from many geographic spaces—Afghanistan, India, Africa, Indonesia, Latin America. Ethnographic exhibitions in Kenya typically cover a more limited range, concerned mainly with Kenya itself, with neighboring countries, or perhaps with other parts of Africa. This difference is related in part to cultural politics, with exhibitions emphasizing and fostering national and regional identities, but the political economy of culture may be even more relevant. First of all, resources and opportunities for covering the world through exhibitions are less available to Kenyans. Further, exhibitions circulate through distribution networks created to reach the audiences imagined.[8] These are often audiences and institutions that can help support exhibitions and pay exhibition fees. Networks too may be nationally or regionally shaped or bounded by national or regional economic and logistical considerations and constraints.[9] Some cultural flows have more roadblocks and bottlenecks than others.

Though SITES advised signaling clearly and quickly what institutions could expect in *Okiek Portraits,* the ethnographic exhibition has always been attended by ambiguities, both as category and genre. The provocative 1988 exhibition *Art/Artifact* highlighted paradoxes in the ways objects are defined by presenting the same objects in several ways: as typically displayed in art exhibitions, in natural history exhibitions, in a "curiosity room" from 1905, and as they might be seen in their original contexts (Vogel 1988, 195–201). The show demonstrated "the way perception of a work of art is conditioned by its presentation" (Vogel 1988, 10).[10] Similar paradoxes of placement arise from the history of museums and display: why are exhibitions about some cultures ("primarily Native Americans and peoples of the Third World") shown regularly in natural history museums while others appear primarily in museums of history and art (Karp 1991, 377–79; Karp and Kratz 2000, 194, 198)? Ethnographic photography aggravates these ambiguities with perennial debates over whether photography is art and where the boundaries lie between art photography, ethnographic photography, and photojournalism.[11] Roland Barthes even declares, "Photography evades us. . . . Photography is unclassifiable" (1981, 4).

All this was involved at least implicitly in finding and negotiating venues for *Okiek Portraits,* perhaps even magnified by its deliberate recasting of certain exhibitionary conventions and stereotypical images. When exhibitors declined to show *Okiek Portraits,* their explanations often offered interesting articulations of the categories and specializations that define exhibition markets. Not surprisingly, most objections came from the side of art. Art museums typically reject exhibitions on two fundamental grounds. Either they do not accept the material included as art, or they do not consider the quality of work up to their standards.[12] These were indeed the main stumbling blocks for art galleries and museums that considered *Okiek Portraits*. If committees objected to the quality of work, however, they tactfully framed their comments in other terms:

- Several university art galleries found the exhibition unacceptable on a priori terms: ethnographic photography is not "art."[13]
- One California venue was interested provided *Okiek Portraits* could be combined with appropriate objects; some board members were biased against photography as a whole, not just ethnographic photography.
- In a gracious letter, the Minnesota Museum of Art declined the exhibition because of its full schedule, many planned photography exhibitions, and upcoming relocation. They did, however, forward the exhibition proposal to the Science Museum of Minnesota.

By contrast, the American Museum of Natural History—a museum that produces and shows ethnographic exhibitions—found *Okiek Portraits* "too existential," a judgment probably based on the captioning and presentation (Schildkrout p.c.). "The Exhibition Advisory Committee [at AMNH] . . . felt it would not be appropriate for our institution" (Jonaitis p.c.).[14] That committee was composed largely of natural scientists, not anthropologists. *Okiek Portraits* did not meet one of their fundamental criteria—to illustrate scientific principles—any better than it met those of art. Neither clearly art nor clearly nomothetic science, ethnographic exhibitions often get caught between these two sides of the museum world. The ways different kinds of institutions handle ethnographic exhibitions bring into relief these divisions, along with the values and criteria of judgment associated with them. The AMNH decision "also underlines the often uneasy existence of cultural anthropology in natural history museums" (Karp p.c.). As one curator (Schildkrout p.c.) said, "The anthropologists have to juggle the discourse a lot."

Whether or not particular institutions decided to show *Okiek Portraits,* each decision and the reasoning behind it were part of broader processes through which exhibition genres, institutions, and audiences are defined, debated, and transformed. The processes are structured and linked through interchanges among the producers, distributors, audiences, and critics of exhibitions (Ennis 1992). Yet each of these social positions and relations also contains significant diversity. For example, some exhibition visitors may be more tolerant and appreciative than museum professionals of efforts to critique strict genre definitions or conventions. Others object or may be more resistant. *Okiek Portraits* became one nexus for such interchange as I sought to intervene in some small way in processes through which stereotypes and exhibitions are defined and understood.

The very first American showing of *Okiek Portraits* took place before I turned close attention to U.S. venues or made the second set of captions. As it turned out, the exhibition was displayed at the University of Texas at Austin in a very peculiar way, with no captions or texts at all. Ironically, what should have been a propitious U.S. debut at my graduate alma mater instead became the occasion for a minor commotion. In the process, it lost sight of my own aims and efforts to personalize Okiek and question stereotypes. Precisely because of this, the Austin episode highlights important issues in exhibit communication and interpretation. At the same time, it epitomizes particular debates about the politics of representation prominent in the late 1980s and early 1990s, part of the larger context for considering *Okiek Portraits* in the United States. After discussing the Austin showing, I turn to more conventional American showings of *Okiek Portraits*.

ARBITRARY DISPLAY
AND ACADEMIC DEBATE IN AUSTIN

When I went to Austin in May 1989 to print Cibachromes for the exhibition, I had nothing confirmed for the U.S. showing promised to sponsors. Plans were made during that visit to show *Okiek Portraits* at the University of Texas in my former department. The anthropology department was moving that autumn into new quarters that would allow small exhibitions; work by a recent alumna seemed a fitting first display. The showing was scheduled for November, following the Nairobi exhibition. When I returned to Kenya in late May, I left a set of framed photographs at the department.[15]

In early September, after the Nairobi opening, I sent the other exhibition materials to Austin: a duplicate set of mounted captions, introductory texts, map, and panels showing title and sponsors. I also included a guide with explicit installation instructions. Exhibition posters had already been delivered in mid-August. The University of Texas showing was intended to duplicate the Nairobi version of *Okiek Portraits*. When I sent the final materials, I also wrote to the Africanist faculty member handling logistics in Austin, reviewing installation instructions again and asking about a security question being resolved when I left in May. Hearing nothing back, I assumed everything in Austin was on track.

In late November, I learned that things had not transpired as planned.[16] The security question, still unresolved, had created complications. The photographs were to be hung along a wide hallway leading to the department office, but this was right next to an unsecured building entrance. Picture-molding was to be installed in the hall with a lock/alarm system so that exhibitions like *Okiek Portraits* could be hung. Whether this proved impracticable, costly, or simply too much trouble, the finishing was not done and security problems remained. Yet my former teachers were still enthusiastic about showing *Okiek Portraits*. Their solution resulted in a truly postmodern mode of display.

Instead of installing the complete exhibition, they hung a number of photographs just outside the departmental office and in glass cases in the nearby seminar room. The photographs had no labels or identification of any kind. At the end of the day, someone put away the photographs in a secure place. Another group of photographs appeared the following day. This rotation continued until some faculty and graduate students in the department protested. They said this arbitrary manipulation of unidentified African images was offensive. It reproduced primitivist images and anthropology's worst colonialist legacy; placing photographs in glass cases, they said, was like putting people in cages.[17] Eventually, after some acrimonious exchanges, a panel discussion was held to clear the air by addressing general issues in the politics of representation.

When I heard about these events later that month, people assured me repeatedly that they did not know the photographs were part of an exhibition, that there were texts to accompany them, or that I was the photographer. It was unclear to me why people had protested without even asking about the pictures and their peculiar display. Neither was it entirely clear what difference the photographer's identity should make. The most striking aspect of the whole situation to me was the apparent lack of communication between those who hung the photographs and those who protested the display. The photographs were indeed shown in a strange way, but I suspect that other issues and political divisions within the department were also being played out through the debate and controversy raised.

This episode demonstrates how critical installation design and manner of display can be in interpreting exhibits. Textual framing, image choices, arrangement, and order of exhibition materials are all important in shaping visitors' understandings. John Berger could be speaking to exhibition developers when he says, "The aim must be to construct a context for a photograph, to construct it with words, to construct it with other photographs, to construct it by its place in an ongoing text of photographs and images" (Berger 1980, 64). But that context is only a guide offered with hope and optimism; the use and interpretation of images cannot be controlled. The most carefully constructed context is still liable to reconfiguration, omission, miscontrual, and multiple interpretations.[18]

Visitors, of course, bring their own knowledge and expectations when they encounter the context offered in the exhibition; their knowledge, expectations, and interpretations are also related to sociopolitical currents. In this case, there were at least three stances toward the photographs. The random display suggests that some people thought the photographs by themselves would convey a universalist reading. Shown in the context of an anthropology department, a humanistic message portraying unity across the diversity of humankind would be obvious. A common message in cross-cultural exhibitions, this interpretation ignores historical differences and inequalities (Barthes 1957, 100–102; Berger 1980, 60–61).[19] A second group probably paid the photographs no more heed than wallpaper. The random appearance, disappearance, and rotation of photographs would have been apparent only to those in the building regularly. As reported later, this aspect of the display was central to the objections. A third, vocal segment of the audience was clearly conversant with contemporary debates on representation, particularly those in the academy and within anthropology itself (see appendix A). Similar concerns were current—and charged—in domains of civil society as well.

In late 1989, museum displays and representations were not yet as prominent an arena of public controversy as they have become since then. Vociferous public debates about *The West as America* did not begin until early 1991; the *Enola Gay* controversy was still several years in the future. But contention over National Endowment for the Arts funding and exhibitions of Robert Mapplethorpe's work was in full swing at the time and important, though less well known, debates about the topics and control of exhibitions were widespread (e.g., in mid-1980s exhibitions such as *Te Maori, Hispanic Art in the United States,* and *Chicano Arts: Resistance and Affirmation*). Writing in 1989, Lavine and Karp characterized the situation:

> In the United States at this historical moment, especially given the heightened worldwide interest in multicultural and intercultural issues, the inherent contestability of museum exhibitions is bound to open the choices made in those exhibitions to heated debate. Groups attempting to establish and maintain a sense of community and to assert their social, political, and economic claims in the larger world challenge the right of established institutions to control the presentation of their cultures. . . . Inevitably, even those curators and museum directors who respond to these concerns find themselves in difficult territory, fearful of the passion of the debates and often insufficiently aware of the unconscious assumptions that underlie their own exhibitions. (1991, 1–2)[20]

Lavine and Karp highlight situations of direct engagement between those creating exhibitions and those represented in them. In Austin, the dynamics were somewhat different. Those represented were not involved; the debate was internal to the department. Colleagues who protested the arbitrary display were probably concerned about some of the very issues that I sought to address as I created the exhibition. They, too, were attuned to debates about representation and power relations in scholarly research and writing. But they did not exactly raise objections "on behalf of" people shown either, when they did not know or ask who they were. Rather, the Okiek pictured entered this debate chiefly in a more abstract sense, as the Other. Complaints—or at least questions—about the puzzling manipulation of their images were certainly in order, but the departmental debate seems to have borrowed some rancor from identity politics. In contests over ownership and power, identity politics prime people to interpret images through a hermeneutic of suspicion and blame that usually also assumes those whose images are presented are innocent or duped. As Lavine and Karp suggest above, those who do an exhibition are the ones under particular scrutiny, especially if they are not from the community represented. In this case, those who installed the exhibition came under question.

With little contextual guidance, the photographs shown in Austin were more open than usual to interpretation. This meant viewers' understandings were based on preconceptions and expectations they brought to the pictures (cf. Shapiro 1988, 150). The

Austin display thus became more like Lutz and Collins's study of *National Geographic* photographs. "[I]nterested in how the photographic elements themselves affect readers," they showed respondents photographs without captions because "of how powerfully captions constrain the reading of a photograph" (1993, 225). The Austin display was not presented as an interpretive experiment, however, nor as installation art or postmodern commentary, nor in an interview setting (like Lutz and Collins's). The mode of display was as open to interpretation as the images themselves. In fact, the random image rotation drew particular attention to the mode of display. In the end, the Austin episode offered poignant support for Susan Vogel's wry comment: "While I feel the authoritative voice inhibits visitors, I hardly recommend uninformed free association before African objects [or images] . . . as a particularly full way to experience them if other means are available" (1991, 195).[21]

Even within this single small-scale setting, concern with and awareness of the politics of representation were uneven. And the display of photographs from *Okiek Portraits* crystallized and problematized the different perspectives and judgments born of that unevenness. In the charged situation created, the different positions fused with other departmental rifts. Nonetheless, the situation also became an occasion for disseminating and heightening awareness by raising questions about modes of display, representation, and the use of images. In some ways the discussion it stimulated may have ultimately been more useful than the display of *Okiek Portraits* as an exhibition. It certainly made an impression on people there, though not the one I intended the exhibition to make.

In contrast to Kenya, where ethnicity, age, and nation defined salient positions, the positions at issue in Austin formed in scholarly debates about the very strategies and effects of exoticizing. Not surprisingly, perhaps, the Austin controversy also shared some of the foibles of those debates. Participants tend to practically preinterpret representations at times, with a predefined priority for reading them in terms of race and gender hierarchies (class analysis is rarely prominent).[22] This conflation of representational forms or techniques and their interpretive effects and connotations sets up a socially and historically impoverished model of communication. Race, class, and gender are critical dimensions for analysis, differing from case to case in their specific interrelations, relevance, and particular meanings, along with the ways they articulate with other concerns. It is equally important to analyze their uses and examine the various forms and techniques of representation combined at different times and in different settings to various purposes and effects.

In political debates over representation, preinterpretation might also include a readiness to assign bad intentions to those who use certain representational forms and techniques. This interpretive grid disregards viewers' own interpretive abilities and involvement while projecting a determining power onto others. But onto whom? Those who arranged the display? The photographer? Those photographed? Exhibitions might also include writers, designers, consultants, and so forth. Exhibitions have multiple producers, just as they have multiple visitors and audiences. In a display like the one in

Austin, with no textual framing or explicit contextual guidance, viewers may be especially involved in and responsible for interpretation. But all these multiple mediations, complex agencies, and systematic linkages disappear from view when the politics of representation play out in this way (Kratz 1994b, 182–83, 194).

Further, the ascription of bad intentions stresses exoticizing tendencies alone. It typically ignores the complex dynamic between exoticizing and assimilating interpretations, though most exhibitions accommodate both simultaneously, in varying degrees. Exotic "Others" always share some aspects of our self-understanding (Nandy 1983, 1996; Karp 1991; Karp and Kratz 2000), creating a dynamic that may lead to assimilation and recognition. Finally, this focus tends to ignore the very subjects and objects on display. Okiek had very little part in the Austin debate. Accounts addressed neither photographic content—scenes and subjects depicted—nor formal composition. Rather, controversy centered on the mode of display and the intentions and assumptions of colleagues who arranged it. With this single aspect dominating discussion, other interpretive possibilities were closed down.

This interpretive foreclosure and controversy had a lasting effect in the department, as I realized years later when I heard of a student exhibition held there in 1996. The display cases in the department seminar room remained vacant and unused, for the most part, after the 1989 controversy. Pauline Turner Strong, who had joined the Austin department four years later, heard vague references to the events and was told the cases had not been touched since then. Discomfort and sensitivity around questions of display remained a remarkably persistent undercurrent. In spring 1996, Strong set students in her graduate class on museums and representation to find out what the department wanted to do with the cases, including dismantling them. As they interviewed faculty, students, and staff, oblique and fragmented accounts of the controversy came out; nearly everyone claimed not to have been there when it happened.

In their class exhibition, *DisPlay/DisPlacement,* the students included a case with a copy of my first book (1994) and the *Okiek Portraits* poster, both bearing photographs.[23] A transparent label on the front of the case superimposed on these a text created from interview quotes, showing the contradictory stories and reactions the controversy still evoked. Response to the student exhibition was positive. Strong thought it seemed to break an impasse and have a cathartic effect by addressing a painful moment that continued to resonate but had never been fully addressed (p.c. [1998]).[24] The label from the exhibition evokes the fraught nature of the memory quite clearly:

> well, . . . I wasn't here exactly . . . I was here before and after it occurred . . . I know a lot about it . . . a student wanted to hang some photographs of some African people . . . we thought this would be a great place to have it first . . . to exhibit here because this was her department of origin . . . an exhibit of photographs . . . they were hung up, as sort of color in the hallway . . . no texts or introductions . . . they were photos . . . from Africa or such, someone's field photographs . . . they were really beautiful . . . very artful photographs, sort of National Geographic-y . . . they

didn't have any captions . . . then there was the big blowup . . . the big dispute . . . the big controversy . . . the big departmental row . . . over them . . . everything was taken down . . . she had to quickly take them down . . . up in the morning . . . down in the afternoon . . . the students objected to these photographs . . . it was mistaken for something else by some of the people we call . . . the counter-hegies . . . I remember the woman who complained . . . she's no longer here . . . said the photographs objectified the woman . . . to put a frame around them is to essentialize them . . . and when it comes to Africa, there's a real tendency to ethnographize . . . hunters and gatherers . . . what are we representing here . . . this kind of myth of the isolated, ahistorical hunter-gatherer now being discovered . . . a lot of animosity generated . . . some of us thought this objection was ridiculous . . . others felt passionately about this issue . . . the reaction against the displays were grossly exaggerated . . . if you've read her ethnography, she's very tied to these people . . . Corie [*sic*] never expected to generate this kind of response . . . now she would try to deconstruct some of her images . . . two of the junior faculty members who objected are no longer with us . . . there was a lot of conflict going on in the department . . . it was a very stressed out time . . . a lot of different factions . . . I don't think it was a constructive debate at all . . . a political attack . . . but they were photos . . . the discussion went on for a considerable period . . . it didn't really go anywhere . . . there was some controversy . . . the issue was never debated, never resolved . . . I've forgotten what the controversy was . . . I only vaguely remember that . . . I don't remember the controversy exactly . . . some things you try to forget . . . what was the controversy . . . I'm not even aware there was one.[25]

This first U.S. showing might suggest that American audiences could find no way to relate to the Okiek portraits. Or it might simply confirm that unlabeled photographs of unidentified people are open to interpretive projections of all sorts.[26] The strange display opened the photographs to many understandings and misunderstandings. The ensuing debate filled the void, effectively replacing the absent contextualizing material to produce a very different focus that limited the range of interpretation. We can only wonder how the display would have been understood if it had shown photographs of people from France or Germany instead.

Some time later, an anthropologist at least as well versed in and sensitive to the politics of representation as those in Austin reviewed *Okiek Portraits*. His interpretive evaluation was the polar opposite of theirs, but it was strongly influenced by contextual material absent in Austin. Nonetheless, the contrast is striking. The review underlines the active, open, and processual nature of exhibit interpretation, as well as the critical interaction of text and image in the way he came to see the exhibition and Okiek:

> The more one reads, the more these pictures become interconnected lives, socially patterned, undergoing institutional and personal change that is connected to neighboring peoples, the national polity, and the international market. . . . [The different aspects of the exhibition] allow multiple accesses to ethnographic reality, unlike

so many picture-books and museum exhibits where texts either merely caption pictures, or more often take off in flights of nonethnographically controlled fancy, stereotype, or typology. (Fischer 1991, 269)

NEGOTIATING DISTANCE
AND DIFFERENCE

The Austin controversy was instructive and revealed assumptions and positions that may have been relevant for American viewers who later saw *Okiek Portraits* in its intended form. Other U.S. showings included all captions and texts, also incorporating the new Okiek/English conversational captions. I added a copy of the Nairobi poster to the introductory material as well, with a short label noting that the exhibition originated in Kenya (in part to prompt visitors to wonder why more exhibitions from Africa don't tour in the United States). *Okiek Portraits* went to three venues in 1990–91: Fairbanks (May–June 1990), Washington, D.C. (June–November 1990), and Philadelphia (February–March 1991). It had two additional showings somewhat later, in East Lansing, Michigan (February–May 1993), and Atlanta, Georgia (September 1997–January 1998). I consider the U.S. venues in two clusters, following the exhibition chronologically but also reflecting the development of my own thinking while traveling the exhibition. The rest of this chapter discusses the three earliest venues.

Taking *Okiek Portraits* to those sites and interacting with exhibition visitors led me to reflect further on exhibition communication and the exhibition process. In 1992 I wrote a long essay on the production, travel, and reception of *Okiek Portraits* (which eventually became this book). In doing so, I found information on visitors' understandings frustratingly fragmentary and incomplete, though many issues and interests mediating U.S. interpretations came through in conversations I had with visitors, in press coverage, and in telegraphic comments in the Fairbanks visitors' book.[27] I sought to explore visitors' understandings more systematically when the exhibition went on to Michigan in 1993 and gathered additional information at its final venue in Atlanta. I turn to the Michigan and Atlanta showings in the next chapter.

In considering each cluster of venues, I begin by describing *Okiek Portraits'* installations and settings, much as I did in considering displays in Austin and Kenya.[28] *Okiek Portraits'* small scale created an intimate exhibition to which visitors might relate more readily (cf. Vogel 1994, 104), but its size and relative simplicity also make it possible to consider installation variations and how they might have affected what the exhibition conveyed. The range of visitors' responses and interpretations was similar across U.S. venues, but I learned about them in different ways at different places.

When *Okiek Portraits* went to Fairbanks, it was shown in the Fine Arts Gallery of the University of Alaska, a small room near the Great Hall.[29] The Great Hall is a major campus center where the Sixth International Conference on Hunting and Gathering Societies was then being held. *Okiek Portraits* was part of the conference's cultural programming, on display from 25 May to 1 June. Most exhibition visitors were probably conference participants and members of the university community, though other

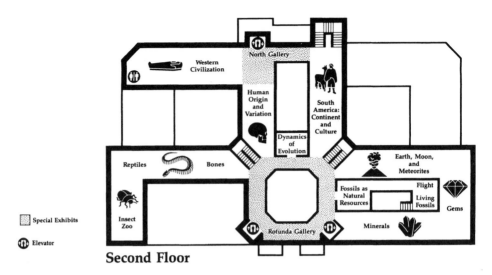

Second Floor

Figure 13. Floor plan showing the location of *Okiek Portraits* on the second floor of the National Museum of Natural History, Smithsonian Institution.

area residents came as well.[30] The exhibition photographs were equally spaced around the square gallery space, beginning to the left of the door. A visitors' comment book stood on a small stand near the end of the exhibition.

Two weeks later, *Okiek Portraits* opened at the Smithsonian Institution's National Museum of Natural History (NMNH), where it stayed for five months, its longest exhibition period. This installation was in the North Gallery, a space dedicated to temporary exhibitions, located on the second floor at the Constitution Avenue end of the building. Visitors could enter from two adjacent exhibition halls (Human Origin and Variation, and Western Civilization); an elevator also opened directly onto *Okiek Portraits,* taking up one gallery wall. One of the world culture halls, South America: Continent and Culture, was around the corner from the elevator foyer (see figure 13).

In the North Gallery, the exhibition was hung along the three walls and on both sides of a room divider angled through the center of the gallery. With this layout and multiple entries, there were many possible exhibition paths. Instead of spacing photographs evenly, the NMNH installation created small groupings of three or four photographs each. These groups cut across life-cycle categories, also clouding that aspect of the exhibition. The multiple paths may have obscured the life-cycle organization as well.

Okiek Portraits undoubtedly had its largest audience at NMNH. The museum has over six million visitors each year, with highest visitation during summer (though visitors rarely look at every exhibition in the museum) (Doering and Bickford 1994, 10; Bielick, Pekarik, and Doering 1995, 3). Divided roughly equally by gender, the overall audience is overwhelmingly nonminority, largely American by residence, and well educated.[31] Most visitors are adults: 71 percent are over 20 years old; 52 percent are between the ages of 25 and 54. Most groups visiting NMNH are composed of adults and children, but a significant number are made up of adults alone (Bickford et al. 1996, 63–64).[32] These figures suggest that NMNH visitorship would resemble that of university museums where *Okiek Portraits* was later shown.[33] Unfortunately, I have little specific information about visitors for *Okiek Portraits* at NMNH or their impressions. There was no opening and NMNH's public relations efforts bore little fruit in the local press. I requested an exhibition comment book, but NMNH staff thought it would be unsafe. Neither was it important to them to solicit responses to a minor traveling exhibition. Had I known then that I would write this book, I would have tried to resolve the staff's concern by following procedures from other Smithsonian museums that have comment books. As a Research Fellow at NMNH at the time, I would also have observed and spoken with exhibition visitors while *Okiek Portraits* was on display.

By the time *Okiek Portraits* opened in Philadelphia the following February at the University of Pennsylvania's University Museum of Archaeology and Anthropology, I *was* thinking of writing a retrospective account of the exhibition. When I spoke with people after gallery talks or at the opening, I noted questions and reactions more carefully. There the exhibition was installed in the Sharpe Gallery, a long hallway gallery much like the original display space in Nairobi. *Okiek Portraits* remained at the University Museum for two months and was included in activities for Black History Month.

The Philadelphia exhibition received more media attention than previous U.S. venues. The public information officer worked hard on promotion and a local angle added interest to the story (I was born near Philadelphia and have family in the area). The *Philadelphia Enquirer* featured a long front-page story in the Saturday "Daily Magazine" section and many smaller newspapers also ran stories, reviews, or listings.[34] Just before the opening, Marty Moss-Coane interviewed me on *Radio Times,* a popular local radio program. This thorough publicity brought *Okiek Portraits* to the attention of museum visitors and the general public. It might even have attracted some visitors as a "destination exhibition" (one visitors come specifically to see) in a way unlikely at NMNH. But again, while I spoke with visitors on several occasions and collected press coverage, I have little information about most people who saw the exhibition there.[35]

Such were the general circumstances of these 1990–91 showings of *Okiek Portraits.* It is hard to tell how differences of setting (conference, national museum, university), installation layout (square room, long two-sided gallery, and the variable paths through NMNH's space), or adjacent exhibitions might have influenced visitors at these venues. However, later showings in Michigan and Atlanta and other research on museum exhibitions and display design (Harris 1990, 70–77; Falk and Dierking 1992, 55–66; Falk and Holland 1993, 15; Karp 1996) both suggest that these factors help shape visitors' views. Often part of the background or implicit taken-for-granted knowledge about exhibition contexts, they are incorporated into visitors' understandings though visitors themselves may not identify them as salient features (cf. Silverstein 1977; Bourdieu 1993, 228; see chapter 5).

At each venue, visitors' interpretive work included negotiating understandings of the cultural difference presented by *Okiek Portraits* and negotiating their own personal distance and stance toward it. "The exotic is the place where nothing is utterly ordinary. Such encounters force us to make comparisons that pierce the membrane of our own quotidian world, allowing us for a brief moment to be spectators of ourselves . . . one becomes increasingly exotic to oneself, as one imagines how others might view that which we consider normal" (Kirshenblatt-Gimblett 1998, 48, 52). Visitors at these American venues generally seemed to approach this negotiation in three ways. Some emphasized individual people, scenes, and personal interaction; others formulated more general conclusions about Okiek or the enterprise of learning about other cultures. Still others filtered the exhibition through quite specific concerns, making particular fragments of the exhibition paramount to them. These approaches are *not* exclusive, but the information available for these venues tends to provide glimpses of visitors' understandings at particular moments rather than a more extensive sense of interpretive processes through which visitors combine and relate them. As I discuss now how visitors saw *Okiek Portraits,* I will dwell at times on extended responses that provide some sense of how understandings are formed and conveyed and the ambiguities involved.

Many visitors to *Okiek Portraits* seemed to regard the exhibit as an encounter with Okiek individuals. Comment book remarks emphasized the interactive nature of the exhibition, combining emotional and intellectual engagement:[36] "Not photographs—conversation"; "Wonderful—both the portraits and the linguistic presentation!"; "Very exciting and moving—good concept"; "Immensely evocative!" A woman in Philadelphia elaborated further, telling me the photographs and commentaries reminded her of her rural Midwest family—her parents, uncles and aunts—sitting around the kitchen table and talking. Such comments indicate that visitors found they could assimilate Okiek to their own experience through dimensions related to domesticity and family relations.[37] Note, however, that she likened Okiek to *rural* family of her *parents'* generation. Okiek were brought home, but in a way that simultaneously maintained a certain difference and distance. She situated them in a distinct social world where she no longer lived, but one she remembered fondly. The past (even our own childhood), another generation (even our parents'), and another region (even one we grew up in) can all be "foreign countries" (Lowenthal 1985). But some foreign countries seem close enough to visit.

Rather than focus on personal encounters, other visitors commented mainly on the exhibit as a whole, generalizing about effect and message. In doing so, they drew on conventions, language, and expectations associated with popular ethnographic representations: "A wonderful glimpse into the world of the Okiek"; "You have captured life on film." Emphasizing informational aspects, such commentaries seem to take a neutral or relativistic stance toward cultural difference yet keep a clear distance. The other world seems not to touch visitors' own world, yet a notion of social evolution is often the underlying framework through which they are related. A sentimentally tinged version of this interpretation is common in popular ethnography, though rare in material available about *Okiek Portraits* visitors. Its nostalgic sense connects these more distanced, general interpretations to the more personal sense expressed by the woman with rural Midwestern family. But the nostalgia is somewhat different in each case.

Nostalgia always involves looking back, idealizing certain aspects of the past that crystallize an ambivalence toward the present. The Midwestern woman encountered Okiek through remembrance of a recent past, part of her own past experience, with a focus on family and personal relations. The other, ethnographic nostalgia is closer to what Rosaldo (1989) called "imperialist nostalgia."[38] Commonly part of Euro-American attitudes toward people in former colonial settings, this nostalgia sees other cultures through a regretful, sentimental scrim. It mourns the loss of "traditional" life's supposed simplicity and naturalness, even while recognizing changes wrought through Western contact as inevitable "progress" toward "modernity." By contrast, then, this is nostalgia for an imagined past projected onto present-day people, a past that is not part of the nostalgic person's experience, and a more distant past seen in social evolutionary terms that encapsulate entire cultures. As part of popular representations, this stance also helps reproduce stereotypes of other cultures.

It may, in fact, be remarkable that such nostalgic regret was *not* prominent in written comments in Fairbanks, in conversations, or in U.S. reviews.[39] Several reviews discussed changes in Okiek life during the past fifty years—in economic pursuits, land holding, education, roads—but they were presented as contextual information, not lament. A certain nostalgia did surface in occasional comments by Philadelphia visitors who assumed Okiek once lived "in harmony with nature." It also appeared in interesting ways in a student paper about the exhibit written for an undergraduate course on "Art and Culture" at George Washington University. Looking at the paper provides a glimpse of the interpretive shifts and process involved as the author developed her point of view.

Jane Lusaka decided to write about *Okiek Portraits* after visiting the exhibit in Washington, then contacted me at the Smithsonian and requested an interview to learn more about it. Increasingly interested in how people understand exhibitions, I agreed and asked her to send me the finished paper and let me refer to it. She came to my home one afternoon and tape-recorded as we talked in the kitchen. Lusaka's paper describes the NMNH installation carefully and makes good use of exhibition texts and captions to summarize information and consider Okiek views.[40] She also comments on the strange juxtaposition of exhibitions ("set up on the second floor of the museum, somewhere between the South American Indians and the beginnings of Western Civilization" [Lusaka 1990, 1]) and visitors' selective attention in the vast Smithsonian museum: "Many tourists hurry through trying to get through to the mummies, or to the gem collection on the other side. They glance at the pretty pictures and move on. But the museum visitors who stop and read the captions stick around to see the entire exhibit" (13).

In three places near the beginning, however, Lusaka uses the formulas of "imperialist nostalgia" to discuss the exhibit.[41] Most occur in an early transitional passage, an awkward break where the author is still seeking her voice and stance. Falling back on clichés from popular ethnography, she asserts that I did the exhibit because "the Ok-iek way of life is gradually disappearing" and that my main interest is "capturing this society in transition, how a people handle the conflict between tradition and change" (Lusaka 1990, 2–3).[42] Much like Wakanyote (1989) in Kenya, she sees costume juxta-positions as evidence of "external" influence (3–4), but she discusses this in local and stylistic terms rather than falling back on ready images of tradition, change, and West-ernization. By the end of the paper, she has a vivid sense that the photographs pre-sented "a contemporary culture . . . a living, breathing community. . . . [and] a personal sense" (13), but the ambivalence of imperialist nostalgia was still part of her starting point, providing tropes for her introduction and early transitions.

Lusaka's paper shows her moving from a somewhat uncertain, but distant stance that generalizes about "dying cultures" to one that places Okiek firmly in the contem-porary world, seeing them as interconnected individuals. The more she thinks about the exhibition and engages with it specifically, the more she leaves behind hackneyed phrases and stereotypical descriptions. The interpretive process in this case seems to combine the two general approaches described, moving from one to another over the course of her paper. Like visitors who regarded the exhibition as conversational en-counter and those who took an overall ethnographic perspective, Lusaka sought to sum-marize her experience of the overall exhibition.

Another set of visitors filtered the exhibition through narrower, more specific con-cerns when they spoke with me, focusing on particular facets of Okiek life. Some sought clarification or elaboration of particular points. For instance, a woman working in en-vironmental law and a man involved with the Sierra Club discussed highland Kenyan forests with me. The exhibit made them realize that *people* live in the forests, they said. They would have to rethink environmental priorities and question ecological policies that take no account of such people. In other cases, the Kenyan setting had attracted visitors, usually people who had lived, worked, or traveled there. A few visitors were Kenyan, pleased to see a display from home.

At every U.S. venue, there were also some visitors who fixed on one particular as-pect of Okiek initiation: circumcision. A single sentence in the introductory text men-tions, without emphasis, that Okiek initiation includes circumcision for boys and girls alike, as noted above. But only the girls' operation caught U.S. visitors' attention.[43] Several Philadelphia visitors wanted to discuss this practice—ranging from a woman who asked me to "explain what female circumcision means" because her gynecologist couldn't, to people seeking "reasons" for the practice, to people who had worked in Kenyan clinics and wanted to compare notes. For Okiek, circumcision is a critical part of making boys and girls into men and women (Kratz 1994a); its principal "purposes" are social and ceremonial. What is self-evident to Okiek, however, was neither sufficient nor satisfying to American visitors. They sought "rational" reasons they could under-stand and accept, based on environmental/ecological reasoning or hygienic concerns.[44] Okiek characterize the surgical results as clean and smooth, aesthetic descriptions of the body that seemed more acceptable to Americans as "reasons" than its essential role in defining adulthood.[45] These visitors questioned me after gallery talks that discussed the dramatic form and meanings of initiation ceremonies; many then went on to view the exhibition from other perspectives, later commenting on the individuals shown and other aspects of Okiek life.

Some visitors, however, were so focused on circumcision that they appeared to see no other aspect of Okiek life. As with Okiek viewers, initiation was their central focus but for them female circumcision alone mattered. It created a sense of strangeness and distance they could not overcome. By synecdoche, it came to stand for and overpower all other aspects of Okiek life and any possible common ground.[46] In Fairbanks, one anonymous visitor felt Euro-American views of female circumcision should be prominent in every visitor's experience. In a kind of guerrilla review, s/he posted a large, public, but unsigned comment in the middle of the exhibit. Written in the authoritative form of a dictionary entry, the comment "defined" excision: "Removal of the entire clitoris, usually together with the adjacent parts of the labia minora and sometimes all of the external genitalia, except parts of the labia majora. These operations are performed without anesthetic, frequently on the ground under highly septic conditions."[47]

While the comment affected the rhetorical form of objective academic authority (medicalized, scientist language and the dictionary as "the codified authority on what words *really* mean" [Silverstein 1979, 193]), the definition was hardly neutral. Nor did it closely resemble actual dictionary definitions.[48] Rather, it was precisely the sensationalistic definition and kind of tactic common in Euro-American anti-circumcision campaigns (see note 43). These campaigns are waged through intense politics of representation that simultaneously combine and redefine diverse cultural practices, horrify with grisly images, and create a spurious notion of "third world women" (Mohanty 1988; Stephens 1989; Kratz 1994a, 341–47, 1999a). Their success at getting these images into public circulation over the last twenty-five years has created a new slant on old stereotypes, demonizing practitioners in ways reminiscent of both colonial rhetoric and anti-abortion fanatics. Having herself made assumptions like those in the guerrilla definition initially, Melissa Parker (1995) investigated biomedical and anthropological research on female circumcision. She found that the extreme assertions about its circumstances and effects are assumed rather than demonstrated, and convincingly relates this suspension of critical judgment to links between identity and sexuality that have become central in Euro-American settings (cf. Obermeyer 1999).

> [The] intense emotions aroused by the subject among Western researchers [and others] are, to a large extent, influenced by Euro-American discourses and debates which have little or nothing to do with the study populations. When such strong emotions are brought to bear in unreflexive ways, understandings of female circumcision will continue to be inadequate and misleading. (Obermeyer 1999, 520)

The synecdoche dictated and championed by this particular example of the politics of representation would close down other interpretations of *Okiek Portraits,* reducing all Okiek to women alone, and recognizing *them* only as victims. The Austin controversy was rather different, yet there is a striking similarity. In both cases, synecdochal reduction served a particular position in one politics of representation by elevating a single aspect of the exhibition above others, mode of display in one case and female circumcision in the other. The major difference is that the circumcision focus had to counter or ignore other information in the exhibition to so narrow interpretive possibilities, while those in Austin saw only selected photographs with very limited contextualizing material.[49]

One newspaper review also parroted the circumcision synecdoche, using the same definition almost verbatim. Tellingly, this was in a Washington, D.C., weekly, *City Paper,* an alternative paper that often includes ironic commentary on the city, federal officials, and cultural programs and whose reviewers often affect a blasé, worldly outlook, through glib, patronizing sarcasm. The reviewer was equally unimpressed by the exhibition's multilingual "shtik," citing a remark made by a five-year-old Okiot girl as evidence of a "Hardy Boys tone" in the captions (Jenkins 1990).

Other U.S. reviews were kinder and took the exhibition more seriously. Philadelphia coverage was most extensive; many stories simply reprinted the museum's press release. Ironically, the small bits added by several local papers illustrated the very assumptions the exhibition hoped to address. One story's headline was "Fascinating Photo Exhibit on Primitive Culture Opens This Weekend"; another ran a large photograph with the simple caption "Primitives."

A long human interest story in the *Philadelphia Inquirer* was among the most thoughtful (Keating 1991). Keating asked me to walk through the exhibition with him before he wrote the article. Much as I had done with Okiek, he wanted me to comment on particular photographs, my relations with people shown, and to recount some of the circumstances surrounding the pictures. His article used this material to build a sense of relatedness across difference and distance, developing an assimilating perspective. Like the student paper discussed above, Keating's review shows how an interpretation and stance toward *Okiek Portraits* develops, negotiating cultural and geographic distance in interesting ways. His overall thematic movement is signaled by the title, "Family Portraits."

Keating begins by placing me in the midst of a trying incident shortly before one photograph was taken (as I filmed someone collecting honey, the bees attacked me). This opening scene joins me with named Okiek individuals in common endeavor and shared peril and allows Keating to introduce a first dollop of information about the Okiek. The first third of the article then forges U.S.-Okiek connections through biographical experience, constructing around me a family that crosses continents and links my biological family in the Philadelphia area and my Okiek family and friends. This construction takes the familiar form of an adventure tale, here with anthropologist as heroine. Okiek become supporting cast in this section, which establishes the distance to be bridged. Rather than exoticizing Okiek, it exoticizes my own experience—through descriptions of distance, harsh conditions, and unusual first encounters common in such stories. In the next section Keating balances his opening with information on recent Okiek history and land politics. He then completes his narrative movement from exotic encounter to assimilated family by turning to specific portraits and captions in the exhibition. Keating sets several photographs in dialogue with one another through their captions and finds Okiek to be perceptive commentators with "a wry sense of humor" (8C).

Keating's article creates a three-part movement, an interpretive process that brings readers progressively closer to Okiek. The structure and presentation are more polished, but the interpretive movement parallels the direction of Lusaka's student paper. Keating's article exemplifies the tensions and interplay of exoticizing and assimilating interpretations, as well as their familiarity. But it is worth noting that Keating uses these popular, and often problematic, tropes *without* slotting Okiek directly into the exotic role.[50] He uses the difficulties of travel itself to evoke distance but maintains the human sense of those encountered throughout. Underlining difference at the start, he telegraphs the final familiarity by recognizing Okiek individuals by name. Like the woman from the Midwest, he mediates distance and difference through personal biography and family images, stressing commonality through personal relations. This is certainly one avenue to understanding Okiek that I tried to make possible in *Okiek Portraits*. And it may be among the most common and effective ways that visitors create interpretive bridges across cultural difference. Keating's description of my own connections with Okiek further presented readers with an illustration of the engaged recognition they might sense through the exhibition.

A review that appeared about the same time in a professional journal reassured me that visitors who took time to look and listen to the exhibition might indeed get the impression I wanted to convey. Based on the Smithsonian installation, Michael Fischer's review was the fullest, most perceptive analysis *Okiek Portraits* received (1991). Evaluating the exhibition within more general reflections on museums, ethnography, and photo-essays, he considered relations between its visual and verbal aspects and presented formal analysis of some images (plate 11):

> a dramatic freeze-frame of an initiation dance, composed of four balanced vortexes drawing the viewer's eye back and forth: a black and white monkey skin costume flashes in the lower left pointing the eye along a diagonal towards red-and-white shawls of viewers in the upper right, while along the recessive other diagonal a fire illuminates squatting children's entranced faces in the lower right, their eyes pointing up towards the dancer and, behind her, in the upper left young men dressed in Western casual style. (Fischer 1991, 267)

Few others—reviewers or other visitors—tried to examine the formal, aesthetic, cognitive, and emotional factors combined in the work of interpreting exhibitions. To understand the communicative processes involved in that work, it is helpful to distinguish these different aspects analytically. Visitors experience them simultaneously when going to an exhibition, however, so it is hardly surprising that few differentiated them systematically. Several people commented on aspects of exhibition design, particularly the multilingual labels and their synergy with the photographs. But most visitors concentrated on the information conveyed, the overall understanding produced, and their own interaction and engagement with the exhibition.

Although information about visitors to these early venues is sparse and uneven, it nonetheless provides some sense of how they understood and experienced *Okiek Portraits*. But in looking back at that material in 1992, I found frustratingly little to answer the many other questions it raised. For instance, the history and politics of race in America surely figured in the interpretive framework visitors brought to the exhibition, but how? Lutz and Collins found that "few people explicitly discussed" race in looking at *National Geographic* photographs, but that "racial categories, though denied, are key to people's experience of the photos" (1993, 254). Precisely how these factors filtered and shaped visitors' understandings of *Okiek Portraits* was not clear from the limited testimony available.

One hint came from an article by Tamsin Newman (1991) in the *Daily Pennsylvanian,* the independent student newspaper of the University of Pennsylvania. The article also provides interesting counterpoint to the Keating article discussed above. Newman's lead paragraph links the exhibition with the celebration of Black History Month and asserts that the Swahili language is one of the exhibition's chief subjects. By thus elevating Kiswahili from simply a language used in labels, Newman situates Okiek as speakers of that language (incidentally obscuring the fact that their first language is Okiek). This places them squarely in a national Kenyan context and connects them to a linguistic symbol of pan-African, diasporic identity that has been incorporated into African American identity and politics (e.g., Kiswahili words used or invented for Kwanzaa ceremonies or as names).[51]

Through this opening paragraph and her headline ("U. museum exhibit examines Kenyans"), Newman identifies the people in the exhibition as *Kenyans* first and foremost. After another echo of national identity in the exhibition's name (*A Kenyan People Look at Themselves*), she begins to refer to them as Okiek in the third paragraph but continues to highlight their position vis-à-vis other Kenyans. The rest of the article has two emphases: the goal of challenging and changing stereotypical representations of Africa and of Okiek; the relations among people that emerge in conversational captions and perhaps in exhibitionary dialogue between visitors and Okiek. Newman's article suggests several intersecting dimensions that could provide links and affinities for African American visitors to *Okiek Portraits*. Personal and domestic relations are again one dimension, also noted by the Augusta students interviewed at the Carlos Museum. Here, however, these are secondary to an emphasis on African national identity and subtler connections to common concerns and symbols of diasporic connection.

Yet accounts like this contain only hints, and occasional conversations with visitors remain suggestive moments. They are not a "cross-section" of those who saw the exhibition, let alone an imaginary entity called "the American audience." My conversations with people attending museum events and conferences and the perspectives available in press coverage each have their own accidents of selection. "If you want to know what's really going on you need to go beyond anecdotal evidence. You need to choose a representative sample in which there is no selection bias, in other words, absolutely no favoritism towards the opinion of any particular type of visitor" (Doering and Pekarik 1996, 18). Exhibition evaluation studies provide more methodical coverage and often point to general patterns in visitors' responses. Yet the surveys common in these studies typically provide little sense of the detail, texture, interpretive ambiguity, or communicative process involved in visitors' interpretation.[52]

When *Okiek Portraits* went to Michigan State University Museum several years later, I had an opportunity to explore questions of visitor understanding and interpretive process more systematically. I worked with the curator of education, Kris Morrissey, in planning and conducting a small visitor study. When I visited MSUM, I also paid more systematic ethnographic attention to the exhibition. Later still, when the exhibition went to the Michael C. Carlos Museum in Atlanta, I asked museum docents to complete a questionnaire about their experience with visitors to *Okiek Portraits* and acquired twenty-six student papers about it. At both sites, I also collected material comparable to that from the earlier venues. All this augmented the preliminary analysis of the first U.S. venues but raised other questions as well, discussed in the next chapter.

To look at the portrait of an individual is to invite oneself to all sorts of speculations as to who they were, how they would have spoken, what they would have thought. To look at a family group is to add the assumption of a whole thicket of connections between the sitters.

PHILIP STOKES, "THE FAMILY PHOTOGRAPH ALBUM"

5

THE FINAL VENUES

Designing and
Defining Interpretation

OKIEK PORTRAITS had shown in Kenya and at four U.S. venues when I wrote a first essay reflecting on the exhibition in 1992. Looking back, I was able to recognize my own naïveté about certain aspects of exhibitions and to examine issues not fully thought through while I worked on *Okiek Portraits*. But I found I did not have enough systematic material about how visitors experienced and understood *Okiek Portraits* to really address fundamental questions about exhibition interpretation. When the exhibition went on to its final two venues, I gathered more information about visitors and paid closer attention to details of installation design. Both final venues were university museums: Michigan State University Museum (MSUM) at a large public land-grant university in East Lansing and the Michael C. Carlos Museum at Emory University, a mid-sized private school in Atlanta, Georgia. *Okiek Portraits* showed at each for about three months, at Michigan State in 1993 and at the Carlos in 1997–98. The two museums' different configurations of gallery space also yielded interesting variations in the exhibition's installation.

Michigan State University Museum is a museum of natural and cultural history, "one of the oldest university museums in the country," founded in 1857 (www.museum.msu.edu). It is one of two museums at Michigan State University, along with Kresge Art Museum. Each floor has permanent exhibitions on ecology and adaptation as well as cultural history displays. For instance, the main floor concentrates on Michigan with the Hall of Michigan Vertebrates and Heritage Hall, "with an authentic fur trader's cabin similar to those found along the Grand River in the late 1700s; a nineteenth-century print shop; and a turn-of-the-century general store." The ground level

Hall of Great Lakes Indians adds "the culture and history of Native Americans of Michigan from the arrival of the Paleo-Indians . . . through the creation of reservations in the nineteenth century" (exhibit guide, n.d.).[1]

Okiek Portraits was placed in the East Gallery on the second level, down the corridor from the North American Habitat Hall's biome dioramas and Jurassic dinosaurs. Immediately adjacent, in the other half of the gallery, was another temporary exhibition, *Cuadros de Pamplona Alta, Peru,* showing textile arts made by women in shantytowns outside Lima.[2] The museum held a joint reception for the two in mid-February. On the invitation the *Okiek Portraits* subtitle was changed to *Peoples of Kenya,* perhaps because of space and design constraints. The exhibition itself and other publicity used the regular U.S. subtitle, *A Kenyan People Look at Themselves.*[3]

The Michael C. Carlos Museum is a museum of art and antiquities; recent temporary shows there have included exhibitions on surrealism, French salon painting, outsider art, Yoruba beadwork, and Ghanaian textiles. However, the Carlos was a more comprehensive museum for its first hundred years, acquiring major collections in ornithology, natural history, and archaeology after its 1876 founding. The museum's mission was redefined as art and archaeology in 1974; the natural history collections went to other Georgia institutions on permanent loan. Currently, permanent exhibitions emphasize the art and archaeology of classical and pre-Columbian cultures, as well as a significant collection of African art acquired in 1994 (Michael C. Carlos Museum 1996, 6–8) and spectacular Egyptian material acquired in 1999.[4]

As described at the start of chapter 4, *Okiek Portraits* was shown in the hinge galleries on the first floor of the Carlos (see figure 14). Two small rooms located on either side of a ramped corridor to the Ancient American Galleries, the hinge galleries present the design challenge of signaling visitors that an exhibition continues in a nearby but nonadjacent gallery. An alcove off the second gallery also offered the possibility of adding a reading room to the exhibition for the first time. There were two openings for *Okiek Portraits* at the Carlos, the first hosted jointly by the museum and several Emory programs and the second held by the provost in an initiative to involve faculty more closely with the museum and its resources.

As a traveling exhibition is reconfigured in each display space, its installation develops idiosyncrasies. These design differences, minor or major, contribute to visitors' experiences and interpretations, though perhaps in subtle ways. It is worth looking more closely at the two cases to see how relatively minor design decisions and details help shape exhibition communication. In addition, they show how decisions about one design/space constraint might reverberate to affect and raise questions about other aspects of an installation. At Michigan State University Museum, some installation particularities resulted from adapting two exhibitions to a shared gallery space with one entrance. Others issued from judgments about how best to balance texts and images and other constraints of gallery space. I focus here on three aspects of the Michigan State installation: exhibition entries, photographic order and inclusion, and text placements (see figure 15).

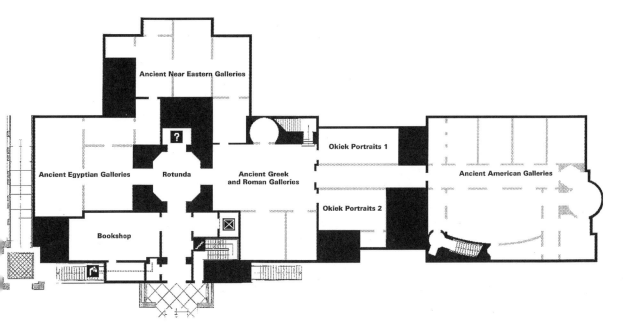

Figure 14. First-level floor plan showing the location of *Okiek Portraits* at the Michael C. Carlos Museum. The alcove off the second *Okiek Portraits* gallery was a reading room for the exhibition.

The main entrance presented an initial design conundrum for museum staff: a single corridorlike entry for a gallery with two temporary exhibitions. Had there been one wide central doorway, entering visitors could have seen clearly that there were two displays. The space could have simply been split, presenting each independently. The corridor entry meant introductory material from the two had to be integrated somehow. *Okiek Portraits* was in the front half of the gallery. If its title and opening text panels were hung in order along the entry hall, effectively drawing visitors into its photographic sequence, the Peruvian exhibition might have remained hidden in the back.

The solution adopted was to mount the *Okiek Portraits* title and a first photograph at the entryway, visible on approach (T_1 in figure 15). Immediately to the left were the title and a large textile from *Cuadros de Pamplona Alta, Peru* (T_2 in figure 15). The Peruvian show began on the opposite wall of the short entrance corridor, its introductory text panels leading to textiles. After an opening on the right into the front of the gallery and *Okiek Portraits,* textiles continued down both sides of the corridor, leading back to the rest of the Peruvian exhibition. A reasonable compromise, this showed there were two exhibitions, giving each some entrance emphasis. But this solution created another problem, discussed below: where to put *Okiek Portraits'* introductory texts. This

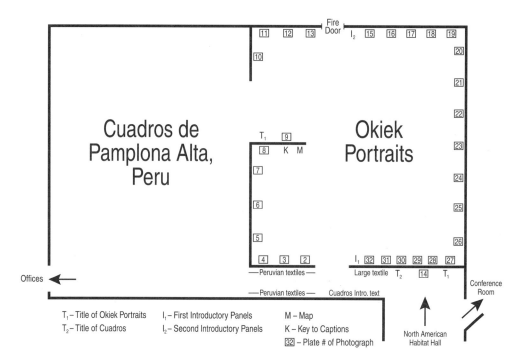

Figure 15. *Okiek Portraits* installation at Michigan State University Museum.

question was further complicated by a second entrance that led from the back of the gallery (where the Peruvian exhibition ended) into *Okiek Portraits* after the first ten photographs or so. The second title panel was hung here with the next photograph in the sequence, clearly marking the boundary between exhibitions.[5]

The main exhibition entrance was also a factor in questions of photograph order and inclusion. Plate 2 usually opens the exhibition, paired with the title panel to start the exhibition's life-cycle sequence with young Kirorua. At Michigan State, however, plate 14 was hung at the entrance instead; other photographs followed in the designated sequence. The staff wanted to start the exhibition with the image most common in their advertising, they explained later.[6] At the back entrance from *Cuadros,* plate 9 was paired with the second title panel. Although the match was fortuitous, the two photographs hung with the title panels did form a pair, a male and female initiate. This choice may have inadvertently emphasized initiation and ceremonial dress.

Michigan State also omitted one piece: the mounted poster from the National Museum in Nairobi (plate 1). It had been part of the introductory material in U.S. showings and so was part of the placement puzzle created by the corridor double-entry at MSUM. The poster's placement was also complicated by the substitution in the opening photograph. The Nairobi poster features the young man in plate 14, showing Keleges Kiamar as an initiate. Having moved this photograph to the beginning, museum staff may have felt the poster rendition would be too close to the original. The omission meant visitors had no indication that the exhibition originated in Kenya, though the effect on the exhibition's representation of Okiek was likely minimal.

The third distinctive aspect of the Michigan installation concerned text placement: decisions had to be made about how to position multilingual labels for individual photographs and the introductory text panels. In other U.S. venues, individual captions were arranged side by side, as in books with translations on facing pages to facilitate comparison. English versions were on one label, the Kiswahili and Okiek on another. A line separated descriptive captions, on top, from commentary captions; typography also distinguished them, with commentary captions in italics. Photographs at Michigan State were closely spaced, however, so the two labels were instead placed vertically, to the right of each photograph, with English versions on top. Visitors who whisked through might have thought each photograph had one long explanatory label; the vertical placement might also have made it more difficult to compare Okiek or Kiswahili with English translations.

The installation guide I sent for U.S. venues discussed the introductory material: a map, the Nairobi poster omitted in Michigan, and five short text panels (two three-paragraph panels in English, corresponding Kiswahili panels, and a key to captions, added for U.S. venues). The guide suggested hanging the map between the two English/Kiswahili pairs, followed by the key to captions. The multilingual panels were meant to lead visitors into the exhibition, but at Michigan State the space after the exhibition title was devoted to *Cuadros,* the second exhibition. This left two options: either hang introductory material together inside the gallery as a clear opening section or split it up. The choice was complicated by different paths visitors might follow (figure 15). Entering from the front, they could either walk straight, begin at the first left wall, and continue clockwise, or they could turn right and move through the gallery counterclockwise. The photographic sequence assumed the first path, going clockwise from children to elders. Still other visitors would enter from the back, through *Cuadros,* and continue clockwise after the second title panel, starting with photographs of initiation.

MSUM chose to divide the introductory material among three places. The first three paragraphs in English and Kiswahili (I_1 in figure 15) were hung to the right of the front entry, next to the exhibition's last photograph. The last three paragraphs (I_2) went on the opposite wall, about halfway through the photographic sequence but soon after the back entry. The map and key to captions (M and K) were joined as a third pair, placed at the end of the first alcove of photographs. This placement balanced the distribution of texts and images; it avoided a text-laden first wall and provided a fragment of orientation along every path. The trade-off was that visitors had no clear guidance about the exhibition's subject or arrangement unless and until they completed the circuit. Those following the intended photographic sequence, in fact, had the least information about whom they were seeing. They would encounter introductory material in reverse order as they moved through the exhibition.[7] Reviewing the exhibition in this venue, Sobania emphasized problems with text placement and other installation features:

> But understanding would have been greatly enhanced by a more logical placement of the text panels and a less cramped gallery space. With little space between photographs one was pulled to the next image rather than to the commentary. Text panels did a good job of explaining why different languages had been used in the captions and commentary. They also offered information on the nature of cultural change, life cycles and initiation, and on the Okiek as forest people involved in trade and contemporary Kenya. But the text panels did not indicate a clear way through the exhibition. A less haphazard placement of these panels might have served, for example, to reduce the prominence of ritual. It was not necessary to have the opening text panel mounted twice, each time next to an initiation photograph. (1993, 73)

As Sobania notes, exhibition texts are more than a source of information. They are also design elements whose placement, order, and typography might signal beginnings and endings, differential emphases, sectional shifts, and appropriate paths through an exhibition (though the Michigan State arrangement generally offered little clear guidance). Sobania also recognized the fortuitous emphasis that came from pairing photographs of initiates with both title panels. The entry marks an exhibition's focus and definition—both textually, through its title, and materially, by the object or image that announces the start. The designed space of an exhibition is full of such metacommunicative features, which might be altered subtly or radically with each new installation when it travels.

The Michael C. Carlos Museum installation of *Okiek Portraits* had its own unique characteristics and quirks. Overall it was an attentive installation. Introductory text panels were placed together at the beginning. The individual labels were redone, returning to the original format used in Nairobi. Descriptive captions appeared on top, in both languages, followed by the multilingual conversational captions. The new reading room off the second gallery was a significant addition, offering visitors opportunities to learn more about Okiek and Kenya. I selected books for the reading room and kept in mind the same concerns that had shaped the exhibition, but with more attention to visitors' age range.[8] The Carlos also announced and advertised the exhibition with large banners outside both building entrances. The banner graphic was based on the initiation dance headdress shown in several photographs in the exhibit (see figure 16; plates 9 and 10).

As already noted, the chief conundrum presented by the two hinge galleries in Atlanta was that visitors had to follow a discontinuous path to see the entire exhibition. Further, some might enter the right gallery first, beginning halfway through. Carlos staff addressed these challenges through several details of installation design. The title of the exhibition appeared in large letters on the back wall of each gallery (see figure 17),

Figure 16. *Okiek Portraits* banner outside the Michael C. Carlos Museum, 1997.

both visible as visitors approached and offered an initial clue that the two galleries were linked. The headdress graphic used on the banner appeared over the initial text on the wall of each gallery and again as a decorative band in the reading room (see figure 18). This motif subtly tied the three rooms together and linked them to the exhibition banners. Still, some visitors might miss these discreet design indicators.

The first text on the wall in each gallery was the short biographical blurb that explained who had taken the photographs (as usual, in English and Kiswahili). I rewrote the text for the Carlos installation, updating the description to indicate I had joined

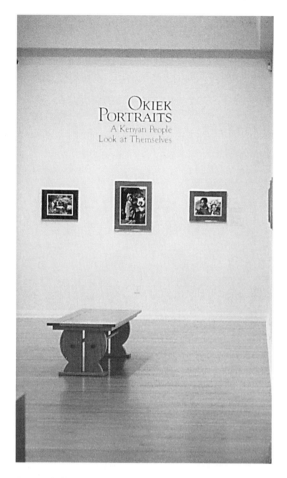

Figure 17. *Okiek Portraits* installation at the
Michael C. Carlos Museum, 1997.

the Emory faculty.[9] This was the only installation where this text was placed first or repeated. However, it was an astute decision given the problem created by the use of two
separate hinge galleries. Visitors who began at the beginning, in the left gallery, and
continued on to the end of the exhibition would encounter the second text as they entered the second gallery. To them, it would show that they were still in the same exhibition. The headdress motif at the beginning and the text itself created a parallel and
link back to the start of the exhibition, reinforcing their choice of a discontinuous exhibition path. If they missed the second gallery, they had still visited what could be
seen as a small but complete exhibition, one with a relatively high proportion of textual introduction relative to photographs and a visual emphasis on young Okiek. Visitors who entered the right-hand gallery first would have the biographical text as their
initial orientation. If they continued on to the beginning of the exhibition in the other
gallery, they would find the same confirming parallel and link, followed by the full in-

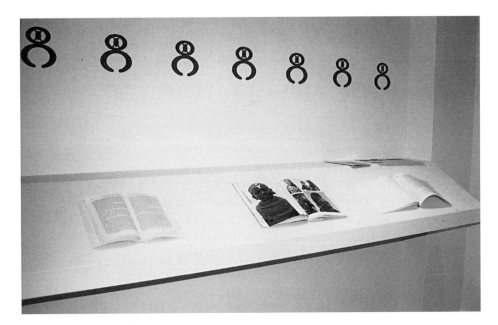

Figure 18. Headdress motif in the reading room
of *Okiek Portraits*, Michael C. Carlos Museum, 1997.

troductory material and the rest of the photographs (and probably realize they had visited the galleries in reverse order). Should they miss the other gallery, these visitors would also have seen something they could consider a full exhibition, but one framed more like an art exhibition with its sole introductory emphasis on the photographer.

These small adjustments and additions in the Carlos installation created cohesion by enhancing features that underlined and reinforced the unity of the exhibition yet at the same time produced a modular design adaptable to the diverse paths through which visitors would encounter the exhibition. Two other details further illustrate the different assumptions, contingencies, and adaptations involved in the installation process. First, while planning the reading room, Carlos staff asked me for an Okiek proverb that might be stenciled on the entry wall. Those I came up with either were not quite appropriate or needed explanation to make sense to American visitors. We decided instead to hang the Nairobi poster on that wall, showing the exhibit's place of origin. The final example involved a last-minute change.

The day the exhibition was hung, Carlos staff asked me to stop by during initial layout. I knew the exhibition order by heart and could sort photographs quickly and easily as they were unpacked, while they would have to refer repeatedly to the installation guide. At the end of the day, I returned for a walk through and noticed that the text thanking exhibition sponsors had been omitted. Assuming it was an oversight, I alerted Carlos staff. It turned out the director had omitted the credits since those Kenyan sponsors were unlikely to see the show in Atlanta and the Carlos itself had received no support from them. Yet I felt a continuing obligation to recognize those who made the exhibition possible in the first place. When the director realized it was important to me, the credits were added. However, we agreed to display them in the reading room, near the Nairobi poster. They were less prominent there yet also appropriately linked to the exhibition's original location. This final adaptation reconciled our slightly different assumptions about credits and attitudes toward the original sponsors.

It is difficult to determine precisely how all the installation idiosyncrasies may have shaped visitors' experiences and understandings at Michigan State and the Carlos Museum. Nonetheless, there are hints in the visitor study, student papers, and other material discussed below. It is clear, for instance, that visitors used all possible paths through the exhibition. Produced in the dynamic between what they bring to the exhibition and vice versa, visitors' understandings and misunderstandings have many sources. While *Okiek Portraits* was in East Lansing and Atlanta, I tried to gain a better understanding of these interpretive processes and experiences.

LEARNING ABOUT VISITORS: HINTS, CLUES, METHODS, AND INDETERMINACY

My reflection on the earlier showings of *Okiek Portraits* had raised questions about how to characterize and understand the experiences of exhibition visitors and audiences.[10] These questions of definition and epistemology are fundamental to exploring how communication and the politics of representation come together in an exhibition. The later venues provided further opportunities for such exploration yet also demonstrated how vexed these issues can be. Collecting more systematic information about visitors to *Okiek Portraits* meant defining questions more precisely, trying to identify various aspects and components of exhibition communication and interpretation and develop appropriately linked methods.

Exploring interpretations of exhibitions requires knowledge of several kinds, including knowledge of visitors' general patterns of understanding and how those understandings vary, as well as information about how visitors reach such understandings through various exhibition experiences.[11] Visitor studies have typically concentrated on the first two, seeking information on interpretive outcomes through demographic profiles, surveys, questionnaires, and observations that track and time visitors. After burgeoning in the 1970s, formative and evaluative visitor studies have become standard practice in large exhibitions, institutionalizing the reliance on these methods and questions.[12] In the last decade, some visitor studies have begun to include focus groups and more qualitative and ethnographic methods; some too now ask basic but surprisingly unexamined questions about what happens in museum exhibitions. This more open-ended "phenomenologically oriented inquiry" (Harris 1990b, 53) is also concerned with interpretive process and the third kind of knowledge.

In designing the Michigan State University Museum visitor study of *Okiek Portraits,* we tried to incorporate techniques to gather all three sorts of information. When the exhibition later went to the Michael C. Carlos Museum, I added a survey of museum docents and a set of papers written by students who visited *Okiek Portraits.* These sources fleshed out impressions based on reviews, discussions with museum staff, my own interactions with visitors at openings, gallery talks, classes, and the analysis of earlier venues. A sketch of how these studies developed will illustrate questions and difficulties involved in producing knowledge about visitors and my own efforts to grapple with them.

Planning for the MSUM visitor study began in mid-December 1992, when I first contacted Kris Morrissey, curator of education.[13] Over the next few months we designed an exploratory study, identifying key questions and devising ways to address them.[14] From the start, we decided to approach visitors' experiences from different directions, combining several methods. We considered various ways to solicit visitor comments (sheets by each photograph, comment books, dialogue kiosks), questionnaires, short interviews about particular issues, mail-in postcards to illuminate longer-term responses, and comments and reactions visitors would tape as they went through the exhibition. I went to East Lansing soon after *Okiek Portraits* opened, saw the installation, spoke with visitors, and talked extensively with Kris about the study. Afterward, I summarized the central questions (letter, 15 February 1993):

1. interpretive processes involved as people visit the exhibit; how they interact with the exhibit

2. what notions of Africa/Africans people have, and how these relate to interpretations of *Okiek Portraits*

3. what difference (if any) the multiple captions . . . make in visitor understandings

4. whether gaze and eye contact in photographs make any difference in the ways people relate to them

5. how to uncover the way understandings of race in America filter interpretations of Africa/Africans

6. what understanding visitors have of the exhibition frame and the museum setting in general, [and] whether they question certain aspects of it

The agenda was ambitious for a small study, but we thought a manageable combination of three methods would begin to address these questions. First, an exit survey asked visitors nine questions.[15] Second, we planned stands in the gallery for visitor comments on particular images and labels. Concerned about visitor flow, the exhibits department suggested we substitute an in-gallery interpretive survey.[16] Visitors were given clipboards and first asked to write comments, questions, and impressions while going through the exhibition, and then asked to create a reduced exhibition of six to eight images. We thought this unusual final question might elucidate responses to different kinds of photographs. Both survey forms are included in appendix C. The third, rather experimental method would ask people to tape-record impressions during their visit.[17] We expected the recorded commentaries and in-gallery surveys to provide the richest material on interpretive process.

Plans were finalized early in March, but nothing went quite as expected. An experienced graduate student was to begin the surveys, but he got chicken pox and then left the museum for another job. As this was "one of the first efforts of the Michigan State University Museum to begin to provide avenues for dialog between visitors and the staff" (Morrissey n.d., 2), there were no other experienced staff or students immediately available to conduct the study. Surveys with adult visitors finally began in early April, conducted by two museum students during two-hour periods spread over four weeks.[18] Tape-recording was scheduled for three periods in late April. We sought taped results from twelve to fifteen people since transcribing and analyzing tapes would be time-intensive. Shortly before the first trial, I returned to Kenya to do further research with Okiek for a year. On return, I found logistical concerns had precluded taping.

In the end, the MSUM study resulted in forty-eight exit surveys and eighteen in-gallery surveys.[19] They suggest patterns in interpretation related to those from earlier venues and an interesting counterpoint to the *National Geographic* study discussed above (see chapter 2; Lutz and Collins 1993).[20] When *Okiek Portraits* went to the Carlos Museum several years later, I asked museum docents to assist in another study. Docents observe and interact regularly with exhibition visitors, so I wanted to draw on their experience to learn more about visitors. Building on the Michigan surveys, I developed ten questions for Carlos docents (see appendix C). When I provided docent training and materials about *Okiek Portraits,* I also explained my project and asked them to answer the questions after taking visitors through the exhibit for at least a month. Mail-in surveys have notoriously low response rates, but I thought the personal contact and appeal, with follow-up reminders through the docent coordinator, would improve returns. The low response rate proved me wrong (just 3 out of 45). Yet those received were interesting, informative, and thoughtful, underlining the importance of docents' experience with visitors and the loss of other equally valuable data through low response.

Yet the Carlos showing also brought unexpected sources on how people experienced and interpreted the exhibition, such as the videotaped encounter described early in chapter 4. In addition, a colleague at Emory decided to use the exhibition in an extra-credit essay for her introductory anthropology class. She set three questions for students to address: on *Okiek Portraits* compared to other exhibits and the effects of multiple languages and dialogue; on clothing patterns and styles; and on genealogical relations among those seen and heard in the exhibition (see appendix C). Twenty-six students wrote papers, at times also describing their visits and responses to the exhibition; all agreed to let me quote their papers.

Let me turn now to patterns in visitors' experience and interpretation found in the various sources from Michigan State and the Carlos Museum.[21] Visitors' encounters with *Okiek Portraits* were shaped in the first instance by design differences in the two installations. It is often hard to tell just how idiosyncrasies of layout and presentation colored visitor understandings, but it is also clear that they did. For instance, my brief observations of visitors at Michigan State showed that they used all three possible paths through the exhibition; one person noted her realization that she was going in reverse order in an in-gallery survey. Several Michigan visitors also suggested rearranging or supplementing texts, most likely reflecting the dispersed introductory panels, and three respondents were strongly influenced by the Peruvian exhibition.[22] Similarly, a Carlos docent noted the difficulty presented there by the unconnected galleries. Four student papers show that they started in the exhibition's second room, but only one noticed the fact. The other three wrote papers without realizing they had seen just half the exhibition and did not understand the different captions and languages or some obvious aspects of Okiek life.[23] These observations alone underline that visitors are not homogeneous in their understandings of exhibitions, and that exhibition viewing is a varied and skilled activity.

Docents provided further glimpses of some visitors' experience: on many tours, roughly five minutes are spent in temporary exhibition galleries; visitors on tour rarely have time to read labels; the reading room was appreciated. One described talking with 4th- to 6th-grade groups about the museum's role as "interpreter" and asking them to figure out the exhibition's arrangement. Many Emory students also noted the life-cycle order, some contrasting this to what they considered random arrangement in other exhibitions. Like the students from Augusta (chapter 4), one docent emphasized visitors' appreciative comments about showing positive images of Africans. But how did visitors to Michigan State University Museum and the Carlos Museum see Okiek? To begin with, how did visitors place Okiek in time and space?

The exit survey began by asking where and when the photographs were taken. Kenya was mentioned in the title and introductory texts, but visitors might locate Okiek in ways that exaggerated or minimized their distance, providing potential clues to how they related to Okiek. In fact, most people did identify Kenya as the location, sometimes including Africa as well, and most knew the photographs were recent. Just one person said "Africa" alone, a vaguer identification, and another claimed the exhibit was about 1954 Nigeria! This specificity of place contrasts with studies that show Americans' first responses to questions about Africa rarely name particular African nations (Falk and Holland 1992; Field Museum 1991) and often place people shown in African displays in a distant, unpleasant past (Perin 1992, 208). Yet it may simply suggest that most visitors read and remembered exhibit texts (though gallery observations and student papers both suggest that some do not) or that survey respondents paid particular attention.

When visitors were asked to characterize Okiek, their answers were quite interesting. Descriptions varied, but family orientation, tradition, and culture were prominent themes in question 3. As an overall gauge, I coded responses positive, negative, or neutral.[24] Characterizations were predominantly positive (53.3 percent; e.g., intelligent, kind, very wise, happy, family oriented, peaceful, and caring) and neutral (39.3 percent; e.g., self-contained, not primitive–not modern, agricultural, normal). Only 7.4 percent were negative, most calling Okiek "primitive." Describing what they thought Okiek found important (question 4), most people used phrases that "suggested that visitors connected or saw Okiek as similar to them" (Morrissey n.d.). Family and friends were mentioned most (29 percent), with notions related to tradition, heritage, and culture a close second (27 percent).[25] No negative values were named. These patterns differ strikingly from the *National Geographic* study, where people said they avoid articles about Africa, ranked Africa last as a place to visit, most associated "primitive" with Africa, and "forty-three percent of the attributional responses to pictures of people perceived as 'African' were negative compared to only twelve percent of those made to lighter-skinned people" (Lutz and Collins 1993, 256–58, 236).

These themes and codings sketch visitors' impressions overall, in aggregate, but the surveys also suggest diversity and ambiguity in how particular people engaged the exhibition. In-gallery surveys show visitors moving among comments curious about people shown, empathetic characterizations, aesthetic judgments, and ruminations on various issues. Here is the range in one (plate numbers in square brackets):

> [3] The mother looks proud of her family. [8] I like this one better than the posed ones. [13] I like the comments of the Okiek looking at this one! This initiation thing might be good for girls and boys here! Not the physical part but the education and seclusion! [16] They are beautiful. [27] I'm glad there was a photograph for her family to see later. *General comment:* I preferred the traditional dress photos but after seeing all I appreciated everyone and the brief visit I was able to have with some beautiful people who I knew nothing about prior to this exhibit.

Lutz and Collins emphasized that their interviews "involve[d] a subtle and complex dialogue carried on both with the interviewer and between the variety of positions the interviewee has entertained over a period of time" (1993, 244–46, 226–27). Short survey responses do not show these contradictions and perspectival shifts as clearly as extended discussion and narrative, though one called Okiek both primitive and spiritual and another incorporated a stand-up comedy formula to broach the touchy subject of race. To *How would you describe the Okiek people?* he replied, "Black. But seriously, proud and rich in culture." His joking reply might have been poking fun at the survey form too.

However, other sources do capture changing interpretations and moments of uncertainty, sometimes presented in personal and emotional terms. At the Carlos opening, for instance, an academic confided her representational anxiety to me. Photographs of secluded initiates (plates 12 and 13) were making her uncomfortable, but she didn't know why. After she found Okiek talking in captions about how others would see them, she realized that *they* recognized the strangeness. This made a real difference, she said with relief, and helped her understand her own discomfort.

Student papers held other examples. One found "it was upsetting to see them wear the modern clothing. For example, in [plate 11] . . . I did not like the men in the back wearing baseball caps either. I don't know why this photo upset me so much, but it seems as if they were not giving respect to the ancient traditions." Yet she found kindred spirits in other photographs and described her absorption: "as I walked through the exhibit I forgot about my own life and problems and got to spend a few hours in a place I had never been before." Another student explained, "The captions and dialogue made the tour of the exhibit more emotional and I felt myself sad about some photos but happy about others. [This] helped to make me feel like more of a participant in the exhibit." Some students were puzzled when the exhibition contradicted their preconceptions (e.g., "though the Okiek are somewhat primitive people . . . they do still have feelings of vanity" and appreciate beauty). Others held steadfastly to their ideas, though the exhibition's contradictory evidence seemed to inspire tiny caveats ("Clothing, although possibly valued to a small extent for its art, served more of a functional purpose to the people, as opposed to an aesthetic purpose as in the United States. . . . Unlike many Americans, attracting people by a style of dress is not important in Okiek culture").

As visitors developed understandings of and through the exhibition, the space of interpretation held room not only for ambiguity and contradiction, but also for simple misunderstanding. Some misconceptions involved the exhibition itself, such as missing the first of the two galleries at the Carlos Museum. One repercussion of this, noted above, was that such visitors did not know what languages were being used or fully understand what they were seeing. But others also misconstrued exhibition languages. When I met with Anthropology Club members, it was clear that some had read captions simply as English/non-English, as did several student papers, without differentiating Okiek and Kiswahili. This was surely true at other venues, too, though not evident in other sources. The multiple temporal frames embedded in the exhibition diverted some visitors as well. For instance, I realized in talking to docents that they did not immediately grasp that the initiation photographs covered a four- to six-month process. Similarly, one student conflated the present of the moment photographed and the moment of later caption commentaries, interpreting Keleges's expression (plate 14) as sorrowful foreknowledge of his own premature death.

Other misunderstandings sprang from disjunctions between American and Okiek cultural understandings and conventions. For instance, foreign bodies, bodily practices, and body art always spark curiosity, but are often read in terms of viewers' own habitual practices and notions of beauty. The elongated earlobes of older Okiek elicited questions and comments from Carlos docents, students, and Michigan respondents, but beaded ear ornaments were easily related to familiar American modes of adornment.[26] However, exhibition visitors often had trouble identifying the gender of Okiek pictured because of different customs related to hair. Okiek shave their heads in normal circumstances, keeping their hair very short. Americans often took this to indicate maleness, reading through their own conventions associating women with longer hairstyles and men with shorter ones. Without this familiar pattern of cues, visitors often mistook the delicate features of young Keleges as female too (plate 14).[27]

Genealogies included in student papers provide a final example. Here again, students often misidentified gender identity, for another set of gender moorings usually provided by names was also missing. Unfamiliar Okiek names offered no hints to them;

gender signals that Okiek and other Kalenjin-speakers would recognize were unknown. Though novices in charting kinship, students tried seriously to diagram relations among those shown and heard in the exhibition. One consistent cultural disconnection across all attempts, however, involved classificatory kinship. Students had no way to tell what the relations identified as father, mother, brother, or sister actually meant without further information, but only one noted the text panel warning that what Okiek call "brother" could refer to what Americans call "cousin." Others charted relations strictly according to American kinship reckoning.[28] For instance, Kirutari says, "They're all my children" in one caption and is identified as a father to initiates shown (plates 15 and 16). Both statements are true, but he was biological father to none. One initiate was his deceased brother's daughter, while others were daughters through more distant links.[29] This exercise helped teach introductory anthropology students why such distinctions matter, though few general visitors would concern themselves with intricacies of kinship. Yet everyone, students and other visitors alike, realized how important the web of kinship is in Okiek life and most formed impressions stressing community interconnection and interaction.

Such impressions had also featured in previous venues. In fact, material from the final venues corresponded in general to my triadic sketch of how visitors negotiated cultural difference and distance at earlier U.S. venues. These three broad patterns, outlined in chapter 4, included those who discussed the exhibition as a direct encounter with Okiek individuals, stressing personal and conversational aspects; those presenting a more distant, generalized perspective, drawing on the language of popular ethnography; and a few who elevated a single aspect of Okiek life into an imagined totality. My conversations with visitors tended to foreground one of these at a time, catching visitors at particular interpretive moments. Yet these were not exclusive ways of approaching the exhibition; visitors might combine them in various ways or move back and forth among different stances. I've already noted the diversity and ambiguity evident in visitors' comments about *Okiek Portraits,* but how does material from the later venues relate to and further illuminate this triad?

As elsewhere, the exhibition reminded Michigan visitors of "pleasant conversations with friends," "looking through a family album," "family," and "friends of ours in Africa." Some even called Okiek in photographs and labels by name or commented on their relations, conversations, or personal situations ("nice Mom!," "I'm glad there was a photograph for her family to see later," "I too admire my older friends"). Emory students made similar comments: "I felt as if I was walking into the middle of a family album"; "It made me feel as if the Okiek people are surrounding me trying to make a conversation." Many students (about 25 percent of papers) used the language of personality to highlight Okiek subjectivity and individuality as well. For one, this was a point of significant cross-cultural connection: "They are people just like you and I, and they have personalities just the same." These comments and visitors' strong emphases on family and friends in describing Okiek echoed the sense of direct encounter and individual connection prominent in the first approach.

The multilingual dialogue captions also drew repeated comment in all sources. Identified as distinctive and unusual, their everyday sense was delightfully fascinating to visitors. Their observations often provided an analytical corollary to the first approach, elaborating the sense of encounter and connection by discussing *how* the exhibition fostered a lively, personalized sense of Okiek. Visitors most often mentioned the conversational captions but noted other features that contributed to this sense as well: the emphasis on portraits and faces, close-ups, color, the human scale of enlargements, informal tone in descriptive captions, inclusion of names, and hanging photographs at eye level.

Visitors also remarked on the content and tone of Okiek conversations, appreciating the wit and sophisticated understanding of representation, but especially their humor and the way Okiek teased and talked back to me. As an Anthropology Club member said, "They're funny, looking at their pictures and making jokes, and laughing at you, saying, 'You take pictures of anything.' It's like something I could say if I was being kind of sarcastic." By making apparent Okiek involvement with the photographs, the exhibition, one another, and me, captions contributed to visitors' own sense of connection. They provided means through which visitors could compare themselves to Okiek and find common ground, and thus occasioned many comments, at times surprised, "that they were not as different as they seemed at first." Such statements are a sign of visitors' interpretive movement from a more exoticizing stance toward a more assimilating one over the course of their visit. Perhaps that dynamic involved a kind of recognition for some.

While visitors at the final venues made generalizing comments like the ones I characterized above as the second approach, they often took a more philosophical, humanistic form. Tropes from popular ethnography were less prominent, and they used broad connective comparisons as well as seemingly neutral, distanced relativism. For instance, in answering *What does this exhibit remind you of?* (question 9):[30] "[Reminds me] of the poverty we have in our own country"; "Makes my everyday problems very minute"; "We're only here on this earth for a short while. We're young and old and that doesn't change in any culture"; "Similarity of *all* human affairs." Such responses dominated when visitors considered connections between Okiek and Americans (question 6), emphasizing broad universals: "similar human values," "basic human connections," "all are mankind," "all have traditions."

We had thought answers to this question might illuminate ways that race figured in visitor interpretations (see note 15). Indeed, a few (15 percent) did focus only on race, claiming that any connections would be with African Americans. One person also foregrounded race by explicitly denying its relevance: "Through my life the one thing I have learned is that ALL people feel the same hurt, hunger, enjoyment, and goals. No matter what color or facial features, all are the same inside." While American understandings of race likely informed visitors' impressions of *Okiek Portraits,* in sources available they emerged explicitly only in isolated instances, usually hedged by denial or humor (cf. Lutz and Collins 1993, 254–58; Handler and Gable 1997, 225–26). The video interview with young African Americans at the Carlos Museum (chapter 4) showed how clearly they related representations of Africans to their own sense of racial politics and identity. We might ask, then, whether the predominant move to broad humanistic connections in response to this question also suggests an oblique commentary on understandings of race in the United States, reflecting a habitual and sometimes uncomfortable avoidance among the larger demographic group (white, middle-class) from which most respondents came?[31]

The question about Okiek-American connections also evoked answers emphasizing contrasts between the two groups. These introduced an interesting twist on the ambivalent ethnographic nostalgia discussed earlier, seeing *Americans* as those who suffered loss: "There may have been [connections] at one time. I think we're losing our traditional sense, though"; "We're just caught up in the trappings of a materialist society, but we value the same things"; "We are very away from the close society they look to be." This perspective casts Okiek life in somewhat romantic, Edenic terms, like a student paper contrasting Okiek attention to family "with some other cultures which may place more emphasis on careers, money, or other endeavors which demand intense attention and therefore take away from the family as the center of one's life." But again, explicit statements of ethnographic nostalgia were surprisingly rare in sources from later venues. Only two comments from all MSUM surveys clearly conveyed this attitude. One summarized the common trope of disappearance (Fabian 1983): "Stories of cultures must be collected—even tho it helps to destroy a culture as we invade their sacredness of the rituals. Too bad 'progress' must destroy a people, a culture." The other echoed, "The initiation costumes and marriage dress are very beautiful. I am glad they continue their customs in the face of 'modernization.'" Note, however, that both use quotation marks to indicate a critical stance to certain concepts, if not to the overall story. A docent at the Carlos showed similar skepticism, "I fully appreciate the need to document these people, especially as our (middle-class American) only contact is to 'help' them in some way."

Though critical distance marked the few full narratives of ethnographic nostalgia, its constituent elements were much in evidence, including category distinctions such as modern/Western/civilized versus traditional/non-Western/primitive and a social evolutionary framework. "Civilization, evolution, development, acculturation, modernization (and their cousins, industrialization, urbanization) are all terms whose conceptual content derives, in ways that can be specified, from evolutionary Time. . . . A discourse employing terms such as primitive, savage (but also tribal, traditional, Third World, or whatever euphemism is current) does not think, or observe, or critically study, the 'primitive'; it thinks, observes, studies *in terms* of the primitive. *Primitive,* being essentially a temporal concept, is a category, not an object, of Western thought" (Fabian 1983, 17–18 [original emphasis]). These categories were basic to visitors' understandings of *Okiek Portraits,* much as studies elsewhere have found. "The categories of primitive or traditional, civilized or modern, were assumed by virtually everyone we talked to. . . . Ideologies of social evolutionism are not always clearly *in* the picture, but are read in"

(Lutz and Collins 1993, 236–38 [original emphasis]; cf. Falk and Dierking 1992, 6; Field Museum 1991).

One sign of the virtually automatic, "instinctive" adoption of this framework was the use of the term "native" in student papers on *Okiek Portraits.* Over a third used phrases like "native people," "native Okiek," "the native's dialogue," and "native garb" to refer to Okiek at some point. While the word "native" may carry the relatively neutral meaning of local inhabitant, their usage seemed to draw more on the second sense listed in the *Concise Oxford Dictionary:* "often offensive, (a) a member of a non-White indigenous people, as regarded by the colonial settlers; (b) South Africa, a Black person." I am quite sure students did *not* intend to disparage Okiek and did *not* see themselves as using racially coded language of colonial intolerance but simply availed themselves of a term that seemed "natural" for talking about the kind of people shown. Its main effect in the papers was to distance and differentiate Okiek from "us." It seemed "natural" because such phrases recur in many contexts, media, and popular ethnographic representations—an example of the dispersed repetition of the countless details that sustain stereotypes as part of a broader framework of social categories, as discussed in chapter 2. A few students and survey respondents also used the category "primitive" to contrast Okiek and Americans, some again using quotation marks to show uncertainty about the term.

Many comments also showed that people expected and preferred photographs that support these deep-seated categories and maintain clear distinctions among them. Broad human values might unite us all, but visitors were interested in cultural diversity and wanted it to be visible and unambiguous. These expectations have long sustained an American "thirst for exotica." In 1876 commentators on the Philadelphia Centennial Exposition were disappointed at the "lamentable lack of foreignness in the dress at the Centennial. The costumed peoples have all put on European wear" (quoted in Harris 1990, 35). Manufactured clothing (usually identified as "Western" or "European") was commonly cited as an unsettling sign in *Okiek Portraits,* too. As elsewhere, some at the final venues read it as showing inevitable change or "outside contact" (cf. Lutz and Collins 1993, 247–53). More often, however, survey reactions were phrased in aesthetic terms. A few thought the combinations "interesting," but most found such "mixture" unpleasing. Nearly half the survey comments on this, in fact, were from question 8, identifying photographs people liked least:

> [Plate 29 or 31]: "The 'Grandpa' wearing what appears to be a very Western-looking coat. Seems out of context to the others."
>
> [Plate 5, noted frequently]: "It could have been a father and son anywhere"; "Put us off because of Western dress, especially the man."

By contrast, several photographs were identified as favorites (question 7) because of beautiful ceremonial dress or ornate beaded jewelry. That attire includes beads from the Czech Republic and manufactured cloth, but it is visually distinctive and read as a clear sign of cultural identity—by Okiek and visitors alike (Klumpp and Kratz 1993; Kratz and Pido 2000).[32]

More than half the student papers addressed the clothing question. Again, variations and combinations in Okiek styles occasioned similar comments; terms like "primitive," "assimilation," "Americanization," "acculturation," and "imposition of Western culture" occurred most commonly in these passages. One student, quoted above, found these styles upsetting, yet a number saw them as self-expression, "their own personal tastes," and thought that "by having such contact with other cultures and societies (and therefore other material goods) they can better express their personalities and their feelings and perceptions."

The many comments on Okiek dress also underline the kind of aesthetic stance toward cultural difference that often accompanies cultural relativism and American multiculturalism. This stance does not necessarily imply trying to understand the aesthetics, morality, or social and cultural imperatives operative for those living in other cultural settings. Rather, an aesthetic stance might emphasize difference and maintain distance rather than encourage the kind of engagement apt to call one's own views into question. This possibility was clear in instances discussed above where the third interpretive approach to *Okiek Portraits* was prominent, elevating some facet of Okiek life or the exhibition synecdochically into the whole. Some visitors at the final venues took that third approach as well, though it was rare in material available to me. As described in chapter 4, circumcision was again the topic on which students fixed during the class interview at the Michael C. Carlos Museum. Similarly, the academic uncomfortable with certain images, described earlier, voiced reactions that might have resonated within the University of Texas debate. Beyond these, however, visitors who asked questions and commented on circumcision and the politics of representation did not fix on them as their chief concern.[33]

The aesthetic stance is also related to the way museums and exhibitions are understood: first and foremost as educational institutions. Despite the politics of representation that are inevitable—and sometimes intense—in making and interpreting exhibitions, outright calls for political action or social justice are not expected, sometimes specifically disallowed. Such understandings were apparent in the virtually unanimous response to *What do you think was the purpose of this exhibition?* (question 2). Virtually everyone responded that it was meant to educate, show, or enhance appreciation and understanding of cultural diversity.[34] Roughly a third answering question 9 also noted similarities between museums and other documentary forms understood as educational in intent (though they are also businesses, as museums are).[35]

Carlos Museum visitors likewise identified the purpose of museums and galleries as educating the public and demonstrated familiarity with different kinds of exhibitions and their conventions. Student papers made clear that experience varied and there were different degrees of critical awareness about exhibition practice.[36] We may not always know how to interpret a particular exhibition or understand what is shown or why, then, but we certainly have notions about what exhibitions and museums themselves are.

An Atlanta review found that *Okiek Portraits* confounded all kinds of conventions. Before discussing how it departed from his own expectations for an exhibition of art photography, the reviewer described how it deviated from popular representations:[37]

[V]iewers are set up to expect the sort of exotic photo-journals of native life that are published by the hundreds every day. Those visually seductive essays, perfect shots every time, show hosts of eager natives crowding the camera, smiling and posing for the photographer. It is therefore something of a shock to find that this exhibition does not belong to that genre. Instead, we are given photos of African people that appear to originate very much in the eyes of the subjects themselves. . . . [W]e have for many decades had our sensibilities altered by *National Geographic* commentary and images, which seem to get more slick and silky each year. It is therefore not possible, except under special circumstances, to take pictures of native peoples *au naturel,* as it were. Corinne Kratz goes as far as is reasonably possible, and the results, if not quite works of art, must have been keenly enjoyed and understood by the people involved. (Locke 1997)

What did Michigan State University Museum visitors do, then, when asked to make their own exhibition? The final in-gallery survey question asked people to make their own exhibition by selecting a subset of pictures. Only eleven did so, but their selections again show different approaches to an exhibition. Half justified their selection with a topical emphasis or general philosophy.[38] Others emphasized a particular topic without explicit explanation (one on initiation, another on children and old women) or replicated the original life-cycle structure.

With so few responses, this final question is difficult to interpret. Yet an interesting, clear, and suggestive pattern emerges in relation to eye contact and direct gaze in photographs chosen. Eye contact and gaze were not overt, stated criteria of selection for these visitors, any more than they were when I first selected photographs for *Okiek Portraits.* But their selections consistently intensified the emphasis I had created, stressing photographs where a main subject faces the camera and visitors can look directly into the eyes of someone shown. This characterized about 60 percent of *Okiek Portraits* photographs, compared to 24 percent of *National Geographic* photographs (1950–86) (see chapter 2). In these smaller selections, one group was comparable to the overall exhibition at 57 percent (4 of 7 photographs). All others created small exhibitions with higher proportions of direct eye contact: 5 of 7 photographs (71 percent) in four cases, 8 of 11 photographs (72 percent) in one case, and 6 of 7 photographs (86 percent) in five cases. Visitors re-created common exhibition narratives, then, and related the exhibition to other educational and documentary representations, but their exhibitions maximized direct photographic contact with individuals, an approach less typical of the frameworks they used.

Where does material from the final venues leave us in understanding how visitors experienced *Okiek Portraits?* The picture that emerges shows visitors taking a range of interpretive stances, often shifting and combining perspectives as they moved through and reflected on the exhibition. The three approaches sketched for earlier venues were also evident at later ones but elaborated in other ways as well. In her preliminary report on the MSUM study, Kris Morrissey noted:

> The general tone and nature of comments suggested to me that most visitors did indeed personally connect to the exhibit, that they saw the people in the photos as individuals rather than homogeneous stereotypes of "Africans" and they seemed to connect to and become engaged in the lives and personalities of the people in the photos [and labels]. . . . While we did not do any tracking or timing of individuals, the gallery is off my office and I spend considerable time in the gallery. I felt that individuals spent an unusual amount of time in the gallery compared to other exhibits, reading labels, discussing and gazing at photos. (n.d., 2–3)[39]

Material from the later venues suggests that many visitors engaged sympathetically with Okiek, but it also raises questions. What difference does it make if people seem to relate and engage with Okiek individuals if they still locate this engagement through social evolutionary narratives and categories like primitive and modern? Should it be regarded as an achievement if a newspaper article on the exhibition refers to "Okiek civilization" and quotes comments in the Okiek language (Perry 1993)? In many ways, information about visitor understandings of *Okiek Portraits* leads back to questions about how stereotypes are reproduced and how they might be countered and transformed. It contains a sober reminder that efforts to understand the interpretive dynamic between visitors and exhibitions cannot "underestimate the absorptive power of ideology, the extent to which the 'facts' themselves become sensible as they take shape within already existing narratives" (Reed 1996b). It brings us to the broader questions: what kinds of knowledge are produced through exhibitions and how do such experiences relate to stereotypes that *Okiek Portraits* originally sought to challenge?

One of visitors' first impulses in encountering the exhibition was comparative, relating Okiek to their own lives and experience in ways that emphasized various similarities and differences, relative closeness and distance. Though exoticizing and assimilating are part of all exhibitions, especially those where cultural difference is prominent, the portrait emphasis and different captions of *Okiek Portraits* seemed to heighten this inclination. Further, while visitors placed Okiek and themselves into familiar narratives, they also introduced caveats and signaled uncertainty about categories and elements of those same narratives. As noted in chapter 2, no single, isolated effort can topple representational habits and understandings embedded in stereotypes and institutional structures that support them, but *Okiek Portraits* might have provided some visitors with ways to recognize some of their chinks and contradictions.

In the end, material from later venues does not provide absolute, clear answers about how visitors interpreted and experienced *Okiek Portraits*. This should not be surprising for "[t]he museum visit may well be . . . a continually revised set of transactions between exhibitor and visitor, with constant renegotiations of meaning and value. . . . But the impact or the intensity of [museum experience] . . . remains, perversely enough, mysterious" (Harris 1990b, 53; cf. Ang 1991, 97, 161–63). After clues are gathered and certain patterns in visitor encounters with the exhibition are sketched, indeterminacy remains. This indeterminacy parallels the relative openness inherent in exhibition communication and the dynamic between what exhibitions bring to visitors and vice versa. As I continue to argue below, politics of representation constrain that dynamic in various ways, shaping interpretive possibilities and sometimes limiting them.

INTERPRETIVE WORK:
SOCIAL PROCESS, EXPERIENCE,
AND KNOWLEDGE IN EXHIBITIONS

In considering *Okiek Portraits'* visitors and audiences, I reflected on my own initial ideas about exhibition visitors and described how various institutions and visitors imagined Okiek, the exhibition, and themselves, often tacking back to consider my attempts to discern and understand visitors' imaginings through comments, conversations, reviews, papers, and surveys.[40] Exhibitions provide occasions and means through which visitors, curators, and others produce knowledge, forming identities and values. Many individuals and institutions become involved over the life of an exhibition, for exhibitions are part of broader histories and political economies of cultural production. Tracing *Okiek Portraits* from initial planning through final exhibition provided a lens through which to examine these processes and some basic assumptions and disjunctures in exhibition practice.

Along the way, I foregrounded two fundamental conditions of exhibitions: their communicative nature and the politics of representation with which they are inevitably engaged. Exhibitions employ diverse communicative resources and conventions. The multiple media, modularity, varied paths and other aspects of "designed space"—all characteristic of exhibitionary communication—together create an interpretive openness that offers visitors occasions for synthetic, synesthetic, and/or disjunctive experiences. How different visitors actually engage and use exhibitions, however, depends on what they bring to the encounter, how their background, history, and ideas bear on their understanding of what is shown. Contingency and creative potential are always part of the meanings and uses of exhibitions. The openness and unpredictability they generate inevitably contend with the politics of representation involved.

Politics of representation involve contests over meaning, competing attempts to heighten particular issues and favor certain interpretations—whether my own efforts to question stereotypes and personalize impressions of Okiek or others' attempts to define *Okiek Portraits* in terms of expatriate influence, academic debates, or international controversies about circumcision. Such politics define boundaries for interpretive openness and limits to the unpredictability of exhibitions. I have argued that politics of representation are inherently uneven and multiple. The unevenness results from differential degrees of knowledge, engagement, power, and authority, from the distinct concerns, social locations, and cultural understandings of those involved. And politics of representation are multiple because the definition and contours of the issues and representations too vary within the debates, as seen in tracing *Okiek Portraits*.

Okiek Portraits sought to engage the politics of representation surrounding stereotypes of Okiek and Africans by presenting images and texts that challenged some of their taken-for-granted aspects. At the same time, it brought attention to certain exhibition conventions by offering different perspectives on both the images displayed and the exhibition itself. Such conventions, too, are usually taken-for-granted, tacit knowledge about how to understand exhibitionary communication. For instance, distinctions among museum genres and various exhibition design components influence exhibition production initially by shaping which exhibitions to present and how. They are already part of what visitors encounter when they come to an exhibition, as well as part of the tacit knowledge visitors themselves bring. Directing critical attention to conventions and expectations allows us to raise questions about them—what is their history, how have they come to seem "natural" or "universal," whose perspectives and interests do they emphasize?

Among an exhibition's many components and effects, some tacit knowledge may be easier to identify and make explicit for discussion. In *Okiek Portraits,* for instance, most visitors focused on the people who were the explicit subject of the exhibition, and more visitors commented on representations of Africans than exhibition design. Though a number remarked on the multilingual double labeling and exhibition arrangement, visitors did not remark on the nature of exhibitions, the authority and role of museums, or the very framework behind exhibitions and museums. They took these fundamental assumptions that grounded and enabled the experience as background, not open for comment (cf. Bourdieu 1993, 228–34).[41]

It may be more common in general for people to contest the content of exhibits than to raise questions about some aspects of presentational form.[42] It may also be easier to question what to enshrine in museums and who is to be in charge than to challenge the very basis and authority of museums themselves as institutions. All this suggests another facet of unevenness in the politics of representation, one related to the communicative nature of exhibitions and how institutional authority is constituted as given. It suggests that different aspects and effects of exhibitionary communication vary in the extent to which they are liable to discussion and description.[43] Identifying these differences would help explicate how exhibitions communicate and how visitors interpret and experience them.[44]

Negotiating cultural difference and distance are a critical part of visitors' interpretive work (Karp and Kratz 2000). This work involves relating oneself to what is shown, and perhaps changing in the process. The multivalent nature of exhibitions provides a range of dimensions and idioms on which visitors might draw in creating exoticizing and assimilating stances. The tension between exhibition communication and politics of representation provides interpretive space for this dynamic, a process through which visitors form identities (individual and collective), constitute different values and narratives, and also place the exhibition and themselves in a range of politics of representation. Lata Mani found that in different countries, people "seized on entirely different aspects of [her] work," prompting "different 'modes of knowing'" set in "different 'configurations of meaning and power'"(1990, 27). Likewise, different issues, dimensions, and identities might come into play when an exhibition is shown in different settings or visited by different people.

When *Okiek Portraits* was shown in Kenya, for instance, questions of cultural difference and distance entwined with other questions quite directly and pointedly, including national pride, ethnic identity and equality, and expatriate influence. Okiek viewers, reminiscing and characterizing friends and kin, also remarked on propensities to stereotype and identified images easily exoticized. Kenyans' concern with these issues varied, charting some of the uneven terrain involved. In the United States, questions of ethnicity and nationalism were rarely apparent in interpretations I encountered, though there were hints that some African American visitors might assimilate the exhibition through a nationalist or pan-Africanist lens. The memory and legacy of colonial relations were also absent from most U.S. comments, again showing asymmetrical concern with politics of representation, rooted in different experiences. Rather, American identities and experience were the counterpoint for most U.S. visitors. Race figured in U.S. interpretations yet was rarely mentioned explicitly.

The visual and experiential fields represented in *Okiek Portraits* offered fewer obvious and familiar entrées for most American visitors than for Kenyans. The environments, ceremonies, costumes, and activities shown—often topics through which people constitute notions of tradition and history (Kratz 1993, 57–58; Handler and Linnekin 1984)—figured far less in assimilating analogies there. Instead, visitors made connections through more general domains of domesticity, social relations, and individual character or personality. U.S. visitors may have drawn more heavily on textual framing in constructing such understandings as well, particularly the conversational captions. The very elements and domains salient in self-representations of tradition and identity in Kenya, however, defined dimensions along which U.S. visitors could construct exoticizing interpretations of Okiek. Okiek and other Kenyans also recognized and drew on the double-sided interpretive possibilities of "traditional" dress and activities. But there was a clear interpretive disjunction over initiation ceremonies for some U.S. visitors. For them, a textual fragment in the exhibition made circumcision the overriding issue in their understanding of Okiek initiation and Okiek life. Yet the concern U.S. visitors showed with academic politics, circumcision debates, representations of Africans, and debates about ethnographic photography was also uneven in each instance—vital for some, irrelevant for others.

Issues central in the Kenyan context, then, figured more distantly in the United States, when they figured at all. Similarly, issues central in the United States were less prominent in Kenya. Visitors' responses to *Okiek Portraits* covered a range of positions, using various assimilating and exoticizing dimensions to understand and position themselves vis-à-vis Okiek. *Okiek Portraits* contained material through which visitors could address questions and values related to cultural identity, tradition, family relations, friendship, national heritage, race, Africa, portraiture, and other practices of representation. "The camera's twin capacities, to subjectivize reality and to objectify it" (Sontag 1977, 178), were one foundation for the range of interpretations, values, and identities invoked, though particular meanings varied in different cultural arenas.[45] But exoticizing and assimilating stances are neither stable nor mutually exclusive. Material on *Okiek Portraits* suggests that people respond in multiple ways as they visit exhibitions, moving among different interpretive emphases and nuances. Selective attention and interest are important in this, making certain aspects of an exhibition prominent for different visitors at different times. Interpretive understandings of exhibitions might continue to shift and develop later, perhaps in discussions with others after visitors leave.

Okiek Portraits provided hints about how such interpretive movement and development may proceed, as people connect their own experience and concerns with exhibitions. My efforts to plumb visitor experiences and understandings combined a variety of sources and methods. These different ways of learning about visitors illuminated different facets and moments of their experience, simultaneously underlining the indeterminacy involved and the difficulty of describing such processes fully. Visitor surveys are often constrained by their design. They are usually administered fairly quickly, at some particular moment in exhibition experience (most commonly entry/exit surveys). They often encourage visitors to summarize and synthesize their response in particular ways, often rather telegraphically; succinct responses seem most suitable to their questions. Brief conversations and comment books also present rather limited impressions, again capturing aspects most salient to visitors at particular moments and magnifying the opinions of self-selected visitors who decide to comment. These sources help explain general patterns and themes in visitors' responses, but they do not show how people constitute such interpretations as they engage with an exhibition.

Longer conversations and reviews often include similar efforts to summarize an exhibition's effects and meanings. These accounts have different, less constraining parameters, however, and typically include other kinds of commentary as well. They allow visitors to develop, justify, and qualify different perspectives. In effect, they provide opportunities to create, weigh, and reflect on such summaries and syntheses. Some of the most clearly developed examples for *Okiek Portraits* involved extended discussions in written narratives formulated after leaving the exhibition, whether for reviews or student papers. Nonetheless, they provided little information about what visitors experience as they go through exhibitions, how they work through various components, integrate them, and progressively try out or reinforce different stances. The in-gallery surveys at Michigan State University Museum, completed as people visited *Okiek Portraits,* suggested similar movement, but no narrative development or presentation integrated their movements. Those surveys had the more disjointed sense of snapshots, combining multiple stances and foci. The play of difference is not unidirectional, but exhibition experience needs fuller exploration to learn how interpretations change as people visit an exhibition, in relation to different photographs and captions, and how people proceed to broader conclusions.

Most of the more fully developed narratives about *Okiek Portraits* seemed to move from relatively distant, exoticizing stances to more assimilative understandings of Okiek. But interpretive movements may also include or end with more exoticizing readings. Exoticizing interpretations of *Okiek Portraits* tended to reduce complexities, emphasize externalities, and narrow the number of dimensions taken into account. Whether summarizing with the simple label "primitive" or seizing on certain practices as bizarre and unsettling, these usually disregarded the particularities of life and the social relations that the exhibition tried to show. They dealt with Okiek neither as individuals nor as Okiek, a self-identified people with a shared history, located in particular social and political circumstances in Africa.

Many aspects of exhibition experience can be summarized and illuminated through the broad contrast of assimilating and exoticizing strategies of interpretation (see chapter 3; Karp 1991; Karp and Kratz 2000). Beyond this entry point to exhibition experience and interpretation, however, lie further questions about how visitors and curators negotiate the distance and difference portrayed in exhibitions. How can exhibitions encourage some ways of understanding rather than others? What issues, dimensions, and cultural idioms are involved in these dynamics? When and why do visitors tend toward more distant, negatively stereotypical, or exotic interpretations and when do they emphasize commonalities within cultural difference? Through what modes of engagement do people complicate that dichotomy and move toward recognition that somehow changes visitors' minds, feelings, or sense of themselves and others? If "[recognition] is achieved through exchanges that have startling, upsetting, sometimes profoundly disturbing consequences for all participants" (Fabian 1999, 66), what are the possibilities and limits for recognition through exhibitions?

Answers to these questions do not lie within exhibition walls alone, nor only in the personal histories of exhibition visitors. Broader social and political circumstances and involvement are central and also shape visitors' understandings of exhibitions (cf. Karp 1992), again returning us to the politics of representation and cultural conventions involved in exhibition communication. In each case, the question is how do the particulars of an exhibition and of visitors' interpretations relate to specific politics of representation? How do politics of representation intersect in various ways, narrowing an exhibition's interpretive potential to promote particular readings from the multiple approaches and wide-ranging content possible?[46] Stereotyping is but one example of how the politics of representation can arrest interpretive processes.

Like other forms of communication, exhibitions do more than simply convey information, and they do many things simultaneously. In addition to providing means for showing, knowing, and forming identities and social relations, they communicate values (Kratz n.d.), familiarize visitors with institutional settings, contribute to and help recreate those same institutions, illustrate and teach analytical skills, and hone particular ways of seeing and kinds of attention.[47] Through these functions and effects, exhibitions are a kind of social action as well as forums for the production of knowledge. To understand an exhibition and its interpretations, then, requires more than discussion of what it is about. It is also important to examine how diverse, multimedia communicative resources are combined and used, how they make possible a range of interpretive directions, emphases, and conclusions, and when and how exhibitions have these various effects.[48] Both unspoken, affective meanings and referential meanings must be considered (cf. Kratz 1994a; Poole 1997, 166). The politics of representation that contain and shape these communicative resources and possibilities are equally important to chart, defining different positions and constituencies and their involvement in wider social, historical, and political economic settings.

Exhibitions are implicated in various ways with education, entertainment, museums, processes of cultural production, and modes of authority. Knowledge, values, and identities produced through exhibitions—by visitors, by exhibition curators and designers, by exhibiting institutions, and by the very act and mode of exhibiting certain objects and subjects—are connected in diverse ways to social and political spheres. When I began work on *Okiek Portraits*, I hoped it would help confound and undermine problematic stereotypes, ways of thinking that can have far-reaching consequences. Some years later, after following *Okiek Portraits* and exploring the exhibition through the writing of this book, I know that the question of how to achieve that hope is, in fact, a very complex and vexed issue. Stereotypes and their ready narratives are undeniably powerful and resilient, reproduced and repeated in myriad ways and forms, through many details, media, and contexts, until they come to seem "natural," ahistorical and apolitical truths. Exhibitions are but one small facet of those larger cultural and political processes. As I considered *Okiek Portraits'* production, travel, and visitors, different questions came to the fore as it (and I) became enmeshed in those processes in changing ways. Exploring *Okiek Portraits* as a case study has shown some of these complexities and the importance of tracing the uneven politics of representation at issue in any exhibition, examining an exhibition's many-layered communicative resources, and recognizing the diverse ways that visitors engage and understand these through exhibitions.

APPENDIX A:
THE POLITICS OF REPRESENTATION
AND IDENTITIES

Our identities are fluid, and they encompass competing
claims, each vying for the mantle of universality. There's
no such thing as authenticity; it's only a marketing ploy.
No coherent group perspectives are decreed automatically
by nature or by social and economic "law," and this applies
to class consciousness as well as identity politics.

ADOLPH REED, JR., *CLASS NOTES*

DEBATES OVER the politics of representation have proliferated in diverse cultural arenas over
the past two decades, arenas that include daily encounters and academic settings, span the arts
and sciences, cut across scholarly distinctions, and involve multiple communities, whether in
the United States, Europe, Africa, or elsewhere. These contests have changed the terrain and
terms of academic practice, saturated museum practice, inspired artistic imagination, and at
times supplied rhetoric to justify government policy or budgetary shifts and cuts.[1] The opening pages of chapter 1 give some examples of the politics of representation, but it is worth paus-
ing to ask explicitly: what *are* the politics of representation and why have they received so much
attention in recent years?

"Representation" has several senses in English, with somewhat different histories and fields
of common usage. In government and law, representation means speaking or substituting for
others, acting as a proxy, as in representative democracy. This political meaning has coexisted
for several centuries with another sense, in which representation is something that stands for
something else, symbolizing it or calling it to mind through depiction or portrayal.[2] This sense
has been associated particularly with the realms of art, theater, symbolism, and philosophy. In
art history it became linked with realism and naturalistic depiction after the mid-nineteenth

century.[3] Clearly, the political and symbolic senses have conceptual ties. An anthropological sense of representation also developed early this century from the symbolic, theatrical meaning. Emile Durkheim and others used it initially to discuss ritual and religious beliefs as individual and collective representations (i.e., shared cultural understandings) (Durkheim [1915] 1965; Herbert 1991). At the risk of exaggerating the differences, these three senses might be called political, artistic, and cultural in their emphases.

In the late 1970s and early 1980s, scholarly attention turned increasingly to the intersections and convergences among these meanings and fields of activity. Political and cultural mediations involved in art and literature became important topics, as did the cultural assumptions and aesthetic-poetic aspects of political action. Reflecting this interest, a raft of scholarly books and articles began to appear from the mid-1980s on "the poetics and politics" of literature, ethnography, museum display, and other topics, with a distinct emphasis on intersections between politics and various forms of writing.[4] Shortly after came an increasing number of titles using the phrase "the politics of representation." As these phrases crystallized and gained popularity, the general concerns that these rubrics signal also became common across scholarly disciplines and cultural arenas.

These phrases, "poetics and politics" and "politics of representation," make the double sense of representation explicit and thus include questions related both to symbolic-artistic forms *and* the social relations and differences of power that practices of representation involve. The politics of representation, then, center on debates about how particular topics, perspectives, and images become prominent, how their depictions are formed and interpreted, and the social relations and inequalities reproduced through representational practices, including their institutional settings. These issues "open questions about rights, authority, and the power to control which voices talk when, how much, in what order, in what language" (Feld 1990, 241).

As this quote suggests, issues of communication are fundamental to the politics of representation. All communication involves representation, using various kinds and combinations of signs, but communication is also a process that draws in a number of people in various ways. Different people may be involved in various moments of production, circulation, and reception/interpretation, and the dynamics of each of these moments influences the others. Communicative processes are also dialogic in the sense that they are always located in social worlds that are themselves in part reshaped by those communicative interactions (Hall 1993, 1994; Mannheim and Tedlock 1995). Feld draws particular attention to the production of representation, including both social aspects (who does what, who controls access, etc.) and formal aspects (e.g., what languages, media, and genres are used—elements that also have social meanings). But politics of representation also address other moments of the communicative process. Representations are interpreted and understood in different ways, depending on the people, contexts, and histories involved. The ways representations are distributed and circulate have patterns and politics as well, with certain images, codes, and places more familiar and accessible to some constituencies than others. These moments are linked and further mediated by the knowledge, experience, interests, and intentions of the people involved and their larger circumstances. The politics of representation may crystallize around any of these aspects in a particular case, but they will be best understood by considering the interrelated processes of representation, mediation, and interpretation involved.

Scholarly interest in the politics of representation can be partially traced through keywords and phrases, but these concerns reach beyond the academy. Contemporary politics of representation have had a range of public faces, often popularized through the most contentious debates. In the mid- and late 1980s, public disputes arose in the United States over multiculturalism and school curricula (the so-called "canon wars"), government support through the National Endowment for the Arts for various kinds of artistic expression, control of the content and perspectives of museum exhibitions, and so forth.[5] Media coverage of clashes over "political correctness" peaked in 1990–91 (Gitlin 1994, 150; Stimpson 1994, 8–9), though such "culture wars" continue to simmer and erupt. Their contours and vocabularies have also continued to shift over time. "Identity politics" is a version that has become increasingly prominent since the early 1990s, though questions of identity and perspective have been important issues since the 1970s.[6]

The social movements of the late 1960s and early 1970s—particularly the civil rights movement, the New Left, and feminism—were the ideological cauldron in which both the politics of representation and identity politics eventually formed. These movements began with progressive aims and made a real difference nationally in the issues discussed, in understandings of community and polity, and in some institutional structures. They had an interest group structure that emphasized identity, communities of difference, and the personal-as-political, all foci later adopted and developed by others across the political spectrum. When taken to extremes, however, "entrancement with the polarities of identity and difference" can be counterproductive.[7]

One repercussion of the 1960s–70s movements was the start of important new work in the human sciences in the 1970s–80s. Now a vast corpus, this work introduced new perspectives and topics by focusing on the history, literature, and lives of women, African Americans, Native Americans, and other minority groups. The new perspectives often led to reassessment and reinterpretation of previous work as well, including literary classics and received historical wisdom.

> *Moby Dick* is a different, richer text when read through a lens sensitive to the significance of race in mid-19th century social thought. On arriving in New Bedford, in the second chapter, and after several evocative references to Native Americans, Ishmael has a pregnant encounter with a black congregation; the Pequod's journey illustrates the realities of economic globalization already, and Melville's descriptions of the crew reflect both the era's equivalent of liberal multiculturalism and the racialism from which it emerged. (Reed 2000, 175–76)

This new work contributed to broader theoretical trends at the time, trends that questioned seemingly universal generalizations and claims and looked for alternative perspectives, internal differences, and qualifications that might have been glossed over. The social constructionist approaches so prominent today also developed out of this work.[8] To some, these perspectives, questions, and reinterpretations seemed threatening, fueling the disagreements of the 1980s canon wars. In the human sciences, all these developments also contributed to what has been called a "crisis of representation," a rather melodramatic phrase for a heightened and widespread critical concern with social, political, and historical factors in the practice of scholarly research. This was seen to have an epistemological effect that "dislodge[d] the ground from which persons and groups securely represent others" (Clifford 1986, 22). Scholarly attention to the practices and politics of representation, outlined above, were one outgrowth of this concern.

It seems now, in the new millennium, that the politics of representation have always been with us. Indeed, in some ways they have; the issues involved are not new.[9] But they have not always received as much attention in and of themselves, and the current configuration of the "politics of representation" is relatively recent. This review of how they came to prominence provides a frame for the period during which the *Okiek Portraits* exhibition was shown in the United States and for questions considered in later chapters. But *Okiek Portraits* began in other circumstances, in Kenya, where issues of representation had rather different settings, histories, and resonances. For instance, ethnicity has long played an important role in Kenyan politics, but it is important to note that the exhibition took place there in 1989, before multiparty politics returned to Kenya, before heightened splintering of the opposition parties along ethnic lines, and before the ethnic clashes preceding the 1992 elections.[10] Similarly, Kenya's colonial history is far more recent than that of the United States (independence from Britain in 1963 rather than 1776).

Writing about identity politics, Micaela di Leonardo asserts that "[i]t is a primarily American phenomenon because the United States is arguably the site of its invention and of its primordial application" (1994, 165). The same might be said of the politics of representation as a precursor of identity politics in the United States. But even though the particular profile and heightening described above emerged from an American political and academic crucible, some formulations and concerns also took root elsewhere, transformed in relation to other national settings and issues. Brazilian Indian activism provides one example. Beth Conklin (1997) describes how connections with international arenas have simultaneously strengthened activists' hand and fostered a politics of representation that plays to Euro-American ideas about identity, authenticity, and appropriate Indian dress. She discusses the "political price for cultural politics that are heavily constrained by Western ideas about Indians" (ibid., 725) as well as important changes that burgeoned in the 1980s and enabled these links.[11] Similarly, Nicholas Thomas discusses the politics of representation and identity in New Zealand and Australia, where Maori and Aborigines since the mid-1980s have sometimes promoted essentialist notions of identity for political ends (1994, 173–88). The politics of representation is a general rubric for talking about heightened awareness of and increased attention to the ways that images and interpretations are constructed, negotiated, presented, and used,[12] but the politics of representation and identity provide idioms through which other political issues are posed and negotiated in many settings.

While it is possible to point to key concerns that help define "the politics of representation," then, the phrase is actually used to refer to many different situations, contexts, constituencies, issues, and positions. There are, in fact, multiple politics of representation that intersect and interact in various ways, in diverse cultural arenas. They may center on race, ethnicity, gender, religion, sexuality, regions of the world, or other issues of difference and diversity (though class is more rarely an overt focus). At any particular time and place several different politics of representation are likely to intersect in various ways. The crucial question is which ones and how.[13] The images, people, histories, and political economies involved must be examined in every case in order to answer these questions. Because the *Okiek Portraits* exhibition appeared in different settings, this case study considers several such configurations.

Politics of representation are neither singular nor stable. As examples in this appendix have shown, the people and key issues involved shift over time, arenas widen and narrow, and the vocabulary and modes of argumentation also change over time and vary in different places. Every politics of representation is also inherently uneven. People's awareness of and engagement with the concerns at issue are not all the same. Some might be preoccupied with them, while others are unmindful or indifferent. Asymmetries of power are also pervasive, at times bolstering or bolstered by uneven involvements. Precisely how power, knowledge, and engagement are related in any politics of representation, and how such unevenness is reproduced are questions that always need to be examined. In relation to museum exhibitions, we might begin by asking how settings such as exhibitions help produce and modify certain kinds of unevenness. What shape do politics of representation take in museums and exhibitions? How do exhibitions become a nexus in the distribution of representations and knowledge (cf. Karp, Kreamer, and Lavine 1992)? This book begins to address these questions by looking at the politics of representation entwined in a specific case, the *Okiek Portraits* exhibition.

APPENDIX B:
KEY RELATIONSHIPS REPRESENTED
IN OKIEK PORTRAITS

THE KAPLELACH AND KIPCHORNWONEK OKIEK whose photographs and comments appear in the *Okiek Portraits* exhibition are part of several communities that are densely interconnected through kinship, marriage, shared initiations, friendship, and history. *Okiek Portraits* provides a strong sense of these relationships, but this appendix shows the actual kinship links among those in the exhibition. The diagram on the next page uses information available in the exhibition, but it also shows intervening links that would not be clear from the exhibition alone. For example, women identified as sisters might be sisters because their fathers are brothers, rather than because they were born of the same mother (the key to captions in the exhibition shows a similar example). To make it easier to relate the diagram to the exhibition, names are shown only for those who are part of the exhibition (not all members of the families charted here are included).

Okiek are members of patrilineages, that is, kinship groups traced through males, with children belonging to their father's patrilineage. What I call families here usually include members of an Okiek patrilineage (*kap*) along with a number of people who have married patrilineage members. The chart does not identify the patrilineage of origin for all those who have married into the families. In order to include most people in the exhibition, it concentrates on portions of the lineages most densely represented there, Kap Leboo and Araapkiplet. Where relevant it also shows small portions of other lineages, which are demarcated by dotted lines and identified by name. A few individuals from the exhibition are not shown because they are members of entirely different lineages or because their connections to the main families were too complicated or distant to show here (e.g., Naoroy, Kibarua, Kopot Mbosholo).

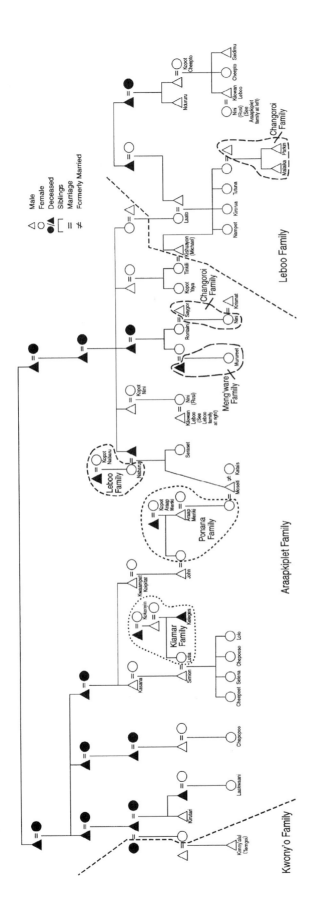

N.B. Families shown are actually larger. This diagram only names people included in the *Okiek Portraits* exhibition.

THE TWO FINAL VENUES for *Okiek Portraits* offered several opportunities to learn systematically about visitors to the exhibition, as described in chapter 5. At Michigan State University Museum, I worked with the curator of education, Kris Morrissey, to design an exit survey and an in-gallery survey for visitors to complete. At the Michael C. Carlos Museum in Atlanta, docents were asked to answer ten questions after a month of taking visitors through the exhibition. A colleague in the anthropology department of Emory University also gave her students an extra-credit exercise on *Okiek Portraits;* students were to visit the exhibition and then write a short essay answering two of three questions. This appendix reproduces the questions asked in each of these venues, beginning with the exit survey and in-gallery survey from the Michigan venue.

OKIEK PORTRAITS VISITOR SURVEY

1. Where were these photographs taken? When?

2. What do you think was the purpose of this exhibition?

3. How would you describe the Okiek people?

4. What do you think is important to the Okiek people?

5. Do you think the Okiek are representative of other African cultures? Explain.

6. Do you think there is any connection between Okiek and Americans?

7. Which photograph or label was your favorite? Why?

8. Which photograph or label was your *least* favorite? Why?

9. What does this exhibit remind you of?

Number of adults in your group: _____ Number of children in your group under 18: _____

Number in your group who are   _____ African American   _____ Euro-American (Caucasian)

_____ Asian American   _____ Hispanic/Latin American

_____ other:

Number of: ___ Females ___ Males

Has anyone in your group spent time in Africa?

Date: *Time:*

OKIEK EXHIBIT VISITOR COMMENTS

As you walk through the exhibit, write any comments or questions you have. Please tell us your impressions of the people in this exhibit. Identify the number of the photograph you are looking at. Include all comments from everyone in your group. Write as much as you like and use the attached sheet if needed.

Photo
number   Comments or Questions

___   _____

___   _____

___   _____

• • •   • • •   • • •   • • •

If this exhibit were reduced to 6 or 8 photographs, which would you include?

_____

Why these photos?

_____

Number of adults in your group: _____ Number of children in your group under 18: _____

Number in your group who are   _____ African American   _____ Euro-American (Caucasian)

_____ Asian American   _____ Hispanic/Latin American

_____ other:

Number of: ___ Females ___ Males

Has anyone in your group spent time in Africa?

Date: *Time:*

DOCENT SURVEY AT THE MICHAEL C. CARLOS MUSEUM

29 September 1997

Dear MCCM Docents:

As we discussed today, I am writing a book about the *Okiek Portraits* exhibition, including information about how visitors in different places understand the exhibition, its photographs, and its texts. As MCCM Docents, I want to ask your help in learning about visitors to *Okiek Portraits* at the Carlos. After you have talked to visitors and taken them through the exhibition for at least a month, would you please answer these ten questions? Please return your answers sometime after 15 November, but before 20 December. The attached envelope can be used to return responses. Your help will be greatly appreciated. Cory Kratz

Date _____

Name (optional) _____

Note: Please be as specific as possible in your descriptions (e.g., "A number of adult women asked about . . ." or "I had many 4th–6th grade student groups. They often commented on . . ."). It is important to include both negative and positive comments on the exhibition if you heard both. Feel free to continue your responses on another sheet of paper if you need more room.

1. What were visitors most interested in? What did they want to know about Okiek, about Kenya, about Africa, or about the exhibition?

2. What questions were commonly asked by visitors? Were there any unusual comments or questions that you particularly remember?

3. What aspects of the exhibition did visitors seem to like especially (photographs, captions, arrangement, particular images, etc.)? Why? Do you remember any specific comments?

4. What aspects of the exhibition did visitors seem to dislike especially (photographs, captions, arrangement, particular images, etc.)? Why? Do you remember any specific comments? What aspects did visitors find difficult to understand?

5. What did visitors have to say about the photographs in the exhibition (in general and about particular images)?

6. What did visitors have to say about the labels in the exhibition (in general and about particular captions or texts)?

7. Did visitors compare the exhibition to any other exhibitions, books, films, travel, or other experiences they have had? Which ones?

8. What did visitors think of the Okiek people after seeing the exhibition?

9. Docents spend more time with an exhibition than most museum visitors and become more familiar with its particular images and texts. Please describe your own reactions to *Okiek Portraits* and how they may have changed over time as you led visitors through the exhibit and came to know it better. Do any particular images, characters, or texts stand out for you now? Which ones, and why?

10. Any other comments?

Thank you for your help!

EXTRA CREDIT ASSIGNMENT FOR INTRODUCTION TO ANTHROPOLOGY CLASS, FALL 1997

Extra Credit Assignment #6: Okiek Portraits

In the Carlos Museum this semester is a temporary exhibit mounted by Dr. Kratz that introduces us to some interesting issues about museum representations of other cultures. Go see the *Okiek Portraits* exhibit and write answers to two of the following three questions. This assignment may be a good one to do in a small group, to share your reactions and opinions. Be sure to write your own original essay.

1. Museum Anthropology: How is this exhibit different from ordinary exhibits of photos in museums or galleries? What effect does the dialogue in the captions have on you? How does the exhibit frame our understandings differently? Try to use an example or two to illustrate specifically what you mean. Why do you think Dr. Kratz used all three languages in the captions?

2. Clothing: Discuss what you see in the portraits about Okiek dress. In some foraging societies, wearing Western clothing represents an imposition of another culture by missionaries or an imitation of high-status outsiders such as government officials or tourists. Among the Okiek, however, most are wearing clothes manufactured in Kenya and purchased in markets. Their beads come mostly from the Czech Republic, though historically they also came (since the late 1800s) from Venice. What variations do you see among individuals in their clothing and adornment? How do they mix styles? What do you think they are *doing* (in a cultural sense) with the clothing they wear? As you speculate, think about what evidence you have to back up your opinion.

3. Make a genealogy chart of the individuals in the portraits, to the best of your ability, given the information in the captions. (You will get instructions on how to make a kinship chart in class.)

Length: approx. 3–4 pages. Maximum 6 points.

Dr. Kratz is writing a book on people's reactions to exhibits and would like to know whether she has your permission to use any of your comments in her book. Please put on the cover of your extra credit paper, "Yes, ok to quote" or "No, please don't quote," to guide her about your preference.

NOTES

PROLOGUE

1. See chapter 1's epigraph for the fuller context and exchange from which this phrase is taken. Okiot is the singular form of Okiek.

2. Conversational hesitations and qualifications have been edited out. As actually spoken in conversation, this would read: "I kinda like expected them to be all, you know, skinny, you know like—but they are really beautiful, you know? I never really have seen this side of the people."

3. Karp discusses these differences in terms of identity formation and museum-community relations (1992, 21–24).

4. On these central questions of personhood, see Fortes (1973, 1983), Jackson and Karp (1990), and Kratz (2000).

5. Fabian (1996b) discusses different types of "recognition" and the ambiguity and ambivalence often characteristic of encounters with people whose lives and customs seem so different that they become Others, their alterity helping define their observers' own identities. As discussed below, Okiek have long been such an Other, their forest-based hunting life a contrast to that of other Kenyans.

6. The Nairobi exhibition placed the title panel with plate 2, followed by opening texts (with the map between paired multilingual text panels) and then the other photograph and caption pairings. In this book texts are gathered at the beginning so that all the color plates fall into the color printing signature.

7. Chapter 3 describes how plans failed to bring Okiek to the Nairobi exhibition.

8. I use the terms "Asian" and "European" in the Kenyan sense. "Asian" refers to people and communities with origins in the Indian subcontinent; "European" includes people from both Europe and North America. The total Okiek population is hard to estimate because national

census information combines Okiek with other people who have been called "Dorobo." Each Okiek group includes about six hundred to one thousand people.

9. Okiek is a Kalenjin language, closely related to other Kalenjin languages such as Kipsigis and Nandi. Linguists classify Kalenjin languages as Southern Nilotic; they are also related, more distantly, to Eastern Nilotic languages (such as Maasai, Turkana, or Teso) and Western Nilotic languages (such as Luo, Nuer, or Dinka). Several Okiek groups (e.g., Digiri, Omotik, and some eastern Mau groups) now speak Maasai as their first language.

10. *Il Torrobo* often becomes *Dorobo* or *Wandorobo* in Bantu languages and English.

11. In the colonial period these moves focused especially on Kapchepkendi Okiek north of Nakuru (Huntingford 1929) and Okiek groups in what became the Southwest Mau Nature Reserve, south and southwest of Nakuru. Later operations to remove the latter in the 1970s and 1980s included having General Service Unit personnel burn Okiek houses. Other areas north of Narok where Okiek landowners sold plots to Kikuyu settlers were subject to similar forest protection policies in the 1980s. The ramifications of these moves and other colonial and postcolonial policies affecting Okiek land are among the most critical issues facing Okiek today. It is important to stress that the contemporary circumstances of Okiek in different local groups vary widely because of historical differences in land policies in their particular areas. In 1996 Maresionik, Tinet, and other Okiek from the Nakuru area formed the Ogiek Welfare Council. Though their applications for official registration have been denied, they began to publicize their land problems through press conferences, demonstrations, delegations to the president, petitions to Parliament, and a lawsuit (still under appeal in May 2000). They do not yet include or address the circumstances, problems, and needs of other Okiek groups, but their systematic efforts may make a difference in their own difficulties and help change the way other Okiek areas are handled.

12. The Kenyan Parliament legislated general land demarcation in 1969. Before that, a group-owned ranch policy was developed for Maasai-dominated districts in an effort to maintain and manage grazing pastures and access to water resources. Kaplelach and Kipchornwonek land was included in this scheme because both Okiek groups live in Narok District, despite differences between highland forested land and semiarid savanna grasslands or the varying uses to which Okiek and Maasai put them. Group ranch demarcation began in the 1970s, crossing what had been boundaries for lineage land holdings, registering some Okiek land to individuals who had never lived there, and incorporating non-Okiek into some groups. The highest altitude forests became reserves. In the 1980s, Okiek began subdividing group ranches into individually owned plots (as did Maasai). Settlement patterns shifted again as people moved onto the land they claimed. Subdivision enables individuals to sell or lease land, which Kipchornwonek and Kaplelach began to do well before subdivisions were official. In the late 1980s and 1990s, settlers from other parts of Kenya who had purchased land (mainly but not only Kipsigis) began to move onto their new plots and clear forest for gardens. By the mid-1990s vast areas of forest had been cleared and there were at least as many settlers in the area as Okiek. Christian missionary activity is relatively recent in Kaplelach and Kipchornwonek areas, quickening after 1980 with the influx of the new settlers who purchased land. Churches were established in the Kipchornwonek area first and have had greater influence there to date.

13. My research and writing about Okiek have been continuous since 1974, but my residence in Okiek communities has been intermittent: in 1974–75, 1982–85, and 1993–94. Between

1985–90, I lived in Nairobi but visited the same communities regularly for periods ranging from a few weeks to a few months at a time. I also spent part of summer 1991 with Okiek.

14. I will say more in chapter 2 about the collection from which the *Okiek Portraits* photographs were selected.

15. Other Kipchornwonek live farther west, stretching to Mulot, while other Kaplelach communities stretch farther east toward Narok. In this brief introduction, I cannot describe fully the changing history of each area where I lived. The Kipchornwonek communities are about an hour's walk from Sogoo, where the first school in this immediate Okiek area was opened (in 1978) and a commercial center developed after a road connected Sogoo to Mulot and Olololunga (in 1979). By the mid-1990s, Nkaroni itself was well on the way to similar development, with shops and a full primary school. As with the general history of Okiek economic diversification in this region, the Kaplelach communities seemed to be undergoing similar processes about a decade later. In the mid-1990s, several small clusters of shops had opened, starting the formation of commercial trading centers, and there were many primary schools in this Kaplelach area, but they did not yet cover all grades.

16. Roland Barthes (1957) is often cited for developing this point in relation to the 1950s photographic exhibition, *The Family of Man,* which combined a family life cycle arrangement (beginning with courtship and marriage) with thematic areas such as work, education, strife, and enjoyment. Barthes's point is important, though as Sandeen (1995, 174–77) discusses, that exhibition also made a strong political statement against nuclear arms and war. Later discussions and critiques of *The Family of Man* usually overlook this feature and pay little attention to the context and historical moment in which it was produced and shown. See chapter 4, note 19.

17. Child and adult are both further differentiated by gender and age: infant (*inkateet*), girl (*ceepta*), boy (*weeriit*), big girl (*ceepta inka oo, melyaat,* or *mebayt*), big boy (*weeriit inka oo*), young woman (*murereet*), mature woman (*ceepyooseet*), old woman (*intasatet*), young man (*muran*), mature/old man (*paayaat*).

18. More detailed discussions of Okiek society and history can be found in Kratz (1990, 1994a, 2000), Klumpp and Kratz (1993), Kratz and Pido (2000), and Blackburn (1976, 1982a).

19. Seven photographs show children (sometimes with adults), ten feature initiation, and fourteen are adults after initiation (including young adults, mature adults, and older adults).

CHAPTER 1. TRACING OKIEK PORTRAITS

1. Beckwith does not specify particular locations and circumstances for her photographs, but the book's acknowledgments mention Lemek, Siyabei, Loita, Magadi, and Ewasoongidongi in Kenya (the first two within about twenty-five miles of Kaplelach and Kipchornwonek Okiek, others ranging from fifty to a hundred miles away).

2. "Insider" status does not automatically guarantee engagement or superior knowledge either. "Insider" is shorthand for a presumed combination of certain kinds of knowledge, ongoing relations within a particular community, and a density of interaction that results from various kinds of socialization and shared life experience. Some who might claim to be "insiders" may not, in fact, have gained and maintained that combination of knowledge, relations, and experience, while others, even a seeming "outsider," may dedicate themselves to learning as much as they can and establishing relations and interactions that over time might come to be like those of an "insider."

3. As noted in the prologue, I use "European" here in the Kenyan sense, which includes all Americans. The corresponding terms in Okiek (*cumpeek,* pl.) and Kiswahili (*wazungu,* pl.) may also refer to Japanese or Kenyans in government positions. The meanings and uses of ethnic and racial categories are discussed in chapter 2.

4. In some cases, stereotypes about Okiek have been reinforced by and reinterpreted in light of historical circumstances. For instance, the name *il Torrobo* means "poor people" in the Maa language. Both English senses of poor would apply to Okiek, according to Maasai: because they had no cattle, they were both impoverished and pathetic. Under colonial administration, roads, health services, markets, and education were developed in other areas of the country to a much greater extent than in forested Okiek areas. Postcolonial policies have only begun to redirect development efforts there. As a result, the measure of Okiek poverty today is not simply a lack of cattle (in fact, many Okiek have cows) but that of other material goods and infrastructure. They have less relative to other areas of Kenya in part because of this history of political and administrative decisions, but material differences are nonetheless interpreted in terms of ethnic character at times. In terms of development, both Maasai *and* Okiek are considered "backward" by some Kenyans and by the international development community.

5. My approach to exhibitions represents an amalgam of perspectives and material drawn from a number of fields and builds on my mode of analyzing ritual performance (1994a). Elsewhere (Kratz 1996), I review several bodies of work of particular relevance to understanding the *Okiek Portraits* exhibition, including analyses of ethnographic writing, cross-cultural research on visual images, the growing literature on museums and cultural display, and critical work in art history and film on the social relations and power involved in looking at images.

6. This aspect of my approach resembles and draws on work that traces the "social life of things" (Appadurai 1986; Miller 1998) and multisited ethnography (Marcus 1995), but I stress the communicative nature of exhibitions and of these processes. I also emphasize broader historical settings and the politics of representation involved in exhibitions.

7. The recent era of public controversies over exhibitions gathered momentum in the 1980s and carried through the 1990s, including disputes over Robert Mapplethorpe's exhibition *The Perfect Moment, The West as America,* the *Enola Gay* exhibition (originally called *The Last Act: The Atomic Bomb and the End of World War II*), and many others. This is not the first time such debates over exhibition representations have figured prominently in U.S. politics. In the years leading up to the McCarthy hearings, "a major art exhibition, Advancing American Art, was not only criticized but investigated by Congress because some of its offending, modernist works had been produced by political leftists" (Sandeen 1995, 110); similar objections were raised about works initially selected by a committee supervised by the Whitney Museum for the 1959 American National Exhibition in Moscow (ibid., 127–29).

8. As U.S. museums developed in the nineteenth century and people learned the conventions associated with them, museums came to be seen this way (Lavine 1988). Museums are institutions with varied social histories and changing relations to a number of constituencies and communities (Harris 1990a; Karp, Kreamer, and Lavine 1992; Bennett 1995).

9. This apparent contradiction is a perennial condition of writing and cultural display. The aim of showing how knowledge is constituted and how social relations figure in the writing/

production process, however, is important. Authority here should not be glossed only as a coercive kind of power. In such enterprises authority always entails an author-ing that involves differences of knowledge, produced through investment and effort and rooted in particular vantage points. But this author-ity—the power, opportunity, and capacity to present a particular viewpoint—need not obliterate other perspectives or always imply immutable power differences. Like power, authority is (and should be) essentially contested, inevitably caught up in disputes about proper use and appropriate perspectives (Arens and Karp 1989, xii; Lukes 1978, 26; Briggs 1996, 236–37). Competing claims to authority and perspective are at the core of the politics of representation; they require persuasion, choices, and judgments. Author-ity, then, entails responsibility for the claims made and for their implications. In trying to simultaneously question stereotypes of Okiek/Africans *and* exhibition conventions, I was making claims about representations but trying to show explicitly that other perspectives and framings were possible. The Okiek viewings and comments discussed in chapter 3 provided some of those perspectives. Two notable exhibitions mounted by the Center for African Art at about the same time also included multiple perspectives: *Perspectives* (1988) and *Art/Artifact* (1989). Fred Wilson also plays several perspectives against one another in his artwork and exhibitions.

10. The path a visitor follows is not necessarily the one exhibition makers envision, introducing multiple spatiotemporal flows that can affect visitors' construal of implied narratives in exhibitions. My discussion of exhibition communication rests on a semiotic approach that Kratz (1994a, 10–11, 20–24) explains in more detail in relation to ritual performance. It draws on Jakobson's model of the multifunctionality of language and understandings of language as social action. These have been developed by many scholars, particularly in linguistic anthropology, including Jakobson (1960); Silverstein (1976); Bauman (1986); Mannheim and Tedlock (1995); and Briggs (1996).

11. Not unique to exhibitions, these communicative features are one foundation of oft-noted similarities between museum exhibitions and ritual. Comparisons between the two typically identify broad correspondences, such as the creation of liminal time and space, potentially transformative effects, and a performative element (Duncan 1988, 1995). However, they do not ask what makes these analogies possible. Multilayered, multimedia communicative structures are one such foundation, relating not just exhibition and ritual, but performance as well. All three are also communicative events framed in ways that distinguish them from daily interaction, even though ordinary interaction continues during an exhibition, ritual, or performance. Further, all three feature metacommunicative aspects: they represent cultural knowledge, values, and/or social life, drawing explicit attention to them in ways that combine conceptual, emotional, and social effects (though in varied ways). Taken together, these features underlie the familiar structural and functional comparisons between exhibition, ritual, and performance: distinctive framing, representational character, and—fundamental to these—their multilayered, multimedia, spatiotemporal communicative structure.

Exhibition, ritual, and performance are related and sometimes blend together, but they are not identical. In specific times and places, they may differ in the degree to which participation is optional, the nature of their institutional siting and definition (religious, political, educational, entertainment etc.), in their locations, topics, the media they combine, transformative intent and effect, and how intentionally constructed their representations are. These dimensions are all factors that may differentiate various kinds of ritual, performance, and exhibition as well (see Abrahams 1976). Few scholars of museums draw explicitly on literature about performance to understand the nature and experience of exhibitions. However, they do sometimes draw on the same sources. For instance, Chambers (1997, 14) turns to Csikszentmihalyi's notion of "flow experience" in an effort to find critical standards for exhibitions, just as Scheckner (1985) did earlier in exploring links among performance, theater, and ritual.

12. Exhibition genres are related to different kinds of museums and settings, but not absolutely tied to them (e.g., a history museum might show art, though it would probably have a history theme or use historical materials) (Karp and Wilson 1996, 252, 261).

13. Andrew Pekarik (1999), curator and scholar of museums, has identified a range of visitor orientations based on their comments about different exhibition components. These different modes of approaching the experience help define what a visitor wants to find and will find satisfying. For instance, visitors oriented particularly to information may appreciate contextualizing videos and long texts, while those who approach an exhibition primarily as an aesthetic, imaginative, or spiritual experience may dislike such material, find it distracting, or ignore it entirely. Visitors may even draw on several orientations in a single exhibition. Pekarik argues, however, that all visitors will have some primary emphasis in approaching particular exhibitions, and perhaps even in how they decide which exhibitions and museums to frequent. Such different patterns of expectation and desire are an important part of what visitors bring to exhibitions and another source of diversity in how people interpret and experience them.

14. Many of the issues united through the notion of "the politics of representation" have been around a long time, but they have received heightened attention in recent decades. The "politics of representation" phrase itself gained currency during this same period. I discuss these developments in appendix A.

15. To be effective, politics of representation must go beyond debates over particular images and matters of content in exhibitions or other cultural forms. They should also include critique of structures and institutions that perpetuate social inequality and problematic representations, as well as action to change these. Adolph Reed (1997a, 1997b, 2000) presents cogent and compelling analysis of the problems with political critique that remains limited to images and lifestyle issues.

16. Writing of the *Enola Gay* exhibition controversy, Martin Harwit (1997) shows that one key tactic is to narrow the definition and number of issues that can be raised. Simplifying subtle arguments and casting aspersions on opponents' intentions and character have also been tactics in public disputes that embroil exhibitions (cf. Lanouette 1997).

17. Of course Americans also go to Kenya for other reasons and often combine tourism, business, development work, education, etc. But the overall contrast remains. Note also that this contrast focuses on a certain range of people in both countries; most Americans and Kenyans will probably never have the opportunity to make such trips. Most Okiek assumed that all Americans are rich because these were the representatives they saw and heard about, presenting the flip side of touristic images of Kenya in the United States.

18. The exhibitionary frame also entails a related tension between pedagogy and performance, a distinction I adapt here from Homi Bhabha's work (1990, 297) on how notions of the nation are constructed. Bhabha identifies this antinomy in the way narratives represent the

nation and how they deal with "the people" (who sometimes stand in for "the nation"). National narratives move between a pedagogical perspective and a performative stance but do not resolve the tension between them. The former emphasizes unity, continuity, cumulative progress, and a totalizing view of nation where the people are "pedagogical objects" (ibid., 302) to be shaped for national identity and allegiance. By contrast, the performative highlights the nation's internal differences, disjunctions, and margins to show that the whole is not just the sum of its parts and that the people are also "performative subjects" who question and decenter any totalizing identification with the nation. Bhabha is not writing about exhibitions, but the tension between pedagogy and performance applies to exhibitions as well. One way people understand exhibitions is by inferring or imputing various exhibition narratives. Those narratives, too, can be both pedagogical and performative, as can interpretative processes involved in exhibitions more generally.

The pedagogical face of exhibits, then, features holistic interpretations, longer temporal trajectories and continuities, and it conveys information in a complete, developed sense. The pedagogical face is clearly part of most exhibitions as their creators envision them. As they develop an exhibition, they usually develop a sense of it as a whole, its general significance, and an overall "story line" that synthesizes its parts. But there is a pedagogical side to visitors' interpretative narratives as well, whether or not they follow the intended paths. The social evolutionary framework that some visitors used to understand *Okiek Portraits* is one example; reviewers also construct encompassing exhibition narratives.

The performative face, in contrast, emphasizes differences and particularities within the exhibition. It highlights the way visitors encounter and appropriate the exhibition: constructing meanings and interpretations as they move through it, following different paths, attending to some parts and not others, attributing various meanings to the exhibition or portions of it. Multiple, discontinuous dimensions of time and space are especially salient here. Exhibition makers, too, fashion performative exhibition accounts, e.g., as they work on particular objects and sections. With its emphasis on interpretive process, this performative face draws particular attention to the diverse aspects of exhibitions. By highlighting differential engagements, it points again to complexities accompanying multiple politics of representation as formulated and communicated through exhibitions.

19. Trachtenberg's history of photography in the U.S. (1989, 21–32) shows that these contrasts framed debates about uses of photography from the start, not least because of market competition between photographers and artists who made portrait miniatures. In a marvelous essay on different interpretations of the interconnected histories of photography and anthropology, Pinney (1992) develops the argument that contrasts drawn between photography and painting parallel those made between speaking and writing, and that both contrasts are illusory. At times some boundary questions might seem resolved, but photography always raises more. Debates about whether or not photography is art were most heated in the late 1800s and the 1920s, "with Edward Weston accusing pictorialist photographers of making 'pseudo-paintings' instead of 'photographs'" (Barrett 1990, 132), but such debates are far from over. Richard Woodward wrote about these questions in the *New York Times* in 1988: "It isn't clear anymore how photography should be valued or looked at, where within our museums it should be exhibited—even what is or is not a photograph." Jeff Wall's photography illustrates this: "Straddling the boundaries between photography, painting, and film, Wall's work also extends into areas typically considered outside the realm of fine art"

(Viso 1997). Michael Kimmelman, chief art critic for the *New York Times* in 1997, made a similar observation (1997, 44): "The old wall separating traditional documentary photography from art photography has clearly come down—for better and worse, meaning that too many artists today think their snapshots are art just because they took them, and too many photojournalists seem to forget that documentary photography done well is art already and needn't be gussied up with artsy touches to make it so. Then again, there are photographers . . . who now move easily between documentary and art photography and understand the distinctive merits of each."

20. For Okiek viewers, this cross-cultural aspect was not based on the photographs themselves but on recognizing that their images and lives would seem strange to others.

21. Schildkrout perceptively describes such differences in two installations of *African Reflections: Art from Northeastern Zaire,* an exhibition she co-curated (quoted in Vogel et al. 1994, 14–15).

CHAPTER 2. PRODUCING OKIEK PORTRAITS

1. My early reflections on these issues produced a slide-sound work included in *Monuments,* a juried exhibition of visual sociology shown in two venues in 1976.

2. In addition to the *Okiek Portraits* exhibition, I wrote articles (Kratz 1988, 1992) for *Kenya Past and Present,* a journal addressed to a general audience published by the Kenya Museum Society. After my initial research in the 1970s, I published a two-part article on Okiek birthing and parenting in a popular U.S. magazine, *Mothers' Manual.* When I was contacted by the *Disappearing World* television series in 1988, I also wrote a scenario for consideration (though it did not portray Okiek as "disappearing" or "endangered"—perhaps one reason it was not produced).

3. O'Hanlon (1993, 82) also saw his exhibition about New Guinea Highlanders as an opportunity to question popular images and stereotypes. His fine book is one of several new ethnographic and historical studies of particular exhibitions (Sandeen 1995; Fienup-Riordan 1999).

4. Lawuyi (1991) discusses congratulatory newspaper advertisements in Nigeria; such advertisements are part of relations between business and government in Kenya as well.

5. Feld translated his book about Kaluli people in Papua New Guinea and discussed it with them after it was published (in 1982). He calls (1990, 241) dialogic editing the "discourse that developed in these encounters, . . . negotiations of what Kaluli and [he] said to, about, with, and through each other, juxtapositions of Kaluli voices and [his] own." Unlike Feld's situation, however, I could consult Okiek at various points along the way to the finished exhibition.

6. Fienup-Riordan (1999) describes such disjunctions in a local exhibition that began with Yup'ik Eskimo collaboration and traveled to national museums.

7. Large Cibachromes were not yet being produced in Kenya. Lufthansa German Airways provided transportation for this trip as exhibition sponsorship.

8. The group included Jackie Davis of the Kenya Museum Society, Ivan Karp, Donna Klumpp, Fiona Marshall, Christine Obbo, and Aidan Southall.

9. Ten days later, a young man from the area passed through Nairobi to return to secondary school; he brought a report of what had happened and a note saying, "They are proposing to come [still] but I don't know when." A letter with further explanations and apologies came in late September, before I returned to visit again.

10. "Market" is not always the best metaphor for talking about cultural production, circula-

tion, exchange, and consumption; economic dimensions that can make it apt sometimes recede into the background. Identities can become defined in commodity terms, or cast as "symbolic capital," and figure as images and objects in commodity flows. But identities also shape the interactions through which those flows, images, and objects are created in ways not reducible to commodification and market logics alone. Freeman's (1999) study of women workers in the Caribbean's growing off-shore informatics industry illlustrates this point.

11. Apart from sponsorship, the exhibition had two economic aspects that I did not anticipate at the start. Poster sales subsidized exhibition costs in Kenya and also raised money for Okiek schools. U.S. venues paid an exhibition fee that I used to cover costs in the U.S.; the balance again went to support Okiek schools.

12. Coffee-table books include Jones 1977; Fedders and Salvadori 1984; Fisher 1984; Beckwith and Saitoti 1980; Beckwith and Fisher 1990; and Magor 1994. *Images of Kenya* (1986) was one comparable exhibition in Kenya. Other media images include films such as *Out of Africa, Kitchen Toto, The Ghost and the Darkness,* and *The Air Up There,* as well as television shows, advertising campaigns, etc.

13. Tracing such connections would require a detailed social history of visual resources, identifying their sources and implications in diverse institutions and relations of power and knowledge. "What lies 'behind' the paper or 'behind' the image is not reality—the referent—but reference: a subtle web of discourse through which realism is enmeshed in a complex fabric of notions, representations, images, attitudes, gestures, and modes of actions which function as everyday know-how, 'practical ideology,' norms, within and through which people live their relations to the world" (Tagg 1988, 100).

14. Appiah's distinction (1990; 1992, 13–14) between intrinsic and extrinsic racism can be extended to biases associated with stereotypes generally. Racialist assumptions provide the problematic cognitive basis for both, but extrinsic racism (or extrinsic stereotypes) *are* abandoned in the face of contradictory evidence. Appiah shows (1992, 34) how closely related racial and ethnic distinctions were for W. E. B. DuBois, a matter of different emphases and distinctive features marking group boundaries in different sociopolitical contexts. While reading about stereotypes, I dipped into related work on race and racisms as well, though I certainly do not attempt here a thorough review of either literature.

15. This tenacity is so salient that it is part of the definition of stereotype in the textbook *Theory and Problems in Social Psychology:* "a tendency for a belief to be oversimplified in content and unresponsive to the objective facts" (Krech and Crutchfield 1948, cited in the *Oxford English Dictionary;* see note 34). In relation to exhibitions, one must ask how the ephemeral experience of an exhibition can alter something defined by cognitive tenacity?

16. Both images are prominent through centuries of European representations of Africans; Africans serve as contrast for European ideas about themselves (Hammond and Jablow [1970] 1992, 11; White 1978, 150–96).

17. See Wilmsen and McAllister (1996) on power in ethnic politics.

18. They have some limited currency beyond Kenya in fiction and early travel literature, portrayals that seem to derive from ethnic characterizations made by other Kenyans.

19. Ndegwa (1997) examines the dual citizenship of nation and ethnicity in Kenya. Ndegwa (1998, 361–64) discusses how ethnicity figures in the discourse of citizenship and economic rights.

20. Evidence for this point is scattered and fragmentary; little systematic research has been done. Falk and Holland (1992) and research for the Field Museum's permanent exhibition on Africa

(1991) both provide support. Perin (1992, 208, 197–99) offers evidence on African American notions about Africa (emphasizing missionaries, apartheid, and romantic fantasies) and anecdotes about visitors who comment, while looking at exhibits about African life, "We wouldn't want to be there—it's scary. There's nothing similar in our experience."

21. *Okiek Portraits* could be seen through a range of named identities and groups, in increasing specificity: black people, Africans, Kenyans, Kalenjin-speakers, Okiek, Kaplelach and Kipchornwonek, people of specific settlements and families, particular individuals. As later chapters discuss, U.S. visitors emphasized the most general categories, never more specific than Okiek and usually not including Kalenjin. Kenyan visitors focused especially on the interplay between ethnic identities (Okiek and Kalenjin) and national identity. Okiek themselves commented on every kind of identity possible when they looked at the photographs.

22. British images of Africa followed their geographical progress into the continent. West Africa, central to the slave trade, attracted attention first, followed some fifty years later by South Africa, and later still Central and East Africa. "With each new dimension, the image spread and took on local variations, but for Britain itself the early-nineteenth-century image of Africa was, in fact, the image of West Africa" (Curtin 1964, xii). Curtin and Hammond and Jablow were among the first studies to focus on such images and representations; Jordan (1968), too, finds it necessary to justify his focus on "attitudes." Such topics have become the norm today, but rarely contain the careful historical, ethnographic, and analytical grounding of these earlier studies. Mphahlele (1962) also wrote about political and literary images of Africans at this time.

23. Appiah (1992, 62) summarizes the argument: "the very invention of Africa (as something more than a geographical entity) must be understood, ultimately, as an outgrowth of European racialism; the notion of Pan-Africanism was founded on the notion of the African, which was, in turn, founded not on any genuine cultural commonality but, as we have seen, on the very European concept of the Negro." Pan-Africanist ideas were reinterpreted and adapted in later formulations of African nationalism and over time gained further meanings and resonances on the African continent. Appiah notes, for instance (44), "If DuBois's race concept seems an all-too-American creation, its traces in African rhetoric are legion." Appiah sees this problematic racialist basis as a continual plague to concepts of pan-Africanism and ideas about African commonalities (62): "Simply put, the course of cultural nationalism in Africa has been to make real the imaginary identities to which Europe has subjected us."

24. The historian Frances White (1990) offers trenchant analysis of how stereotypes of Africa figure in recent versions of African American nationalism and the conservative positions they espouse on gender and sexuality.

25. See Kratz (1981, 360–61) on Okiek as Kenya's autochthonous people.

26. For instance, the forested nature of Okiek areas contributes to Kenyan evaluations but not American ones.

27. Munasinghe (1997), Coetzee (1996), Segato (1998), Poole (1997), and Brodkin (1998) show how race and ethnicity have been defined and interconnected in other settings and times.

28. Many people were brought from India to work as laborers, artisans, and clerks while building the railroad from Mombasa to Uganda in the late 1890s. Of about 30,000 workers (mainly Punjabi), roughly 6,000 stayed on. People from Gujerati, Goa, and other parts of India also came to Kenya for other reasons, at earlier and later times (Salvadori 1983, 9).

29. See Ambler (1988), Spear and Waller (1993), Lonsdale (1977), Berman and Lonsdale (1992), and Bravman (1998).

30. The phrasing is from Homi Bhabha (1986, 150): "epithets racial or sexual come to be seen as modes of differentiation, realized as multiple, cross-cutting determinations . . . crucial to the binding of a range of differences and discriminations that inform the discursive and political practices of racial and cultural hierarchization."

31. South African philosopher David Goldberg (1990, xii–xiii) makes the same argument about forms and effects of racisms.

32. Philosophical work on racism offers another synthesis (Goldberg 1990).

33. Paul (1995, 4) and Gardner (1991, 3) illustrate this by listing vapid attempts to do so. Gardner identifies a simple core agreement, that stereotypes are beliefs, with variation in whether they are individual beliefs or shared, communitywide beliefs. He argues that the consensual nature of stereotypes has important implications.

34. According to the *Oxford English Dictionary* (2d ed.), the word "stereotype" was initially used in the late 1790s to describe a new printing method that used a plate cast from a mold. It could also refer to the plate used in the process. By 1850 the word also had a figurative sense based on such mechanical reproduction, meaning a phrase or manner of speaking that was constantly used, repeated without change. The sense of stereotype now most familiar, i.e., "a preconceived and oversimplified idea of the characteristics which typify a person, situation, etc., and attitudes based on such preconceptions," is first cited in 1922. A 1935 text in social psychology emphasizes the results of such prejudgment, linking stereotype with bias and prejudice. A 1948 text definition incorporates the much remarked resilience of stereotypes in the face of counterevidence (see note 15). Prototypes may represent the "typical," but a "prototype effect" is a generalization that might be based on a variety of case examples or experiences: the best case, the first case, the most frequent, the most notorious, the most recent, etc. (B. Shore, p.c.).

35. This higher taxonomic unity provides the means to simultaneously deny the distinctions created through stereotypes, stressing universal humanism. The taxonomic boundary between human and animal is questioned in some stereotypes. One way to rank a type of people as low as possible is to deny their very humanity (cf. Balibar 1990, 290).

36. As a mode of reasoning, essentializing is not limited to social stereotypes, but "virtually all systems of racial thinking share a commitment to essentialism, a commitment to the notion that members of any particular group share a common essence that underlies the group's nature and development" (Hirschfeld 1997, 64). Like Hirschfeld, Stoler (1997) emphasizes the interplay of visible and nonvisible criteria in constituting the resilience of racist reasoning; this is related to what I call projecting explicit criteria of ranking onto other domains.

37. This helps explain why historicizing stereotypes is a common strategy in countering their misrepresentations. Demonstrating historical change for those stereotyped or stereotypes themselves helps undercut premises that might otherwise seem "natural" or taken for granted. "Classification and hierarchy are above all else operations of naturalization, or more accurately, the projection of historical and social differences onto an imaginary nature" (Balibar 1990, 290). But note that stereotyping and representations of "tradition" can overlap in this (Kratz 1993).

38. Brilliant (1991, 105) discusses stereotyping of public figures (e.g., royalty, movie stars), where viewers project cognitive representations onto familiar, omnipresent images. Public rela-

tions managers try to shape and control both the images and the characters attributed to them.

39. The dynamics of social interaction and subject formation associated with stereotypes can produce an enduring ambivalence that is also part of this fixity-fluidity amalgam, making "the stereotype . . . an ambivalent mode of knowledge and power. . . . It is the force of ambivalence that gives the colonial stereotype its currency; ensures its repeatability in changing historical and discursive conjunctures; informs its strategies of individuation and marginalization; produces that effect of probabilistic truth and predictability which, for the stereotype, must always be in *excess* of what can be empirically proved or logically construed" (Bhabha 1986, 148–49 [original emphasis]).

40. Wilmsen (1996, 4) stresses this for ethnicity: "Ethnicity arises in the exercise of power. It has no singular construction; there must always be two, usually more, ethnicities to be defined against each other."

41. Category domains related to social groups interlock with other kinds of categories, too, making links yet more pervasive. Gupta (1995, 393) finds connections between notions of "the state" and the imagination of a range of social groupings.

42. Foucault (1970, 1972) brought attention to the important role such dispersal plays in cultural formations. It is a foundational concept for his later studies of institutions and discursive formations related to madness and to sexuality. Fabian (1978) uses the notion of dispersal to look at cross-media relations and thematic developments in African popular culture. Fabian's paper remains one of the clearest examples of the methodological implications of Foucault's notion for anthropology. Pinney (1997, 37–38, 190) cites Said to make a similar point about the parallel "proofs" that texts, museum artifacts, and other modes of documentation provide for social typologies, and emphasizes the "inter-ocularity" of popular visual culture in India.

43. Hammond and Jablow ([1970] 1992) and Curtin (1964) trace the history of representations of Africa in Britain. Gordon traces another such history in *Picturing Bushmen* (1997). He considers how representations of Africa circulate by focusing on the Denver African Expedition of 1925, how it was reported, and its photographs. He identifies an important shift toward the romantic image of Bushmen and the "disappearing culture" theme that now permeate popular culture and explores sources of this shift. A *New York Times* article on the commodification of identity politics considers multicultural fashion styles (e.g., collections based on Maasai dress styles by Ralph Lauren and others) and how models of color are used to promote them. The opening line states, "stereotypes are the shorthand of sitcoms and stylists" (Spindler 1997); *Harper's Bazaar* (1992) also extols Maasai taste as a fashion design source. In related work elsewhere, Dominy (1993, 326–28) looks at how images and narratives representing New Zealand's high country have circulated among photojournalism, newspaper accounts, films, novels, and anthropology from at least the 1940s until now. She shows how images and narratives are used and reused with little sense of their prior history or the different perspectives they promote, buying into existing iconography without critical consideration. Gupta's (1995) analysis of notions of corruption and the state in north India offers another example of key images and narratives circulating across contexts and media, and how such dispersal features in cultural understandings and social action and institutions. One might adapt the concept of the "public historical sphere" from Tony Bennett's superb work to see these as various examples of "public ethnographic/ his-

torical spheres." Like Foucault's notion of dispersal, Bennett's concept (1995, 132, 146) refers to the way historical representation occurs across a range of institutions, texts, and media.

44. The following example shows that a single site is not sufficient, that exhibition influence depends on visitors' initial knowledge and frames of reference, and that repetition and multiple sites can maintain or strengthen visitor orientations as well as change them. A 1988 study (Fronville and Doering, cited in Perin 1992, 194–96) of a tropical rainforest exhibition found that visitors already knowledgeable and concerned about rainforests considered the exhibition informative, clear, and used images from the exhibition in their post-visit discussion. Visitors with little or no prior interest or knowledge understood the basic message that rainforests are disappearing but found the exhibition confusing and had no opinions about rainforests on the exit survey. "The more familiarity visitors have with its topic, the greater an exhibition's influence."

45. Fabian (1996b) develops the concept of "recognition" for situations of actual encounter; exhibitions present a situation of displaced encounter, with parties from both sides imagining the other. Okiek commentaries in labels, however, brought impressions from their side of the interaction to visitors. Fabian considers possibilities for "recognition" as mediated through objects.

46. Such images were prevalent in 1992 visitor research for *African Voices,* the new Africa Hall at the Smithsonian's National Museum of Natural History (opened in 1999). It suggested that notions of "tribe" and cultural evolution are important in American ideas about Africa, and that the past is the "default" temporal orientation to Africa. Wild animals figured in 22 percent of visitor responses; images of violence and starvation were also mentioned by those interviewed. "Visitors, regardless of race/ethnicity, recognized that the United States media and educational system had not provided adequate information about Africa" (Falk and Holland 1992). The Field Museum (1991) reached similar conclusions. International media images from mid- or late 1980s crises of drought and starvation may have been especially prominent in the late 1980s and early 1990s. Conflict images were hardly absent when I produced *Okiek Portraits* in 1989, but many long-term conflicts that contribute to images of war, violence, and refugees now so prominent had not yet begun (Liberia 1989, Sierra Leone 1991, Somalia 1992, Rwanda 1994, Zaire/Congo 1997). Ebron (2000, 916) notes that U.S. images of Africa can have a romantic, spiritual side as well.

47. "Similarly, the editors of the 1983 book *El Salvador* found that, even with the work of thirty [media] photographers to draw from, there were not enough images that delved into the daily lives of the country's inhabitants, so insistent and repetitive were the publications in their assignments" (Ritchkin 1999, 32).

48. Unlike Okiek, the Bushmen peoples in parts of southern Africa were subjects of considerable photography from the beginning of the century (Gordon 1997).

49. There were other reasons for using only color. Photographers advised me that successfully mixing the two is hard in a single exhibition unless it is broken into sections; *Okiek Portraits* would be small and the layout simple.

50. Abu-Lughod (1993, 7–32) emphasized personal narratives in a similar strategy suited to written form, also drawing strength from humanistic appeals while wary of their potential for veiling social, political, and economic inequalities.

51. The emphasis on people and portraits eliminated other formally interesting images, but aesthetics were just one concern I sought to balance in the exhibition. The contrast be-

tween research archive and exhibition archive here generally parallels a distinction Barrett (1990, 71) draws between explanatory photographs and ethically evaluative photographs.

52. Hagaman's account of the conventions of photojournalism and her development of a different photographic vocabulary for photographically exploring religion in America present a similar juxtaposition of visual conventions. My portrait choices may have been influenced by some of the very photojournalistic conventions she describes (1996, 10, 22), e.g., personalizing images and having the central visual focus "pop" against a slightly blurred background.

53. The cracked skin on her legs, most likely pellagra, also introduces a reddish tone; exhibition visitors in the U.S. often brought this detail to my attention.

54. Ritchkin (1999, 73–76) describes a 1947 *Life* magazine test that asked readers to decide, on the basis of image alone, which of twenty-eight people were criminals and which mystery writers. He notes how photographic angle, lighting, and backdrop influenced the decisions readers made.

55. In a study of *National Geographic* photographs discussed below, Americans often saw such costume combinations as incongruous and used them to construct social evolutionary readings (Lutz and Collins 1993, 238, 241, 247–53). Wakanyote's full review draws on the traditional/modern categories to construct a related reading, phrased in terms of "development" (see Karp 1993). See Landau (1987) on evolutionary narratives and Kratz (1993) on notions of tradition.

56. Bennett examines how such displays proliferated in the nineteenth century into an exhibitionary complex (1988, 1995). As Hall states this general argument (1996, 252): "The very notion of an autonomous, self-produced and self-identical cultural identity . . . had in fact to be discursively constructed in and through 'the Other,' through a system of similarities and differences."

57. To Kenyans, "European" includes all Americans.

58. A study (Csikszentmihalyi and Rochberg-Halton 1981, 69) of the meaning of objects for contemporary (1970s) urban Americans stressed the importance of family photographs: "More than any other object in the home, photos serve the purpose of preserving the memory of personal ties. In their ability to arouse emotion there is no other type of object that can surpass them." It also described the interactions people have with photographs and their effects (224): "Through these photos this woman's identity and sense of self have been enlarged to include experiences that have been transmitted indirectly to her through symbols and which give her a broader perspective in which to confront life." Cohen et al. (1992, 213–14) note that photographs of the exotic and strange are another favorite subject matter, in addition to "faces you know."

59. Technological shifts have been important conditions in the histories of photographic portraiture. These include "the fully corporate stage of dry-plate, camera and photofinishing industries of the 1880s and 1890s" (Tagg 1992, 172) that helped make worldwide spread of photography possible and the later proliferation of color photographs and automatic processing, which began in the 1970s and 1980s in Africa. The latter has been seen as threatening the livelihood of African studio photographers (Werner 1996; Magnin 1995; Azaglo 1996, 90), or at least their practice as developed between the 1930s and 1970s. Hagaman (1996, 8–11) discusses a technological shift within U.S. newspaper photography in the 1960s with implications for photographic conventions. These are only one part of diverse histories and photographies. With characteristic incisiveness, Tagg comments (173): "To talk about

the emergence of amateur photographies is to talk of the tracing out of new levels of meaning and practice, new hierarchies of cultural institutions, and new structures and codes of subjectivity: processes unquestionably bound up with technological innovation and the restructuring of production and marketing, but equally part of the momentum of a reconstitution of the family, sexuality, consumption and leisure that plots a new economy of desire and domination. . . . [I]t is never . . . a simple unrolling, economically and technologically driven process. The formation of amateur photographies had always to be negotiated in and across the fields of specific national structures, cultural conventions, languages, practices, constructed traditions and institutions" (cf. Clarke 1997, 19).

60. Some scholars simply assert "the power of a facial expression to compel attention, even (or perhaps especially) when it is mediated by the photographic medium" (Poignant 1992, 44) or note "our extraordinary sensitivity to [the] nuances [of the human face]" (Ritchkin 1999, 65). Others explain the attraction of faces (and portraiture generally) in terms of the communicative role facial expression plays in human interaction, early childhood bonding, and socialization (Brilliant 1990, 12–13; 1991, 9–10). In 1901 social theorist Georg Simmel (1959, 279–80) noted, "The face is the most remarkable aesthetic synthesis of the formal principles of symmetry and of individuality."

61. How mimetic resemblance should be is variable. African portraits that use photographs as models seem like relatively generalized representations to some viewers (see the 1990 special issues of *African Arts* on portraiture in Africa). Fifteenth-century religious painting provides another example. Michael Baxandall (1972, 40–56) describes active interaction between painters' representations of religious figures and the devotional conventions of the time, which included intense, personal, detailed visualization during meditation. "The public mind was not a blank tablet on which the painters' representations of a story or person could impress themselves; it was an active institution of interior visualization with which every painter had to get along" (45). In this situation, popular religious painters did not create detailed, lifelike images, but rather "painted people who are general, unparticularized, interchangeable types. They provided a base . . . on which the pious beholder could impose his personal detail, more particular but less structured than what the painter offered" (47).

62. Oguibe's argument is interesting, if problematic. It is based almost entirely on limited Yoruba examples, and those examples do not include discussions with Yoruba about photography. Though the notion of a unitary Yoruba people did not develop until after 1900 (Peel 1989), Yoruba loom large in studies of African art history because they are well documented—their art can be traced over six centuries—and because some ancient Yoruba art had a naturalistic tradition. Nonetheless, generalizing about all twentieth-century Africa on the basis of Yoruba is like generalizing about all Europe on the basis of Yorkshire, England. The only non-Yoruba example cited is Pankhurst's (1992) fascinating discussion of photography's role in Ethiopian political struggles in the early twentieth century. That example, however, relies centrally on understanding photographs as representing reality as well as trying to legitimize particular political outcomes.

63. In other cases, these are the primary means of associating image, identity, and individual. Borgatti distinguishes three kinds of portraits: generalized portraits with generic physical features whose identification with particular individuals depends on naming and context; emblematic portraits that represent individuals by including things associated with them but do not necessarily resemble them physically; and representational portraits that por-

tray individuals through visual correspondence with their physical appearance (Borgatti and Brilliant 1990; Borgatti 1990a; Brilliant 1991, 46–49). In semiotic terms, these different kinds of portraits emphasize indexical, symbolic, and iconic associations respectively, but all combine several sign modes. Clarke (1997, 109) describes examples of portrait association through objects.

64. This is widely recognized in literature on portraits and photography, though various terms are used (Tagg 1988, 37; Mohr 1992, 37–39; Brilliant 1991, 10; Clarke 1992). Trachtenberg (1989, 27) discusses the development of understandings of surface appearance as a sign of inner truth and individual character (cf. Clarke 1997, 101–2). Anthropological work on personhood, distinguishing person and individual, is highly relevant (Jackson and Karp 1990; Karp 1997).

65. Photographer and subject do not always have the same understanding of conventions either, so portraits cannot be assumed to have been produced through a single set of codes or conventions portraying identity. For instance, my sense of portraiture differed from that of Okiek whom I photographed (chapter 3). Clarke (1992, 74) describes the complexity of such signs: "The portraits are full of visual codes in which social identity and position at once establish significance and declare status: clothes, of course, but equally rings and medals; the merest detail is often a sign of a collective code affirming significance."

66. Others also note these temporal ambiguities and how they encompass the future (Barthes 1981, 95–99; Edwards 1992, 7). Samuel (1994, 315–36) discusses how understandings of history are related to photography and popular culture.

67. Different ways of looking and viewing are also appropriate to different settings and objects, as art historian Susan Vogel (1997) shows through subtle exploration of Baule art in Côte d'Ivoire.

68. This general sketch simply notes several issues and variables involved. As Tagg (1998, 18–19) observes, "the field of portraiture . . . is divided, over its entire range, into a number of zones defined by different forms of practice, different economies, technical bases, semiotic resources, and cultural statuses. No absolute set of criteria crosses these zones. Nor can their separation be seen as a ready-made basis for evaluation. Rather, we must try to grasp their historically produced relations not only as levels in the market, but as levels in a hierarchy of practices whose most privileged strata, increasingly sustained by post-market institutions, are called 'Art,' whose middle ground ranges from 'commercial art' to 'craft,' and whose lower registers are designated 'kitsch,' 'vernacular,' 'amateur,' or 'popular culture.'" Information on photographic histories in Africa is still too limited to fully describe the diversity found there.

69. Contemporary ethnographic photography, for instance, has roots in all three. John Tagg (1988) has written splendid and influential essays on the social history of photography in the U.S. and western Europe, considering all these portrait traditions. Trachtenberg (1989) outlines the early development of daguerreotype and photographic studio portraits in the U.S. and considers several case studies in documentary photography. Some examples of photographers from post-1950 Africa who work in several idioms: Ouedraogo (1996) profiles a photographer in Burkina Faso who makes both personal portraits and identity cards; Werner (1996) also finds that identity photographs are an economic staple of studios in Côte d'Ivoire. Cornélius Yao Augustt Azaglo, a Ghanaian national who worked in Togo and Côte d'Ivoire, opened an Ivoirian studio in 1955. Though identity cards may have been his main support, he combined them with personal studio portraits (Azaglo 1996, 92–93). Seydou Keita, fast becoming one of the best-known African studio photographers, did stu-

dio portraits (1948–62) and worked as Mali's official photographer (1962–77). Pinney's (1997) discussion of photographic traditions in India is a valuable comparative source.

70. See Poole (1997, 112–14) on the differences and interactions between personal portraiture and portraits that defined social "types" in *cartes de visite,* the collection and display of both kinds of *cartes* in albums, and the role of *cartes* in defining global conventions of photographic portraiture in the 1860s to 1880s.

71. "The more informal the pose, the more confidence we have in it. But . . . nothing is more contrived than the natural, or more carefully prepared than the spontaneous shot" (Samuel 1994, 366). Informal candids were not adopted uniformly across all classes and social groups.

72. South Africa had fewer than forty studios by 1861 (Bensusan 1966, 13); there were forty-eight studios in the Cape between 1846 and 1870 (Gordon 1997, 177). Traveling photographers served smaller South Africa towns without studios (Bensusan 1966, 22). The history of photography in Africa is woefully uncharted, but studios were also open in Mozambique by 1889 (ibid., 31), in Sierra Leone by the late 1860s (Viditz-Ward 1987), in Zanzibar by at least 1868, and in Kenya by 1899 (Monti 1987). In Namibia, studios had been opened in Windhoek and all large towns by the late 1920s (Gordon 1997, 3). Bensusan (1966) surveys early photographic history in South Africa, particularly among settlers and sojourners. Monti (1987) and Viditz-Ward (1987) identify some of the earliest known professional African photographers: Da Costa (1895, Nigeria), N. Walwin Holm (1883, Ghana), F. R. C. Lutterodt (1889, Ghana), S. Albert St. John, Dionysius Leomy, and W. S. Johnston (all 1880s, Sierra Leone), and Alphonso Lisk-Carew (1905, Sierra Leone). Meïssa Gaye was photographing in Senegal soon after 1915, though he did not open a studio until 1945 (Pivin 1994, 67–69). In 1914, an as yet unidentified photographer in Lomé, Togo, took several portraits shown in *Africa Explores* (Vogel 1991, 138–39). It seems photography became more widespread as a possible profession for Africans in the 1910s to 1930s. Judging from the few biographies of African photographers, there was a surge of studio openings soon after World War II as well (Pivin 1994; Magnin 1995; Azaglo 1996).

73. Yoruba make other kinds of photographic portraits, too, using other poses and conventions. Sprague (1978a) does not discuss these at length but notes that Yoruba photographers and subjects who draw on more Euro-American conventions specialize and adapt them in particular ways.

74. Bensusan (1966, 24–29, 80–86) identifies some early photography by explorers. Gordon (1997, 19–28) reviews part of the history of photographic practice in expeditions and early travelers' accounts, including how these images were linked to popular genres of display. The Denver African Expedition of 1925, his focus, emphasized photographic documentation and pictures of people; its photographs were widely distributed and reproduced, in part by the World Picture Service. Geary (1988) studied German colonial photography in one Cameroon kingdom early this century. To date, scholarship on African photography has focused on work by explorers, missionaries, colonial photographers, and others who produced representations *of* Africa, with little attention to African photographers or African understandings of photography (cf. Jewsiewicki 1996, 7; Werner 1996, 81–82). With the exception of Sprague's early study (reported in two articles with similar texts but different images: 1978a, 1978b), little has been written about African photographic aesthetics or how photographs are used in various African contexts.

New interest in African photography and photographers burgeoned in the early 1990s

(Viditz-Ward 1987; Pivin 1994; Azaglo 1996; Bell et al. 1996; Magnin 1995, 1997), some sparked by work by African photographers included in the 1991 *Africa Explores* exhibition (Vogel 1991). For instance, Borgatti's work on African portraiture, published in 1990, does not explicitly consider photography, though several studies in her guest-edited *African Arts* issues give passing mention to photographs as models for portraits in other media or incorporation of photographic portraits in masquerades and ritual settings. So far the new interest in African photography has revolved around rediscovering early studio photographers (most from francophone West Africa in the 1930s to 1960s). It emphasizes their artistic sensibility and the aesthetic power of their work but these celebratory presentations do not yet include serious explorations of local aesthetics, uses, or histories of photography in Africa. (The 1996 Guggenheim exhibition also includes African photojournalists who worked on *Drum* in the 1950s and early 1960s and more recent African "art" photographers working throughout the world [Bell et al. 1996].)

A few recent studies have begun to trace the contours and meanings of local photographic practice in particular places (Werner 1993, 1996; Ouedraogo 1996; Behrend 1998, 2000; Wendl and du Plessis 1998; Mustafa i.p.) and a multidisciplinary research group on African photography (called Photons) has been formed (Werner 1996, 110). This recent work is strongly biased toward West Africa (as is Borgatti's work on African portraiture). Eastern African photography has received little scholarly attention as yet, apart from a popular biography of photojournalist Mohammed Amin (Tetley 1988). Chapter 3 discusses this further. To my knowledge, no one has followed up Sprague's observation about the difference within Nigeria between Hausa and Yoruba interest in and development of photography either (1978a, 59).

75. Werner notes commonalities of layout and general photographic practice among West African studios and their similarity to European studios of 1860 to 1950 (1996, 101).

76. Keita used his bedspread as a backdrop initially but then changed his background hanging every few years (which allowed him to date images) (Magnin 1995). Viditz-Ward (1987, 516), Wendl (1998), and Appadurai (1997) discuss studio backdrops in Sierra Leone, Ghana, and India.

77. Keita's props and practice suggest success and relative prosperity, and he owns several houses in Bamako today. However, he claims to have profited little from his work (French 1997).

78. Nor is this topic well studied elsewhere. Stokes (1992, 197) describes research on changing conventions for photographic portraits in immigrant and religious groups in Manchester, England.

79. Most observations concern incorporation of photographic portraits into commemorative and funeral contexts, again often for elites, though there is surely a wide and varied range of personal use and display. *Future Remembrance* is an entertaining film that shows studio photographers in relation to commemorative image arts in Ghana (Wendl and du Plessis 1998).

80. Commenting during discussions at the December 1992 visual anthropology conference in San Francisco, Karl Heider (p.c.) noted that a focus on portraits could accentuate a vacuum common in ethnographic photography. Ethnographic photos tend to show isolated individuals, people attending to a task or the photographer, distanced groups, village scenes, and landscapes. Few photographs show intense interaction and discussion among those portrayed, a remarkable absence when people spend a great deal of time in this way.

81. Interviews were conducted in Binghamton, New York, and on the island of Oahu, Hawaii (Lutz and Collins 1993, 223–24).

82. Gaze was a matter of explicit instruction in early American daguerreotype portraits: "the eyes should be directed a little sideways above the camera, and fixed upon some object there, but never upon the apparatus, since this would tend to impart to the face a dolorous, dissatisfied look" (quoted in Trachtenberg 1989, 26). In *The Gallery of Illustrious Americans,* Mathew Brady's ambitious 1850 project, the men shown are "indifferent to spectators (an effect achieved by looking anywhere but into the lens). . . . Not only would an intimate gaze into the eyes of a viewer be unseemly, but the distant look, the guise of introspection or reflection, allows the characteristic lines of the face and the weight of the body to display themselves without distraction" (ibid., 46).

83. They differ in geographic and temporal coverage, total number of photographs, and also their manner of presentation. Lutz and Collins used the photographs without captions in their interviews.

84. *Okiek Portraits* and the interviews were roughly contemporaneous. When I heard of the *Geographic* work in 1993, I contacted Lutz. I thank her for sending several prepublication chapters when I was working on the visitor study described in chapter 5.

85. Visitor profiles can vary considerably, however, for different types of museums. Merriman (1989) discusses visitor profiles in Britain.

86. Of 600 total photographs, 468 were coded for type of gaze within the picture. Comparing photographs before and after 1970, they found no significant difference, though the presence of Westerners in photographs dropped sharply after 1969 (ibid., 143).

87. The 74 percent nonfrontal includes photographs of groups concentrated on a task or event as well as portraits where people turn obliquely from the camera. Smiles were ambiguous in some pictures. I included photographs where people have partially open mouths, though the status of their expression as a smile was not always entirely clear. *National Geographic* figures are based on 436 photographs with visible facial expressions.

88. The chi square is significant at more than a .01 level ($\chi^2_{(1)} = 20.92$). Thanks to Howard Balshem for working through these figures with me.

89. Yet photographic eye contact is paradoxical, Barthes notes, because the subject looks the viewer straight in the eye without seeing her (1981, 111–12).

90. My choices may have been inflected by variations in U.S. photographic conventions related to class, ethnicity, or other distinctions as well, but I am unaware that such variations have been clearly identified. Chalfen considers the themes and organization of Japanese American home photography and albums. He notes a change over time in the extent to which people in these family photographs smile (1991, 211). I calculated the proportion of smiling figures in *Okiek Portraits* to parallel Lutz and Collins's figures, though again smiles might be understood in several ways. Exchanges on the VISCOM (Visual Communication) e-mail discussion list in 1996 considered how and when Americans began to smile for photographs. No answer was proposed, but interesting comments were made. Hess (26 March 1996) recalled John Berger ([1972] 1987, 104) on seventeenth-century Dutch paintings: "The poor smile as they offer what they have for sale. (They smile showing their teeth, which the rich never do.) They smile at the better-off—to ingratiate themselves, but also at the prospect of a sale or a job." Another pertinent quote was from Ray Birdwhistell, a prominent scholar in the study of kinesics: "Only [as a result of my analyses] have I been able to free myself from an ethnocentric preconception that I know what a smile is" (cited by Rickert, 28 March 1996). Fussell (1982, 41, cited in Gordon 1997, 72) provides a clue to

the history of photographic smiles: "The smile was rare in photographs, even in the U.S. metropole, until around 1902, and laughter was a subject of photography only after 1937."

91. Clark (1997, 104–6) discusses differences of eye contact and frontality in Julia Margaret Cameron's portraits of men versus women.

92. "Standard Swahili" is itself a scholarly and political invention based on the Kiswahili of Zanzibar and defined through the decisions of bodies such as the Inter-Territorial Language (Swahili) Committee for the East African Dependencies in the 1930s. John Innis (1992) has been a tireless and erudite advocate for including all varieties of Kiswahili *as actually spoken* in dictionaries and curricula. He distinguishes *Kiswahili sanifu* (standard Swahili), *Kiswahili cha mapokea* (ordinary, conversational Swahili), and *Kiswahili cha mitaani* (slang, "street" Swahili). See also the Archive of Popular Swahili at www.pscw.uva.nl/pca/, the Language and Popular Culture in Africa website.

93. In a more abstract sense, the different sets of multilingual captions emphasized the multiple verbal framings and communicative mediations involved in all photographic exhibitions—before, during, and after viewing. Exhibition labels are only one such frame, supplemented by interactions while photographing, exhibition planning discussions, visitors' conversations, reviews, gallery talks, and so forth.

94. Popular writers signal that they are parodying an anthropological stance by using this style of ethnographic writing (see di Leonardo 1998, 52–55).

95. The present tense can be used for several discursive functions in English. Simple contrasts between use of present and past tense in label copy can be revealing in some cases, but the diverse ways that tense is used to convey differences of aspect, mood, and register need to be taken into account as well.

96. Styles of display and labeling have changed significantly over time as well, even within art museums alone (Bennett 1995, 170–71). Roberts (1997, 67–68) describes the surge of research in the mid-1980s on effectiveness in label style and presentation that began to establish more standardized guidelines now in use for label placement, type size, and rhetorical styles. Schildkrout (1999) is a recent statement on the importance of combining aestheticizing and contextualizing display and breaking from the paradigm that assumes they are separate.

97. The style combination is clear in captions for plates 3, 7, and 12, all introduced by a general normative statement, followed by more personalized description. It is more subtle in other captions, with general context indicated through phrases or the balance carrying across a series of captions (such as those for initiation photographs).

98. In several exhibitions in the late 1980s and early 1990s, the Center for African Art experimented with different tones and styles in exhibition texts. With characteristic insight, Vogel (1988) describes these exhibitions (*Art/Artifact, Perspectives,* and *Africa Explores*) and discusses authoritative, personal, opinionated, informal, and didactic label voices and styles. Her chapters in Vogel et al. (1994) expand on this and also compare European and American approaches to labels, based on different emphases on the educational role of museums.

99. I was also described in third person in a brief biographical text at the end of the exhibition. Barrett (1990, 100) discusses artist Barbara Kruger's use of pronouns to address viewers directly and call attention to dynamics of inclusion and exclusion. Clifford (1988, 232–34) discusses different meanings and impressions conveyed through first and third person in labels for exhibitions at four Northwest coast museums.

100. Exhibition visitors have always been active interpreters, though the interactive nature of this interpretation has only recently been emphasized by museum professionals and academic observers (Lavine 1992, 146; Tomlinson 1991, 45–64). Exhibition viewing was previously considered a passive experience, with visitors simply taking in what was shown. Fuery and Mansfield (1997, 70–84) summarize a diverse literature in film studies and art history on "the gaze" that emphasizes viewers' activity, accentuating power differences between viewer and viewed. These analyses of gazing relations rarely consider how those viewed understand themselves, their images, and the viewings. Similarly, few analysts have noted that the passivity of the viewed is itself a constructed effect. It can be reinforced or weakened by modes of presentation and labeling, photographic selections, attempts to privilege a single viewpoint or interpretation, as well as by different collaborative ways of organizing exhibitions.

CHAPTER 3. IMAGINING AUDIENCES: KENYA

1. It was unlikely that the poster would otherwise reach the area, though a copy might have eventually found its way there. As far as I know, by 1994 the poster still had not been seen by Okiek in the area.

2. The interplay I discussed in stereotypes, however, is primarily concerned with categories and crosses taxonomic levels: difference is emphasized among social categories at one taxonomic level that are nonetheless all similar at a higher level. The interplay of assimilating and exoticizing involves all the media and modes of exhibitionary communication discussed in chapter 1.

3. As Stuart Hall (1996, 249 [original emphasis]) notes, "it is only too tempting to fall into the trap of assuming that, because essentialism has been deconstructed *theoretically,* therefore it has been displaced *politically.*"

4. "Audience" may be the most artificial group imagined in an exhibition, combining people from diverse communities and constituted mainly by coincidence of attendance. Yet exhibition organizers and visitors alike talk about audiences as groups, predicating commonalities. In some circumstances the "*audience,* a passive entity, becomes the *community,* an active agent. This is [often] a process in which self-appointed or delegated representatives of a community contest a[n exhibition's] perspective by articulating a community point of view" (Karp 1992, 12–13 [original emphasis]). Karp also discusses Thomas Crow's work on the notion of "the public," formed in eighteenth-century Paris in conjunction with art salons and art criticism. MacDonald and Silverstone (1990, 185–86) contrast approaches that see those who come to museums as "visitors" and "consumers." Bennett (1996a) considers several notions used to refer collectively to people who come to museums: publics, audiences, communities, and citizens. Each has different histories, connotations and implications for museums' public roles.

   In this study I usually use "visitor" when talking about how people experienced and understood the exhibition. Its sense of hospitality and brief sojourn seem appropriate for discussing a temporary exhibition at several venues, and it improves on the single-sense emphasis of the term "viewer." Further, its foregrounding of individuals rather than collectivities is fitting for a study concerned with interpretive process. I use "audience" to talk about general attendance patterns, groups that I hoped to reach, and other broad senses.

5. Many exhibition-as-text analyses, however, treat exhibitions and museums as if they have no history and are not products of complex social interactions, raising serious questions about the intentions they might attribute to exhibitions (i.e., anonymous curators and administrators at an unnamed time). For instance, Bal (1984) reads messages conveyed by relations among halls in the American Museum of Natural History as if they were all created at one point in time.

6. At the University Museum of Anthropology in Philadephia, I spoke with people at the opening and after a gallery talk several weeks later. In Michigan, I presented a seminar, public lecture, and gallery talk and spoke with people at each; during the three-day visit, I also observed visitors who went through the gallery and spoke with several of them. In Atlanta, a large opening, docent training session, gallery talk, class sessions, and a tour meeting with a student club all provided specific occasions for talking with people; occasional discussions continued throughout the showing.

7. Most discussions took place the month after the Austin display, when I was in the United States for a conference. Much later, in 1998, I spoke with Pauline Turner Strong about her students' interviews and 1996 exhibition about the Austin showing.

8. The Nairobi Museum includes a Snake Park. Regional museums are in Lamu, Kitale, Meru, Kisumu, Kapenguria, Kabarnet, Kariandusi, Gede, Hyrax Hill, Fort Jesus (Mombasa), and the Karen Blixen House outside Nairobi, with a new Museum of Maa Cultures being built in Narok. Sites and monuments include Olorgesailie, Mnarani Ruins, Takwa Ruins, Juma La Mtwana, Koobi Fora, Siyu Fort, and Thimlich Ohinga. Further information on NMK and its galleries can be found at www.museums.or.ke.

9. A government-subsidized museum was approved in 1929. "It was established initially as a memorial to the former Governor of the colony, Sir Robert Coryndon, who had been a staunch friend of the private museum of the East Africa and Uganda Natural History Society, and was constructed with money raised from the Coryndon Memorial Fund" (NMK 1981, 2).

10. Attendance figures show that school groups are a large proportion of museum visitors. Expatriates predominate in the Kenya Museum Society and in some museum programs, e.g., the Know Kenya Course, an annual lecture series on weekday mornings.

11. A review of the *Images of Kenya* exhibition also noted this problem: "The National Museum in Nairobi is a great place but one rarely sees local people visiting there, except for school parties" (Andere 1986).

12. Fewer than a dozen Okiek from the areas where I work had lived in or near Nairobi then, though more had visited for various reasons. I do not know, however, how many Okiek from elsewhere have moved to Nairobi for work, schooling, or other reasons.

13. Talking with proprietors also created a small word-of-mouth campaign about the exhibition.

14. I was out of the country at the time and did not see *Images of Kenya;* no book was produced. Discussion with Coulson first made me consider a poster for *Okiek Portraits.* When full financing for the exhibition did not materialize, I subsidized remaining costs by producing extra posters for the museum shop. Once exhibition costs were covered, I donated all remaining proceeds to Okiek schools in my research area.

15. The photographers responded that many more images were shown in Canada, that they emphasized scenes unfamiliar to urban dwellers in the Kenyan exhibition, and that visitors were fascinated by the "rapidly vanishing culture" shown (Fisher et al. 1986).

16. Saitoti also claims Beckwith included images in their book, against his protests, from the staged Maasai tourist village, Mayer's Ranch, and took advantage of his naïveté in their contract, which now prevents him from publishing his text independently in East Africa.

17. Another letter on the same page as Beckwith's presents another variation on this theme. J. B. Kalule of Karatina writes, "[K]eep on as before, cautioning our rather gullible youth on the dangers imported from overseas. I also appeal to all influential voices in Africa to spearhead a return to purity on our contintent. Let us seek only technology and nothing else from outside."

18. I discuss Kalenjin languages in the prologue, note 8.

19. GL identified himself to me at different times as both Nandi and Kipsigis; he often spoke about "Kalenjin" customs, generalizing across ethnic groups combined in this term.

20. See Amin 1969, 1973, 1975, 1983; Amin, Willetts, and Tetley 1982, 1986, 1990; Amin, Willetts, and Eames 1987; Amin, Willetts, and Shah 1994; and Tetley's (1988) biography of Amin.

21. Presented as a research product, *Okiek Portraits* drew reactions from institutional officials, too. Again, the exhibition was more important to them than specific photographs and mode of representation (although these would have been important if seen as problematic). An undersecretary in the Office of the President (who oversaw research clearance then) and the chair of the sociology department at the University of Nairobi (where I am Research Associate) were openly pleased with the exhibition, a tangible product with greater public visibility than usual for academic projects.

22. Openly exploiting such racial divisions, President Moi used "foreigner" as an epithet when attempting to discredit Richard Leakey, a third-generation Kenyan, when Leakey helped found the opposition party Safina. Obviously, more than race was involved, as Leakey's brother Philip, a KANU party loyalist and member of Parliament, has not been similarly impugned. A particular socioeconomic and educational profile may be implicit in the national "we" as well; KK resembled readers of the *Weekly Review* in those terms.

23. Photographic criticism includes description, interpretation, evaluation, and theorization in various combinations (Barrett 1990, 2–6).

24. Tagg (1988, 8–15) discusses the development and use of different notions of "documentary" photography in the U.S. and Britain.

25. Many Okiek have heard of the National Museum but few had visited apart from some children on recent school trips. I described the museum as a large building where things from Kenya's different peoples had been collected to show Kenyan customs and history to visitors and schoolchildren. When Okiek asked if visitors pay to see them, I explained entrance fees (nominal for Kenyan residents, larger for foreigners, none for school groups).

26. Musello discusses family photography in middle class white American settings, including family viewings. His family viewing events have no obvious Okiek equivalent, and American families have greater access to and familiarity with photography. Photography has not yet become a family activity for Okiek, though they agree with Musello's group about some topics appropriate for photographing. Nonetheless, participant groups and settings for these Okiek viewings often paralleled Musello's. For other comparisons, see *Photo Wallahs'* marvelous depiction of multiple settings and uses of photography in the northern Indian town of Mussoorie (MacDougal and MacDougal 1992; MacDougal 1992) and Pinney's (1997) sensitive account of the "social life of Indian photographs." Chalfen (1987, 1991) develops the related concept of "home mode pictorial/visual communication" in research on mid-

dle class white American and Japanese American photo albums. He focuses on photographs by family members to determine topics photographed, formal patterns, and how people use, store, display, and interpret their pictures, setting photographic behavior in broad social and communicative context. Ben-Ari (1991, 91–92) considers family albums in Japan. Ritchkin (1999, 89–93) discusses differences between Latin American and American approaches to photography.

27. Monti lists these commercial photographers in Zanzibar in the 1890s: A. C. Gomes and his son P. F. Gomes, A. R. P. De Lord, E. C. Dias, and the Coutinho brothers. It is not clear if all had studios. For Uganda, the only commercial photographer listed is Alfred Lobo, working in Entebbe in 1900 to 1920s. The Gomes studio also opened a branch in Dar es Salaam in the 1930s. Behrend (1998) draws attention to Indian traditions of photography in Kenya as well as European ones.

28. Presumably, some railway construction photographs in Beard's *End of the Game* (1988) were by Young. With typical disregard for scholarly documentation, Beard offers no information on historic photographs used (photographers, locations, sources, etc.) and acknowledges no permission to reproduce them.

29. Wildlife photography was popular among tourists and settlers in Kenya from at least the 1920s, and Bensusan (1996, 81–82) notes overlap between big game hunters and members of the Kenya Photographic Society, founded in 1929. Thirty years later "this Society opened membership to all races and changed its name to the Nairobi Photographic Society."

30. Commercial photographers and photographic studios were established in many parts of Africa before 1900, but the history of photography by Africans is more varied and little known. In western Africa, a few African photographers were practicing in Nigeria, Ghana, and Sierra Leone before the turn of the century (ibid., 164–66; Oguibe 1996, 233–34). Elsewhere, local African photographers began practicing at different times (see chapter 2, note 72). Geary (1998) surveys postcard production in Africa early this century, including several African studio photographers, but she ignores eastern Africa. Central questions in the history of photography in Kenya concern when and how Kenyans began to learn photographic skills, open studios, and otherwise make and seek photographs, as well as the cultural and aesthetic understandings that informed these practices and the modes of photographic circulation and use.

31. Kenyans who served in the armed forces during the war may have become more familiar with photography and snapshots, bringing that experience home. This would parallel patterns of technological and stylistic innovation in other domains of Kenyan life at the time and photographic history elsewhere in Africa.

32. The earliest photograph in Oginga Odinga's autobiography (1967, facing page 16) is from 1934, during his schooldays at Maseno.

33. Behrend (1998) discusses some variations in these conventions both over time and in different communities in Kenya. Pinney's (1997) thorough discussion of different moments and traditions of photography in India, the poses, props, and gestures used, and the social and aesthetic interactions that produced new forms of visuality in Indian photography is a valuable comparative resource and model for future work in Kenya. In this cursory outline, I will not give separate consideration to different domains of photographic practice in Kenya, but there too one finds differences and interactions among official, academic, studio, and amateur photography over time.

34. The system originated in the Registration of Natives Ordinance in 1915, requiring males between the ages of fifteen and forty to register, be fingerprinted, and receive a registration certificate (*kipande*) that had to be carried at all times when outside native reserves, usually in a metal container (also called *kipande*) worn like a necklace. "The registration system brought virtually the entire male African population under much more direct administrative control . . . the *kipande* was the most hated of Kenya's labour laws and the one that came to symbolize for Africans their servile status" (Berman and Lonsdale 1992, 112–13). I have not been able to determine exactly when photographs became a regular feature of *vipande* (pl.), but after the colonial government declared a state of emergency in October 1952, a new pass system was established for all Kikuyu, Embu, and Meru people. "New Emergency regulations were introduced making it compulsory for [all Kikuyu laborers] to be photographed. The local leaders of KAU [Kenya African Union] immediately decided that these regulations should be opposed. . . . Thousands of squatters refused to be photographed" (Rosberg and Nottingham [1966] 1985, 285; cf. Kanogo 1987, 140). Kikuyu, Meru, and Embu passbooks issued during the 1950s had spaces for right and left thumb prints and a photograph.

35. I spoke with some in Kenya who believe that each business unit is legally required to display the president's photograph; others thought it a matter of custom rather than explicit requirement. Usually taken for granted, these photographs can be highly charged signs in some circumstances. The transition to President Moi's government after Jomo Kenyatta's 1978 death was one such time, in rural and urban areas alike. Shortly after Moi became president, his pictures were being given to each person who received a new business license in Narok District. Lack of a photograph became a sign for police that a shopkeeper was operating illegally. The photographic transition was even raised in national politics. As one current MP, an admirer of Kenyatta, recounted to me in 1993, shops gradually began to hang Moi photographs but many kept Kenyatta's on display as well. Eventually, a government minister, Arthur Magugu, asked publicly, why are two pictures being shown, does Kenya have two presidents? He may have raised the matter at Moi's instigation: if a Kikuyu did so, it would less likely be seen as "simple tribalism." Police then began going around, telling people to take the Kenyatta photograph down, but they refused. The government had to issue a statement that there was no government policy requiring their removal. Even today, many offices and shops display both photographs or one that shows Kenyatta and Moi together, taken when Moi was still vice president. In some cases, it remains a personal political statement to refuse to show a picture of Moi alone.

36. All were men. Behrend's (2000) recent work on photographers at the Likoni Ferry in Mombasa, Kenya, notes that all ten with small studios were men, but others, including several young women, worked as roving photographers. In Bouaké, Côte d'Ivoire, virtually all studio photographers were also men (Werner 1996, 89). Werner notes that this means that female photographers rarely set up on their own, not that there are none.

37. In the mid-1990s, Kaplelach with photo albums were typically in their teens or early twenties. Kipsigis who have been immigrating to this area, however, have used albums for longer, and older Kipsigis also had albums. See Mustafa (i.p.) on the long established use of photo albums by women in Dakar.

38. Okiek men belong to named age-sets according to their year of initiation; each age-set has two named subsets, right (senior) and left (junior). Each subset includes men initiated over several years, an age-set those initiated during both subsets. Age-sets offer a useful chronol-

ogy for tracing Okiek history and comparing the experiences of different age cohorts. Women are related to age-sets through their fathers, husbands, and lovers. See Kratz (1994a, 61) for a list of Okiek age-sets and corresponding dates, Kratz and Pido (2000) on beadwork that marks age-set identities. For age-sets mentioned here, *il kalikal* is the right subset of *il ny'angusi* age-set; *eseuri* is the next full age-set, followed by *i rambau,* and then *il kishili* (also known as *il kipalit*).

39. Cf. similar comments: "Turkana women in northern Kenya told us in 1973 that they feared photography because it 'might make us weak' or 'make our blood thin'" (MacDougal 1992, 104). "In the 1950s, when photography spread through the villages of western Kenya, many people feared that their likenesses would be used by witches or sorcerers to kill them. As a means to counter this threat, the practice of holding or posing with a Bible while being photographed evolved as a protective device" (Behrend and Wendl 1997, 411).

40. The personal image collections that Pinney (1997, 149–69) describes provide interesting contrasts.

41. The contrast of Inkutukai's studio pictures and his brother's still more recent outdoor photographs corresponds to a gradual increase in the number of itinerant photographers who visit the area and frequent local markets. Another photo album owned by a woman slightly younger than Inkutukai's brother consisted entirely of outdoor group photos. Werner (1996) notes an increase of itinerant photographers in Côte d'Ivoire after 1985, a shift he relates to technological changes that made color photographs more widely available and then allowed color film processing in minilabs. He sees these changes undermining the economic viability of photographic studios.

42. As Pinney (1997, 112) notes for India, associations with "modernity" do not necessarily connect photography to Western values or identities alone; photography in religious imagery there links it to ancient forms of representation as well.

43. Again, it is mostly young men who say they want cameras. Only one Okiot in my immediate research area had a camera between 1982 and 1990, a gift from my sister in 1984. It received little use since the film required was not easily available and his photographs were not very successful.

44. *Okiek Portraits* included several such posed portraits, but my mode of framing often distinguished them from studio portraits. A review of Inkutukai's pictures, those in several other photo albums, and the few photographs on display in Kaplelach houses in 1993–94, suggests fairly clear Okiek photographic conventions. Photographs displayed were all portraits. A few showed individuals, but more were groups with two to six relatives (especially, but not only, brothers, wife/husband and children, cousins, and some affines). (This contrasts with Werner's [1996, 84] review of five albums in Dakar, with only one-quarter photographs of relatives and two-thirds showing friends, schoolmates, coworkers, neighbors, etc. That pattern is more common in the few Kipsigis albums I was able to see.) The Okiek portraits rarely showed older relatives or parents, though schoolmates were included in several pictures. Except for passport and identity pictures and photographs I did, all were full body images. Virtually all people had neutral facial expressions, straight faced or with their mouth slightly open. A few individuals smiled slightly. Most stood for their portraits, though groups sometimes arranged themselves with some standing and some sitting, or sat all in a row. In all these, people faced the camera squarely. In a few cases, young friends squatted, turned diagonally inward towards one another and shook hands, or leaned on a

prop from the studio (a stool with plastic flowers in a pot). Several other pairs also shook hands, greeting one another (*kikatkee*) to show their friendship. One photograph showed a pair of young men shaking hands and making the hand sign of the KANU political party. Most people held their arms straight at their sides or in their laps. A few young men struck a jaunty pose, leaning their arm on one leg or placing hand on hip. Props appear in only a few photographs, including flowers, a radio, a book, records, and one staged exchange between two young men, one giving a leaf and the other a banknote (denomination unclear). Studio backdrops were usually patterned floors with simple curtains, unlike the painted scenes in early Kenyatta portraits. Outside the studio, portraits were taken near home, against maize fields, in schoolyards, and in one case inside a Nairobi building. Even if the format of photographic portraits varies, then, it remains rather well defined and different from most photographs in *Okiek Portraits*. Younger people, especially young men, were more likely to strike poses and use props.

45. These viewings involved (1) a mature Kaplelach woman (my co-wife), her adult daughter, young son, and grandson; (2) a Kaplelach man (one of our neighbors); (3) a woman with four of her daughters (my neighbors and friends in the Kipchornwonek area); (4) a young Kaplelach man (my son) and his Kisii wife; and (5) a young man (with whose family I lived in 1974–75) and a mature man (one of my closest Kaplelach friends) who called his Kisii wife to look at some photographs.

46. I participated in discussions mainly when asked to identify people and places. I did not "probe," ask people to develop points, or focus attention on particular details. I did not want to lead the conversations that would become Okiek commentary captions.

47. For examples of multiple totalities read into photographs, see Jean Mohr's "What Did I See?" (1982).

48. Photographs "cannot escape this pure deictic language" of "look," "here it is" (Barthes 1981, 5).

49. Such performative acts that "create or intensify co-presence pervade all oral texts" (Fabian 1996a, 252). Kratz (2001) considers how communicative patterns and interactions of co-presence shape life histories.

50. The 1920s were a key period for development of this documentary tradition in the U.S. (Tagg 1988, 8ff. and chap. 6). Tagg's periodization corresponds with Edwards's (1992) survey of photography and anthropology. Documentary notions of photography can be well suited to ethnographic projects, but understandings of anthropology, ethnography, and photography all have complex histories, related in interesting ways.

51. This preference may also be associated with class-based differences in photographic practice or with "Western" tastes (cf. Musello 1980, 25), for candids were made possible by technologies that have reached different places and people at different times. Werner (1996, 104) notes greater preference for candids in Bouaké since 1980, a shift he relates to dissatisfaction with the photographic ritual in studios. "Cette désaffection se lit encore dans la manière dont le ritual photographique est tourné en dérision par des sujets qui adoptent des poses moqueuses, décontractées, voire provocatrices, ou bien encore vont jusqu'à demander, dans leur quête d'une expression plus spontanée, d'être photographiés à leur insu ('photo-surprise')."

52. Pinney's (1997, 8–9) photographs were regarded as flawed by their subjects if they were not full-length.

53. Residents of New Zealand's high country were critical of a magazine article about their community because it was not "representative" but focused on a few personalities (Dominy 1993, 322).

54. New Guinea villagers featured in a film trilogy (*First Contact, Joe Leahy's Neighbors, Black Harvest*) also imagined others in New York responding to their images and words (Briggs 1993, 407–8). In 1995, Gordon (1997, 144) showed Hei//omn bushmen in Namibia pictures of people from their area made during a 1925 expedition and noted their reactions.

55. As mentioned, most Okiek in this area did not have extensive experience with government officers before independence. However, they were removed from the forest to a camp during the 1950s Mau Mau freedom struggle.

56. Such activities are decreasingly important economically and involve skills that current school-going Okiek are learning and practicing far less.

57. Like bicycles or the motorbike in Kenyatta's 1920s portrait, the radio–cassette player is a common photographic prop, a sign of modernity and prosperity. "A radio is one of the three big African status symbols,' said Mr. Maluma, a Zambian who has visited fifty African countries. 'If you have one, you are considered above average. A bicycle, even more so. A motorcycle, well, that's a Cadillac. But on the basis of just a radio, make no mistake—you can procure a wife'" (McNeil 1996).

58. Settling on that combination is sometimes problematic, however, particularly when different family members emphasize different orientations.

59. *Living Arctic*, a 1989 exhibition at the Museum of Mankind, had quotations from Native Americans, and Michael O'Hanlon (1993, 87) planned to use quotations from New Guinea Highlanders to counterpoint photographs from the 1933 Taylor-Leahy patrol in his 1993 *Paradise* exhibition there. These were apparently dropped in final installation as the exhibition was reconfigured (Clifford 1997, 167).

60. I did this immediately after moving to Washington, D.C., in 1990 for a fellowship at the Smithsonian Institution.

61. Scholars who have examined the interpretive processes and structures of conversational interaction include Gumperz 1992; Jefferson 1978; Sacks, Schegloff, and Jefferson 1974; Sacks 1972, 1992; Bauman 1986; Grice 1989; Sherzer 1983. Others have considered processes of entextualization and recontextualization involved when discursive products are moved from one interactional context to another (Bauman and Briggs 1990; Briggs 1993, 1996a; Silverstein and Urban 1996, 15).

62. The exhibition languages did not represent the linguistic repertoire most common among Kaplelach and Kipchornwonek Okiek, which would include Maa (Kratz 1986). Had I included commentary captions for the Nairobi showing, they would have been translated into both Kiswahili and English.

63. I could have used "O my," but it did not fit the sentences as well.

64. *Ugali* is the Kiswahili word for the food, also a loanword in Okiek. The Okiek word is *akimny'eet*.

65. A reciprocal form of the verb (i.e., to marry one another) is sometimes used, increasingly it seems. But this is a marked form that emphasizes either that the couple are really just living together without proper marriage protocol (family discussions and bridewealth), or what Okiek see as a recent increase in young people's autonomy in choosing marriage partners (Kratz 2000).

66. A colleague included this challenge in an extra-credit exercise for anthropology students while *Okiek Portraits* was at the Michael C. Carlos Museum. Key relationships that can be mapped from exhibition information are shown in appendix B.

67. It is not surprising that the same photographs are evaluated differently, in almost opposite ways, when seen in relation to different issues. Non-Western clothing was a sign of authenticity and identity and also a sign of the strange and exotic for *National Geographic* viewers as well (Lutz and Collins 1993, 247–53).

CHAPTER 4. IMAGINING AUDIENCES: UNITED STATES

1. These classroom visits also gave me an opportunity to learn how some visitors experienced the exhibition.

2. The following account relies on the videotape and on research notes written the day of the class. In quotations, bracketed ellipses [. . .] show brief portions in the video transcription where I could not hear the exact words used. In the slightly abbreviated exchange with Augusta students included below, unbracketed ellipses show omissions.

3. Di Leonardo discusses how anthropologists are portrayed in the media and recounts her own experience in giving a *Newsweek* reporter a complicated response and trying to retain some of the nuance in the final story (1998, 350–59).

4. An early exhibition proposal and organizational notes indicate that I first sought a venue in Washington, D.C., in November 1989, where I would attend the annual meetings of the American Anthropological Association.

5. Exhibitions shown in unusual settings demonstrate this point. For instance, some Kenyan artists organized exhibitions in schools, social halls, marketplaces, and other open-air sites in 1982. They reached enormous numbers of people who would not usually visit art galleries and museums (Agthe 1990, 146–47). Display sites themselves enter visitors' understandings as part of what exhibitions bring to them. For their part, visitors bring to exhibitions their notions about those sites, and much more.

6. Introductions or support from professional colleagues were often instrumental in arranging venues. *Okiek Portraits* bookings were serendipitous compared to traveling exhibits mounted by major museums. Its schedule took shape in fits and starts, with several long gaps that resulted both from the informal planning and from the constraints of adapting exhibition travel to my other commitments and research schedule. The exhibition was considered seriously by eleven venues (three natural history museums, one culture history museum, one art museum, and six university sites).

7. When first exploring how to bring *Okiek Portraits* to the United States, I considered turning it over to a touring service. SITES tours Smithsonian exhibitions and other small independent exhibits.

8. Jhala (1996) shows how ethnographic films are targeted to metropolitan audiences and the communities filmed, but rarely reach villages, small communities, or even cities in other parts of the world, what he calls the "unintended audience." Himpele (1996) perceptively analyzes the social mapping and cultural negotiations embedded in the Bolivian film distribution system.

9. For instance, a colleague wanted to launch a short European tour for *Okiek Portraits* in Germany, but overseas shipping costs, customs logistics, and complex international arrangements deterred us.

10. Fred Wilson's installation *Rooms with a View: The Struggle Between Culture, Content, and the Context of Art* made a similar point contemporaneously. Vogel (1988, 12) summarizes the problem of categorization from the art history perspective: "Virtually all of the African art works we now know were once classified as artifacts. The problem of distinguishing between the two categories has proven remarkably resistant to clear-cut solutions, and continues to bedevil those who collect and exhibit African and other 'Primitive' arts." On tour until 1990, *Art/Artifact* showed in both art museums and science museums (ibid., 204 n.15), as did *Sacred Arts of Haitian Vodou* more recently. Bal (1996) considers the basic principles and concerns of ethnographic and art museums, finding the distinction an ideological premise in need of critical analysis.

11. Hageman (1996) emphasizes the distinct conventions of photojournalism and ethnographic photography but also identifies features that blur the distinction, creating interesting continua.

12. If the exhibition satisfies these basic criteria, then other considerations such as significance of the topic, quality of scholarship, schedule, etc., become relevant.

13. Letter from Aldona Jonaitis, 30 October 1990. Because of its many uses, photography can signal both documentation and art, perhaps more so than other media. Yet this does not always result in ambiguity. For some people, subject matter can be determinate, e.g., photography + Africa = ethnography, but not art.

14. The Field Museum of Natural History in Chicago consulted previous exhibitors and solicited reviews from nine committee members when considering *Okiek Portraits.* Unfortunately, their letter conveyed none of the substance of their discussion and reviews.

15. Sponsors in Kenya convinced me that producing a duplicate set for the U.S. would be easier and cheaper than shipping the exhibition back and forth.

16. My description of the Austin showing is based on these discussions with faculty and students who were there at the time.

17. Several years later in 1992, Guillermo Gómez-Peña and Coco Fusco did put themselves on display in a golden cage in a performance meant to criticize exoticizing and dehumanizing modes of exhibition (Fusco and Heredia 1993). I do not know which photographs were shown in Austin. If photos with ceremonial dress alone were displayed, then accusations of primitivist imagery might have had some basis. This would be hard to claim, however, if the exhibition's variety was maintained, showing children hoeing, shopkeepers, women in ordinary dresses, etc.

18. This is certainly a potential hazard for traveling exhibitions. One striking example occurred during the tour of the recent exhibition *Baule: African Art/Western Eyes,* curated by Susan Vogel. One way the exhibition illustrated different ways of viewing and contexts for seeing art was to evoke settings and practices that Baule define and restrict by gender. Men's masks were placed in a separate room marked "Baule men do not want women to see their sacred objects." An analogous room with a similar label in red type over the door contained a video of the women's dance. In both cases visitors had to leave the exhibition path and enter a separate room to view these things. Installations in New Haven, New York, and Chicago maintained the concept. When the Museum of African Art in Washington, D.C., installed the exhibition, however, it eliminated the men's room and put the sacred masks out for all to see in the main path through the galleries. Indeed, one large mask was placed especially prominently at a gallery entrance. The catalog and label texts were reproduced

unchanged but referred to the original installation. Similarly, when *African Zion: the Sacred Art of Ethiopia* was shown at the Menil Collection in Houston in 1994, Menil personnel eliminated information panels and contextual photographs in order to make the show conform to their own philosophy and aesthetic of "the sovereignty of each object" (Smart 1997, 120–21).

19. Barthes and Berger both make this valuable point in critiques of Edward Steichen's *The Family of Man* exhibition. However, as Sandeen shows (1995, 50), the antinuclear argument central to this 1950s exhibition has disappeared from later interpretations and representations. Steichen did seek to convey a positive, universalizing sense of "how alike people were in all parts of the world," but he did so "to accomplish my mission . . . [I] incited people into taking open and unified action against war itself." Though inescapable in the exhibition, this message was omitted in the book and later commentaries. Sandeen describes (48) how the exhibition built to its climax, as visitors stepped into a dark space near the end:

> The viewer now stood before the single most arresting and important image of the exhibition. The only color image and the only photograph to command an entire room, it was also, curiously, the only image not reproduced in the book version of The Family of Man. It was a huge, six-by-eight foot color transparency of a hydrogen bomb explosion, glowing red and orange in a darkened enclosure that forced the individual close, close enough to be enveloped by the cloud. The effect of the blast was produced through the new technology of a large color transparency, unfamiliar to most viewers. After perhaps 450 black-and-white images, viewers were shocked back into polychromatic reality with this reminder of life in the modern world.

20. Originally in *Museum News,* March–April 1989.

21. Barrett (1990, 90) describes another striking example of how presentational context affects understanding. A photograph of a man and woman in a bar that first appeared in a magazine story on cafés was then used (without consent) in an article on prostitution, and later still shown at the Museum of Modern Art, conveying very different understandings. "The presentational environment in which this café photograph appeared overrode the content of the photograph and overdetermined its meaning in ways unfair to the photographer, the subjects, and the photograph itself, but that is the power of the external context."

22. Kratz (1994b, 180–84) discusses this tendency to allegorical reading.

23. The case is pictured in Strong (1997, 45).

24. I heard of the student exhibition over a year later, when a colleague reported Strong's mention of it in a conference presentation. The students' aim was to determine what the department wanted to do with the display cases, not to find out what had actually happened. Still, I found it odd that they did not contact me while piecing together the history or let me know they were using my photographs in the display. The politics of representation take shape and play out, often quietly, in many ways and many places.

25. Thanks to Pauline Turner Strong and David Sandell for providing the label text. The other label for this display pieced together interview quotes about use of the display cases.

26. Cf. Byers (1966, 31): "The photograph is not a 'message' in the usual sense. It is, instead, the raw material for an infinite number of messages which each viewer can construct for himself." However, readings are also constrained and influenced by the context in which pictures are shown. "[N]ot all media artifacts are equally likely to have the same cultural

ideas deployed to make sense of them. The *Geographic*'s Arabs and Hollywood Arabs can obviously be read in diverse ways, but sympathetic and relativistic readings of cultural difference are more likely to come with the *Geographic*" (Lutz and Collins 1993, 219; see also Pinney 1992, 87–90). Trachtenberg (1989, xv) summarizes this general condition: "the relation between images and imputed meanings is fraught with uncertainties, for, like opaque facts, images cannot be trapped readily within a simple explanation or interpretation. They have a life of their own which often resists the efforts of photographers and viewers (or readers) to hold them down as fixed meaning."

27. Staiger's (1992, 89) caveat about reviews as a source in film reception is relevant here. With few contemporary sources for her historical materialist study of *Rear Window,* she turned to reviews to reconstruct 1950s interpretations. She notes some of the problems: "[M]y sample is very limited . . . [and] the reading public studied is film reviewers and (later) academic scholars. Finally, the review and scholarly article are genres in themselves; thus their conventions mediate the results."

28. In a recent article, Fienup-Riordan (1999, 353) follows a Yup'ik Eskimo exhibition on tour. She describes how different institutions "changed the exhibit to better fit both their spaces and their ideas of what an exhibit should be and what their viewers would expect" and how the strong Yup'ik collaboration central to the exhibition was attenuated in other settings. Though the overall effect was significant, "changes to the exhibit were handled by design and exhibition team members as 'cosmetic features'—paint color, signage intelligibility, credit placement—for which they felt consultation was unnecessary" (ibid., 354). The National Museum of Natural History was a venue for both the Yup'ik exhibition and *Okiek Portraits.*

29. Organizers first planned to show it at the University of Alaska Museum, but that space was already booked during the conference.

30. Half the comments in the visitors' book were written by Alaskan residents, 14 percent by residents of other U.S. states, and 36 percent by people from other countries.

31. Over 90 percent of those 25 or older have finished high school; 64 percent hold a bachelor's or graduate degree. Merriman (1989, 152, 158) found education and age to be key variables in museum visitorship in the United Kingdom in the mid-1980s and cites Bourdieu on the importance of education as a factor in art museum visitorship in France (ibid., 162–63).

32. Citing a year-long Smithsonian study of the NMNH audience during 1994–95, Bickford et al. provide the following figures. *Okiek Portraits* was shown during the same seasons as the exhibition they evaluated, so I reproduce here their general NMNH information on summer, autumn, and total visitorship:

DEMOGRAPHIC CHARACTERISTICS (IN PERCENT) OF VISITORS TO NMNH

	Summer	Autumn	Total
Gender			
Male	50.5	54.3	51.8
Female	49.5	45.7	48.2
Age			
0 to 11	18.1	14.0	16.7
12 to 19	15.0	8.0	12.5

20 to 24	7.1	6.9	7.0
25 to 34	13.4	19.7	15.6
35 to 44	22.8	19.7	21.7
45 to 54	14.4	15.6	14.8
55 to 64	5.2	9.0	6.5
65 or over	4.0	7.0	5.1
Race/Ethnicity			
Non-Minority/White	80.4	84.7	81.9
Minority	19.6	15.3	18.1
Residence			
Foreign	9.8	12.2	10.7
Other U.S.	73.5	62.8	69.7
Washington, D.C.	2.8	4.7	3.5
MD/VA Suburbs	13.9	20.3	16.2
Education (Age 25 and over)			
Less than High School Grad	2.9	2.5	2.8
High School Graduate	35.5	28.9	33.2
Bachelor's/Some College	30.8	33.9	31.9
MA/Ph.D./Professional	30.8	34.7	32.2
Occupation (Age 18 and over)			
Executive/Management	16.4	12.6	15.1
Professional Specialties	33.1	44.6	37.2
Sales, Technical/Admin.	17.1	15.5	16.5
Other	13.5	15.6	14.2
Non-Labor Force	20.0	11.8	17.1
Visiting Group Composition			
Alone	8.9	18.8	12.4
Two Adults	17.7	26.0	20.6
3+ Adults	9.8	14.9	11.6
Adults and Kids	53.7	30.9	45.7
Teens/Child(ren)	4.5	3.2	4.0
School/Tour Group	5.3	6.1	5.6
Visitor Type			
New	51.3	47.7	49.9
Repeat	27.6	27.4	27.5
Frequent	21.1	25.0	22.5

33. The visitor profile for university museums may be slightly younger, with higher average education for those over 25 (Pekarik p.c.).

34. The "Daily Magazine" subtitle emphasized the local connection: "A University Museum exhibit grew from a special spirit of kinship between an Abington [local town where I was born] anthropologist and a Kenyan branch of the human family" (Keating 1991).

35. I gave two gallery talks in Philadelphia: one at the exhibition opening (a members' preview and reception) and another at the end of February during the World Culture Program, an activity-packed Saturday with events throughout the museum. Those who came to the talks

probably had greater initial interest in the exhibition than visitors who just happened on it during a museum visit. My conversations, then, may have been with a subset of visitors who were especially attentive and articulate about the exhibition, but their understandings seemed similar to other responses.

36. The exhibition included a comment book only in Fairbanks. Comment books are interesting but incomplete sources of information on visitor responses. "Only individuals who feel very strongly about an exhibition, either strongly positive or strongly negative, are likely to take the trouble to write what they think. In addition, these voluntary, self-selecting methods give greater weight to the opinions of those who have the time to spend on them, and to those who feel comfortable writing. A small, vocal minority of either enthusiasts or critics can easily distort your impressions of the audience's responses to your work. Comment books are important, but they are not reliable sources for understanding what visitors as a whole think" (Doering and Pekarik 1996, 18). Nonetheless, without more systematic information, the specific phrasings and emphases of comments offer insight into how some visitors interpret exhibitions, the issues they find important or controversial, and the possible range of visitor interpretations. This is the primary way I use comment book remarks here.

37. Americans associate photographs with memory and immediate family, sometimes evoking strong emotional responses (Csikszentmihalyi and Rochberg-Halton 1981, 67–68). This may have contributed to such associations with Okiek portraits as well.

38. Though widely cited, Rosaldo's (1989) discussion of the notion is somewhat problematic. He moves from his personal distress at nostalgic representations of colonialism in contemporary popular culture, to the nostalgia of those imperialists for the past of those they ruled, to a similar romanticizing of "tradition" in scholarly writings. Following Lowenthal, he notes that the concept of "nostalgia" itself has changed significantly over time: from a physical ailment in the seventeenth century to the current sense of nostalgia as a state of mind (Lowenthal 1985, 10–11). This lesson does not carry into Rosaldo's analysis, however, even though elsewhere (1994) he champions careful historical and contextual specificity. Rosaldo moves deftly among his three instances of nostalgia, finding ways that they implicate one another, but he does not consider how these nostalgias relate to their own times and locations or how they relate to one another.

"Imperialist nostalgia thus revolves around a paradox: . . . someone deliberately alters a form of life and then regrets that things have not remained as they were prior to his or her intervention" (Rosaldo 1989, 108). But the nostalgia Rosaldo describes here for those involved in colonial ventures was not confined to "traditional" cultures in the colonies or to imperialist Europeans overseas. Lowenthal (1985, 8–10, 96–99) notes that nostalgia was rampant in Victorian times, particularly late Victorian, and into the early twentieth century, in Anglo-American and Continental contexts alike. Fabian (1985, 10–12) also cites eighteenth-century formulations of "disappearance" as fundamental in European understandings of "primitive" societies. Lowenthal identifies another increase in nostalgia from the 1970s, as disillusionment with modernity began to set in. From this time, he traces the development of a virtual nostalgia industry and something that might be called "nostalgic creep," as an ever broader range of time, space, and theme become incorporated into nostalgic representation. Samuel (1994, 322) discusses this same phenomenon in relation to historic photographs, dating the disillusionment to the late 1960s.

Rosaldo's first nostagia, then, the nostalgic contemporary representation of colonial situations, is a nostalgia for another period of widespread nostalgia, as well as a manifestation of this second period of heightened nostalgia. Nostalgia does not always express malaise with modernity, but Lowenthal makes a good case that these two periods are tied up with such concerns. But is the malaise of early modern times really the same as that of late modernity and postmodernity? We might think so from the way Rosaldo collapses them.

39. But "just because no one mentioned a particular response does not mean that no one felt it, only that they didn't mention it" (Pekarik p.c.).

40. In trying to understand Okiek comments, however, Lusaka (1990, 13) encountered the ethnographic limits of exhibitions: "there isn't enough information to give you a full picture of Okiek philosophy." Her paper also made good use of quotes from our interview, but not in the sections discussed below where she resorts to the nostalgia of popular ethnography. In fact, I explained my motivations for doing *Okiek Portraits* to her much as I presented them in chapter 2.

41. I maintain Rosaldo's (1989) term since it has gained wider currency, but also because it underlines connections between the "decline" of "traditional" societies and larger political and economic circumstances.

42. She later asserts instead that the community is "changing rapidly and faces the risk of disappearing altogether" (Lusaka 1990, 5), and that "It is through the young people that adaptations will be made so that the Okiek will live on in a new society" (ibid., 14). All these are part of the repertoire of formulas in nostalgic popular representations.

43. The term "female circumcision" includes three kinds of operations, each practiced in various countries connected to diverse cultural beliefs and involving different institutional, social, and ceremonial structures. In sunna circumcision the tip of the clitoris and the prepuce are cut. The most common operation, excision, removes the clitoris and labia minora. Infibulation, the most severe of the three, also removes the labia majora and then joins the sides of the vulva, leaving a small opening for urine and menstrual blood. Sensationalistic accounts of these practices emphasize this last operation and refer to them all together as "female genital mutilation." In the mid- and late 1990s journalists and others began using other, somewhat more neutral, cover terms: "female genital cutting" (e.g., Dugger 1996) or "female genital modification" (Kratz 1994a; Shweder 2000). On recent politics surrounding these operations see Kratz (1994a, 341–47; 1999a; 1999b; i.p.); Parker (1995); Washington (1996); Gruenbaum (1996); and an issue of *Africa Update* with articles by Emeagwali (1996), Iweriebor (1996), Matias (1996), and Apena (1996). Cf. also Brumberg (1982) and Murray (1976).

44. One gentleman anticipated an explanation similar to the ritual analysis in *Pigs for the Ancestors* (Rappaport 1967). He somehow thought I would explain circumcision in terms of a regional ecological balance maintained through the exchange of women. Viewers also evoked ecological models when looking at *National Geographic* photographs (Lutz and Collins 1993, 233), but in a social evolutionary framework rather than the functionalist approach this man's remarks suggested.

45. Even this miscommunication arose from an assimilating gesture on their part; they assumed a universal practical rationality would apply. They did not recognize that Western body modifications (present and past) often lack such "rational" justifications too.

46. Myers (1991, 34–37) discusses a similar process through which art becomes a synecdochal practice that makes Australian aborigines acceptable to whites.

47. Phillips (1995, 13–15) describes a similar encounter. *The Family of Man* was also subject to a kind of guerrilla review after it opened in Moscow in 1959, showing that the politics of representation were alive and well then as well (Sandeen 1995, 155): "Theophilus Neokonkwo, a young Nigerian, tore down several pictures," later declaring, "The collection portrayed white Americans and other Europeans in dignified cultural states—wealthy, healthy and wise, and Americans and West Indian Negroes, Africans, and Asiatics as comparatively social inferiors—sick, raggerty [*sic*], destitute, and physically maladjusted. African men and women were portrayed either half clothed or naked. I could not stand the sight. It was insulting, undignified and tendentious."

48. "Excise: v.tr. (1) remove (a passage of a book etc.); (2) cut out (an organ etc.) by surgery. Derivative: excision n." (*Concise Oxford Dictionary*); "excision, n.: the act or procedure of removing by or as if by cutting out" (*Webster's Collegiate Dictionary*, 10th ed.).

49. The question remains: is there a better way to frame Okiek initiation, with its male and female circumcision, for American audiences without turning *Okiek Portraits* into an exhibition on genital modification and Euro-American concerns about it? Would an extra paragraph or label addressing the concerns heighten attention to them and make synecdochal interpretations more common? Alternatively, would deletion in U.S. venues of the single sentence on male circumcision and female excision enable a wider range of American visitors to engage with Okiek? Would it also distort the importance of the practice for Okiek?

50. An article in the University of Pennsylvania student newspaper accomplished this in other ways (see below).

51. Kente cloth from Ghana plays a similar symbolic role (Ross 1998). Cf. also Ebron (2000).

52. Some evaluation researchers have begun increasingly to include more ethnographic methods, in-depth interviews, and discourse analysis to better understand these questions. Andrew Pekarik is one of the most thoughtful and inventive proponents of these methods.

CHAPTER 5. THE FINAL VENUES

1. Ground level also includes Discovery Theater, a hands-on education Family Room, and two other exhibitions covering broad expanses of time (Hall of Evolution) and/or space (Hall of World Cultures).

2. The two showed together for most of their exhibition periods: *Cuadros de Pamplona Alta, Peru* from 23 January to 25 April, *Okiek Portraits* from 7 February to 3 May.

3. This subtitle change shows how easily museum professionals too fall into tropes of popular ethnography. The substitution (*Peoples of Kenya*) was a classic way of presenting and emphasizing cultural diversity, even retaining the plural form for an exhibition primarily about Okiek. But it removed the active sense of Okiek involvement and looking stressed with *A Kenyan People Look at Themselves.*

4. As part of Emory University, the Carlos gives special consideration to exhibitions mounted by Emory faculty and to those that can be integrated into teaching there. These considerations were decisive in overriding concern by some on the exhibition review committee that *Okiek Portraits* was not "art" (as several art museums had objected; see chapter 4).

5. The second panel was originally created because of two entries at the Smithsonian. In the far back corner, *Cuadros* included a few color photographs of Peruvian women making textiles, but the material in the two shows (textiles vs. photographs) was distinctive enough to signal the boundary to some visitors.

6. That image was used in about half the articles and announcements collected from Michigan State University Museum. In Nairobi, plates 2 and 14 were both used in promotional material. For instance, both appeared on invitations to the opening, one with Kiswahili text and the other with English.

7. I visited Michigan State shortly after the exhibition opened. When I saw how texts had been distributed, I suggested exchanging the first text paragraphs (I_1) and key to captions so the initial text would be near the map and near the start of the photographic sequence. I do not think this change was made. Further rearrangement would have required rehanging the entire show.

8. The final selection included a short book about Okiek written for late primary students (Blackburn 1982b), my own book (Kratz 1994a), and an overview of Kenya with striking color photographs of urban and rural scenes, showing the country's social and geographical diversity (Tomkinson 1988). We considered including schoolbooks in Kiswahili and Kalenjin—continuing the exhibition's multilingual emphasis—but decided the smaller selection suited the alcove.

9. This description is part of the exhibition text that begins this book.

10. Scholarly interest had turned to audiences in other media as well in the 1990s (Ang 1991, 1996; Bennett 1996a, 1996b; Abu-Lughod 1997; Moores 1993; Fiske 1998).

11. In theoretical terms, the latter requires understanding the semiotics, rhetoric, and pragmatics of exhibition communication. Doering and Pekarik (1993) approach exhibitions through a semiotic and communicative framework.

12. Some of the earliest museum visitor studies were conducted in the 1920s and 1930s. Harris (1990b) relates phases in the history of visitor studies to the broader history of public opinion survey research, psychologically based market research, and shifting notions of authority in U.S. public institutions. He links the rise of visitor studies in the 1960s and 1970s to a museum period he characterizes as "populist deference," with new funding sources and a newly admitted concern with market share. Roberts (1997) recounts the history of visitor studies from a museum educator's perspective, noting shifts in focus from visitor demographics to evaluation of exhibition components. To further recent concern with visitor experience, she advocates incorporating methods of narrative research and analysis into studies of museum visitors.

13. Ray Silverman, a colleague who helped bring *Okiek Portraits* to Michigan, suggested the contact. Morrissey had experience in museum education; her doctoral research (1989) used learning theory and psychological approaches to look at visitors' interaction with exhibits and interactive video in museum settings.

14. In designing the survey, we had to reconcile the open-ended ethnographic research of my anthropological approach with the narrower methodological range (mainly surveys and questionnaires) more common and manageable in visitor studies and rooted in cognitive psychology. For instance, visitor studies typically distinguish three types of goals, effects, and experience in exhibitions: intellectual, emotional, and behavioral (Doering and Pekarik 1993, 10; Falk and Dierking 1992, 135). Yet recent anthropological work questions the basis of this analytical distinction; it emphasizes confluences among affect, morality, meaning, and social action, as well as the cultural construction of emotion (Lutz and Abu-Lughod 1990; Lutz and White 1986). "[T]he view that affective experience and motivational force are analytically and/or ontologically distinct from cognition is now being questioned on the ba-

sis of ethnopsychological research showing that cultural schemata have many of the directive and morally persuasive qualities once associated primarily with affect" (Lutz and White 1986, 430). Comparative research on museum exhibitions and other cultural display offers fruitful ground for such dialogue. Doering and Pekarik (1996, 5), for instance, also recognize overlap and interaction among the three, providing examples that stress these aspects differentially.

15. Here are the exit survey questions we planned to relate to our research questions:

1. Where were these photographs taken? When? Apart from determining whether visitors noted this basic information, how they located Okiek in space and time might suggest how visitors saw them (e.g., Africa, Kenya, highland forest, another part of the world, in the past, or as contemporary with themselves) (cf. Fabian 1983).

2. What do you think was the purpose of this exhibition? These responses might suggest what goals people find appropriate for museums and exhibitions as well as their interests and attitudes toward the exhibition.

3. How would you describe the Okiek people? 4. What do you think is important to the Okiek people? These questions were framed to solicit characterizations and attributions about Okiek. Responses might indicate whether people saw them positively, negatively, through stereotypes, and whether they responded to individuals shown and related them to their own lives.

5. Do you think the Okiek people are representative of other African cultures? Explain. 6. Do you think there is any connection between the Okiek and Americans? These open-ended questions sought comparisons and contrasts that would illuminate visitors' ideas about Africa and Africans. We thought they might also provide oblique comments on how race influenced interpretation. Participants found the phrasing of question 5 puzzling; it should have asked, "Do you think the Okiek people are like other people in Africa? Explain."

7. Which photograph or label was your favorite? Why? 8. Which photograph or label was your least *favorite? Why?* These questions might illuminate reactions to certain kinds of pictures. The *least* favorite question was also intended to encourage critique and identify features people found unpleasant or problematic. I received a draft chapter from Lutz and Collins's *National Geographic* study while finalizing survey questions. Since they also asked these questions, we thought a comparison would be interesting.

9. What does this exhibit remind you of? Visitors were again asked for comparisons in this final question, intended to clarify how they understood exhibitions in relation to other kinds of representation. We also envisioned responses that suggested visitors' overall impressions of the exhibit, similar to remarks elsewhere likening *Okiek Portraits* to a conversation.

16. This plan also addressed one weakness of comment books, i.e., their primarily self-selected respondents (see chapter 4, note 36).

17. Independently, in 1993 Mike McGovern (1996, 7–11) used a similar method to study a block of 42d Street in New York. He gave pedestrians a small tape recorder and walked down the block with them as they commented. People talked about art installations, sex work, real estate maneuvers, street life, New York history, and issues of class, gender, and sexuality. He asked few questions, but they talked as if in an interview.

18. Survey periods ranged across museum hours on weekdays and weekends. We concentrated on adults to gather information comparable to related studies at other venues. Spring is also "a time when the Michigan State University Museum is filled to capacity with active

school groups and we didn't have the resources to adequately access the experience of these groups" (Morrissey n.d., 1).

19. Samples are small, but the first is typical of exhibition studies that are exploratory or emphasize qualitative data. For example, forty-five interviews were done in a preliminary visitor study for the Africa Hall at the National Museum of Natural History (Falk and Holland 1992). Participants might not answer everything, so some questions have smaller samples. In our in-gallery survey, for instance, only eleven people answered the final question about creating a reduced exhibition.

20. As noted in chapter 2, the *Geographic* study also clarifies the broader interpretive background visitors brought to *Okiek Portraits*. That study included comparable numbers of interviews (55) and photographs (20), though its setting and goals were rather different (Lutz and Collins 1993, 224). The makeup of MSUM visitors, judging from study participants, was comparable to those in the *Geographic* study. They were overwhelmingly Euro-American, about evenly divided by gender, and most had not been to Africa. Participants in the *Geographic* study were all white adults over eighteen, evenly divided by gender, split into two age cohorts. Lutz and Collins conducted interviews in two places, Binghamton, New York, and Oahu, Hawaii, in order to "include people in our sample with a range of experience with racially and culturally diverse people" (ibid.). There is no information on education for either group.

21. In addition to the visitor/docent studies and student papers, I collected press coverage from Michigan State University Museum and the Carlos Museum, spoke with people at Michigan State after three presentations (public lecture, gallery talk, seminar), and did gallery observations at Michigan State and at the Carlos. At the Carlos, I spoke with people at the openings, a gallery talk, at docent training, and in three Emory classes. Students in the Anthropology Club also invited me to talk with them. Finally, I received letters and notes from several who visited *Okiek Portraits* in Atlanta.

22. One focused responses on *Cuadros,* one identified both Kenya *and* Latin America as locations, and another transferred *Cuadros'* emphasis on women to *Okiek Portraits* ("enhance a greater appreciation of the life of cultures of primarily women").

23. For instance, one asserted that Okiek initiate only men and that no initiation photographs were included.

24. Thirty-four people responded to question 3 with a total of sixty-one characterizations. Thirty responded to question 4, listing a total of fifty-six qualities. Codings were determined by asking a class of fifty-four Emory students to evaluate a complete list of responses. Codings generally agreed across the group, except for nearly equal splits in question three on "realists," "traditional" (both positive/neutral), and "skinny" (neutral/negative), and in question four on "fascinations of daily life," "ritual" (positive/neutral), and a three-way split, weighted to neutral, for "attractive children."

25. Responses to question 4 were over 90 percent positive and also included religion, work, land, life, love, and ceremonies.

26. Elongated earlobes were also a sign of social and ritual maturation. Though rarely practiced now, an ear-piercing ceremony once preceded initiation into adulthood.

27. Lacking signals recognizable to Americans, visitors may also have assumed Keleges was female because other initiates pictured were. For Okiek, longer hair marks ritual states and is sometimes a sign of ritual impurity. For example, Okiek mothers grow their hair while their children are in initiation seclusion, as do the ritual teachers involved. Long hair is also

associated with young men (*murenik*), who once wore shoulder-length braided styles, colored with red ochre. Okiek sometimes have reverse problems of gender identification. For instance, I had long hair and usually wore pants while doing research. Many Okiek mistook me initially for male because of my hair and clothing.

28. The actual kinship relations are shown in appendix B.

29. Genealogical relations among the initiates are shown in Kratz (1994, 100).

30. This question also elicited some responses that seemed to bridge the first two approaches, e.g., "pages out of an encyclopedia with a personal touch." Those likening it to personal travel integrated the two through a kind of intimate tourism.

31. Handler and Gable (1997) note similar avoidance in displays at Colonial Williamsburg. A voluminous literature (Rone i.p.), largely in psychology and sociology, finds focusing on human values and discounting the importance of race to be one of three general patterns of racial socialization in the United States.

32. Conklin (1997, 712) discusses the revival of Amazonian body decoration in the context of international ecopolitics, responding to "Western notions of cultural identity that privilege exotic body images as an index of authenticity," and how this politics of representation constrains who can raise what issues.

33. The single in-gallery survey that mentioned circumcision asked searching, empathetic questions ("How long after excision, or is this before? Are they depressed and sad [appearance] due to pain of excision or are they instructed that this is a solemn period?" [plates 15 and 16]). Only one woman, an environmental lawyer, discussed the practice during my three Michigan presentations, and members of the Anthropology Club at Emory asked whether anyone refuses the operation. Members also noticed that photographs covered everyday and ceremonial contexts alike, contrasting with many popular representations. Of course, the African American students interviewed at the Carlos also discussed American politics of representation surrounding Africa.

34. The three exceptions (a) related the exhibition to doctoral research; (b) considered the purpose artistic; and (c) identified aesthetic and communicative impulses ("Just aesthetic joy and affection for the people. To share *their* lives with North Americans").

35. These answers also showed familiarity and exposure to popular ethnography: films, television shows, other exhibits, and most commonly *National Geographic.*

36. For instance, *Okiek Portraits* was the second photographic exhibition one student had ever attended.

37. Most press coverage at later venues consisted of exhibition announcements. This was the only review in Atlanta; an article about the MSUM showing also appeared in the student newspaper.

38. For instance, "cross-section and honesty of life is seen in pride of people"; "show the personality of the people." It is interesting that the "cross-section" and three responses emphasizing "traditional customs" included no photographs of young children. Photographs of children were seen as having universal appeal, sometimes picked as favorites but apparently did not fit images of "tradition."

39. But, Morrissey (n.d., 2–3) also notes, "this may be related to the fact that it was a special exhibit and located somewhat 'off the beaten path' of the museum and therefore, most likely the visitors in the exhibit had specifically chosen to see this exhibit and may have been particularly interested in the content."

40. Ang (1991, 21) contrasts the notion of television audience created through quantified technical "measurement" and the more intuitive notion used by those creating television programs, both located within an institutional perspective but at different moments and for distinct purposes.

41. The viewers at the University of Texas constitute an exception. Presented with a peculiar and problematic mode of presentation, they paid attention almost exclusively to exhibitionary form and its definitional power. Similarly, the anthropologist-reviewer at the Smithsonian (Fischer 1991, 266) saw possibilities for "the ethnographic photographic exhibit [as] a site of resistance within museums" noting that the "double-voiced, multilingual captions, and double-gazed photos [of *Okiek Portraits*] suggest supplementary re-viewings, call attention to multiple registers of reading, and call out from beyond the frame."

42. Questions about presentational form do arise, of course. Strong reactions can result when assumptions about what is "right" are violated. These situations usually involve both what is shown and how it should be presented. For instance, some protests about the controversial *Miscast* exhibition at the South African National Gallery in 1996 centered on placement of "a montage of news stories and photographs [about the San people, on the floor] which the visitor was forced to walk upon. It was this that the San . . . found so humiliating, and other visitors found either irritating or uncomfortable" (Kasfir 1997, 6; see Lane 1996, 8, for a photograph). Khoisan comments were critical of display form, e.g., "I do not want to walk on this floor, because I am walking on my people. Their suffering is too important. It should have been shown on the wall" (Kasfir 1997, 4; Lane 1996, 9). Similar issues have arisen when American artists use the national flag in their work, again sometimes on the floor. After visiting *Okiek Portraits* at the Carlos Museum, one thoughtful colleague wondered what visitors would think of an alternative installation that reversed image/text size emphases by using relatively small images and much larger labels.

43. In making this argument, I draw on Bourdieu's (1993) analysis of art and class and on Silverstein's (1977) work on the pragmatics of language.

44. To argue that certain aspects of exhibition communication are easier to recognize and more available to description is *not* to argue that people (visitors, curators, etc.) don't understand them or that an exhibition's communication is not effective. Nor is it to argue that there is a special cadre of professional "experts" who alone can and should interpret exhibition experience and communication. This unevenness does not fall neatly along professional lines. Curators and museum professionals are "often insufficiently aware of the unconscious assumptions that underlie their own exhibitions" (Karp and Lavine 1993b, 4), whether these assumptions are about content, presentational form, or pragmatic and rhetorical effects. The communicative forms, conventions, impressions, and effects of exhibitions are culturally grounded but may be taken as "natural," "normal," or inherently right. Cross-cultural and historical comparisons help throw these cultural groundings into relief (cf. ibid., 5) and in the process bring to awareness facets that might be more difficult to recognize. The politics of representation sometimes provide occasions that require such comparison when they bring together people of different communities, with different priorities, interests, and communicative conventions, grounded in different social and historical contexts.

45. Fred Myers (1991) makes a similar point about acrylic paintings by Aboriginal artists in Australia: the paintings' connection to religious activities is a major source of value in all their settings, but Aborigines and whites understand that value differently.

46. Cf. Berger, "Words, comparisons, signs need to create a context for a printed photograph in a comparable way; that is to say, they must mark and leave open diverse approaches. A radial system has to be constructed around the photograph so that it may be seen in terms which are simultaneously personal, political, economic, dramatic, everyday, and historic" (1980, 67).

47. Alpers calls the cultivation of particular ways of seeing and kinds of attention "the museum effect" (1991).

48. The question of when and how exhibitions create their various effects concerns the pragmatics of exhibitions as communication. In relation to language, the study of pragmatics concerns language in use, how certain "speech forms are used as effective action in specifiable cultural contexts" (Silverstein 1977, 1). For example, speech might indicate ethnic or regional identity, regardless of referential content. Such indexing of identity is a pragmatic meaning. Similarly, poetic patterns of repetition, alliteration, rhythm, and other aspects of discourse structure in ritual speech or political rallies can contribute to a speaker's persuasive power, to pragmatic effects on those present. The rhetorics and pragmatics of exhibitions involve the combination of a range of communicative forms in addition to language (see Kratz 1994, 12–13; Kratz n.d.).

APPENDIX A. THE POLITICS OF REPRESENTATION AND IDENTITIES

1. Academic research and writing practice have been the subject of critical attention in many disciplines (literary studies: Ashcroft et al. 1989, Black 1992, Pratt 1992, Said 1979; anthropology: Fabian 1983, Clifford and Marcus 1986, Fardon 1990, Kratz 1994b, 2001, Marcus and Cushman 1982, Marcus and Fischer 1986, di Leonardo 1998; science: Franklin 1995, Haraway 1989, 1991, Harding 1987, Landau 1987; philosophy: Mudimbe 1988, 1994; history: Chatterjee 1993, Denning 1996; Guha 1988, 1989, Guha and Spivak 1989, Scott 1988, Stone 1979, White 1973, 1987). None of these examples fits neatly or solely into such disciplinary pigeonholes, however. Such work seems to stimulate interdisciplinary thinking. Two fertile collections addressed the politics of representation in museum settings (Karp and Lavine 1991; Karp, Kreamer, and Lavine 1992), spawning many other studies and collections. Harris (1990a) and Bennett (1995) are key works in the history of museums and display and their political effects, and important monographic studies of particular exhibitions have begun to appear (O'Hanlon 1993; Sandeen 1995; Handler and Gable 1997; Gaspar de Alba 1998). Museum exhibitions have also come under scrutiny from local constituents. Examples of this scrutiny include protests over the Royal Ontario Museum's exhibition *Into the Heart of Africa* (Schildkrout 1991), and Afrocentric critiques of Smithsonian displays published in the TuWaMoja newsletter in Washington, D.C. (1992a, 1992b). Some museums have tried to address such critiques with exhibitions, not always successfully (see, for example, discussion of the *CARA* exhibit and *Hispanic Art in America* by Livingston and Beardsley 1991; Ybarra-Frausto 1991; Gonzalez and Tonelli 1992; and Gaspar de Alba 1998).

Issues in the politics of representation are central to work by artists such as Andrea Fraser (1991, 1997, 1999), Guillermo Gómez-Peña and Coco Fusco (1992–93), James Luna (1992a, 1992b), and Fred Wilson (1991, 1992–93). See also commentaries on Gómez-Peña and Fusco by Obejas (1993a, 1993b) and Sommers (1992), commentaries on Luna by Durham (1990, 5–6) and Reid (1991, 62), and commentaries on Wilson by Kimmelman (1992), Schildkrout (1991), and Corrin (1994). The same issues have featured in programs sponsored by arts institutions (e.g., the Atlanta College of Art's 1992 lecture series on "Art in Context: reThinking the New World"). Such programs also reflect the links to budgetary issues, often framed as attention to multiculturalism. Budgets are also cut in reaction against such attention (e.g., Smithsonian federal funding was reduced after "controversial" exhibitions in the late 1980s and 1990s). There are, of course, multiple intersections and overlaps among all these arenas.

2. Williams (1977, 222–25) describes these histories and meanings. Spencer (1997, 10–12) discusses several ways that political representation can be understood and notes the tension between political and symbolic senses. Spivak (1988, 275–79) also discusses ambiguities between political and symbolic senses, distinguished in German as *vertreten* and *darstellen,* and their importance for understanding ideology.

3. The title essay in Gombrich (1963) is a perceptive discussion of representation in relation to art.

4. Before the 1980s, most works with these title words were by or about Aristotle. These observations are based on searches of the library holdings at Emory University, the Arts and Humanities Index database (1980–), and Current Contents (1990–). Examples of early "poetics and politics" titles in anthropology, literature, and museum studies would include Clifford and Marcus 1986, Stallybrass 1986, Karp and Lavine 1991.

5. These national debates were replicated many times over at state and municipal levels. Kramer (1994) details one such dispute over public sculpture commissioned from John Ahearn for a neighborhood in the South Bronx. Her description captures the shifts in awareness and increasing sensitivity over representation and identity that developed between the mid-1980s and early 1990s. She cites similar disputes about art, identity, and power at the time (ibid., 48).

6. Di Leonardo (1994) and Reed (1997a; 2000) are particularly cogent on the development of identity politics and on its problems. Calhoun (1994) discusses the longer history of the politics of identity and difference. Shotter notes particular shifts between the 1960s–70s and the mid-1990s in the language used to frame questions of identity: "motifs governing the critical thought of this time [late 1960s and early 1970s] were: similarities rather than differences; harmony and agreement rather than conflict and discord; homogeneity rather than heterogeneity; order rather than chaos; structures and products rather than formations and processes; unity and stability rather than plurality and instability; finding and discovering rather than inventing and making; already shared foundations rather than living *in medias res;* already existing forms and frameworks rather than formative processes or resources; explanations rather than descriptions; logic and mathematics rather than rhetoric and poetry. In short, there was the assumption that, in fact, we all already lived in a common world, if only we could discover what it was" (1993, 191). These articles are sources for the following discussion.

7. The philosopher Kwame Anthony Appiah (1992, 72) uses this phrase in identifying one pitfall: "Yet I, at least, worry about our entrancement with the polarities of identity and difference; partly because the rhetoric of alterity has too often meant the evacuation of specificity." He quotes (26–27) the literary scholar Werner Sollors on another problem: "The heart of the matter is that in the present climate consent-conscious Americans are willing to perceive ethnic distinctions—differentiations which they seemingly base exclu-

sively on descent, no matter how far removed and how artificially selected and constructed—as powerful and crucial; . . . and even the smallest symbols of ethnic differentiation . . . are exaggerated out of proportion to represent major cultural differences, differences that are believed to defy comparison or scrutiny."

8. A further historical marker of these developments was the 1983 founding of the journal *Representations,* an outlet for work associated with the New Historicism and interdisciplinary work that was historical, visual, and literary.

9. See chapter 1, note 7, for two U.S. examples from the 1940s to 1950s.

10. See the first three chapters of Haugerud (1995), Ogot (1995), and Throup and Hornsby (1998) on the transition to multipartyism and these events.

11. These include activists' stress on global ecology rather than human rights and the spread of communication technologies in Indian villages (Conklin 1997, 718–21).

12. All these are issues related to communication. The politics of representation involves talking *about* representation, meaning it is a kind of metalanguage.

13. Intersections and articulations among race, class, and gender are often invoked, but the larger point is to analyze whether or not particular dimensions of difference and inequality interact and how. We cannot assume a priori that these three dimensions will always be the most relevant ones or that they will have the same meanings in different times and places. Nor are these the only dimensions of identity whose representations become politicized; ethnicity, religion, and sexuality are other obvious possibilities.

BIBLIOGRAPHY

BOOKS AND ARTICLES

Abrahams, Roger. 1976. The Complex Relations of Simple Forms. In *Folklore Genres,* ed. D. Ben-Amos. Austin: University of Texas Press.

Abu-Lughod, Lila. 1993. *Writing Women's Worlds.* Berkeley: University of California Press.

———. 1997. The Interpretation of Culture(s) after Television: Anthropology, Ethnographic Studies, Egyptian Mass-Media. *Representations* 59:109–34.

Agthe, Johanna. 1990. *Signs: Art from East Africa 1974–89.* Frankfurt am Main: Museum für Völkerkunde.

Ahmadu, Fuambai. 2000. Rites and Wrongs: An Insider/Outsider Reflects on Power and Excision. In *Female "Circumcision" in Africa: Culture, Change, and Controversy,* ed. B. Shell-Duncan and Y. Hernlund. Boulder, Colo.: Lynne Rienner.

Alpers, Svetlana. 1991. The Museum as a Way of Seeing. In *Exhibiting Cultures: The Poetics and Politics of Museum Display,* ed. Ivan Karp and Steven D. Lavine. Washington, D.C.: Smithsonian Institution Press.

Ambler, Charles. 1988. *Kenya Communities in the Age of Imperialism.* New Haven: Yale University Press.

Amin, Mohamed. 1969. *Tom Mboya: A Photographic Tribute.* Nairobi: East African Publishing House.

———. 1973. *Mzee Jomo Kenyatta: A Photobiography.* With text by Peter Moll. Nairobi: Transafrica.

———. 1975. *One Man, One Vote: A Photorecord of Kenya's 1974 General Elections.* With text by Peter Moll. Nairobi: East African Publishing House.

———. 1983. *Cradle of Mankind.* Woodstock, N.Y.: Overlook Press.

Amin, Mohamed, Duncan Willetts, and John Eames. 1987. *The Last of the Maasai.* London: Bodley Head.

Amin, Mohamed, Duncan Willetts, and Tahir Shah. 1994. *Journey through Namibia.* Nairobi: Struik.

Amin, Mohamed, Duncan Willetts, and Brian Tetley. 1982. *Journey through Kenya.* London: Bodley Head.

———. 1986. *Karachi.* Karachi, Pakistan: Pak American Commercial Ltd.

———. 1990. *Journey through Zimbabwe.* Ashbourne: Moorland.

Andere, Amboka. 1986. A Chance to View Kenya's Beautiful Scenery and Faces. *Daily Nation,* 6 November, 14.

Ang, Ien. 1991. *Desperately Seeking the Audience.* London: Routledge.

———. 1996. Hemispheres of Scholarship: Psychological and Other Approaches to Studying Media Audiences. In *Audience and Its Landscape,* ed. J. Hay, L. Grossberg, and E. Wartella. Boulder, Colo.: Westview Press.

An-Na'im, Abdullahi, ed. 1992. *Human Rights in Cross-Cultural Perspectives: A Quest for Consensus.* Philadelphia: University of Pennsylvania Press.

Apena, Adeline. 1996. Female Circumcision in Africa and the Problem of Cross-Cultural Perspectives. *Africa Update* 3, no. 2:7–8.

Appadurai, Arjun. 1997. The Colonial Backdrop. *Afterimage* 24:4–7.

———, ed. 1986. *The Social Life of Things: Commodities in Cultural Perspective.* Cambridge: Cambridge University Press.

Appadurai, Arjun, and Carol Breckenridge. 1992. Museums Are Good to Think: Heritage on View in India. In *Museums and Communities: The Politics of Public Culture,* ed. Ivan Karp, Christine M. Kreamer, and Steven D. Lavine. Washington, D.C.: Smithsonian Institution Press.

Appiah, Kwame Anthony. 1990. Racisms. In *Anatomy of Racism,* ed. David Theo Goldberg. Minneapolis: University of Minnesota Press.

———. 1992. *In My Father's House: Africa in the Philosophy of Culture.* Oxford: Oxford University Press.

Arens, William, and Ivan Karp. 1989. Introduction to *The Creativity of Power,* ed. W. Arens and I. Karp. Washington, D.C.: Smithsonian Institution Press.

Ashcroft, Bill, Gareth Griffiths, and Helen Tiffin. 1989. *The Empire Writes Back: Theory and Practice in Post-Colonial Literatures.* London: Routledge.

Azaglo, Cornelius Yao Augustt. 1996. *Cornelius Yao Augustt Azaglo: photographie, Côte d'Ivoire, 1950–1975.* Paris: Éditions Revue Noire.

Bal, Mieke. 1996. The Discourse of the Museum. In *Thinking about Exhibitions,* ed. R. Greenberg, B. Ferguson, and S. Nairne. London: Routledge.

Balibar, Etienne. 1990. Paradoxes of Universality. In *Anatomy of Racism,* ed. David Theo Goldberg. Minneapolis: University of Minnesota Press.

Barbash, Ilisa, and Lucien Taylor. 1996. Reframing Ethnographic Film: A Conversation with David MacDougall and Judith MacDougall. *American Anthropologist* 98, no. 2:371–87.

Barrett, Terry. 1990. *Criticizing Photographs: An Introduction to Understanding Images.* Mountain View, Calif.: Mayfield Publishing.

Barthes, Roland. 1957. The Great Family of Man. In *Mythologies,* trans. Annette Lavers. New York: Hill and Wang.

———. 1981. *Camera Lucida.* Trans. Richard Howard. New York: Hill and Wang.

Bauman, Richard. 1977. *Verbal Art as Performance.* Rowley, Mass.: Newbury House.

———. 1986. *Story, Performance, and Event: Contextual Studies of Oral Narrative.* Cambridge: Cambridge University Press.

———. 1992. Performance. In *Folklore, Cultural Performances, and Popular Entertainments,* ed. Richard Bauman. Oxford: Oxford University Press.

Bauman, Richard, and Charles Briggs. 1990. Poetics and Performance as Critical Perspectives on Language and Social Life. *Annual Review of Anthropology* 19:59–88.

Baxandall, Michael. 1972. *Painting and Experience in Fifteenth-Century Italy.* New York: Oxford University Press.

Beard, Peter. 1988. *The End of the Game.* San Francisco: Chronicle Books.

Becker, Howard S. 1998. Categories and Comparisons: How We Find Meaning in Photographs. *Visual Anthropology Review* 14, no. 2:3–10.

Beckwith, Carol. 1987. Cultural Exploitation. *The Weekly Review,* 30 January, 2–3.

Beckwith, Carol, and Angela Fisher. 1990. *African Ark.* New York: Harry Abrams.

Beckwith, Carol, and Tepilit ole Saitoti. 1980. *Maasai.* New York: Harry Abrams.

Behrend, Heike. 1998. Love à la Hollywood and Bombay in Kenyan Studio Photography. *Paideuma* 44:139–53.

———. 2000. "Feeling Global": The Likoni Ferry Photographers in Mombasa, Kenya. *African Arts* 33, no. 3:70–76.

Behrend, Heike, and Tobias Wendl. 1997. Photography, Social and Cultural Aspects. In *Encyclopedia of Africa South of the Sahara,* ed. John Middleton. New York: Charles Scribner's Sons.

Beidelman, T. O. 1986. *The Moral Imagination in Kaguru Modes of Thought.* Bloomington: Indiana University Press.

Bell, Clare, Okwui Enwezor, et al., eds. 1996. *In/sight: African Photographers, 1940 to the Present.* New York: Guggenheim Museum.

Bellman, Beryl, and Bennetta Jules-Rosette. 1977. *A Paradigm for Looking: Cross-Cultural Research with Visual Media.* Norwood, N.J.: Ablex Publishing.

Ben-Ari, Eyal. 1991. Posing, Posturing, and Photographic Presences: A Rite of Passage in a Japanese Commuter Village. *Man* 26, no. 1:87–104.

Bennett, Tony. 1988. The Exhibitionary Complex. *New Formations* 4:73–102.

———. 1995. *The Birth of the Museum: History, Theory, Politics.* London: Routledge.

———. 1996a. Museums and Their Constituencies: Citizens, Publics, Audiences, and Communities. Keynote address, National Museums Conference, New Zealand.

———. 1996b. Figuring Audiences and Readers. In *Audience and Its Landscape,* ed. J. Hay, L. Grossberg, and E. Wartella. Boulder, Colo.: Westview Press.

Bensusan, A. D. 1966. *Silver Images: History of Photography in Africa.* Cape Town: Howard Timmins.

Berger, John. 1980. *About Looking.* New York: Vintage.

———. 1982. Stories. In *Another Way of Telling,* by John Berger and Jean Mohr. New York: Pantheon.

———. [1972] 1987. *Ways of Seeing.* London: British Broadcasting Corporation.

Berman, Bruce. 1990. *Control and Crisis in Colonial Kenya: The Dialectic of Domination.* London: James Currey.

Berman, Bruce, and John Lonsdale. 1992. *Unhappy Valley.* London: James Currey.

Bhabha, Homi. 1984. Of Mimicry and Man: The Ambivalence of Colonial Discourse. *October* 28:125–33.

———. 1986. The Other Question: Difference, Discrimination and the Discourse of Colonialism. In *Literature, Politics, and Theory,* ed. F. Barker et al. London: Methuen.

———. 1992. DissemiNation: Time, Narrative and the Margins of the Modern Nation. In *Nation and Narration,* ed. Homi K. Bhabha. New York: Routledge.

Bickford, Adam, Andrew Pekarik, Zahava Doering, and Steven Yalowitz. 1996. Ocean Views: A Study of Visitors to the "Ocean Planet" Exhibition at the National Museum of Natural History. Report 96–5. Institutional Studies Office, Smithsonian Institution.

Bielick, Stacy, Andrew Pekarik, and Zahava Doering. 1995. Beyond the Elephant: A Report Based on the 1994–95 National Museum of Natural History Visitor Survey. Report 95–6B. Institutional Studies Office, Smithsonian Institution.

Black, Edwin. 1992. *Rhetorical Questions: Studies of Public Discourse.* Chicago: University of Chicago Press.

Blackburn, R. H. 1976. Okiek History. In *Kenya Before 1900,* ed. B. A. Ogot. Nairobi: East African Publishing House.

———. 1982a. In the Land of Milk and Honey. In *Politics and History in Band Societies,* ed. Eleanor Leacock and Richard Lee. Cambridge: Cambridge University Press.

———. 1982b. *Okiek.* London: Evans Brothers Ltd.

Boddy, Janice. 1997. Writing Aman. *Anthropology Today* 13, no. 33:9–13.

Borgatti, Jean. 1990a. Portraiture in Africa. *African Arts* 23, no. 3:34–39.

———. 1990b. African Portraiture: A Commentary. *African Arts* 23, no. 4:38–41.

———. 1990c. African Portraits. In *Likeness and Beyond: Portraits from Africa and the World,* by Jean Borgatti and Richard Brilliant. New York: Center for African Art.

Borgatti, Jean, and Richard Brilliant. 1990. *Likeness and Beyond: Portraits from Africa and the World.* New York: Center for African Art.

Bourdieu, Pierre. 1993. *The Field of Cultural Production: Essays on Art and Literature.* Ed. Randal Johnson. New York: Columbia University Press.

Bravman, William. 1990. Using Old Photographs in Interviews: Some Cautionary Notes about Silences in Fieldwork. *History in Africa* 17:327–34.

———. 1998. *Making Ethnic Ways: Communities and Their Transformations in Taita, Kenya, 1800–1950.* Oxford: James Currey.

Briggs, Charles L. 1993. Metadiscursive Practices and Scholarly Authority in Folkloristics. *Journal of American Folklore* 106, no. 422:387–434.

———. 1996a. The Politics of Discursive Authority in Research on the "Invention of Tradition." *Cultural Anthropology* 11, no. 4:435–69.

———. 1996b. Conflict, Language Ideologies, and Privileged Arenas of Discursive Authority in Warao Dispute Mediation. In *Disorderly Discourse: Narrative, Conflict, and Inequality,* ed. Charles L. Briggs. New York: Oxford University Press.

Brilliant, Richard. 1990. Portraits: A Recurrent Genre in World Art. In *Likeness and Beyond: Portraits from Africa and the World,* by Jean Borgatti and Richard Brilliant. New York: Center for African Art.

———. 1991. *Portraiture.* Cambridge, Mass.: Harvard University Press.

Brodkin, Karen. 1998. *How Jews Became White Folks and What That Says about Race in America.* New Brunswick: Rutgers University Press.

Brown, Roger. 1965. *Social Psychology*. New York: Free Press.

Brumberg, Joan. 1982. Zenanas and Girlless Villages: The Ethnology of American Evangelical Women, 1870–1910. *Journal of American History* 69, no. 2:347–71.

Byers, Paul. 1966. Cameras Don't Take Pictures. *Columbia University Forum* 9:27–31.

Calhoun, Craig. 1994. Social Theory and the Politics of Identity. In *Social Theory and the Politics of Identity,* ed. Craig Calhoun. Cambridge, Mass.: Blackwell.

Chalfen, Richard. 1987. *Snapshot Versions of Life*. Bowling Green, Ohio: Bowling Green State University Popular Press.

———. 1991. *Turning Leaves: The Photograph Collections of Two Japanese American Families*. Albuquerque: University of New Mexico Press.

Chambers, Marlene. 1997. What Manner of Beast Is This? Exhibition Criticism and the "Intentional Fallacy." *Exhibitionist* 16, no. 1:13–15.

Chatterjee, Partha. 1993. *The Nation and Its Fragments: Colonial and Postcolonial Histories*. Princeton: Princeton University Press.

Ciira, Wanjiru. 1986. Impressive but Unrepresentative. *The Weekly Review,* 14 November, 24.

Clarke, Graham. 1997. *The Photograph*. Oxford: Oxford University Press.

———, ed. 1992. *The Portrait in Photography*. London: Reaktion Books.

Clarke, Kamari. 1999. To Reclaim Yoruba Tradition Is to Reclaim Our Queens of Mother Africa. In *Feminist Fields: Ethnographic Insights,* ed. R. Bridgman, S. Cole, and H. Howard-Bobiwash. Peterborough, Ontario: Broadview Press.

Clifford, James. 1986. Introduction to *Writing Culture: The Poetics and Politics of Ethnography,* ed. James Clifford and George Marcus. Berkeley: University of California Press.

———. 1988. Four Northwest Coast Museums: Travel Reflections. In *Exhibiting Cultures: The Poetics and Politics of Museum Display,* ed. Ivan Karp and Steven D. Lavine. Washington, D.C.: Smithsonian Institution Press.

———. 1997. Paradise. In *Routes: Travel and Translation in the Late Twentieth Century*. Cambridge, Mass.: Harvard University Press.

Clifford, James, and George Marcus, eds. 1986. *Writing Culture: The Poetics and Politics of Ethnography*. Berkeley: University of California Press.

Coetzee, J. M. 1996. Apartheid Thinking. In *Giving Offense: Essays on Censorship*. Chicago: University of Chicago Press.

Cohen, Erik, Yeshayahu Nir, and Uri Almagor. 1992. Stranger-Local Interaction in Photography. *Annals of Tourism Research* 19:213–33.

Collier, John. 1967. *Visual Anthropology: Photography as a Research Method*. New York: Holt, Rinehart and Winston.

Collins, Jane, and Catherine Lutz. 1992. Becoming America's Lens on the World: *National Geographic* in the Twentieth Century. *South Atlantic Quarterly* 91, no. 1:161–92.

Conklin, Beth. 1997. Body Paint, Feathers, and VCRs: Aesthetics and Authenticity in Amazonian Activism. *American Ethnologist* 24, no. 4:711–37.

Cooper, Frederick, and Randall Packard, eds. 1997. *International Development and the Social Sciences: Essays on the History and Politics of Knowledge*. Berkeley: University of California Press.

Corbey, Raymond. 1988. Alterity: The Colonial Nude. *Critique of Anthropology* 8, no. 33:75–92.

Cosentino, Donald. 1989. Midnight Charters: Musa Wo and Mende Myths of Chaos. In *Creativity of Power,* ed. W. Arens and Ivan Karp. Washington, D.C.: Smithsonian Institution Press.

Cowen, M. P., and R. W. Shenton. 1996. *Doctrines of Development.* New York: Routledge.

Creider, Chet. 1977. Towards a Description of East African Gestures. *Sign Language Studies* 14:1–20.

———. 1978a. Quantitative Aspects of Conversational Interaction. In *Linguistic Variation: Models and Methods,* ed. David Sankoff. New York: Academic Press.

———. 1978b. Language Differences in Strategies for the Interactional Management of Conversation. Paper presented to the annual meeting of the American Anthropological Association, Los Angeles.

Crow, Thomas. 1985. *Painting and Public Life in Eighteenth-Century Paris.* New Haven: Yale University Press.

Csikszentmihalyi, Mihaly, and Eugene Rochberg-Halton. 1981. *The Meaning of Things: Domestic Symbols and the Self.* Cambridge: Cambridge University Press.

Curtin, Philip. 1964. *The Image of Africa: British Ideas and Action, 1780–1850.* Madison: University of Wisconsin Press.

Dening, Greg. 1996. *Performances.* Chicago: University of Chicago Press.

di Leonardo, Micaela. 1994. White Ethnicities, Identity Politics, and Baby Bear's Chair. *Social Text* 41:165–91.

———. 1998. *Exotics at Home: Anthropologies, Others, American Modernity.* Chicago: University of Chicago Press.

Doering, Zahava. 1999. Strangers, Guests or Clients? Visitor Experiences in Museums. *Curator* 42, no. 2:74–87.

Doering, Zahava, and Adam Bickford. 1994. Visits and Visitors to the Smithsonian Institution: A Summary of Studies. Report 94–1. Institutional Studies Office, Smithsonian Institution.

Doering, Zahava, and Andrew Pekarik. 1993. The Exhibition Dialogue: An Outline. *Exhibitionist* 12, no. 2:8–11.

———. 1996. Assessment of Informal Education in Holocaust Museums. RN 96–2. Institutional Studies Office, Smithsonian Institution.

Dominguez, Virginia. 1997. The Racialist Politics of Concepts, or Is It the Racialist Concepts of Politics? *Ethos* 25, no. 1:93–100.

Dominy, Michèle. 1993. Photojournalism, Anthropology, and Ethnographic Authority. *Cultural Anthropology* 8, no. 3:317–37.

Dugger, Celia. 1996. African Ritual Pain: Genital Cutting. *New York Times,* 5 October, A1.

Duncan, Carol. 1988. Art Museums and the Ritual of Citizenship. In *Exhibiting Cultures: The Poetics and Politics of Museum Display,* ed. Ivan Karp and Steven D. Lavine. Washington, D.C.: Smithsonian Institution Press.

———. 1995. *Civilizing Rituals: Inside Public Art Museums.* London: Routledge.

Duranti, Alesandro. 1986. The Audience as Co-Author. *Text* 6, no. 3:239–48.

Durham, Jimmie. 1990. Cowboys and. . . . *Third Text* 12:5–20.

Durkheim, Emile. [1915] 1965. *The Elementary Forms of Religious Life.* New York: Free Press.

Ebron, Paulla. 1991. African Music and the Marketing of Past and Future. Paper presented at the annual meetings of the American Anthropological Association, Chicago.

———. 1997. Traffic in Men. In *Gendered Encounters: Challenging Cultural Boundaries and Social Hierarchies in Africa,* ed. M. Grosz-Ngate and Omari Kokole. New York: Routledge.

———. 2000. Tourists as Pilgrims: Commercial Fashioning of Translatlantic Politics. *American Ethnologist* 26, no. 4:910–32.

Edwards, Elizabeth, ed. 1992. *Anthropology and Photography 1860–1920*. New Haven: Yale University Press.

Emeagwali, Gloria. 1996. Female Circumcision in Africa. *Africa Update* 3, no. 2:1.

Ennis, Philip. 1992. *The Seventh Stream: The Emergence of Rocknroll in American Popular Music*. Middletown, Conn.: Wesleyan University Press.

Escobar, Arturo. 1995. *Encountering Development: The Making and Unmaking of the Third World*. Princeton: Princeton University Press.

External Review Panel. 1992. Report and Recommendations, National Museums of Kenya.

Fabian, Johannes. 1978. Popular Culture in Africa: Findings and Conjectures. *Africa* 48:315–34.

———. 1983. *Time and the Other*. New York: Columbia University Press.

———. 1985. Culture, Time and the Object of Anthropology. *Berkshire Review* 20:7–23.

———. 1996a. *Remembering the Present: Painting and Popular History in Zaire*. Berkeley: University of California Press.

———. 1996b. The "Ethnic Artefact" and the "Ethnographic Object": On Recognizing Things. Paper delivered at workshop on Modern Culture and the Ethnic Artefact, Vienna.

———. 1998. *Moments of Freedom: Anthropology and Popular Culture*. Charlottesville: University of Virginia Press.

———. 1999. Remembering the Other: Knowledge and Recognition in the Exploration of Central Africa. *Critical Inquiry* 26:49–69.

Falk, John, and Lynn Dierking. 1992. *The Museum Experience*. Washington, D.C.: Whalesback Books.

Falk, John, and Dana Holland. 1992. Preliminary Findings: Visitor Research for the Africa Hall. Memo, 9 December.

———. 1993. Content Planning Research: "Africa Hall." Unpublished report on visitor survey at National Museum of Natural History.

Fanon, Frantz. 1967. *Black Skin, White Masks*. New York: Grove Press.

Fardon, Richard. 1990. *Localizing Strategies: Regional Traditions of Ethnographic Writing*. Washington, D.C.: Smithsonian Institution Press.

Fedders, Andrew, and Cynthia Salvadori. 1984. *Peoples and Cultures of Kenya*. Nairobi: Transafrica.

Feld, Steven. 1982. *Sound and Sentiment*. Philadelphia: University of Pennsylvania Press.

———. 1990. Postscript, 1989. In *Sound and Sentiment*. 2d ed. Philadelphia: University of Pennsylvania Press.

———. 1994. From Schizophonia to Schismogenesis: On the Discourses and Commodification Practices of "World Music" and "World Beat." In *Music Grooves,* by Charles Keil and Steven Feld. Chicago: University of Chicago Press.

Field Museum of Natural History. 1991. *Analysis of Visitor Attitudes about Africa for the Africa Exhibit*. Northampton, Mass.: People, Places & Design Research.

Fienup-Riordan, Ann. 1999. Collaboration on Display: A Yup'ik Eskimo Exhibit at Three National Museums. *American Anthropologist* 101, no. 2:339–58.

Fischer, Michael M. J. 1991. Review of Okiek Portraits. *American Anthropologist* 93:265–69.

Fisher, Angela, David Coulson, and Carol Beckwith. 1986. Photo Exhibition. *The Weekly Review,* 28 November, 3.

Fisher, Philip. 1991. *Making and Effacing Art*. Oxford: Oxford University Press.

Fiske, John. 1998. Audiencing: Cultural Practice and Cultural Studies. In *The Landscape of Qualitative Research,* ed. N. Denzin and Y. Lincoln. New York: Sage Publications.

Fortes, Meyer. 1973. The Concept of the Person among the Tallensi. In *La notion de personne en Afrique noire,* ed. G. Dieterlen. Paris: Éditions du Centre National de la Recherche Scientifique.

———. 1983. Problems of Identity and Person. In *Identity: Personal and Sociocultural; a Symposium,* ed. A. Jacobson-Widding. Uppsala: Humanities Press.

Foucault, Michel. 1970. *The Order of Things.* New York: Vintage Books.

———. 1972. *The Archaeology of Knowledge.* Trans. A. M. Sheridan Smith. New York: Harper Colophon.

———. 1977. *Discipline and Punish.* Trans. Alan Sheridan. New York: Pantheon Books.

———. 1980. *Power/Knowledge: Selected Interviews and Other Writings, 1972–1977.* Trans. Colin Gordon, Leo Marshall, John Mephan, and Kape Soper. New York: Pantheon.

Franklin, Sarah. 1995. Science as Culture, Cultures of Science. *Annual Review of Anthropology* 24:163–84.

Fraser, Andrea. 1991. Museum Highlights: A Gallery Talk. *October* 57:103–22.

———. 1997. Inaugural Speech. Delivered at the San Diego opening of inSITE97, 26 September.

———. 1999. Where Have We Gotten With Institutional Critique? The Baby and/or the Bath Water (Revisited). Paper presented at workshop on Critical Conjunctions: Institutional Critique, Cultural Brokerage, and Cultural Display, Emory University.

Freeman, Carla. 1999. *High Tech and High Heels in the Global Economy: Women, Work and Off-Shore Informatics in Barbados.* Durham, N.C.: Duke University Press.

French, Howard W. 1997. Here, an Artist's Fame and Fortune Can Be Fatal. *New York Times,* 11 September, A5.

Fuery, Patrick, and Nick Mansfield. 1997. *Cultural Studies and the New Humanities: Concepts and Controversies.* Melbourne: Oxford University Press.

Fusco, Coco, and Paula Heredia. 1993. *The Couple in the Cage: A Guatinaui Odyssey.* Authentic Documentary Productions. Video.

Fussell, Paul. 1982. *The Boy Scout Handbook and Other Observations.* New York: Oxford University Press.

Gaither, Edmund Barry. 1992. "Hey! That's Mine": Thoughts on Pluralism and American Museums. In *Museums and Communities: The Politics of Public Culture,* ed. Ivan Karp, Christine M. Kreamer, and Steven D. Lavine. Washington, D.C.: Smithsonian Institution Press.

Galaty, John. 1979. Pollution and Anti-Praxis: The Issue of Maasai Inequality. *American Ethnologist* 6:803–16.

———. 1982. Being "Maasai," Being "People of Cattle": Ethnic Shifters in East Africa. *American Ethnologist* 9:1–20.

Gardner, R. C. 1994. Stereotypes as Consensual Beliefs. In *The Psychology of Prejudice: The Ontario Symposium,* ed. M. P. Zanna and J. M. Olson. Vol. 7. Hillsdale, N.J.: Lawrence Erlbaum Associates.

Gaspar de Alba, Alicia. 1998. *Chicano Art Inside/Outside the Master's House: Cultural Politics and the CARA Exhibition.* Austin: University of Texas Press.

Geary, Christraud. 1988. *Images from Bamum: German Colonial Photography at the Court of King Njoya.* Washington, D.C.: Smithsonian Institution Press.

———. 1998. Different Visions? Postcards from Africa by European and African Photographers and Sponsors. In *Delivering Views: Distant Cultures in Early Postcards,* ed. C. Geary and V. Webb. Washington, D.C.: Smithsonian Institution Press.

Gitlin, Todd. 1994. From Universality to Difference: Notes on the Fragmentation of the Idea of the Left. In *Social Theory and the Politics of Identity,* ed. Craig Calhoun. Cambridge, Mass.: Blackwell.

Goldberg, David Theo. 1990. Introduction to *Anatomy of Racism,* ed. David Theo Goldberg. Minneapolis: University of Minnesota Press.

Gombrich, E. H. 1963. *Meditations on a Hobby Horse and Other Essays on the Theory of Art.* London: Phaidon.

Gonzalez, Alicia, and Edith Tonelli. 1992. Compañeros and Partners: The CARA Project. In *Museums and Communities: The Politics of Public Culture,* ed. Ivan Karp, Christine M. Kreamer, and Steven D. Lavine. Washington, D.C.: Smithsonian Institution Press.

Gordon, David. 1986. *Decolonization and the State in Kenya.* Boulder, Colo.: Westview Press.

Gordon, Robert J. 1997. *Picturing Bushmen: The Denver African Expedition of 1925.* Athens: Ohio University Press.

Goswamy, B. N. 1991. Another Past, Another Context: Exhibiting Indian Art Abroad. In *Exhibiting Cultures: The Poetics and Politics of Museum Display,* ed. Ivan Karp and Steven D. Lavine. Washington, D.C.: Smithsonian Institution Press.

Greenblatt, Stephen. 1991. Resonance and Wonder. In *Exhibiting Cultures: The Poetics and Politics of Museum Display,* ed. Ivan Karp and Steven D. Lavine. Washington, D.C.: Smithsonian Institution Press.

Grice, Paul. 1989. *Studies in the Way of Words.* Cambridge, Mass.: Harvard University Press.

Gruenbaum, Ellen. 1996. The Cultural Debate over Female Circumcision: The Sudanese Are Arguing This One Out for Themselves. *Medical Anthropology Quarterly* 10, no. 4:455–75.

Guha, Ranajit. 1988. The Prose of Counter-Insurgency. In *Selected Subaltern Studies,* ed. Ranajit Guha and Gayatri Spivak. New York: Oxford University Press.

———, ed. 1989. *Subaltern Studies VI.* New York: Oxford University Press.

Guha, Ranajit, and G. Spivak, eds. 1989. *Selected Subaltern Studies.* New York: Oxford University Press.

Gumperz, John. 1992. *Discourse Strategies.* Cambridge: Cambridge University Press.

Gupta, Akhil. 1995. Blurred Boundaries: The Discourse of Corruption, the Culture of Politics, and the Imagined State. *American Ethnologist* 22, no. 22:375–402.

Gutman, Judith Mara. 1982. *Through Indian Eyes.* New York: Oxford University Press.

Guyer, Jane. 1996. *African Studies in the United States.* Atlanta: African Studies Association.

Hafsteinsson, Sigurjon. 1996. Introduction to *The Construction of the Viewer: Media Ethnography and the Anthropology of Audiences,* ed. Peter Crawford and Sigurjon Hafsteinsson. Højbjerg, Denmark: Intervention Press.

Hagaman, Dianne. 1996. *How I Learned Not To Be a Photojournalist.* Lexington: University Press of Kentucky.

Hall, Stuart. [1980] 1993. Encoding, Decoding. In *The Cultural Studies Reader,* ed. Simon During. London: Routledge.

———. 1994. Reflections upon the Encoding/Decoding Model. In *Viewing, Reading, Listening: Audiences and Cultural Reception,* ed. Jon Cruz and Justin Lewis. Boulder, Colo.: Westview Press.

———. 1996. When Was "The Post-Colonial"? Thinking at the Limit. In *The Post-Colonial Question,* ed. Iain Chambers and Lidia Curti. London: Routledge.

Hammond, Dorothy, and Alta Jablow. [1970] 1992. *The Africa That Never Was: Four Centuries of British Writing about Africa.* Prospect Heights, Ill.: Waveland Press.

Handler, Richard, and Eric Gable. 1997. *The New History in an Old Museum: Creating the Past at Colonial Williamsburg.* Durham, N.C.: Duke University Press.

Handler, Richard, and Jocelyn Linnekin. 1984. Tradition, Genuine or Spurious. *Journal of American Folklore* 97, no. 385:273–90.

Hannerz, Ulf. 1987. The World in Creolization. *Africa* 57:546–59.

Haraway, Donna. 1984. Teddy Bear Patriarchy: Taxidermy in the Garden of Eden, New York City, 1908–1936. *Social Text* 11:21–64.

———. 1989. *Primate Visions: Gender, Race, and Nature in the World of Modern Science.* New York: Routledge.

———. 1991. *Simians, Cyborgs, and Women.* New York: Routledge.

Harding, Sandra. 1992. Inside Fashion. *Harper's Bazaar,* April, 44.

———, ed. 1987. *Feminism and Methodology.* Bloomington: Indiana University Press.

Harris, Neil. 1990a. *Cultural Excursions: Marketing Appetites and Cultural Tastes in Modern America.* Chicago: University of Chicago Press.

———. 1990b Polling for Opinions. *Museum News* 69, no. 5:46–53.

Harwit, Martin. 1997. *An Exhibit Denied: Lobbying the History of the* Enola Gay. New York: Copernicus.

Haugerud, Angelique. 1995. *The Culture of Politics in Modern Kenya.* Cambridge: Cambridge University Press.

Herbert, Christopher. 1991. *Culture and Anomie: Ethnographic Imagination in the Nineteenth Century.* Chicago: University of Chicago Press.

Himpele, Jeffrey. 1996. Film Distribution as Media: Difference and Discourse in the Bolivian Cinemascape. *Visual Anthropology Review* 12, no. 1:47–66.

Hirschfeld, Lawrence. 1997. The Conceptual Politics of Race: Lessons from Our Children. *Ethos* 25, no. 1:63–92.

Howarth, Anthony. 1967. *Kenyatta: A Photographic Biography.* Nairobi: East African Publishing House.

Huntingford, G. W. B. 1929. Modern Hunters: Some Account of the Kamelilo-Kapchepkendi Dorobo (Okiek) of Kenya Colony. *Journal of the Royal Anthropological Institute* 59:333–76.

Innis, John Mtembezi. 1992. Mkono Mmoja Haulei Mwana. Paper presented at annual meetings of African Studies Association, Seattle.

Irvine, Judith. 1989. When Talk Isn't Cheap: Language and Political Economy. *American Ethnologist* 16, no. 2:248–67.

Iweriebor, Ifeyinwa. 1996. Brief Reflections on Clitorodectomy. *Africa Update* 3, no. 2:2.

Jackson, Michael, and Ivan Karp. 1990. Introduction to *Personhood and Agency: The Experience of Self and Other in African Cultures,* ed. Michael Jackson and Ivan Karp. Uppsala: Smithsonian Institution Press Distributors.

Jakobson, Roman. 1960. Concluding Statement: Linguistics and Poetics. In *Style in Language,* ed. T. Sebeok. Cambridge, Mass.: MIT Press.

Jefferson, Gail. 1978. Sequential Aspects of Storytelling in Conversation. In *Studies in the Organization of Conversational Interaction,* ed. J. Schenkein. New York: Free Press.

Jenkins, Mark. 1990. Okiek Portraits: A Kenyan People Look at Themselves. *City Paper* (Washington, D.C.), 17–23 August.

Jewsiewicki, Bogumil. 1996. Présentation. *Cahiers d'Études africaines* 141–42, XXXVI–1–2:7–24.

Jhala, Jayasinjhi. 1996. The Unintended Audience. In *The Construction of the Viewer: Media*

Ethnography and the Anthropology of Audiences, ed. Peter Crawford and Sigurjon Hafsteinsson. Højbjerg, Denmark: Intervention Press.

Jones, David Keith. 1977. *Faces of Kenya.* New York: Mayflower Books.

Jordan, Winthrop. 1968. *White over Black: American Attitudes toward the Negro, 1550–1812.* Chapel Hill: University of North Carolina Press.

Kanogo, Tabitha. 1987. *Squatters and the Roots of Mau Mau.* London: James Currey.

Karp, Ivan. 1991. Introductions: Culture and Representation; Other Cultures in Museum Perspective. In *Exhibiting Cultures: The Poetics and Politics of Museum Display,* ed. Ivan Karp and Steven D. Lavine. Washington, D.C.: Smithsonian Institution Press.

————. 1992. Introduction to *Museums and Communities: The Politics of Public Culture,* ed. Ivan Karp, Christine M. Kreamer, and Steven D. Lavine. Washington, D.C.:Smithsonian Institution Press.

————. 1993. Development and Personhood. Manuscript.

————. 1996. Public Scholarship as a Vocation. In *Proceedings of the Museums New Zealand 1996 Conference.*

————. 1997. Notions of Person. In *Encyclopedia of Africa South of the Sahara,* ed. John Middleton. New York: Charles Scribner's Sons.

Karp, Ivan, and Corinne A. Kratz. 2000. Reflections on the Fate of Tippoo's Tiger: Defining Cultures in Public Display. In *Cultural Encounters: Communicating Otherness,* ed. E. Hallam and B. Street. London: Routledge.

Karp, Ivan, and Steven D. Lavine. 1993a. Museums Must Take on New Roles in this Multicultural Society. *Chronicle of Higher Education* 39, no. 32: B3 and B6.

————. 1993b. Museums and Society in Crisis. Manuscript.

Karp, Ivan, and Fred Wilson. 1996. Constructing the Spectacle of Culture in Museums. In *Thinking about Exhibitions,* ed. R. Greenberg, B. Ferguson, and S. Nairne. London: Routledge.

Karp, Ivan, Christine M. Kreamer, and Steven D. Lavine, eds. 1992. *Museums and Communities: The Politics of Public Culture.* Washington, D.C.: Smithsonian Institution Press.

Karp, Ivan, and Steven D. Lavine, eds. 1991. *Exhibiting Cultures: The Poetics and Politics of Museum Display.* Washington, D.C.: Smithsonian Institution Press.

Kasfir, Sidney. 1997. Cast, Miscast: The Curator's Dilemma. *African Arts* 30, no. 1:1, 4–9.

Keating, Douglas. 1991. Family Portraits. *Philadelphia Inquirer,* 9 February, C1.

Kenny, Michael. 1981. The Mirror in the Forest: The Dorobo Hunter-Gatherers as an Image of the Other. *Africa* 51, no. 1:477–96.

Kenyatta, Jomo. 1968. *Suffering without Bitterness: The Founding of the Kenyan Nation.* Nairobi: East African Publishing House.

Kimmelman, Michael. 1992. An Improbable Marriage of Artist and Museum. *Baltimore Sun,* 2 August, H1.

————. 1997. Assignment: Times Square. *New York Times Magazine,* 18 May, 43–44.

Kirshenblatt-Gimblett, Barbara. 1998. *Destination Culture: Tourism, Museums, and Heritage.* Berkeley: University of California Press.

Klumpp, Donna, and Corinne A. Kratz. 1993. Aesthetics, Expertise, and Ethnicity: Okiek and Maasai Perspectives on Personal Ornament. In *Being Maasai: Ethnicity and Identity in East Africa,* ed. Thomas Spear and Richard Waller. London: James Currey.

Korn, Randi. 1997. Reading the Museum. Paper presented at annual meetings of the American Association of Museums, Atlanta.

Kramer, Fritz. 1989. The Influence of the Classical Tradition on Anthropology and Exoticism. In *The Humanities between Art and Science: Intellectual Developments 1889–1914*, ed. Michael Harbsmeier and Mogens Larsen. Copenhagen: Akademisk Forlag.

Kramer, Jane. 1994. *Whose Art Is It?* Durham, N.C.: Duke University Press.

Kratz, Corinne A. 1977. The Liquors of Forest and Garden: Drinking in Okiek Life. Master's thesis, Wesleyan University.

———. 1981. Are the Okiek Really Masai? or Kipsigis? or Kikuyu? *Cahiers d'Études africaines* 79, xx–3:355–68.

———. 1986. Ethnic Interaction, Economic Diversification and Language Use: A Report on Research with Kaplelach and Kipchornwonek Okiek. *Sprache und Geschichte in Afrika* 7, no. 2:189–226.

———. 1988. Okiek Ornaments of Transition and Transformation. *Kenya Past and Present* 20:21–26.

———. 1990. Sexual Solidarity and the Secrets of Sight and Sound: Shifting Gender Relations and Their Ceremonial Constitution. *American Ethnologist* 17, no. 3:31–51.

———. 1992. Okiek of the Mau: Shared Memories in Changing Lives. *Kenya Past and Present* 24:19–23.

———. 1993. "We've Always Done It Like This . . . Except for a Few Details": "Tradition" and "Innovation" in Okiek Ceremonies. *Comparative Studies in Society and History* 35, no. 1:28–63.

———. 1994a. *Affecting Performance: Meaning, Movement, and Experience in Okiek Women's Initiation.* Washington, D.C.: Smithsonian Institution Press.

———. 1994b. On Telling/Selling a Book by Its Cover. *Cultural Anthropology* 9, no. 2:1–22.

———. 1994c. Imagining the Rural Mother: Communication and Educational Images in Primary Health Care. Paper presented at SSRC Workshop, "Languages of Development," Berkeley.

———. 1996. Okiek Portraits: Representation, Mediation, and Interpretation in a Photographic Exhibition. *Cahiers d'Études africaines* 141–42, xxxvi–1–2:51–79.

———. 1999a. Contexts, Controversies, Dilemmas: Teaching Circumcision. In *Great Ideas for Teaching about Africa,* ed. Misty Bastian and Jane Parpart. Boulder, Colo.: Lynne Rienner.

———. 1999b. Female Circumcision in Africa. In *Encarta Africana,* ed. Kwame Anthony Appiah and Henry Louis Gates, Jr. Redmond, Wash.: Microsoft.

———. 2000. Forging Unions and Negotiating Ambivalence: Personhood and Complex Agency in Okiek Marriage Arrangement. In *African Philosophy and Cultural Inquiry,* ed. Dismas Masolo and Ivan Karp. International African Institute Monograph. Bloomington: Indiana University Press.

———. 2001. Conversations and Lives. In *Words and Voices: Critical Practices in African Oral History,* ed. David William Cohen, Luise White, and Stephan Miescher. Bloomington: Indiana University Press.

———. In press. Circumcision Debates and Asylum Cases: Intersecting Arenas, Contested Values, and Tangled Webs. In *Engaging Cultural Differences,* ed. Richard Schweder, Hazel Markus, and Martha Minow. New York: Russell Sage Foundation.

———. N.d. Rhetorics of Value: Constituting Quality, Worth, and Meaning through Cultural Display. Manuscript.

Kratz, Corinne A., and Ivan Karp. 1992. Islands of Authenticity: Museums in Disney's World. Paper presented to the annual meetings of the American Anthropological Association, San Francisco.

———. 1993. Wonder and Worth: Disney Museums in World Showcase. *Museum Anthropology* 17, no. 3:32–42.

Kratz, Corinne A., and Donna Pido. 2000. Gender, Ethnicity, and Social Aesthetics in Maasai and Okiek Beadwork. In *Rethinking Pastoralism in Africa: Gender, Culture, and the Myth of the Patriarchal Pastoralist,* ed. Dorothy Hodgson. London: James Currey.

Kurin, Richard. 1997. *Reflections of a Culture Broker: A View from the Smithsonian.* Washington, D.C.: Smithsonian Institution Press.

Landau, Misia. 1987. Paradise Lost: The Theme of Terrestiality in Human Evolution. In *The Rhetoric of the Human Sciences,* ed. John Nelson, Alan Megill, and Donald McCloskey. Madison: University of Wisconsin Press.

Lane, Paul. 1996. Breaking the Mold? Exhibiting Khoisan in Southern African Museums. *Anthropology Today* 12, no. 5:3–10.

Lanouette, William. 1997. Catching the Flak: Review of *An Exhibition Denied,* by Martin Harwit. *Washington Post,* 2 March, WBK1.

Lavine, Lawrence. 1988. *High Brow, Low Brow: The Emergence of Cultural Hierarchy in America.* Cambridge, Mass.: Harvard University Press.

Lavine, Steven D. 1992. Audience, Ownership, Authority. In *Museums and Communities: The Politics of Public Culture,* ed. Ivan Karp, Christine M. Kreamer, and Steven D. Lavine. Washington, D.C.: Smithsonian Institution Press.

Lawuyi, Olatunde Bayo. 1991. The Social Marketing of Elites: The Advertised Self in Obituaries and Congratulations in Some Nigerian Dailies. *Africa* 61, no. 2:247–62.

Livingston, Jane, and John Beardsley. 1991. The Poetics and Politics of Hispanic Art: A New Perspective. In *Exhibiting Cultures: The Poetics and Politics of Museum Display,* ed. Ivan Karp and Steven D. Lavine. Washington, D.C.: Smithsonian Institution Press.

Locke, Donald. 1997. Mirror Images. *Creative Loafing* (Atlanta,Ga.), 22 November, 31, 94.

Lonsdale, John. 1977. When Did the Gusii (or any other group) Become a "Tribe"? *Kenya Historical Review* 5:123–33.

Lowenthal, David. 1985. *The Past Is a Foreign Country.* Cambridge: Cambridge University Press.

Lukes, Steven. 1978. Power and Authority. In *A History of Sociological Analysis,* ed. T. Bottomore and R. Nisbet. New York: Basic Books.

Lusaka, Jane. 1990. Okiek Portraits: A Kenyan People Look at Themselves. Student paper for course on Art and Culture, George Washington University.

Lutz, Catherine, and Jane Collins. 1991. The Photograph as an Intersection of Gazes: The Example of *National Geographic. Visual Anthropology Review* 7, no. 1:134–49.

———. 1993. *Reading National Geographic.* Chicago: University of Chicago Press.

Lutz, Catherine, and Geoffrey White. 1986. The Anthropology of Emotions. *Annual Review of Anthropology* 15:405–36.

Lutz, Catherine, and Lila Abu-Lughod, eds. 1990. *Language and the Politics of Emotion.* Cambridge: Cambridge University Press.

MacDonald, Sharon, and Roger Silverstone. 1990. Rewriting the Museum's Fictions:Taxonomies, Stories and Readers. *Cultural Studies* 4, no. 2:176–91.

MacDougal, David. 1992. Photo Hierarchicus: Signs and Mirrors in Indian Photography. *Visual Anthropology* 5:103–29.

———. 1998. Subtitling Ethnographic Films. In *Transcultural Cinema.* Princeton: Princeton University Press.

MacDougal, David, and Judith MacDougal. 1992. *Photo Wallahs.* University Media Extension, Berkeley. Filmstrip.

Magnin, André. 1995. Seydou Keita. *African Arts* 28, no. 4:90–95.

———, ed. 1997. *Seydou Keita.* Zurich: Scalo.

Magor, Thomasin. 1994. *African Warriors.* London: Harville.

Mani, Lata. 1990. Multiple Mediations: Feminist Scholarship in the Age of Multinational Reception. *Feminist Review* 35:24–40.

Mannheim, Bruce, and Dennis Tedlock. 1995. Introduction to *The Dialogic Emergence of Culture,* ed. D. Tedlock and B. Mannheim. Urbana: University of Illinois Press.

Marcus, George. 1995. Ethnography in/of the World System: The Emergence of Multi-Sited Ethnography. *Annual Review of Anthropology* 24:95–117.

Marcus, George, and Dick Cushman. 1982. Ethnographies as Texts. *Annual Review of Anthropology* 11:25–69.

Marcus, George, and Michael M. J. Fischer. 1986. *Anthropology as Cultural Critique.* Chicago: University of Chicago Press.

Matias, Aisha Samad. 1996. Female Circumcision in Africa. *Africa Update* 3, no. 2:3–6.

McGovern, Michael. 1993. The Garden of Earthly Delights: An Experimental Ethnography of Times Square. Manuscript.

———. 1996. Discourse Analysis. Manuscript.

McNeil, Donald G., Jr. 1996. A Crank-up Radio Helps Africa Tune In. *New York Times,* 16 February, A1.

Merriman, Nick. 1989. Museum Visiting as a Cultural Phenomenon. In *The New Museology,* ed. P. Vergo. London: Reaktion Books.

Messaris, Paul. 1994. *Visual Literacy: Image, Mind, and Reality.* Boulder, Colo.: Westview Press.

Messaris, Paul, and Larry Gross. 1977. Interpretations of a Photographic Narrative by Viewers in Four Age Groups. *Studies in the Anthropology of Visual Communication* 4, no. 2:99–111.

Michael C. Carlos Museum. 1996. *Handbook.* Atlanta.

Miller, Daniel, ed. 1995. *Worlds Apart: Modernity through the Prism of the Local.* London: Routledge.

———. 1998. *Material Cultures: Why Some Things Matter.* Chicago: University of Chicago Press.

Mohanty, Chandra. 1988. Under Western Eyes: Feminist Scholarship and Colonial Discourse. *Feminist Review* 30:61–88.

Mohr, Jean. 1982. "Beyond My Camera" and "What Did I See?" In *Another Way of Telling,* by John Berger and Jean Mohr. New York: Pantheon.

Monti, Nicolas. 1987. *Africa Then: Photographs 1840–1918.* London: Thames and Hudson.

Moores, Shaun. 1993. *Interpreting Audiences: The Ethnography of Media Consumption.* London: Sage.

Morrissey, Kristine A. 1989. Interactive Video within the Museum Setting: The Attracting Power, Use, and Effect on Visitors' Interaction with an Exhibit. Ph.D.dissertation, Michigan State University, Department of Counselling, Educational Psychology, and Special Education.

———. N.d. Okiek Exhibition Visitor Survey Report (1995).

Mphahlele, Ezekiel. 1962. *The African Image.* New York: Praeger.

Mudimbe, V. Y. 1988. *The Invention of Africa.* Bloomington: Indiana University Press.

———. 1994. *The Idea of Africa.* Bloomington: Indiana University Press.

Müller, Chris. 1994. Exhibition-ism: The Design Approach. In *Exhibition-ism: Museums and African Art,* by Susan Vogel and Mary Nooter Roberts, with C. Müller. New York: Museum for African Art.

Mulwa, David. 1979. *Master and Servant.* Nairobi: Longman.

Munasinghe, Viranjini. 1997. Culture Creators and Culture Bearers: The Interface between Race and Ethnicity in Trinidad. *Transforming Anthropology* 6, nos. 1–2:72–86.

Murray, Jocelyn. 1976. The Church Missionary Society and the "Female Circumcision" Issue in Kenya. *Journal of Religion in Africa* 8, no. 2:92–104.

Musello, Christopher. 1980. Studying the Home Mode: An Exploration of Family Photography and Visual Communication. *Studies in Visual Communication* 6, no. 1:23–42.

Mustafa, Hudita. In press. Portraits of Modernity: Fashioning Selves in Dakarois Popular Photography. In *Images and Empires in Africa,* ed. D. Kaspin and P. Landau. Berkeley: University of California Press.

Myers, Fred. 1991. Representing Culture: The Production of Discourse(s) for Aboriginal Acrylic Paintings. *Cultural Anthropology* 6, no. 1:26–62.

Myers-Scotton, Carol. 1993. *Social Motivations for Code Switching: Evidence from Africa.* Oxford: Clarendon Press.

Nandy, Ashis. 1983. *The Intimate Enemy: Loss and Recovery of Self under Colonialism.* Delhi: Oxford University Press.

———. 1996. A Report on Religion, Culture, and Civil Society in India. Lecture at Emory University, 7 October.

National Museums of Kenya. 1981. *Souvenir Guidebook to the National Museums of Kenya.* Nairobi: Kenya Museum Society.

———. 1990. *A Commemorative Guidebook to the National Museums of Kenya 1930–1990.* Nairobi.

Ndavu, Eva. 1989a. Okiek: A Journey through Life. *Daily Nation,* 15 August.

———. 1989b. Okiek Life and Culture Brought Out in Pictures. *Daily Nation,* 12 September.

Ndegwa, Stephen. 1997. Citizenship and Ethnicity: An Examination of Two Transition Moments in Kenyan Politics. *American Political Science Review* 91, no. 3:599–616.

———. 1998. Citizenship amid Economic and Political Change in Kenya. *Africa Today* 45, nos. 3–4:351–68.

Newman, Tamsin. 1991. U. Museum Exhibit Examines Kenyans. *The Daily Pennsylvanian,* 12 February, 8.

Obejas, Achy. 1993a. Live Art Framed by Bars: Cage Comes to Field Museum. *Chicago Tribune,* 18 January.

———. 1993b. Pushing the Borders of Art: Caged Players Reach across Cultural Chasms. *Chicago Tribune,* 28 January, 5–1.

Obermeyer, Carla Makhlouf. 1999. Female Genital Surgeries: The Known, the Unknown, and the Unknowable. *Medical Anthropology Quarterly* 13, no. 1:79–106.

Odinga, Oginga. 1967. *Not Yet Uhuru.* London: Heinemann.

O'Doherty, Brian. 1986. *Inside the White Cube: The Ideology of the Gallery Space.* Berkeley: University of California Press.

Ogot, B. A. 1995. Transition from Single-Party to Multiparty Political System 1989–93. In *Decolonization and Independence in Kenya 1940–93,* ed. B. A. Ogot and W. R. Ochieng'. London: James Currey.

Oguibe, Olu. 1996. Photography and the Substance of the Image. In *In/sight: African Photographers, 1940 to the Present,* ed. Clare Bell et al. New York: Guggenheim Museum.

O'Hanlon, Michael. 1993. *Paradise: Portraying the New Guinea Highlands.* London: British Museum Press.

Ouedraogo, Jean-Bernard. 1996. La figuration photographique des identités sociales: valeurs et apparences au Burkina Faso. *Cahiers d'Études africaines* 141–42, XXXVI–1–2:25–50.

Pankhurst, Richard. 1992. The Political Image: The Impact of the Camera in an Ancient Independent African State. In *Anthropology and Photography 1860–1920,* ed. Elizabeth Edwards. New Haven: Yale University Press.

Parker, Melissa. 1996. Rethinking Female Circumcision. *Africa* 65, no. 4:506–24.

Paul, Robert. 1995. Stereotypes and Prototypes. Paper presented at the Biennial Meetings of the Society for Psychological Anthropology.

Peel, J. D. Y. 1989. The Cultural Work of Yoruba Ethnogenesis. In *History and Ethnicity,* ed. Elizabeth Tonkin, Maryon McDonald, and Malcolm Chapman. London: Routledge.

Pekarik, Andrew J., Zahava D. Doering, and David A. Karns. 1999. Exploring Satisfying Experiences in Museums. *Curator* 42, no. 2:152–73.

Perin, Constance. 1992. The Communicative Circle. In *Museums and Communities: The Politics of Public Culture,* ed. Ivan Karp, Christine M. Kreamer, and Steven D. Lavine. Washington, D.C.: Smithsonian Institution Press.

Perry, Rachel. 1993. Exhibit Offers Glimpse of Kenya. *State News* (East Lansing, Mich.), 17 February.

Phillips, Ruth. 1995. *Representing Women: Sande Masquerades of the Mende of Sierra Leone.* Los Angeles: UCLA Fowler Museum of Cultural History.

Pinney, Christopher. 1992. The Parallel Histories of Anthropology and Photography. In *Anthropology and Photography 1860–1920,* ed. Elizabeth Edwards. New Haven: Yale University Press.

———. 1997. *Camera Indica: The Social Life of Indian Photographs.* Chicago: University of Chicago Press.

Pivin, Jean Loup, ed. 1994. *Mama Casset et les précurseurs de la photographie au Sénégal, 1950.* Paris: Éditions Revue Noire.

Poignant, Roslyn. 1992. Surveying the Field of View: The Making of the RAI Photographic Collection. In *Anthropology and Photography 1860–1920,* ed. Elizabeth Edwards. New Haven: Yale University Press.

Poole, Deborah. 1997. *Vision, Race, and Modernity: A Visual Economy of the Andean Image World.* Princeton: Princeton University Press.

Pratt, Mary Louise. 1992. *Imperial Eyes: Travel Writing and Transculturation.* New York: Routledge.

Preston, George. 1990. People Making Portraits Making People: Living Icons of the Akan. *African Arts* 23, no. 3:70–76.

Ragan, Janet Mills, and Albert Smouse. 1981. Pose Preference in Social and Business Photographs. *Studies in Visual Communication* 7, no. 3:76–82.

Rappaport, Roy. 1967. *Pigs for the Ancestors.* New Haven: Yale University Press.

Reed, Adolph, Jr. 1996a. Skin Deep. *Village Voice,* 24 September. Reprinted in *Class Notes* (New York: New Press, 2000).

———. 1996b. Race and Medical Research. Manuscript.

———. 1997a. Token Equality. *The Progressive* 61, no. 2:18–19. Reprinted in *Class Notes* (New York: New Press, 2000).

————. 1997b. Hallmark Card Politics. Manuscript.

————. 2000. Ethnic Studies and Pluralist Politics. In *Class Notes.* New York: New Press.

Reid, Calvin. 1991. Inside/Outside (Multi-Site Exhibitions). *Art in America* (January):56–63.

Richards, Paul. 1996. *Fighting for the Rain Forest.* Oxford: James Currey.

Ritchin, Fred. 1999. *In Our Own Image: The Coming Revolution in Photography.* New York: Aperture.

Roberts, Lisa. 1997. *From Knowledge to Narrative: Educators and the Changing Museum.* Washington, D.C.: Smithsonian Institution Press.

Rone, Tracy. In press. The Socialization of Academic Achievement and Racial Consciousness in a Black Community-Based Youth Organization. In *New Perspectives on African American Education: Race, Human Development, and Social Policy,* ed. W. R. Allen, M. B. Spencer, and C. O'Connor. Stamford, Conn.: JAI Press.

Rosaldo, Renato. 1989. Imperialist Nostalgia. *Representations* 26:107–21.

————. 1994. Whose Cultural Studies? *American Anthropologist* 96, no. 3:524–29.

Rosberg, Carl, Jr., and John Nottingham. [1966] 1985. *The Myth of "Mau Mau."* Nairobi: Transafrica.

Ross, Doran. 1998. *Wrapped in Pride: Ghanaian Kente and African American Identity.* Los Angeles: UCLA Fowler Museum of Cultural History.

Ruffins, Fath Davis. 1985. An Elegant Metaphor: The Exhibition as Form. *Museum News* 64, no. 1:54–60.

————. 1998. Reflecting on Ethnic Imagery in the Landscape of Commerce, 1945–1975. In *Getting and Spending: European and American Consumer Societies in the Twentieth Century,* ed. S. Strasser, C. McGovern, and M. Judt. Cambridge: Cambridge University Press.

————. In press. *Ethnicity in American Advertising.* New York: Harry Abrams.

Sacks, H., E. Schegloff, and G. Jefferson. 1974. A Simplest Systematics for the Organization of Turn-taking in Conversation. *Language* 50:696–735.

Sacks, Harvey. 1972. On the Analyzability of Stories by Children. In *Directions in Sociolinguistics: The Ethnography of Communication,* ed. J. Gumperz and D. Hymes. New York: Holt, Rinehart and Winston.

————. 1992. *Lectures on Conversation,* ed. Gail Jefferson. Oxford, Mass.: Blackwell.

Said, Edward. 1979. *Orientalism.* New York: Vintage.

Saitoti, Tepilit ole. 1987. Clipping the Eagle's Wings: Ending Cultural Exploitation by Foreigners. *The Weekly Review,* 23 January, 26–27.

Salvadori, Cynthia. 1983. *Through Open Doors: A View of Asian Cultures in Kenya.* Nairobi: Kenway Publications.

Samuel, Raphael. 1994. *Theatres of Memory: Past and Present in Contemporary Culture.* London: Verso.

Sandeen, Eric J. 1995. *Picturing an Exhibition:* The Family of Man *and 1950s America.* Albuquerque: University of New Mexico Press.

Schechner, Richard. 1985. *Between Theater and Anthropology.* Philadelphia: University of Pennsylvania Press.

Schildkrout, Enid. 1991. Ambiguous Messages and Ironic Twists: Into the Heart of Africa and the Other Museum. *Museum Anthropology* 15, no. 2:16–23.

————. 1999. Challenging Exhibitions: New Paradigms, Same Old Questions. *African Arts* 32, no. 3:1–8.

Schudson, Michael. 1997. Paper Tigers. *Lingua Franca* 7, no. 6:49–56.

Schwartz, Dona. 1992. *Waucoma Twilight: Generations of the Farm.* Washington, D.C.: Smithsonian Institution Press.

Scott, Joan Wallach. 1988. *Gender and the Politics of History.* New York: Columbia University Press.

Segato, R. L. 1998. The Color-Blind Subject of Myth; Or, Where to Find Africa in the Nation. *Annual Review of Anthropology* 27:129–51.

Shanklin, Eugenia. 1990. The Odyssey of the Afo-A-Kom. *African Arts* 23, no. 4:62–69.

Sherzer, Joel. 1983. *Kuna Ways of Speaking.* Austin: University of Texas Press.

Shotter, John. 1993. *Cultural Politics of Everyday Life.* Toronto: University of Toronto Press.

Shweder, Richard. 2001. What about FGM? And Why Understanding Culture Matters in the First Place. *Daedelus* 129, no. 4:209–32.

Silverstein, Michael. 1976. Shifters, Linguistic Categories, and Cultural Description. In *Meaning in Anthropology,* ed. K. Basso and H. Selby. Albuquerque: University of New Mexico Press.

———. 1977. The Limits of Awareness. Lecture given to Harvard Anthropology Seminar.

———. 1979. Language Structure and Language Ideology. In *The Elements: A Parasession on Linguistic Units and Levels,* ed. P. Clyne, W. Hanks, and C. Hofbauer. Chicago: Chicago Linguistic Society.

Silverstein, Michael, and Greg Urban. 1996. The Natural History of Discourse. In *Natural Histories of Discourse,* ed. Michael Silverstein and Greg Urban. Chicago: Chicago University Press.

Simmel, Georg. [1901] 1959. The Aesthetic Significance of the Face. In *Georg Simmel, 1858–1918,* ed. K. Wolff. Columbus: Ohio State University Press.

Sims, Patterson. 1993. *The Museum: Mixed Metaphors, Fred Wilson.* Seattle: Seattle Art Museum.

Smart, Pamela. 1997. Sacred Modern: An Ethnography of the Menil Collection. Ph.D. dissertation, Anthropology Department, Rice University, Houston.

Sobania, Neal. 1993. Review of "Okiek Portraits: A Kenyan People Look at Themselves." *African Arts* 26, no. 3:73–74.

Sommers, Pamela. 1992. The Couple in the Cage. *Washington Post,* 20 October, E3.

Sontag, Susan. 1977. *On Photography.* New York: Delta.

Spear, Thomas, and Richard Waller, eds. 1993. *Being Maasai: Ethnicity and Identity in East Africa.* London: James Currey.

Spindler, Amy M. 1997. Taking Stereotyping to a New Level in Fashion. *New York Times,* 3 June, B13.

Sprague, Stephen. 1978a. Yoruba Photography: How the Yoruba See Themselves. *African Arts* 12, no. 1:52–59.

———. 1978b. How I See the Yoruba See Themselves. *Studies in the Anthropology of Visual Communication* 5, no. 1:9–28.

Staiger, Janet. 1992. *Interpreting Films: Studies in the Historical Reception of American Cinema.* Princeton: Princeton University Press.

Steiner, Christopher. 1994. *African Art in Transit.* Cambridge: Cambridge University Press.

Stephens, Julie. 1989. Feminist Fictions: A Critique of the Category "Non-Western Women" in Feminist Writings on India. In *Subaltern Studies VI,* ed. Ranajit Guha. New York: Oxford University Press.

Stimpson, Catherine. 1994. Introduction to *Whose Art Is It?* by Jane Kramer. Durham, N.C.: Duke University Press.

Stokes, Philip. 1992. The Family Photograph Album: So Great a Cloud of Witnesses. In *The Portrait in Photography*, ed. Graham Clarke. London: Reaktion Books.

Stoler, Ann. 1997. On Political and Psychological Essentialisms. *Ethos* 25, no. 1:101–6.

Stoller, Paul. 1992. *The Cinematic Griot: The Ethnography of Jean Rouch*. Chicago: University of Chicago Press.

Stone, Lawrence. 1979. The Revival of Narrative: Reflections on a New Old History. *Past and Present* 85:3–24.

Strong, Pauline Turner. 1997. Exclusive Labels: Indexing the National "We" in Commemorative and Oppositional Exhibitions. *Museum Anthropology* 21, no. 1:42–56.

Tagg, John. 1988. *The Burden of Representation: Essays on Photographies and Histories*. Amherst: University of Massachusetts Press.

———. 1992. *Grounds of Dispute: Art History, Cultural Politics, and the Discursive Field*. Minneapolis: University of Minnesota Press.

Taussig, Michael. 1996. *The Magic of the State*. New York: Routledge.

Tchen, John Kuo Wei. 1992. Creating a Dialogic Museum: The Chinatown History Museum Experiment. In *Museums and Communities: The Politics of Public Culture*, ed. Ivan Karp, Christine M. Kreamer, and Steven D. Lavine. Washington, D.C.: Smithsonian Institution Press.

Tetley, Brian. 1988. *Mo: The Story of Mohamed Amin, Front-line Cameraman*. London: Moonstone Books.

Theroux, Paul. 1978. *Picture Palace*. London: Penguin Books.

Thomas, Nicholas. 1994. *Colonialism's Culture*. Princeton: Princeton University Press.

Throup, David, and Charles Hornsby. 1998. *Multi-Party Politics in Kenya: The Kenyatta and Moi States and the Triumph of the System in the 1992 Election*. Oxford: James Currey.

Tomkinson, Michael. 1988. *Kenya*. Oxford: Michael Tomkinson Publishing.

Tomlinson, John. 1991. *Cultural Imperialism*. Baltimore: John Hopkins University Press.

Trachtenberg, Alan. 1989. *Reading American Photographs*. New York: Hill and Wang.

Tsing, Anna. 1993. *In the Realm of the Diamond Queen: Marginality in an Out-of-the-Way Place*. Princeton: Princeton University Press.

TuWaMoja. 1992a. Continued Support for White Supremacy. *TuWaMoja Newsletter* 3:1–5.

———. 1992b. An Accurate Interpretation of African Religion vs the Smithsonian Exhibit on That Religion. *TuWaMoja Newsletter* 2, no. 4:1–3.

Tyler, Stephen. 1984. The Vision Quest in the West, or What the Mind's Eye Sees. *Journal of Anthropological Research* 40:23–40.

Viditz-Ward, Vera. 1987. Photography in Sierra Leone, 1850–1918. *Africa* 57, no. 4:512–17.

Viso, Olga. 1997. Jeff Wall. An exhibition at the Hirshhorn Museum, Washington, D.C., February–May 1997.

Vogel, Susan. 1988. Always True to the Object. In *Exhibiting Cultures: The Poetics and Politics of Museum Display*, ed. Ivan Karp and Steven D. Lavine. Washington, D.C.: Smithsonian Institution Press.

———. 1994. Portrait of a Museum in Practice. In *Exhibition-ism: Museums and African Art*, by S. Vogel and M. Nooter Roberts with C. Müller. New York: Museum for African Art.

———. 1997. *Baule: African Art, Western Eyes*. New Haven: Yale University Press.

———, ed. 1988. *Art/Artifact: African Art in Anthropology Collections*. New York: Center for African Art.

———. 1991. *Africa Explores: 20th Century African Art.* New York: Center for African Art.

Vogel, Susan, and Mary Nooter Roberts with Chris Müller. 1994. *Exhibition-ism: Museums and African Art.* New York: Museum for African Art.

Wakanyote. 1989a. The Okiek: Just Who Are They? *Sunday Nation* (Nairobi), 13 August.

———. 1989b. Camera Lens Snaps a Changing Society. *Sunday Nation,* 20 August.

Walker Art Center. 1995. *Dawoud Bey, Portraits 1976–1995.* Minneapolis: Walker Art Center.

Washington, Harriet. 1996. Rite of Female Circumcision. *Emerge,* September, 30.

Wendl, Tobias. 1998. Speaking Grounds: The Semiotics and Aesthetics of Ghanaian Photographic Studio Backdrops. Paper delivered at the Triennial Symposium on African Art.

Wendl, Tobias, and Nancy du Plessis. 1998. *Future Remembrance: Photography and Image Arts in Ghana.* Watertown, Mass.: Documentary Educational Resources. Video.

Werner, Jean-François. 1993. La photographie de famille en Afrique de l'Ouest: une méthode d'approche ethnographique. *Xoana* 1, no. 1:43–56.

———. 1996. Produire des images en Afrique: le cas des photographies de studio. *Cahiers d'Études africaines* 141–42, XXXVI-1–2:81–112.

White, E. Frances. 1990. Africa on My Mind: Gender, Counter Discourse, and African American Nationalism. *Journal of Women's History* 2, no. 1:73–97.

White, Hayden. 1973. *Metahistory: Historical Imagination in Nineteenth-century Europe.* Baltimore: Johns Hopkins University Press.

———. 1978. *Tropics of Discourse: Essays in Cultural Criticism.* Baltimore: Johns Hopkins University Press.

———. 1987. *The Content of the Form: Narrative Discourse and Historical Representation.* Baltimore: Johns Hopkins University Press.

Whitely, Wilfred, ed. 1974. *Language in Kenya.* Nairobi: Oxford University Press.

Wilmsen, Edwin, and Patrick McAllister, eds. 1996. *The Politics of Difference: Ethnic Premises in a World of Power.* Chicago: University of Chicago Press.

Wilson, Fred. 1994. *Mining the Museum: An Installation by Fred Wilson,* ed. Lisa Corrin. New York: Contemporary.

Wolf, Margery. 1992. *A Thrice Told Tale: Feminism, Postmodernism, and Ethnographic Responsibility.* Stanford: Stanford University Press.

Worth, Sol, and John Adair. 1972. *Through Navajo Eyes: An Exploration in Film Communication and Anthropology.* Bloomington: Indiana University Press.

Worth, Sol, and Larry Gross. 1974. Symbolic Strategies. *Journal of Communication* 24, no. 4:27–39.

Yamaguchi, Masao. 1991. The Poetics of Exhibition in Japanese Culture. In *Exhibiting Cultures: The Poetics and Politics of Museum Display,* ed. Ivan Karp and Steven D. Lavine. Washington, D.C.: Smithsonian Institution Press.

Ybarra-Frausto, Tomás. 1991. The Chicano Movement / the Movement of Chicano Art. In *Exhibiting Cultures: The Poetics and Politics of Museum Display,* ed. Ivan Karp and Steven D. Lavine. Washington, D.C.: Smithsonian Institution Press.

PERFORMANCE ART

Gomez-Peña, Guillermo, and Coco Fusco. 1992–93. The Year of the White Bear: Two Undiscovered Amerindians Visit the West. Performances at Columbus Plaza, Madrid, May 1992; National Museum of Natural History, Washington, D.C. 17–18 October 1992; Field Museum of Natural History, Chicago, Ill. 17 January 1993; and other sites.

Luna, James. 1992a. *The Sacred Colors*. Exhibit (12 June–18 July) and brochure. Sacramento, Calif.: Galeria Posada.

————.1992b. Indian Tales: Stories of Native People from the Rez and Cities. Performance, National Museum of Natural History, 14 November.

Wilson, Fred. 1991. *The Other Museum*. Installation at Washington Project for the Arts, 9 February–17 March.

————. 1992–93. *Mining the Museum*. Exhibition at Maryland Historical Society.

ILLUSTRATIONS

Ouedraogo, Jean-Bernard, 121, 246n69
Out of Africa (film), 136

pan-Africanism, 107, 188, 215
Pankhurst, Richard, 245n62
Paradise exhibition, 258n59
Parker, Melissa, 185
pastoralism, 6, 7, 90
patrilineages, Okiek, 6, 224
Paul, Robert, 109, 241n33
Pekarik, Andrew, 189, 236n13, 264n36, 265n39, 267n11, 268n14
Pennsylvania, University of, Museum of Archaeology and Anthropology (Philadelphia), 4, 134, 181, 183, 186, 188, 252n6, 263n35
Perfect Moment exhibition, 234n7
Perin, Constance, 240n20
Perspectives exhibition, 235n9, 250n98
Philadelphia Centennial Exposition (1876), 209
photography: aesthetics of, 102; archives of, 101; color versus black and white, 112; ethnographic, *see* ethnographic photography; history in Africa of, 5, 120–21; in Kenya, 141–43; Okiek attitudes toward, 143, 146–48; portrait, *see* portraits; Pulitzer prize in, images chosen for, 110; uses as medium of representation of, 96–97; visual anthropology and, 100
photojournalism, 139
Photons, 248n74
Pinney, Christopher, 237n19, 242n42, 254n33, 256n41, 257n52
political economy, 95, 139
politics of representation, 3–5, 13, 89–97, 131–32, 163, 173, 213, 215, 219–23, 236nn14, 15; and aesthetic stance, 210; of anti-circumcision campaigns, 185–86; community involvement in, 101–2; constraints on interpretive possibilities by, 213; exhibition design and, 174–79; exploitation in, 136–37; in Okiek-Maasai relations, 157; photography and, 96–97; in portraiture,

124; senses of identity and, 94; stereotypes and, 90, 168; unevenness of, 3, 89, 95–96, 176, 213–15, 218, 222–23
Poole, Deborah, 240n27, 247n70
portraits, 5, 117–24; formal, 102, 146–48; introduction of individuals to viewers through, 101; in Kenya, history of, 142; labeling of, *see* texts, exhibition; selection of, 112, 114–17
poses, 119, 120; frontal, 122–23
postcolonial era, 7
power, issues of, 89, 95
"primitive" stereotypes, 100, 108–9
props, 120–21, 156
psychology, cognitive, 108

race, 215; ethnicity and, 107–8; history and politics of, 188; stereotypes based on, 106–7; visitor comments on, 207–8
Rear Window (film), 262n27
recognition, 3, 110, 111, 118, 123, 133, 169, 177, 187, 207, 217, 231n5, 243n45
Reed, Adolph, Jr., 219, 221, 236n15, 273n6
Registration of Natives Ordinance (1915), 255n34
representation, 162; ethnic equity in, 104; politics of, *see* politics of representation; production of, 101–2; through selection, 111–17; shaped by circulation and interaction, 103; of stereotypes, 105, 110; visual, 100 (*see also* photography)
reviews, 134; of *Images of Kenya* exhibition, 136; of Nairobi Museum installation, 133, 140; and politics of representation, 178–79, 186; in United States, 181, 186–87, 211
Ritchkin, Fred, 243n47, 244n54, 254n26
Roberts, Lisa, 250n96, 267n12
Rochberg-Halton, Eugene, 244n58
Romans, ancient, 118
Rooms with a View exhibition, 260n10
Rosaldo, Renato, 183, 264n38, 265n41
Royal Ontario Museum, 272n1
Ruffins, Fath, 97, 108

TEXT 10.75/13.5 Adobe Garamond
DISPLAY Akzidenz Grotesk
DESIGNER Nicole Hayward
COMPOSITOR Integrated Composition Systems
COLOR PRINTER Pinnacle Press, Inc.
PRINTER + BINDER Edwards Brothers
INDEXER Ruth Elwell